The Virgin Mary's Book at the Annunciation

The Virgin Mary's Book at the Annunciation

Reading, Interpretation, and Devotion in Medieval England

Laura Saetveit Miles

D. S. BREWER

© Laura Saetveit Miles 2020

All Rights Reserved. Except as permitted under current legislation
no part of this work may be photocopied, stored in a retrieval system,
published, performed in public, adapted, broadcast,
transmitted, recorded or reproduced in any form or by any means,
without the prior permission of the copyright owner

The right of Laura Saetveit Miles to be identified as
the author of this work has been asserted in accordance with
sections 77 and 78 of the Copyright, Designs and Patents Act 1988

First published 2020
D. S. Brewer, Cambridge
Paperback edition 2022

ISBN 978 1 84384 534 8 hardback
ISBN 978 1 84384 628 4 paperback

D. S. Brewer is an imprint of Boydell & Brewer Ltd
PO Box 9, Woodbridge, Suffolk IP12 3DF, UK
and of Boydell & Brewer Inc.
668 Mt Hope Avenue, Rochester, NY 14620–2731, USA
website: www.boydellandbrewer.com

A catalogue record for this book is available
from the British Library

The publisher has no responsibility for the continued existence or accuracy of URLs for
external or third-party internet websites referred to in this book, and does not guarantee
that any content on such websites is, or will remain, accurate or appropriate

For my grandmother,
Nancy Zimmerman Proctor (1925–2011),
who continues to inspire me every day

Contents

	List of Figures	ix
	Abbreviations	xi
	Introduction	1
1	*Imitatio Mariae*: Mary, Medieval Readers and Conceiving the Word	15
2	Performing the Psalms: The Annunciation in the Anchorhold	41
3	Reading the Prophecies: Meditation and Female Literacy in Lives of Christ Texts	79
4	Writing the Book: The Annunciations of Visionary Women	115
5	Imagining the Book: *Of Three Workings in Man's Soul* and Books of Hours	175
6	Inhabiting the Annunciation: The Shrine of Our Lady of Walsingham and the Pynson Ballad	225
	Coda: Mary and Her Book at the Reformation	251
	Acknowledgements	267
	Bibliography	269
	Index	295

Figures

1. Annunciation; margins: various scenes from Mary's life. Matins, Hours of the Virgin. Book of Hours. France, Troyes, *c.* 1470. Walters Art Museum, MS W.249, fol. 37r. © The Walters Art Museum.   3
2. Marginal illumination: Jesus cradled in a book, with Mary looking on. Book of Hours, known as the Rohan Hours. Paris, France, *c.* 1416–35. Paris, BnF, MS lat. 9471, fol. 133r. © Bibliothèque nationale de France.   18
3. Visitation. Lauds, Hours of the Virgin. Book of Hours. Paris, France, *c.* 1425–30. Baltimore, Walters Art Gallery MS W.288, fol. 41r. © The Walters Art Museum.   19
4. Presentation in the Temple; border: Annunciation. None, Hours of the Virgin. Book of Hours. Paris, France, *c.* 1425–30. Baltimore, Walters Art Gallery MS W.288, fol. 68v. © The Walters Art Museum.   20
5. Annunciation. Benedictional of St Æthelwold (971–84, *c.* 973). London, British Library, Additional 49598, fol. 5v. © The British Library Board.   65
6. Annunciation. St Albans Psalter (*c.* 1140–6). Hildesheim, Dombibliothek, MS St Godehard 1, p. 19. © Hildesheim Dombibliothek.   69
7. Mary of Burgundy at Prayer. Hours of Mary of Burgundy, Flanders, *c.* 1470–80. Österreichische Nationalbibliothek, Vienna, Codex Vindobonensis 1857, fol. 14v.   207
8. Annunciation. Matins, Book of Hours. Tournai, Belgium, *c.* 1480–90. New York City, Pierpont Morgan Library, MS M.171, fol. 30v. © The Morgan Library and Museum.   211
9. Annunciation. Matins, Hours of the Virgin. Book of Hours, use of Paris and Le Mans. Paris, France, *c.* 1490–5. Poitiers, Médiathèque François-Mitterrand, MS. 53 (292), fol. 18r.   213
10. Annunciation. Matins, Hours of the Virgin. Book of Hours. Paris, France, 16th century. Amiens, Bibliothèque Municipale, MS 2540, fol. 1r. © Amiens, Bibliothèque Municipale.   214

11 Annunciation. Matins, Hours of the Virgin. Book of Hours, known as the Buves Hours. Hainaut, Belgium, *c.* 1450–60. Baltimore, Walters Art Museum, MS W.267, fols 13v–14r. © The Walters Art Museum. 217

12 Annunciation. Matins, Hours of the Virgin. Book of Hours, known as the Beauchamp Hours. England, *c.* 1430. London, BL, MS Royal 2.A.XVIII, part 2, fol. 34r. © The British Library Board. 219

13 Annunciation. Matins, Hours of the Virgin, use of Poitiers. France, 15th century. Poitiers, Médiathèque François-Mitterand, MS 1096, fol. 43r. 221

14 Copper alloy pilgrim badge from the shrine of Our Lady of Walsingham. Late 15th century. Diameter 37 mm. Museum of London, Item ID 78.84/19. © Museum of London. 224

15 Lead alloy pilgrim badge from the shrine of Our Lady of Walsingham. Late 14th-early 15th century. Height 37 mm, width 31 mm. Museum of London, Item ID 88.53. © Museum of London. 226

16 Detail of Annunciation, stained glass. *c.* 1460–70. Main-light panel (part), South window, Nave, All Saints Bale parish church, Norfolk, UK. Source: CMVA inv. no. 005130. © Crown copyright. Historic England Archive. 231

17 'The Salutation.' Anthony Stafford, *The Femall Glory; or, the Life, and Death of our Blessed Lady, the holy Virgin Mary, Gods owne Mother* (London: Thomas Harper, 1635), p. 30. Reprinted from The Internet Archive, OpenLibrary ID OL25880447M. 263

The author and publisher are grateful to all the institutions and individuals listed for permission to reproduce the materials in which they hold copyright. Every effort has been made to trace the copyright holders; apologies are offered for any omission, and the publisher will be pleased to add any necessary acknowledgement in subsequent editions.

Abbreviations

BL	British Library
BnF	Bibliothèque nationale de France
CCCM	*Corpus Christianorum Continuatio Medievalis*
CUL	Cambridge University Library
Douay-Rheims	*The Holy Bible: Translated from the Latin Vulgate and diligently compared with the Hebrew, Greek and other editions, with notes by Bishop Challoner.* New York: The Douay Bible House, 1945.
	(source for all Bible quotation translations)
EETS e.s.	*The Early English Text Society* extra series
EETS o.s.	*The Early English Text Society* original series
Lewis and Short	Lewis, Charlton and Charles Short. *A Latin Dictionary.* Oxford: Oxford University Press, 1879.
MED	*Middle English Dictionary.* https://quod.lib.umich.edu/m/middle-english-dictionary/dictionary
MVC	*Meditationes vitae Christi*
MDN	*Meditaciones domini nostri*
O3W	*Of Three Workings in Man's Soul*
OED	*Oxford English Dictionary*
PL	*Patrologia Latina*, ed. J.-P. Migne, 221 vols (Paris, 1844–64). http://pld.chadwyck.co.uk
Vulgate	Weber, Robert and Roger Gryson, eds. *Biblia Sacra: Iuxta Vulgatam Versionem*. Stuttgart: Deutsche Bibelgesellschaft, 1969, 2007. (source for all Latin Bible quotations)

In mense autem sexto, missus est angelus Gabriel a Deo in civitatem Galilaeae, cui nomen Nazareth, ad virginem desponsatam viro, cui nomen erat Ioseph, de domo David: et nomen virginis Maria. Et ingressus angelus ad eam dixit: Ave gratia plena: Dominus tecum: benedicta tu in mulieribus. Quae cum vidisset turbata est in sermone eius et cogitabat qualis essit ista salutatio. Et ait angelus ei: Ne timeas Maria, invenisti enim gratiam apud Deum. Ecce concipies in utero, et paries filium, et vocabis nomen eius Iesum: hic erit magnus, et Filius Altissimi vocabitur, et dabit illi Dominus Deus sedem David patris eius: et regnabit in domo Iacob in aeternum, et regni eius non erit finis. Dixit autem Maria ad angelum: Quomodo fiet istud, quoniam virum non cognosco? Et respondens angelus dixit ei: Spiritus Sanctus superveniet in te, et virtus Altissimi obumbrabit tibi. Ideoque et quod nascetur sanctam, vocabitur Filius Dei. Et ecce Elisabeth cognata tua et ipsa concepit filium in senecta sua: et hic mensis sextus illi quae vocatur sterilis: quia non erit impossibile apud Deum omne verbum. Dixit autem Maria: Ecce ancilla Domini, fiat mihi secundum verbum tuum. Et discessit ab illa angelus. (Luke 1:26–38)

(And in the sixth month, the angel Gabriel was sent from God into a city of Galilee, called Nazareth, to a virgin espoused to a man whose name was Joseph, of the house of David; and the virgin's name was Mary. And the angel being come in, said unto her: 'Hail, full of grace, the Lord is with thee: blessed art thou among women.' Who having heard, was troubled at his saying and thought with herself what manner of salutation this should be. And the angel said to her: 'Fear not, Mary, for thou hast found grace with God. Behold thou shalt conceive in thy womb and shalt bring forth a son: and thou shalt call his name Jesus. He shall be great, and shall be called the Son of the most High. And the Lord God shall give unto him the throne of David his father: and he shall reign in the house of Jacob for ever. And of his kingdom there shall be no end.' And Mary said to the angel: 'How shall this be done, because I know not man?' And the angel answering, said to her: 'The Holy Ghost shall come upon thee and the power of the Most High shall overshadow thee. And therefore also the Holy which shall be born of thee shall be called the Son of God. And behold thy cousin Elizabeth, she also hath conceived a son in her old age: and this is the sixth month with her that is called barren. Because no word shall be impossible with God.' And Mary said: 'Behold the handmaid of the Lord; be it done to me according to thy word.' And the angel departed from her.)

Introduction

Luke 1:26–38 preserves the only canonical telling of the Annunciation, when Gabriel arrives to announce to Mary that she will become the Mother of God, and Christ becomes incarnate in her womb.[1] For many Christians the Annunciation is an historical event faithfully recorded by the disciple Luke, an 'educated Greek Christian believer', directly from Mary's telling.[2] We learn next to nothing about the setting, situation or appearance of this young woman – only that she is a virgin, betrothed. Indeed, nothing actually *happens* explicitly in this passage. It is exclusively speech-act, *parole*, out of which centuries of exegesis has spun the mystery of the hypostatic union, the indescribable, ineffable union of God and human.

Despite the gospel's lack of detail we can instantly picture the scene because of its nearly ubiquitous representation throughout western art history over the last two millennia. Since the episode is discourse-driven, concrete iconographic imagery helps to identify it visually. While the setting may vary from chapel to bedroom to study to garden, it is almost always Gabriel flying in, Mary with her book.[3] Thousands of manuscript illuminations, altar paintings, sculptures, relief carvings, rood screens, wall paintings, stained glass, textiles and pilgrim badges depict the Annunciation scene, pervading pre-modern art in the West.[4] As a representative example, the altogether typical Annunciation scene of a fifteenth-century book of hours, Walters Art Museum, MS W.249,

---

[1] On other surviving versions of the Annunciation story, including the apocryphal gospels and the Qu'ran, see Gary Waller, *A Cultural Study of Mary and the Annunciation: From Luke to the Enlightenment* (London: Pickering & Chatto, 2015), ch. 2, 'Multiple Texts, Multiple Stories'.
[2] Waller, *A Cultural Study of Mary*, 60.
[3] On the varying settings of late-medieval Annunciations, especially from the Continent, see David M. Robb, 'The Iconography of the Annunciation in the Fourteenth and Fifteenth Centuries', *The Art Bulletin* 18:4 (1936): 480–526.
[4] In Byzantine art Mary spins instead of reads; see, for instance, Maria Evangelatou, 'The Purple Thread of the Flesh: The Theological Connotations of a Narrative Iconographic Element in Byzantine Images of the Annunciation', in *Icon and Word: The Power of Images in Byzantium. Studies Presented to Robin Cormack*, ed. A. Eastmond and L. James (Aldershot: Ashgate, 2003), 261–79.

fol. 37r (Figure 1), shows Mary in her aristocratic bedroom with one hand still on her open book, the other hand raised in greeting to the angel, while Gabriel wields the banderole of his words to the Virgin which also form the *Ave Maria* prayer. The Holy Spirit in the form of a dove and shafts of light represent divine conception. As in many Annunciation illuminations, Mary's book contains writing that is just barely *illegible*: its unreadability leaves it open to interpretation and allows it to bear multiple layers of meaning. The long, rich tradition of these layers of meaning of Mary's book forms the basis for this study.

On one level Mary's reading could be the Old Testament prophecies foretelling the Incarnation, such as Isaiah 7:14, 'ecce virgo concipiet et pariet filium' (Behold a virgin shall conceive and bear a son) or Psalm verses interpreted allegorically to relate to the Annunciation. On a deeper level Mary's book symbolically represents the theological belief of Christ as the Word of God, as *Verbum* or *Logos*. 'in principio erat Verbum et Verbum erat apud Deum et Deus erat Verbum' (In the beginning was the Word, and the Word was with God, and the Word was God) opens the first two verses of John's Gospel, and he soon after explains the phenomenon of the Incarnation in these terms: 'et Verbum caro factum est et habitavit in nobis' (and the Word was made flesh and dwelt among us) (John 1:14).[5] Because Mary gave her flesh to Christ, Mary's book represents the Word conceived out of her body, the Book of Christ on which the world can be written, and the New Testament conceived out of the Old. Her reading symbolizes not just specific prophecies but the entire exegetical interpretation of every word of the Old Testament as a typological foreshadowing of the coming of the Messiah. And this weighty symbolism is in addition to the weighty symbolism of any representation of this scene: 'The Annunciation is therefore more than just the iconography of a biblical passage, for it thematizes and comments upon the beginning of the figurative process as something that flows forth from the principle of incarnation – the becoming flesh, and thus "becoming image," of Christ himself,' comments art historian Barbara Baert.[6] The hypostatic union of God and man does not just evoke acts of interpretation and figuration: it literally embodies them.

---

[5] Often modern discussions of the Incarnation and Christ as 'Word made flesh' do not include Mary at all; for only two recent examples, see, for instance, Emily A. Holmes, *Flesh Made Word: Medieval Mystics, Writing, and the Incarnation* (Waco, TX: Baylor University Press, 2014) and Mayra Rivera, *Poetics of the Flesh* (Durham, NC: Duke University Press, 2015).

[6] Barbara Baert, 'The Annunciation and the Senses: Late Medieval Devotion and the Pictorial Gaze', in *The Materiality of Devotion in Late Medieval Northern Europe: Images, Objects, and Practices*, ed. Henning Laugerud, Salvador Ryan and Laura Katrine Skinnebach (Dublin: Four Courts Press, 2016), 122.

Figure 1. Annunciation; margins: various scenes from Mary's life. Matins, Hours of the Virgin. Book of Hours. France, Troyes, c. 1470. Walters Art Museum, MS W.249, fol. 37r.

Today all this theology might seem rather esoteric – something only for theologians to play with. And likewise we rather take for granted the ability to have meaning behind language. Of course it is possible to draw multiple layers of interpretation out of a text. But in the Augustinian mindset of the Middle Ages, such interpretation was only possible because of God. 'Per ipsum pergimus ad ipsum, tendimus per scientiam ad sapientiam' (through Him we reach on to Himself: we stretch through knowledge to wisdom) explains Augustine (d. 430) in *De Trinitate*.[7] Michelle Karnes summarizes Augustine's influential epistemology: 'For Augustine, understanding is an act enabled by God, self-understanding resembles God, and from both one might understand, in part, God.'[8] Because the human takes on the divine, signs can take signification, concrete can take on the abstract. Words can work, metaphors can work, interpretation can work – cognition itself can work. This theology was far from obscure; while it was developed by theologians such as Augustine, Aquinas and Bonaventure, its ramifications infiltrated all levels of cultural belief and production. Could we imagine a world where all understanding of meaning was contingent upon a single girl in the distant past saying 'yes' to an angel? To wrap our heads around such a profoundly different attitude towards interpretation we must pay attention to how the Annunciation moment functioned in medieval culture and, in particular, the significance of a very concrete image: Mary's book.

This book (the one currently being read) offers a new contribution to the history of reading, one centred on a reader alone in a room with *her* book, perhaps looking much like the reader reading at this moment. That sense of reflexivity is crucial to this story: because the Virgin saw herself reflected in the virgin of Isaiah's prophecy, medieval readers could see themselves reflected in their books, whether that was the Bible, retellings of the Bible, or other devotional texts. Just as Mary's book merges with all books, so does the conception of Christ in her reading body offer a model of transformative reading for all bodies. She conceives physically, spiritually and intellectually, opening up a rich paradigm of metaphorical conception that medieval authors and theologians embraced. According to Mary's model, Christ could be conceived in the reader's soul, but also a complex new awareness of the self could emerge into the reader's existence. In many ways, devotion centred on the Annunciation, with its combination of divine embodiment and Mary's self-reflective reading, becomes a medium for the production of identity. Literature and art

---

[7] Augustine, *De Trinitate*, VIII.xix.24, from *De Trinitate libri XV, CCSL* 50A, ed. William J. Mountain and François Glorie (Turnhout: Brepols, 1968, 2001), 417. Translation from Gareth B. Matthews, *On the Trinity: Books 8-15* (Cambridge: Cambridge University Press, 2002), 132. Quoted in Michelle Karnes, *Imagination, Meditation, and Cognition in the Middle Ages* (Chicago: University of Chicago Press, 2011), 69.

[8] Karnes, *Imagination, Meditation, and Cognition*, 75.

that promote a participatory piety, such as lives of Christ, often open with the Annunciation scene as a mimetic moment where the meditant is formed in the mould of the praying Mary, thus ensuring his or her successful approach to the devotional exercise. Through Mary, meditants learn how to pray, how to move with Christ's humanity to his divinity, how to move from the bodily to the spiritual. All of this transformation was channelled through the maternity of Mary. David Linton has suggested that medieval art makes Mary's reading 'a marginal act, one which was peripheral to her role as Mother of God, an act of devotion she did in her chamber while waiting for the really important job to begin, that of being a mother'.[9] Actually, Mary's first 'really important job' was that of expert reader, exegete and *maistress* of Scripture, a role that continually undergirds her later 'really important job' of mother. As the following chapters will prove, her textual engagement was in no way marginal: it provides a theologically and devotionally significant representation of the transformation happening in her body, and offers a crucial metaphor for what could happen metaphorically in each believer's soul when they practised an *imitatio Mariae*. While for centuries the Crucifixion had dominated (and would continue to dominate) Christian devotion to Christ in his suffering and Mary in her grief, from the long twelfth century through the early sixteenth century the Annunciation offered an alternative subject for and model of imaginative prayer. The scene of Christ's Incarnation made available a very different *imitatio Mariae*, one devoid of her pain, sorrow and weeping at the scene of Christ's death. Most importantly, the devotional site of the Annunciation offered something the Passion could not: a praying figure engaging a text in an enclosed space – in other words, a suggestively close mirroring of actual meditative practices of medieval men and women.

Like the Incarnation, the iconography of the book in Mary's hands also functioned on the concrete level, as a symbol of medieval women's reading practices. The evidence I gather below shows how the book's function as a theological symbol does not preclude its function as an icon of female literacy, both legitimizing and promoting women's reading of scripture. While texts certainly encouraged her imitation by both men and women, Mary held a different signification for readers who shared her gender. In a society where women generally had more limited access to education and books than men, such a female model of independent literacy could be taken literally by female readers who otherwise had few precedents of literate women. If Mary's saintliness was to be imitated, and she read the Bible unmediated by any man, could medieval women do the same? Could Mary's book challenge the patriarchal hold on textual production and consumption that continues to shape culture

---

[9] 'Reading the Virgin Reader', in *The Book and the Magic of Reading in the Middle Ages*, ed. Albrecht Classen (New York: Falmer Press, 1999), 274.

today? I will show how Mary's book was not only spiritually transformative – it could be culturally radical, disrupting gendered power dynamics that undergirded the medieval world. Thus the new history of reading presented in this study also offers a new history of women readers and women authors that changes how we understand the last 1000 years of literacy.

The story of Mary's book

To contextualize the impact of the motif of Mary's book in the later Middle Ages and beyond, we must reach back a further thousand years to trace its evolution.[10] None of the canonical gospels give us any details on Mary's life or literacy prior to the Annunciation. The non-canonical *Gospel of Pseudo-Matthew*, possibly compiled in the sixth century from various earlier apocryphal texts including the *Protoevangelium Jacobi*, presents her as a virgin dedicated to the temple, where no one was 'In sapientia legis dei eruditior, ... in carminibus dauiticis elegantior' (more learned in the wisdom of the law of God, ... more elegant in the songs of David) than she was.[11] Of all the church fathers, Ambrose (d. 397) most thoroughly develops the portrait of this learned virgin. In a sermon written for a congregation of virgins, he describes Mary as 'legendi studiosior' (most studious in reading) and surrounded by books when Gabriel arrived.[12] Later in his commentary on Luke, Ambrose specifies that Mary had read the prophecy of Isaiah 7:14 prior to the angel's visit, and that she believed it but did not yet know how it would come to pass. The Venerable

---

[10] For a more detailed early history of the motif and further references for the sources included here, see Laura Saetveit Miles, 'The Origins and Development of Mary's Book at the Annunciation', *Speculum* 89/3 (2014): 632–69. On the visual art history, see other sources cited in that article, as well as Klaus Schreiner, 'Marienverehrung, Lesekultur, Schriftlichkeit: Bildungs- und frömmigkeitgeschichtliche Studien zur Auslegung und Darstellung von "Mariä Verkündigung"', in *Frühmittelalterliche Studien: Jahrbuch des Instituts für Frühmittelalterforschung des Universität Münster* 24, ed. Hagen Keller and Joachim Wollasch (Berlin: De Gruyter, 1990), 314–68, as well as his later book, *Maria: Jungfrau, Mutter, Herrscherin* (Munich: Carl Hanser, 1994). For briefer discussions see also Linton, 'Reading the Virgin Reader', and on the German tradition, Winfried Frey, 'Maria Legens – Mariam Legere: St Mary as an Ideal Reader and St Mary as a Textbook', in *The Book and the Magic of Reading*, 277–93, as well as Melissa R. Katz, 'Regarding Mary: Women's Lives Reflected in the Virgin's Image', in *Divine Mirrors: The Virgin Mary in the Visual Arts*, ed. Melissa R. Katz (Oxford: Oxford University Press, 2001), 19–132, esp. 37–41.

[11] *Pseudo-Matthew* 6.2, in *Libri de natiuitate Mariae: Pseudo-Matthaei Euangelium*, ed. J. Gijsel, Corpus Christianorum Series Apocryphorum 9 (Turnhout: Brepols, 1997), 335–6, lines 8–11. See also Miles, 'The Origins and Development', 638.

[12] *De virginibus ad Marcellinam*, 2.2.7; PL 16: 209A. On Ambrose and Bede see Miles, 'The Origins and Development', 639–42.

Bede (d. 735) reiterated Ambrose's detail of Mary's reading, but it would not be further popularized for at least another century and a half.

The real momentum of pictorial and textual references to the Virgin's reading at the Annunciation emerges from male monastic and clerical contexts in the ninth and tenth centuries and can be linked with the new spiritual ideals defining successive waves of religious reforms. On the continent in the mid-ninth century, ivory carvings like the Brunswick Casket and an Old High German gospel harmony by Otfrid von Weissenburg (c. 800–871) pick up the motif of the book, while in the 900s, Annunciation manuscript illuminations from both sides of the Channel begin to feature Mary reading.[13] From out of the surge in Marian devotion on the continent at the turn of the millennium came sermons by Fulbert of Chartres (c. 952–1028) and Odilo of Cluny (c. 962–1048) that perpetuate Ambrose's suggestion of Mary reading the Old Testament prophecy of the Incarnation. Mary, Odilo explains, was reading when Gabriel arrived; 'Quid legebat?' (What was she reading?) he asks. 'Forsitan occurrebant ei divinae Scripturae testimonia ad illud ineffabile sacramen- tum quod in ea gerebatur sine dubio pertinentia' (Perhaps the testimonies of divine scripture occurred to her, concerning that ineffable sacrament that was born in her, of which there is no doubt), including Isaiah 7:14 among others.[14]

Within the next hundred years the Annunciation iconography of a book in Mary's hands, on a stand, or in her lap would permeate art across Europe and England. Its meteoric rise in popularity can be pinpointed to the late eleventh century – a rise concurrent with a dramatic growth in the cult of the Virgin, the expansion of women's religious life and an increase in women's overall literacy and access to books. While representations of Mary's solitary reading were initially directed towards male clerics and monks, in the long twelfth century the use of the motif shifted to include its prominent use as a mimetic devotional moment for enclosed religious women. The symbolic power of a literate Virgin took on new complexities with its new audiences. Mary's engagement with the Bible, long positioned by men and for men as a symbol of monastic reading practices, suddenly became an explicit emblem of literacy for women readers – particularly anchoresses.[15]

Mary's reading could now function in a way it could not for men, as a means of appropriating for a female audience acts normally portrayed as masculine: scriptural study and interpretation. After all, there was no shortage of male iconographic models for reading and writing: portraits of Matthew,

---

[13] Miles, 'The Origins and Development', 643–7.
[14] *Sermon 12, De Assumptione dei genitricis Mariae*, PL 142: 1024B. See also Miles, 'The Origins and Development', 653–4.
[15] Miles, 'The Origins and Development', 659–69, offers a closer analysis of these claims, which are also further explored in Chapter 1 and Chapter 2.

Mark, Luke, John, Augustine and Jerome (to name just a few) with their books heavily populated medieval manuscripts. When female readers opened the anchoritic texts discussed below, they witnessed a portrait of a female reader, perhaps for the first time. When female visionaries sought an inspiration for their channelling of the divine and their own participation in literate culture as both consumers and producers of books, their texts testify that they turned to Mary at the Annunciation. As the only biblical female figure represented reading, by far the most frequently portrayed female reader and the common ideal behind any medieval female saint who might have been able to read, by the end of the twelfth century Mary had come to dominate the readerly self-conception of the medieval religious woman.

Mary's reading at the Annunciation also influenced other relevant aspects of her cult. The late medieval image of St Anne teaching her daughter the Virgin Mary to read is essentially a back-formation to explain her literacy at the Annunciation, and succeeded in offering an unusual and powerful model of women teaching and reading together.[16] The full-page illumination in Figure 1 surrounds the Annunciation with scenes in Mary's life leading up to that decisive moment, including St Anne reading to her daughter in the top right-hand corner. Mary leads an erudite life. Less common but related iconographical traditions include her representation with a book at nearly every other episode in her life shared with Christ: the Nativity, resting beside the infant Christ; at the Visitation,[17] when she meets her cousin Elizabeth, also pregnant (with John the Baptist); the Flight into Egypt; at the foot of the cross at the Passion; and at Pentecost, with a book and surrounded by the disciples.[18] In

---

[16] The earliest images of Anne teaching the Virgin to read are from the late thirteenth century; it was not until the fourteenth century that St Anne's feast day was celebrated throughout England. Pamela Sheingorn makes an argument parallel to mine when she claims that the image of Saint Anne teaching the Virgin Mary 'should be associated with female literacy' and that 'representations of women with books in medieval art have been overlooked, so their implication for female literacy has been neglected'. See '"The Wise Mother": The Image of St Anne Teaching the Virgin Mary', *Gesta* 32, no.1 (1993): 69–83 (69). Also on St Anne, Kathleen Ashley and Pamela Sheingorn, eds, *Interpreting Cultural Symbols: Saint Anne in Late Medieval Society* (Athens: University of Georgia Press, 1990) and Virginia Nixon, *Mary's Mother: Saint Anne in Late Medieval Europe* (University Park: Pennsylvania State University Press, 2004); on images of St Anne and Mary reading, see Miriam Gill, '*Female Piety and Impiety: Selected Images of Women in Wall Paintings in England after 1300*', in *Gender and Holiness: Men, Women and Saints in Late Medieval Europe*, ed. Samantha J.E. Riches and Sarah Salih (London: Routledge, 2002), 101–20.

[17] There is also a rare tradition of depicting Mary writing the Magnificat; see Susan Schibanoff, 'Botticelli's Madonna del Magnificat: Constructing the Woman Writer in Early Humanist Italy', *PMLA* 109.2 (1994): 190–206.

[18] For various examples see Susan Groag Bell, 'Medieval Women Book Owners', *Signs* 4 (1982): 742–68 (762), and Lesley Smith, 'Scriba, Femina: Medieval Depictions of

addition, if the book at the Annunciation constitutes the foremost material expression of the Virgin as the Mother of the Word made flesh, Mary's model of transformative reading and linguistic interpretation underpins her medieval role as 'queen' over the three liberal arts of the *trivium*. It is little known today that in the Middle Ages she was 'imagined to be present as a teacher, muse, and orator at many levels of liberal arts instruction.'[19] Mary's early association with the scriptural figure of Wisdom/Sapientia or the goddess personification of Sophia hovers behind all these facets of Mary's later medieval cult, including Mary's reading.[20]

The current study follows this story through to the eve of the Reformation and focuses on these literary and artistic traditions as they developed in England, or 'Oure Ladyes dowre', in the words of the anonymous fifteenth-century poet of the Pynson ballad, about the Shrine at Walsingham.[21] John Lydgate (d. 1451) similarly invites Mary to 'Entyr in Englond, thy dower with reverence' in his Marian hymn *Ave Regina Celorum*.[22] To think of 'England's green and pleasant land' as Mary's marriage portion expresses the feeling of familial participation which prompted the English not only to recreate Mary's little room on their soil as the shrine at Walsingham, but also in their souls, as they replayed the Annunciation scene over and over again in their devotions. 'The Marian fervor that we associate today with Italy or Spain – or link with the Gothic cathedrals of Our Lady that glorified the plains and the Capetian politics of medieval France – was in the Middle Ages of English renown,' Gail McMurray Gibson rightly claims. Rosemary Woolf, in her study of the English religious lyric, likewise argues that early medieval England was one of the chief

---

Women Writing', in *Women and the Book: Assessing the Visual Evidence*, ed. Jane H.M. Taylor and Lesley Smith (Toronto: University of Toronto Press, 1996), 22.

[19] Georgiana Donavin, *Scribit Mater: Mary and the Language Arts in the Literature of Medieval England* (Washington, DC: The Catholic University of America Press, 2012), 5.

[20] From the turn of the millennium readings from the sapiential books of Proverbs, Sirach and Ecclesiastes mark Marian liturgy; Barbara Newman, *Gods and Goddesses: Vision, Poetry, and Belief in the Middle Ages* (Philadelphia: University of Pennsylvania Press, 2003), 190–206.

[21] J.C. Dickinson, *The Shrine of Our Lady of Walsingham* (Cambridge, 1956), Appendix 1: The Pynson Ballad, 129, stanza 19. On Mary in medieval England, see Gary Waller, *The Virgin Mary in Late Medieval and Early Modern English Literature and Popular Culture* (Cambridge: Cambridge University Press, 2011); Gail McMurray Gibson, *The Theater of Devotion: East Anglian Drama and Society in the Late Middle Ages* (Chicago: University of Chicago Press, 1989); and for the earlier period, Mary Clayton, *The Cult of the Virgin Mary in Anglo-Saxon England* (Cambridge: Cambridge University Press, 1990).

[22] *The Minor Poems of John Lydgate*, ed. H.N. MacCracken, EETS e.s. 107 (London, 1911), vol. 1: Lydgate Canon and Religious Poems, 291–2; quoted in Gibson, *Theater of Devotion*, 212, n. 3.

originators in western Europe of many forms of Marian piety.[23] Both continental texts adapted for English audiences and new English vernacular texts all testify to a growing insular desire for Marian-centred devotional practices. I explore how writings and art originating from both within and outside England influence each other in their representations of a literate, authoritative Mary, together weaving a distinctively English story.

This study begins with an overview of how polysemy and biblical hermeneutics can help explain the importance of the Word, and the book as an object, to our understanding of Christ and Mary in the Middle Ages. The multiple meanings of the verb *to conceive*, in turn, give us a view into the history of the idea of conceiving Christ or God in the soul and its relation to Mary's reading. But could her reading be more than a symbol, and actually imitated by normal men and women? I introduce the long tradition of *imitatio Mariae* to show that it could be a model, and often was, and to provide a foundation for the following chapters proving this claim. Chapter 2, 'Performing the Psalms: The Annunciation in the Anchorhold', focuses on eleventh- and twelfth-century England by examining a series of Latin and vernacular texts and linked images, all associated with enclosed solitary women, which identify Mary's reading as the psalms. I argue that in this period Mary emerged as the foremost model of female literary devotion for anchoresses, or urban recluses, even as she came to resemble an anchoress herself in the literary tradition. Goscelin of St Bertin's *Liber confortatorius* (*c.* 1080) and the anonymous Middle English *Ancrene Wisse* (*c.* 1200–30) invoke the Virgin at the Annunciation as an appropriate model of solitary, enclosed reading for their anchoritic readers. Christina of Markyate's *Vita* (*c.* 1150), meanwhile, describes a scene where the holy woman reacts to a supernatural visit not of an angel, but of demonic toads, with loud chanting of the psalter in her lap – a kind of counter-image of the Annunciation illumination found in the beautiful St Albans Psalter, likely made for Christina herself. In all three texts the vocalized performance and assertive voice of the Virgin offer the anchoress a more sophisticated, transformative engagement with the Word than modern critics have previously acknowledged. As a contrast to the idea of the meditative silence of their enclosure, these female readers find a bold, vocal identity in Mary's example.

From the twelfth century on, however, Mary usually read not the psalms but the prophecies of Isaiah foretelling the Incarnation – the focus of Chapter 3, 'Reading the Prophecies: Meditation and Female Literacy in Lives of Christ Texts'. Mary reading Isaiah can be seen in another text written for anchoresses: Aelred of Rievaulx's *De Institutione Inclusarum* (*c.* 1160), which jump-started a

---

[23] *The English Religious Lyric in the Middle Ages* (Oxford: Oxford University Press, 1968), 114.

popular genre of medieval literature, so-called 'lives of Christ' or spiritual biographies that invite readers to participate imaginatively in the life of Christ as a meditative exercise. I connect Aelred's Annunciation scene with similar ones in the late-medieval pseudo-Bonaventuran *Meditationes vitae Christi* (*MVC*), Nicholas Love's *Mirror of the Blessed Life of Jesus Christ* (c. 1415) and the anonymous *Speculum Devotorum* (c. 1425–50) in order to argue that each encourages their readers to join Mary at the Annunciation in reading the Old Testament prophecies, but with subtle, yet significant differences. This chapter analyses how these depictions of Mary reading Isaiah's prophecy evolved over the twelfth to fifteenth centuries in response to England's shifting religious climate and tolerance of women's reading habits. In fact, her Bible reading was sometimes controversial enough in late-medieval England to warrant its restriction – and even omission, as in one of the later vernacular translations of Aelred's *De Institutione*. Tracking the presence of Mary's book in these devotional texts offers an innovative case study illuminating the history of control over biblical reading and women's literacy in the Middle Ages.

Some medieval Christians took the invitation to participate imaginatively in the Annunciation to a whole new level: they experienced visions where they join Mary in the scene itself. In Chapter 4: 'Writing the Book: The Annunciations of Visionary Women', I shift to consider Mary's role in the visionary writings of four women: Elizabeth of Hungary and Naples (d. 1322) and Birgitta of Sweden (d. 1373), continental visionaries whose works were translated into Middle English; and Julian of Norwich (d. c. 1416) and Margery Kempe (d. after 1438), English visionaries who were very much influenced by Elizabeth and Birgitta as continental foremothers shaping the insular tradition. I discuss how these female authors are united by an *imitatio Mariae* where the Virgin's reception of the Annunciation functions as the primary model for their reception of divine revelation. The process of documenting this mystical presence in a text likewise found a model in Mary: as she conceives and gives birth to Christ, so they conceive the vision and birth a text – their written visionary account. She becomes a visionary just like them. The inherent 'textuality' of the Annunciation – the Virgin's (in)corporation of the divine Word into the speaking 'text' of the corporeal Christ – offered a way for holy women to conceptualize their visionary authorship as an act authorized by God.

Chapter 5 begins by focusing on a single treatise to demonstrate how the devotional traditions and the visionary traditions of the previous two chapters come together to centre Mary in the development of meditational practice in late-medieval England. This previously unrecognized shift is exemplified in a fascinating yet neglected text examined in depth for the first time in this chapter: the fourteenth-century Middle English *Of Three Workings in Man's Soul*, a short prose treatise teaching the basics of meditation for readers new to the practice. The first half of the treatise offers a translation of part of Richard of

St Victor's *Benjamin minor*, and the second half a detailed description of Mary reading and then imagining herself as part of that scripture, contemplating and in ravishment – all just before Gabriel's arrival. Readers are encouraged both to meditate *on* her and meditate *like* her. Here I will present new support for the argument for Richard Rolle's authorship of this work, and its original intended audience of religious women – and also show how manuscript evidence proves it was later adapted for male readers. This unique Annunciation scene was later interpolated into a longer life of Christ compilation, *Meditationes domini nostri*, another understudied Middle English text. This borrowing demonstrates the significance of Mary's model for reading and meditating on the very texts within which she appears.

Through this common locus of Mary's reading, these interconnections between the genres of meditational treatises, lives of Christ and visionary texts change the way we understand late medieval devotion. Chapter 5 moves beyond the previous chapters in showing how Mary's book worked for mixed gender audiences, as demonstrated by both *Of Three Workings* and *Meditationes domini nostri*. By no means was an *imitatio Mariae* of her reading limited only to female readers, though its significance might have varied between men and women, and between lay and enclosed readers. These points are supported by comparison between *Of Three Workings* and a series of unusual Annunciation illuminations from Books of Hours, where the moment *before* Gabriel's arrival is captured, and then the female – or male – reader/owner is added to the scene, re-visioning the imaginative experience of the life of Christ text.

All the Annunciation traditions in England examined thus far – as a part of solitary enclosure, participatory piety, women's devotion, visionary experience and lay spiritual practices – come together in one of the most famous pilgrimage destinations in late-medieval England, the Shrine of Our Lady of Walsingham, the subject of Chapter 6. The shrine claimed to be a re-creation of the house where the Annunciation took place, originally built by an eleventh-century Anglo-Norman noblewoman, Richelde de Faverches, upon the command of a divine vision. The final chapter offers a close reading of the 'Pynson Ballad', a late-fifteenth-century poem that tells the shrine's story. I demonstrate how the shrine's little building provided for pilgrims a simulacrum of the Virgin's private, devotional space. In offering an actual building that pilgrims could inhabit with their physical bodies, the Shrine at Walsingham endorsed the devotional value of envisioning one's self as present at the Annunciation. The vicarious experiences of participative piety, with lives of Christ and other texts, transform into actual performances in this sacred extra-liturgical space – that also represents Mary's womb and her spiritual motherhood of all Christians. In the poem's telling of Richelde's vision, I contend, Mary's interpretive power (rooted in the tradition of her reading at the

Annunciation) enables the construction of the shrine, and connects with the official identification of the building as the place of the Incarnation.

To conclude, the Coda looks forward in time to the Reformation and post-Reformation period in England, and how Mary's image changed in a period of shifting literacies. I end with a challenge to scholars of later periods: how must we re-think the exemplarity of Mary in the intervening centuries, now that we know she offered the Middle Ages such a complex model of reading, interpretation and devotion?

1

Imitatio Mariae:
Mary, Medieval Readers and Conceiving the Word

Polysemy and biblical hermeneutics

Underpinning this book's literary and historical analyses are several intertwined theological matters: the polysemy of language and Scripture, Christ and Mary each as both book and reader, medieval hermeneutics, the fourfold interpretation of Scripture, and what this all means for individual medieval readers. Perhaps it is easiest to start with a single verb whose meaning and nature epitomize the core of this study: *to conceive*. Derived from the Latin *concipere*, from *con-* 'altogether' + *capere* 'to take', conceive supports multiple senses derived from the principal notion of 'to take to oneself, take in and hold'.[1] Gabriel uses the primary sense of 'to become pregnant with young' when he tells Mary, 'ecce concipies in utero' (behold, thou shalt conceive in thy womb) (Luke 1:31). The figurative implications range widely but centre around the sense of 'to take into, or form in, the mind': to understand mentally or intellectually. Medieval authors played with these dual meanings; Julian of Norwich, for instance, deploys both connotations of *to conceive* and their syntactical parallels in the more vernacular *to behold*, a word that comes to define her theology, as I will explore in Chapter 4. *Conceive* is a polyseme: a word with multiple *related* meanings. Literally 'many-signed', a polysemous word 'has a multiplicity of meanings or bears many different interpretations'.[2] In that 'polysemes are etymologically and therefore semantically related,

---

[1] OED, *conceive*, v.
[2] OED, *polysemous*, adj.

and typically originate from metaphorical language',[3] polysemy takes to an extreme the foundational metaphoricity that underlies *all* language. A word's first (usually concrete) sense stretches figuratively to encompass other senses (usually metaphorical), each of which can operate independently of that initial meaning; yet simultaneously, the paranomasic potential – the pun – remains. Medieval authors viewed figurative language and metaphor as 'not primarily ornamental but, rather, fundamental to a way of understanding, and they perceive language, embodiment, and cognition as mutually interrelated'.[4]

In a broader usage, polysemy refers to the layers of meaning which can adhere to a work of art or literature. Dante's epistolary preface to the *Commedia* expresses this idea very clearly: 'sciendum est quod istius operis non est simplex sensus, immo dici potest polysemum, hoc est plurium sensum' (it should be understood that there is not just a single sense in this work; it might rather be called *polysemous*, that is, having several senses).[5] In the Christian tradition, the two-part Bible also operates in this polysemous way. The Old Testament is the signifier, or 'letter', of which the New Testament is the signified, or the 'spirit'. Christ, as *Logos*, or Word, is both the sender of the New Testament and the 'ultimate referent of the Scriptures'.[6] Explained by John as 'the Word was made flesh' (John 1:14), Christ's presence on earth, as both God and man, unlocks the words of the Scriptures in their multiple meanings. 'In short, the spirit of the letter is Christ… he joins together the two Testaments,' summarizes Henri de Lubac, the historian of exegesis.[7] Umberto Eco writes of

---

[3] Yael Ravin and Claudia Leacock, 'Polysemy: An Overview', in *Polysemy: Theoretical and Computational Approaches*, ed. Ravin and Leacock (Oxford: Oxford University Press, 2000), 2.

[4] Cristina Maria Cervone, *Poetics of the Incarnation: Middle English Writings and the Leap of Love* (Philadelphia: University of Pennsylvania Press, 2012), 21, where she continues on to an important discussion of Augustine's role in these issues.

[5] *Epistola X*, ed. E. Moore, in *Tutte le Opere di Dante Alighieri*, 3rd ed. (Oxford University Press, 1904), 415; translation, Robert Haller, *Literary Criticism of Dante Alighieri* (Lincoln: University of Nebraska Press, 1973), 99. The entire passage is a remarkable explanation of different literal and metaphorical senses of reading. Discussed in Brigitte Nerlich, 'Polysemy: Past and Present', in *Polysemy: Flexible Patterns of Meaning in Mind and Language*, ed. Brigitte Nerlich, et al. (Berlin: Mouton de Gruyter, 2003), 49–79, 58–9; Umberto Eco, 'History and Historiography of Semiotics', in *Semiotik/Semiotics: Ein Handbuch zu den zeichentheoretichen Grundlagen von Natur und Kultur* (Berlin: Walter de Gruyter, 1996), vol. 1, 730–46; and R.A. Shoaf, 'Medieval Studies After Derrida After Heidegger', in *Sign, Sentence, Discourse: Language in Medieval Thought and Literature*, ed. Julian N. Wasserman and Lois Roney (Syracuse: Syracuse University Press, 1989), 9–30, 13–14.

[6] Umberto Eco, *Semiotics and the Philosophy of Language* (Bloomington: Indiana University Press, 1984), 148.

[7] Henri de Lubac, *Medieval Exegesis, Volume 1: The Four Senses of Scripture*, trans. by Mark Sebanc (Grand Rapids, MI: Wm. B. Eerdmans, 1998), 237; for more on Christ

the exceedingly complex relationship between Christ as sender, his message as signifier and scriptural content as signified:

> This semiotic web was encouraged by the ambiguous status of the term *Logos*, which is at the same time *verbum mentis* and *verbum vocis*, as well as the name and the nature of the second person of the Trinity. Moreover, the first interpreter of the ancient law was still Christ as *Logos*, and every commentary of the Holy Texts was an *imitatio Christi*, so that in the light of the *Logos* all faithful interpreters can become *Logikoi*. To make the web even more inextricable, Christ, insofar as He was the *Logos*, that is, the knowledge that the Father had of Himself, was the ensemble of all the divine archetypes; therefore he was fundamentally polysemous. Thus both Testaments speak of their sender and of their own polysemous nature, and their content is the nebula of all the possible archetypes.[8]

In this way it is Christ that enables hermeneutic interpretation of the Bible, a tradition at its most dynamic in the Middle Ages.[9] The word 'hermeneutics' draws on the ancient Greek figure of Hermes, the god of translation, who guided souls 'from their carnal dwellings, their somatic tombs, to the place of the spirits, to the spiritual' (i.e. Hades).[10] Thus textual hermeneutics leads us from the literal to the metaphorical; 'the process in question is that of textual interpretation, transferring and translating the flesh of the letter into the sense of the spirit: to its *meaning*'.[11] Christ, as both man and God, as both letter and spirit, not only unlocks exegesis of God's Word, but *is* the Book, embodied on earth. So, while Eco makes the important point that Christ encompasses within himself both book as *Logos* and its interpretation, Jean Leclerq OSB prioritizes the two: 'first and primarily, Jesus is the Book; only secondly and consequently is he the Reader. The whole truth and revelation of God about God meets in Jesus, and he reads this revelation both itself and in the books which announced and prepared for it.'[12] The Annunciation is far from the only moment utilized to represent this central metaphor, as a few Books of Hours illuminations demonstrate. In the early fifteenth-century Rohan Hours, Paris, BnF, MS lat. 9471, fol. 133r, the artist depicts an infant Christ cradled in a clasped

---

in relation to scripture, see 'The Action of Christ', 234–41.

[8] Eco, *Semiotics*, 148–9.
[9] For a clear introduction to the ideas of polysemy and Biblical hermeneutics in general, see Henning Laugerud, 'Polysemi og den dynamiske tradisjon', in *Passepartout: Skrifter for kunsthistorie*, 25 (2005), 94–103.
[10] John Panteleimon Manoussakis, 'On the Flesh of the Word: Incarnational Hermeneutics', in *Carnal Hermeneutics*, ed. Richard Kearney and Brian Treanor (New York: Fordham University Press, 2015), 307.
[11] Manoussakis, 'On the Flesh of the Word', 307.
[12] Jean Leclerq OSB, 'Mary's Reading of Christ', Monastic Studies 15 (1984): 107

book, an adoring Mary looking on from above (Figure 2).[13] His body blends with the book both visually and metaphorically. Another Book of Hours also made in Paris in the first third of the fifteenth century, Baltimore, Walters Art Gallery MS W.288, fol. 41r, presents a very unusual (perhaps unique) twist on the Visitation, where when Mary greets her cousin Elizabeth, instead of sharing their pregnant bodies they both gaze upon and touch a large book cradled in Mary's arms and overlapping both wombs (Figure 3).[14] Christ as foetus becomes externalized as Scripture, making the women look more like serious bibliophiles than expectant mothers. To underscore the Christ as book symbolism, the Presentation in the Temple illumination some folios later in the same manuscript presents the Virgin in the same posture as at the Visitation, this time with her arms in the same position around not the Word but the squirming infant Christ (Figure 4). Just to the top left of the main image, the artist

Figure 2. Marginal illumination: Jesus cradled in a book, with Mary looking on. Book of Hours, known as the Rohan Hours. Paris, France, c. 1416–35. Paris, BnF, MS lat. 9471, fol. 133r.

---

[13] On the Rohan Hours see Millard Meiss, intro., with intro and commentaries by Marcel Thomas, *The Rohan Master: A Book of Hours: Bibliotheque Nationale, Paris (MS Latin 9471)* (New York: George Braziller, 1973). The manuscript is digitized at https://gallica.bnf.fr/ark:/12148/btv1b10515749d (accessed 17 August 2019).

[14] On this Book of Hours see Roger S. Wieck, *The Book of Hours in Medieval Art and Life* (London: Sotheby's, 1988), 11.

Figure 3. Visitation. Lauds, Hours of the Virgin. Book of Hours. Paris, France, c. 1425–30. Baltimore, Walters Art Museum MS W.288, fol. 41r.

Figure 4. Presentation in the Temple; border: Annunciation. None, Hours of the Virgin. Book of Hours. Paris, France, c. 1425–30. Baltimore, Walters Art Museum MS W.288, fol. 68v.

includes a small Annunciation roundel to remind the viewer of Christ's textual origins (the full-page Annunciation being back at the beginning of Matins).

With Christ figured as the book (a metaphor I will return to in a moment), Leclerq then emphasizes Mary as foremost reader: 'For Mary, however, the primary role is to be, not the book but the reader, to read the prophecies about Jesus, then to read Jesus as their fulfillment.'[15] His second use of the verb 'read' here suggests its meaning of 'to interpret'. Mary's reading of Christ as a Book and the Book as Christ represents the original act of hermeneutic interpretation of scripture, in as much as it is Christ's Incarnation in her womb that originally allowed for any act of hermeneutic interpretation. While it is Christ that is the ultimate interpreter, Mary is the first (non-divine) human to perform the cognitive process of textual interpretation, translating the 'letter' to its 'spirit', its meaning. As she reads the Old Testament, the text suddenly achieves its final referent in both her mind and her womb simultaneously: she conceives Christ as she conceives the meaning of the words in front of her. If those words are imagined as one of the verses foretelling the Incarnation, like Isaiah 7:14, 'ecce virgo concipiet et pariet filium' (Behold, a virgin shall conceive and bear a son), she suddenly becomes that virgin – she herself becomes the fulfilment of that prophecy. The connection between Mary's pregnancy and the Old Testament prophecies is made already in Matthew 1:22–3, when the angel cites this prophecy as part of his oneiric explanation to Joseph of the miraculous conception of Jesus: 'Hoc autem totum factum est, ut adimpleretur idquod dictum est a Domino per prophetam dicentem : Ecce virgo in utero habebit, et pariet filium : et vocabunt nomen ejus Emmanuel, quod est interpretatum Nobiscum Deus' (Now all this was done that it might be fulfilled which the Lord spoke by the prophet, saying: Behold a virgin shall be with child, and bring forth a son, and they shall call his name Emmanuel, which being interpreted is, God with us) (Matthew 1:22–3). In contrast, Gabriel's words to Mary in Luke ('ecce concipies in utero, et paries filium, et vocabis nomen ejum Jesum') do not explicitly quote but rather closely echo Isaiah ('ecce virgo concipiet, et pariet filium, et vocabitis nomen ejus Emmanuel'). She is perfectly capable of making the parallel between the angel's words and the Word herself, as it were, without the angel needing to state it. Her skills in recalling – and interpreting – scripture exceed any other human's.

How does Mary's expert reading relate to the four senses of typological interpretation of the Bible? By the high Middle Ages the *quadriga*, or four senses of scripture, had been established: first, the *historia* or *littera*, the letter or literal sense, and then the 'threefold spiritual sense': allegorical,

---

[15] Leclerq, 'Mary's Reading of Christ', 107.

moral or tropological and anagogical or mystical.[16] Thirteenth-century Augustine of Dacia's well-known verses explain the *quadriga* quite concisely: 'Litteras gesta docet, quod credas allegoria; / moralia quid agas, quid speres anagogia' (the letter teaches the facts, allegory what you should believe; / the moral sense what you should do, and anagogy what you should hope for).[17] First I will consider the literal sense as it applies to the actual act of Mary's reading the Old Testament as a foretelling of the Incarnation. The twelfth-century medieval theologian Richard of St Victor (d. 1173) argued that the understanding of Mary as Isaiah's *virgo* was its literal sense, 'because the authors of the text intended it to speak of Christ when they wrote it'.[18] Later this interpretation would be called the 'parabolic' or 'prophetic' literal sense by Thomas Aquinas (d. 1274) in the thirteenth century or, later on, the 'double literal sense' for Nicholas of Lyra (d. 1349).[19] A few commentators explicitly discuss Mary as a reader, and what kind of exegesis she performed in reading the prophecies about herself. Albertus Magnus (d. 1280) describes Mary as *lector*, a reader: 'lector, quantum ad omnium prophetarum expositionem, ad litteram, in se ipsa' (a reader, with respect to the exposition of all the prophets, according to the literal sense, as in her very self).[20] Probably drawing on Albertus Magnus, the Dominican Antoninus of Florence (d. 1459) goes further in identifying Mary as *lectrix*, a gendered female reader: 'lectrix spiritualis, quia eum lectoribus habuit prophetiarum expositionem'

---

[16] On the four senses of scripture, among many sources, see all volumes of Henri de Lubac, *Medieval Exegesis*, but particularly *Medieval Exegesis, Volume 3: The Four Senses of Scripture*, trans. E. M. Macierowski (Grand Rapids, MI: Wm. B. Eerdmans, 2009), 37, 197–9; Beryl Smalley, *The Study of the Bible in the Middle Ages* (Notre Dame, IN: University of Notre Dame Press, 1964); and Frans van Liere, *An Introduction to the Medieval Bible* (Cambridge, MA: Cambridge University Press, 2014), 120–40.

[17] Quoted in van Liere, *An Introduction to the Medieval Bible*, 121.

[18] van Liere, *An Introduction to the Medieval Bible*, 134, based on Richard of St Victor, *De emmanuele*, PL 196: 601 ff.

[19] van Liere, *An Introduction to the Medieval Bible*, 135–6. For more details see *Medieval Literary Theory and Criticism, c. 1100–c.1375: The Commentary-Tradition*, rev. ed. Alastair Minnis, A.B. Scott, and David Wallace (Oxford: Oxford University Press, 1991, rpt 2001), 205–6; as well as Alastair Minnis, *Medieval Theory of Authorship: Scholastic Literary Attitudes in the Later Middle Ages*, 2nd ed. (Philadelphia: University of Pennsylvania Press, 1988, rpt. 2010), 'Preface to the Reiussed Second Edition', ix–xi.

[20] Albertus Magnus, in *Biblia Mariana* (sup. lib. Prov.); cited in Jean Jacques Bourassé, *Summa Aurea de Laudibus Beatissimæ Virginis Mariæ*, Vol. IX (Paris: P. Migne, 1862), col. 1323. Bourassé's *Summa Aurea* is an 'Encomia Mariana', a dictionary of epithets for Mary, and a reprinting of the *Polyanthea Mariana*. This reference and the next are briefly mentioned in Leclerq, 'Mary's Reading of Christ', 107.

(a spiritual reader, because she of all readers had the exposition of the spiritual sense of the prophets).[21]

Two further verses from Luke influenced the medieval development of Mary as not only an interpretive reader, but also as a contemplative reader: Luke 2:19, 'Maria autem conservabat omnia verba haec, conferens in corde suo' (But Mary kept all these words, pondering them in her heart), and Luke 2:51, 'Et mater ejus conservabat omnia verba haec in corde suo' (And his mother kept all these words in her heart). Medieval commentators, Leclerq explains, used these verses to show how, over the course of her life, Mary continually compared what she had read in the prophecies to what she saw in Christ's life: 'as the first witness of these events she was able to understand them progressively and thus to give the exegesis of them'.[22] She is able to take the Old Testament and read its literal, typological meanings as foreshadowing the life of Christ. Indeed, sometimes Mary is depicted holding a Bible at the foot of the cross, recalling her lifelong interpretive relationship to the scriptures as an expression of the Word that is her son. Because she 'kept all these things in her heart', or memory, patristic and medieval authors also figured Mary as a book herself written in by the hand of God (in parallel to the theme of Christ as book, a theme explored below).[23] Perhaps the height of this tradition can be found in Peter of Celle, a Benedictine abbot of the twelfth century, whose Annunciation Sermon 22 elaborates a detailed allegory of the Incarnation as book-making in and on Mary, including all the tools and steps of producing a manuscript.[24] Bernard of Clairvaux (d. 1153), in one of his sermons on Luke's

---

[21] D. Anton. in *Summa Theologica*, part. IV, tit. 15., cap 16; cited with the Albertus Magnus above in Bourassé, *Summa Aurea*, Vol. IX, col. 1323.

[22] Leclerq, 'Mary's Reading of Christ', 111. Leclerq cites, among others, Jerome, Bede, Haymon, Werner and Aelred of Rievaulx as part of this exegetical tradition.

[23] Catherine Keene presents an up-to-date history of this trope in 'Read Her Like a Book: Female Patronage as *Imitatio Mariae*', *Magistra* 24(1) (2018): 3–38. Klaus Schreiner discusses the tradition of Mary as a book in his article '". . . wie Maria geleicht einem puch': Beiträge zur Buchmetaphorik des hohen und späten Mittelalters', *Archiv für Geschichte des Buchwesens* 11 (1971): cols 1437–64, and on Peter of Celle cols 1445–6.

[24] Peter of Celle, Sermo XXVI, *In Annuntiatione Dominica V* on Isaiah 8:1 'Sume tibi librum grandem', PL 202: 718a–720c; discussed in Leclerq, 'Mary's Reading of Christ', 108–9, and Keene, 'Read Her Like a Book', 14. In Sermon XXIV he also refers to Mary as written in by the finger of God (PL 202: 713a-b) as discussed in an article by Mary McDevitt, '"The Ink of Our Mortality": The Late-Medieval Image of the Writing Christ Child', in *The Christ Child in Medieval Culture: Alpha Es et O!*, ed. Mary Dzon and Theresa M. Kenney (Toronto: University of Toronto Press, 2012), 240. On Peter of Celle in general see the introduction to Hugh Feiss OSB, trans., *Peter of Celle: Selected Works* (Kalamazoo, MI: Cistercian, 1987), which does not include these sermons.

Annunciation passage, uses the metaphor when he imagines Mary's thoughts as she responds to Gabriel:

> Fiat mihi non tantum audibile auribus, sed et visibile oculis, palpabile manibus, gestabile humeris. Nec fiat mihi verbum scriptum et mutum, sed incarnatum et vivum: hoc est, non mutis figuris, mortuis in pellibus exaratum - sed in forma humana meis castis visceribus vivaciter impressum: et hoc non mortui calami depictione, sed sancti Spiritus operatione.[25]

> (Let it be to me, [a Word] not only audible to the ear, but visible to the eyes, one which hands can touch and arms carry. And let it not be to me a written and mute word, but one incarnate and living, that is to say, not [a word] scratched by dumb signs on dead skins, but one in human form truly graven, lively, within my chaste womb, not by the tracings of a dead pen, but by the workings of the Holy Spirit.)

Christ's presence on earth, as both divine and human, unlocks the 'dumb signs on dead skins' of the scriptures to be intelligible as the Word of God, 'lively ... by the workings of the Holy Spirit'. Thus while Mary engages with the scriptures in an exemplary way, as the true singular fulfilment of the Old Testament prophecies, she also offers an imitable mode of reading the Bible. Though Mary is *literally* that virgin of the prophecy, her relationship to the Old Testament itself points to several other kinds of biblical exegesis, meaningful for medieval readers. In regards to how we might read in the literal sense, medieval Christians believed Mary existed as an historical figure from biblical history, whose story is preserved in the *historia* of the New Testament. Simultaneously, like Christ, she can be understood in a typological sense as fulfilling some types of the Old Testament – indeed, she stands as a kind of hinge between the Old and the New, as the conception of Christ in her signals the start of the New Law. 'Typological exegesis,' K.J. Woollcombe explains, 'is the search for linkages between events, persons or things *within the historical framework of revelation*, whereas allegorism is the search for a secondary and hidden meaning underlying the primary and obvious meaning of a narrative' (italics original).[26] Albertus Magnus demonstrates a Marian allegorical approach in his *Biblia Mariana*, where he systematically goes through the Old Testament books and interprets each verse as a type of Mary.[27]

---

[25] Bernard of Clairvaux, *Sermones Super missus est* from *Homilia De Laudibus Virginis Matris*, Sermon IV.11, PL 183: 86b. Translation from Marie-Bernard Saïd OSB, *Homilies in Praise of the Virgin Mary* (Kalamazoo, MI: Cistercian, 1993), 57.
[26] 'The Biblical Origins and Patristic Development of Typology', in *Studies in Biblical Theology 22: Essays on Typology* (London: SCM Press, 1957), 40.
[27] The entirety of Albertus Magnus, *Biblia mariana*, can be found in *Opera omnia*, ed. Jammy (Lyon, 1651), volume 20, part c, 1–40.

Such reflectivity of Old onto New Testament, of *historia* shading into *allegoria*, leads also to the idea of a universal history patterned on the Bible and on Christ's life. It was a commonly held medieval belief that

> the Bible did not contain two distinct histories of Israel and the early Church but a single universal history ... Events did stand alone on their historical completeness, but were best understood in relation to the divine purpose in which circumstances, while retaining their historical integrity, figurally re-enacted archetypes. These historical recurrences were regarded as incarnations of divine meaning revealed by God's providence and gesturing beyond themselves, in one direction towards the archetype and the historical fulfilment, in the other towards their ultimate apocalyptic consummation.[28]

Folding time back on itself, in continually smaller increments, meant that in the Christian universe signs could take on very rich signification. This is how the visionary Bridget of Sweden, with her mystical pregnancy experience where a child seemed to quicken in her womb, could see that sign as signifying not merely a similarity to the Mother of God but rather that 'in a real sense she *becomes* the God Bearer'.[29] Events more than parallel each other – they cleave together. This can also be seen in how the liturgical cycle works. Each year maps onto Christ's life: Christ's conception is celebrated on 25 March, the Feast of the Annunciation, while his birth is exactly nine months later, 25 December. The crucifixion must always be celebrated in the context of a calendar week, so Holy Week and the date of Easter are not fixed but calculated. But 25 March, the date of the Annunciation, God made man, was also believed to be the date on which Adam was created (man made man), and the actual historical date on which Christ died. According to Augustine in *De Trinitate*:

> For He is believed to have been conceived on 25 March, and also suffered on this same day; thus the womb of the Virgin, in which He was conceived, where no mortal person was begotten, corresponds to the new tomb in which He was buried, where no deceased person was laid, neither before nor after.'[30]

---

[28] Samuel Fanous, 'Becoming Theotokos: Birgitta of Sweden and Fulfilment of Salvation History', in *Motherhood, Religion, and Society in Medieval Europe, 400–1400: Essays Presented to Henrietta Leyser*, ed. Conrad Leyser and Lesley Smith (Surrey: Ashgate, 2011), 276. See also M.-D. Chenu OP, 'Theology and the New Awareness of History', in *Nature, Man, and Society in the Twelfth Century: Essays on New Theological Perspectives in the Latin West*, ed. and trans. Jerome Taylor and Lester K. Little (Toronto: University of Toronto Press, 1997), 162–201.

[29] Fanous, 'Becoming Theotokos', 277.

[30] Book 4, ch. 5, paragraph 9 of *The Trinity*, trans. Stephan McKenna, C. SS. R. The Fathers of the Church Volume 45 (Washington, DC: The Catholic University of America Press, 1963), 141–2. Also discussed in Georges Didi-Huberman, *Fra Angelico:*

Thus life, death, and salvation layer on one another, all happening simultaneously in the liturgical celebration of the Christian story, all a cohering moment. The medieval Christian belief system is dependent upon the ability of signs to take multiple significations without cancelling out each other, and upon the ability of signs (the Bible as the main sign) to have simultaneously a universal as well as a very personal meaning for each individual.

So Mary's role in the Incarnation, and her reading at that moment, can become a tropological mode of biblical reading and take on that very personal meaning. The moral sense of scriptural interpretation concerns how the Bible might be interpreted as a guide to one's daily actions and lived faith. This includes both a more straightforward *imitatio Christi* – trying to act like Christ or lead a Christ-like life – as well as the more metaphorical interpretations of Old Testament verses as instructions for holy living. *Tropologia* 'is the *sensum quotidie*, the kind of everyday prophecy that Scripture should inspire in every soul, in the entire Church, at every moment in time'.[31] Thus every word of the Bible is, tropologically speaking, 'the most perfectly straight ruler of human life so as to guide it to the heights of perfection'.[32] In their elaborations on Mary's comportment at the Annunciation, the texts I examine in the following chapters inspire their readers to act, pray, read, sing, meditate and contemplate like the Virgin, an *imitatio Mariae* founded in the tropological sense of Scripture. A meta-reflexive motive drives this interpretive mode: the reader is encouraged to see him or herself reflected in the devotional text in their hands just like the Virgin saw herself reflected in the Old Testament text in her hands. Ultimately this is an act of almost interwoven literal and tropological interpretation – or even *interpellation*, with the medieval reader interpellating themselves into the text as a performance of participatory piety. Indeed all of the following chapters, but especially the chapters on meditative guides, showcase how medieval devotional texts developed a mode of dramatically active reading, encouraging the reader to imagine themselves within the biblical scene, right behind Mary when Gabriel arrives, right at Christ's side at the cross. This kind of reading brings alive the multiple senses of scripture: that the actual literal, historical event both happened in a historical past even as it is *always happening* and happens anew for each devotee that imagines themselves at the scene. In many visual representations of the Annunciation from the Middle Ages (indeed most biblical episodes), for instance, Mary dresses like a contemporary viewer not because the painter was painfully unaware

---

Dissemblance and Figuration, trans. Jane Marie Todd (Chicago: University of Chicago Press, 1995), 76 and 124–7.

[31] Didi-Huberman, *Fra Angelico*, 40.

[32] Henri de Lubac, *Medieval Exegesis: Vol. 2, The Four Senses of Scripture*, trans. E.M. Macierowski (Grand Rapids, MI: Wm. B. Eerdmans, 2000), 'Mystical Tropology', 141.

of the anachronism, but because for them the Annunciation event was not 'merely' historical – it was continually recurring, just as Christ is eternal in God, and able to be conceived anew in the soul of each devout Christian.

Conceiving Christ in the soul

That rich, polysemous verb *to conceive* provides the perfect articulation of how it is that Christ could be imagined as being brought alive metaphorically within one's self as a kind of tropological fulfilment of scripture. While *imitatio Christi* might be the main performative mode of medieval Christian practice, the widespread teaching of conceiving Christ in an individual's heart or soul can function as a performance of *imitatio Mariae* rooted in the Annunciation scene.[33] From the earliest Christian traditions, re-enacting the Incarnation in one's self was a significant way to understand godliness. Paul writes to the Galatians 'filioli mei quos iterum parturio donec formetur Christus in vobis' (my little children, of whom I am in labour again, until Christ be formed in you) (Galatians 4:19) and also to the Ephesians, 'habitare Christum per fidem in cordibus vestris' (that Christ may dwell by faith in your hearts) (Ephesians 3:17). According to this disciple, the image of Christ is reproducible within the individual Christian – with the right faith, actions and grace. Origen (c. 184–253) returns again and again throughout his works to the idea of conceiving Christ in the soul, especially in *On Prayer*, and in writings on *The Song of Songs*. He connects the concept closer to Mary in his fragmentary *Commentary on Matthew*: 'And every soul, virgin and uncorrupted, which conceives by the Holy Spirit so as to give birth to the Will [i.e. Word] of the Father, is the mother of Jesus.'[34] Mary's maternal role becomes metaphorically available to any pure soul. Conception and birth, both being metaphorical in this sense, were mutually invoked, making the motif equally appropriate to the Annunciation or the Nativity. Augustine of Hippo (d. 430) expanded on the theme in a Christmas sermon: 'hunc fide concipite, operibus edite; ut quod egit uterus

---

[33] For an overview of this idea and its history among the fathers and other medieval authors, see the section on 'Deification and Birthing' in Bernard McGinn, ed. and intro., *The Essential Writings of Christian Mysticism* (New York: The Modern Library, 2006), 396–425; on the history of metaphorical conception in relation to Bridget's mystical pregnancy, see Claire Sahlin, *Birgitta of Sweden and the Voice of Prophecy* (Cambridge: D.S. Brewer, 2001), 85–90, and 'The Virgin Mary and Birgitta of Sweden's Prophetic Vocation', in *Maria i Sverige under tusen år*, ed. Sven-Erik Brodd and Alf Härdelin, 227–54 (Skellefteå: Artos, 1996). Rosemary Drage Hale offers an extensive treatment of metaphorical maternal *imitatio Mariae* in 'Imitatio Mariae: Motherhood Motifs in Late Medieval German Spirituality' (unpublished PhD dissertation: Cambridge, MA, 1992), 46–110.

[34] McGinn, *The Essential Writings*, 402.

Mariae in carne Christi, agat cor vestrum in lege Christi' (conceive [Christ] by faith, give birth to Him through your works, so that your heart may be doing in the law of Christ what the womb of Mary did in the flesh of Christ).[35] Mary becomes the subject of imitation, though it is her Son that is the object.

The particularly strong influence of Origen on the early medieval development of the spiritual conception of Christ can be seen in the sermons of Guerric of Igny (c. 1087–1157), a French Cistercian Abbot. In his *Sermon 2 on the Annunciation* he elaborates:

> So that you may more fully recognize that the Virgin's conception is not only mystical [i.e. a hidden dogmatic truth] but also moral [a truth for emulation], what is a mystery for redemption is also an example for your imitation, so that you will certainly cancel out the grace of the mystery in you if you do not imitate the virtue given in the example. For she who conceived God by faith promises you the same if you have faith. Hence, if you want to receive the Word from the mouth of the heavenly messenger in faithful fashion, you too will be able to conceive the God whom the whole world cannot contain, but in your heart and not your body. Yet more, even in your body, although not by bodily work or manner, but still certainly in your body, since the Apostle commands us 'to glorify and bear God in our body' (1 Cor 6:20).[36]

Perhaps for the first time, Guerric explicitly comments that conceiving Christ in the soul sets up the Virgin's conception as 'an example for imitation'. He pulls in more details from the Annunciation scene itself to explain how this works, referring to Gabriel as 'the heavenly messenger' who delivers the Word from his mouth. Guerric's explication of the simultaneous distinction and connection between body and soul fits with the decreasingly dualist views after the millennium, and foreshadows how later medieval female visionaries, especially Bridget of Sweden, will express the metaphorical conception of Christ as a quite real physiological conception in the body. Likewise, the paradox that 'you too will be able to conceive the God whom the whole world cannot contain' anticipates Julian of Norwich's vision where Mary marvels over this exact enigma. Guerric returns to this epistomological tension later in his sermon:

> A faithful soul, open wide your breast, enlarge your desire so that you do not become too narrow within; conceive him whom no creature is able to contain! Open the ear of your hearing to the Word of God. This is the way

---

[35] Augustine, *Sermon 192.2*, PL 38: 1012; trans. Thomas Comerford Lawler, *St Augustine, Sermons for Christmas and Epiphany*, Ancient Christian Writers, no. 15 (Westminster, MD: The Newman Press, 1952), 114.

[36] McGinn, *The Essential Writings*, 405; trans. by McGinn from Guerric of Igny, *Sermones per Annum, in Annuntiatione Dominica II,* in PL 185: 120-4.

of the Spirit conceiving in the womb of the heart; for 'this reason the bones of Christ' (that is, the virtues) 'are knit together in the womb of the pregnant woman' (Eccles 11:5).[37]

For Guerric the senses, especially hearing, facilitate conception of the Spirit as Christ, linking both to Mary's aural reception of Gabriel's announcement as well as to the general power of hearing the Word of God uttered or sung liturgically. Such is the potential Goscelin of St Bertin taps into in his nearly contemporaneous *Liber Confortatorius* when he depicts Mary's singing of the psalms as concurrent with – if not precipitating – both Gabriel and God's arrival.

So for the early history of this metaphor, male monks are encouraged to imitate the Mother of God, a woman, and allowed to occupy a feminine position without any conflict. In parallel to the development of the image of Mary's book, the twelfth century also saw the metaphor of conceiving Christ move from a male monastic context to a female one, specifically nuns living a life of vowed virginity, like the intended reader of Goscelin's *Liber*. Conceiving Christ in the soul is a major theme in *Speculum Virginum*, or *Mirror of Virgins*, a twelfth-century text composed by a Benedictine monk for monastic women in Germany. Over the course of the next three centuries it became relatively popular with vernacular translations made for Franciscan, Bridgettine and Augustinian cloisters.[38] Perhaps the most prominent example of the influence of *Speculum Virginum* is the documentation of one of Birgitta of Sweden's confessors reading it to her aloud early in her religious career, and that it is explicitly identified as the inspiration for at least one other revelation.[39] In this guide for virgins, a monk named Peregrinus carries out a dialogue with a nun named Theodora. The author has no problem explicitly encouraging direct emulation of Mary in her role in the Incarnation: 'Hanc uirginum principem, tu uirgo Christi, quantum possibile est, imitare et cum Maria filium dei uideberis spiritualier parturire' (Imitate this chief of virgins as far as possible, virgin of Christ, and you too, with Mary, will seem to give birth spiritually to the Son of God).[40] Again, at another point in the text, he explains that 'Christ, who was once born physically from his virgin mother, is always carried and

---

[37] McGinn, *The Essential Writings*, 406.
[38] Hale, 'Imitatio Mariae: Motherhood Motifs', 62. For an edition of *Speculum Virginum* see Jutta Seyfarth, *Speculum Virginum*, CCCM V (Turnhout: Brepols, 1990).
[39] Claire L. Sahlin, *Birgitta of Sweden and the Voice of Prophecy* (Woodbridge: Boydell Press, 2001), 89; Päivi Salmesvuori, *Power and Sainthood: The Case of Birgitta of Sweden* (New York: Palgrave Macmillan 2014), 41–4.
[40] Barbara Newman has translated selected excerpts of *Speculum Virginum* as the Appendix to *Listen Daughter: The* Speculum Virginum *and the Formation of Religious Women in the Middle Ages*, ed. Constant J. Mews (New York: Palgrave, 2001), 284; *Speculum Virginum* book 5, 114, ll. 1–10.

born spiritually from holy virgins.'[41] While his audience and agenda dictates an emphasis on physical virginity, he is adapting a motif that began, as we have seen, as available to any person pure enough in heart and soul – an understanding clearly held by Birgitta of Sweden, whose lack of virginity actually enabled her to channel her maternal experience into a divine connection. Yet we will also see how Birgitta's adaptation of the motif of conceiving Christ, where Mary herself interprets its significance, transforms the metaphor into a source of female authority over clerics.

Outside the convent, Meister Eckhart (c. 1260–1328) continued to embrace both Origen and Augustine on the idea of conceiving Christ in the soul. One of Eckhart's sermons reflects on the personal nature of Christ's conception as spiritual rebirth: 'What does it avail me that this birth is always happening, if it does not happen in me? That it should happen in me is what matters' (indeed, Eckhart cites Augustine here, when it should be Origin's *Homily 9 in Jeremiah*).[42] Beyond the prospect of salvation, the Incarnation becomes even more immediately relevant to the individual Christian precisely because its eternal nature is reproducible in each person's soul during life. Eckhart, like some other medieval writers in whose works the motif appears, puts the emphasis on Christ rather than on Mary. The *Speculum Virginum* shows how a shift to a female audience can draw the author to bring Mary to the foreground of the motif. In my analysis of specific devotional texts and visionary accounts that tap into Mary's role as reader and vessel of the Word, the Virgin herself functioned as a kind of interpretive 'key' with which medieval readers – both women and men – could unlock the Word of God, and thus, like Mary, conceive the divine within themselves. I show how her maternal, female body plays a vital role in those expressions of the idea of conceiving Christ in the soul. For holy women who shared the female body with Mary, this meant that their experiences of physical motherhood could become not a liability nor an embarrassment but a source of authority. As with Birgitta of Sweden, their motherhood could provide the authorizing motivation not only to pursue a holy life like Mary's, but even to serve as vehicles of divine revelation with the creative agency to produce literary works – often in the face of stifling misogyny. The texts of Margery Kempe, Julian of Norwich and the other visionary authors I examine demonstrate how Christ, conceived in the holy

---

[41] *Speculum virginum* book 3; trans. Sahlin, *Birgitta of Sweden*, 90. Kim E. Power makes the related point that the *Speculum Virginum* also contains an important development of Mary as pre-existent Wisdom, in that just as the Son was always with the Father, so is Mary always with her Son; Power identifies this position as a significant 'quantum leap in Mariology', representing a 'leap of faith' on the part of the author. See 'From Ecclesiology to Mariology: Patristic Traces and Innovation in the *Speculum virginum*', in *Listen Daughter*, 100.
[42] McGinn, *The Essential Writings*, 413.

woman's vision, can be given birth again in the form of a book. The profound significance of Mary's reading as an authorizing mechanism, however, perhaps can best be demonstrated by showcasing what happens in its absence – that there is in fact quite a lot at stake.

One text in particular offers an eye-opening example of how focusing exclusively on Christ as Word made flesh without extending the literary aspect to his mother can disenfranchise women readers and discount the female body. *Book to a Mother*, a Middle English devotional text likely from after 1380, intertwines the motif of conceiving Christ spiritually with the motif of Christ as a book, open for all Christians to read.[43] This thematic metaphor rose to prominence in the twelfth century, developed by Peter Lombard and later Bonaventure (among others), and also reflected in the prominent tradition of charters of Christ where his body becomes parchment for writing.[44] The anonymous priest behind *Book to a Mother* adopts the book theme as a completely polysemous, pervasive structural metaphor for his text, enveloping his own codex, the Bible, Christ as a book, the reader, salvation, and all of creation as the Book of Life: 'þis bok is Crist'.[45] Like many of the devotional works examined in the following chapters, *Book to a Mother* was written for a specific female audience (in this case, the author's actual mother) as well as a broader general audience in mind. Unlike many of those works, however, misogynist tendencies seep throughout this text, which figures female bodies as sinful and in need of physical claustration as well as complete control by husband, father and cleric, as documented by Nancy Bradley Warren.[46] Again and again, the author combines the metaphors of Christ as a book and spiritual conception of Christ in order to devalue physical conception – that is, mothers' womb work. For example, in this passage:

---

[43] On dating, see *Book to a Mother: An Edition with Commentary*, ed. Adrian James McCarthy (Salzburg: Insitut für Anglistik und Amerikanistik, Universität Salzburg, 1981), xxxiv; Fiona Somerset pushes McCarthy's 1370–80 dating back to the 1380s or later, in *Feeling Like Saints: Lollard Writings After Wyclif* (New York: Cornell University Press, 2014), 261–72.

[44] *Book to a Mother*, xxxviii–xxxl. On the parallel and related tradition of Christ writing, see the invaluable discussion by McDevitt, 'The Late-Medieval Image of the Writing Christ Child'.

[45] *Book to a Mother*, 31. For further explication of the manifold meaning of 'book', see Nicholas Watson, 'Fashioning the Puritan Gentry-Woman: Devotion and Dissent in *Book to a Mother*', in *Medieval Women: Texts and Contexts in Medieval Britain: Essays for Felicity Riddy*, ed. Jocelyn Wogan-Browne et al. (Turnhout: Brepols, 2000), 177; and Elisabeth Dutton, 'Christ the Codex: Compilation as Literary Device in *Book to a Mother*', *Leeds Studies in English* ns 35 (2004): 81–100.

[46] Nancy Bradley Warren, *Spiritual Economies: Female Monasticism in Later Medieval England* (Philadelphia: University of Pennsylvania Press, 2001), 85–6.

> þenk hou Crist com into þis world to be conceyued, and hou þis Bok was closid nyne monþe in a litel place of a maide. And ȝif þou wolt þou maist conceyue þe same Crist and bere him not onlich nine monþes but wiþoute ende; and that is better þan to bere him bodiliche as oure Ladi dide, as Crist seiþ in þe gospel. For Marie is as much to seie as a bittur se or a sterre of þe see.[47]

Spiritual conception is not only an option, but a *far superior* option than bodily conception like Mary's. Her motherhood is not to be emulated as an affirmation of the fecundity of the female body but as a purely genderless metaphor disconnected from impure womanly flesh. Warren argues that 'this passage de-genders maternity. When maternity is made spiritual, its female particularity is obliterated. Maternity is removed from the sphere of the carnal and the feminine, a move that enhances its value.'[48] Such a view is a very important critique of how the metaphor of conceiving Christ spiritually has the potential to play out in a misogynistic way when it erases Mary's maternal and intellectual identities. Her body is elided, she performs no actions and displays no agency; she is only represented by the old *maria/mare* pun that colours her with bitterness.

Therefore it should come as no surprise that when *Book to a Mother* represents the Annunciation scene Mary's voice is likewise silenced and the emphasis is on the angel Gabriel:

> Þerfore þenk as þouȝ wendest wiþ Gabriel into þe conclaue þere sche was loke in hure preiers wiþ þe seuene ȝiftis of þe Holi Gost, and gret hure wiþ Gabriel and sei: 'Heil, ful of grace! God is wiþ þe.' And be glad wiþ hure of þe conceyuynge of hure Sone, and preie hure þat sche wol bidde hure Sone þat þou mowe folowe hure in mekenesse, pouert and chastite.[49]

Note that the author does not take the opportunity to invoke the Christ as book motif here, at the Incarnation moment when the Word is made flesh. Perhaps it would remind the reader too much of the Virgin holding her own Bible, performing her own kind of incarnational hermeneutics. For the 'modir' reader to which the *Book* is repeatedly addressed, Mary is not a mother-reader; she is not part of the fulfilment of the prophecies and certainly not an interpreter of scripture. Such a representation should be understood as a deliberate choice to discourage identification with Mary's independent maternal and intellectual powers, even as, Watson notes, the absence of her book fits with the *Book*'s overall replacement of the Bible with Christ himself.[50]

---

[47] *Book to a Mother*, 44–5.
[48] Warren, *Spiritual Economies*, 89.
[49] *Book to a Mother*, 33.
[50] Watson, 'Fashioning the Puritan Gentry-Woman', 178.

Likewise Elizabeth Schirmer explains how 'this model of reading replaces the material text of the Bible with the "true" Bible that is Christ himself, written through imitation and love in the soul of the reader, ultimately striving to render text – of the Bible, of the *Book* – obsolete'.[51] This scene in *Book to a Mother* echoes a closely contemporary text discussed in Chapter 2, the late fourteenth-century Vernon manuscript translation of Aelred of Rievaulx's *De Institutione Inclusarum*. In a very similar way the reader is encouraged to identify with Gabriel, bypassing a blank, non-active Mary who no longer reads as she once did in the original Latin version of Aelred's meditation. Far from showing its limited influence, omissions like these actually serve to underscore the power of the representation of the Virgin with her book, a female figure whose incursion into the male realm of biblical reading and interpretation seemed to be worthy of censorship by some authors.

Part of my underlying argument of the following chapters is that the image of Mary reading was so ubiquitous in medieval art – literally surrounding Christians in church and at prayer, in illuminations, altarpieces, stained glass, sculptures, vestments, etc. – that *all* authors were aware of the motif and made conscious decisions to invoke it or not. For some authors, like the priest who wrote *Book to a Mother* and the Vernon translator of Aelred's gospel meditation, Mary's meekness and chastity were utterly incompatible with her reading and her pregnant body. While the female reader should feel gladness in the Virgin's conception of Christ, nonetheless 'how wide a gulf separates the sinful reader from Mary', Warren remarks.[52] The *Book* author's mother is certainly not urged to ventriloquize Mary's response to Gabriel, which emboldens several female visionaries to view themselves as active participants in a matrilineage of special access to God. Rather, for the *Book* author the best texts require mere mimicry rather than mimetic interpretation from the reader, and the best texts work best when they efface themselves, and disappear.[53] In the end, this text's female readers are encouraged to be 'women who do not claim the benefits of their productivity and power but instead willingly put them, and themselves, under the control of husbands, fathers, and clerics'.[54]

---

[51] Liz Schirmer, 'Reading Lessons at Syon Abbey: *The Myroure of Oure Ladye* and the Mandates of Vernacular Theology', in *Voices in Dialogue: Reading Women in the Middle Ages*, ed. Linda Olsen and Kathryn Kerby-Fulton (Notre Dame, IN: University of Notre Dame Press, 2005), 351.
[52] Warren, *Spiritual Economies*, 89.
[53] Schirmer, 'Reading Lessons at Syon Abbey', 352; on the book seeking to disappear, see Watson, 'Fashioning the Puritan Gentry-Woman', 178.
[54] Warren, *Spiritual Economies*, 92. For a slightly different view of how Mary and exemplarity works in *Book to a Mother*, see Nicole Rice, *Lay Piety and Religious Discipline in Middle English Literature* (Cambridge: Cambridge University Press, 2008), 123–5.

In some ways the Annunciation scene in *Book to a Mother* is entirely typical. Many theological texts go to great lengths to insist that Mary's powers were unique, a point closely tied to the controversies over female priesthood: if even she was denied sacramental powers by Christ, certainly they should be denied to other women.[55] While in medieval orthodox theology Mary's conception of Christ could be made metaphorically available to ordinary women, no women (including Mary) could confect or make the body of Christ in the Eucharist. On the winning side of late-medieval debates 'the roles played by Christ's Mother and Christ's ministers are judged as irreducibly different and distinctive', Alastair Minnis concludes from his examination of Albert the Great's *Mariale super Missus est* as well as a refutation of the heretical views of Englishman Walter Brut, a Lollard tried in 1391.[56] Denying confection of the Eucharist to women was linked to the restriction of formal preaching to male ministers exclusively. While St Paul famously prohibits female preaching (1 Cor. 14:34–5), biblical examples such as Mary teaching the Apostles qualify not as *ex officio et auctoritate*, from the office and authority of a priest, but rather as *ex necessitate et amicabiliter*, out of necessity and as between friends: 'very different from a woman assuming the *magisterium* of teacher, that being contrary to the sexual hierarchy'.[57] Thus Margery Kempe was so careful to declare that she never preached but 'merely' communicated. With all these official avenues closed off to women, the discourse of Mary's book represents a significant means of giving women access to scriptural and spiritual authority.

In their use of the Annunciation scene in particular, many devotional texts entirely bypass Mary's agency, even the agency inherent in her vocal submission as handmaiden, in favour of connecting the reader with Gabriel's praise in the form of the *Ave Maria* prayer. Such examples put in stark relief what the image of Mary reading can achieve: it challenges misogynist oppression by priests like the author of *Book to a Mother*, it bypasses clerical mediation altogether, it gives women access to the raw materials of both clerical authority and divine incarnation – to hermeneutics.

---

[55] On women and the priesthood in general see Alcuin Blamires, 'Women and Preaching in Medieval Orthodoxy, Heresy, and Saints' Lives', *Viator: Medieval and Renaissance Studies* 26 (1995): 135–52, and *The Case for Women in Medieval Culture* (London: Clarendon Press, 1997).

[56] Alastair Minnis, *Translations of Authority in Medieval English Literature: Valuing the Vernacular* (Cambridge: Cambridge University Press, 2009), 101.

[57] Minnis, *Translations of Authority*, 114.

The meaning of Mary and medieval *imitatio Mariae*

As *Book to a Mother* reminds us, Mary was a paradoxically multivalent figure in the Middle Ages, able to be used both in the suppression and the empowerment of women, and whose cult offers a rich variety of material in all media. The history of the Mother of God has long been a source of interest for both academics and believers,[58] as for nearly two thousand years she has been ubiquitous in art and architecture, in music, in liturgy and prayers, in cathedrals and shrines in her name, in more recent visions and miracles[59] in Catholic cultures around the world – and in the use of the name *Mary* or *Maria* for countless women. Two millennia of doctrine and devotion develop (and continue to develop) her powerful roles as Queen, Bride, Intercessor, Mediatrix and, more controversially, Co-Redemptrix.[60] In addition to the Annunciation, the episodes and feasts of the Conception, Visitation, Nativity, Purification, Christ's Crucifixion and Assumption of Mary all offer opportunities for devotion to Mary.

Exaltation of one exemplary woman certainly does not entail equal elevation of all earthly women. While this distinction is true to some extent then and now, in their over-emphasis on this point some contemporary assessments

---

[58] A few of the most influential volumes concerning the history of Mary and Marian devotion to come out over the last 60 years include: Juniper Carol, ed., *Mariology*, 3 vols (Milwaukee: Bruce 1954); Hilda Graef, *Mary: A History of Doctrine and Devotion* (New York: Sheed and Ward, 1964); Marina Warner, *Alone of All Her Sex: The Myth and Cult of the Virgin Mary* (London: Knopf, 1976); Jaroslav Pelikan, *Mary Through the Centuries: Her Place in the History of Culture* (New Haven: Yale University Press, 1996); Sarah Jane Boss, *Empress and Handmaid: On Nature and Gender in the Cult of the Virgin Mary* (London: Cassell, 2000); Sarah Jane Boss, ed., *Mary: The Complete Resource* (London: Continuum, 2007); Miri Rubin, *Mother of God: A History of the Virgin Mary* (New Haven: Yale University Press, 2009); Andrew Breeze, *The Mary of the Celts* (Leominster: Gracewing, 2008); none of these sources closely examines the motif of a literate Mary. Adrienne Williams Boyarin, *Miracles of the Virgin in Medieval England: Law and Jewishness in Marian Legends* (Cambridge: D.S. Brewer, 2010), presents an important intervention concerning hagiographic texts not covered by this current study.

[59] For a survey of Marian visions strong on the modern period see Roy Abraham Varghese, *God-Sent: A History of the Accredited Apparitions of Mary* (New York: Crossroad, 2000).

[60] Works that focus on doctrine and devotion especially include, among many others, Brian K. Reynolds, *Gateway to Heaven: Marian Doctrine and Devotion, Image and Typology in the Patristic and Medieval Periods*, vol. 1: *Doctrine and Devotion* (New York: New City Press, 2012); Juan Luis Bastero, *Mary, Mother of the Redeemer: A Mariology Textbook*, trans. Michael Adams and Philip Griffin (Dublin: Four Courts Press, 2006). On the continuing controversy of Mary as co-redemptrix, see Bastero, *Mary, Mother of the Redeemer*, 228–37; and its medieval antecedents, Reynolds, *Gateway to Heaven*, 107–51, 246–92.

reveal an ignorance of Mary's medieval history as an empowered, active interpreter, the history captured in the following chapters. Mariolatry's objectification of Mary has lately been seen to contribute decisively to 'the oppression of women ... oppression through exaltation'.[61] Many modern theologians view Mary as a major barrier for Christian women, seeing her passive role in the Annunciation as encoding female subjection to the patriarchy, and the incarnation of God in a male body as shutting out women from equal access to divinity. Gary Waller sums up these views as blaming the image of the humble and obedient Virgin Mary for forcing women to accept phallocentric values that pressure them 'to regress into a primitive world of subordination'.[62] The Annunciation emerges for some modern readers, such as Rebecca Sabbath, as 'a romance of a frightened girl, her body possessed by an omnipotent male, submissively, even servilely, consenting to the use of her body as a subject, receptacle, void, and then ultimately rejoicing in her own objectification'.[63] For others, the Incarnation borders on rape. Mary becomes a blank object on which all kinds of male fantasies can be inscribed, exploiting her objectification for their barely concealed sexual and masochistic satisfaction. This situation is so dire as to be 'beyond patching' according to some feminist theologians.[64]

Such a disheartened, and disheartening, assessment is in part a result of centuries of *post-Reformation* shaping of the representation of Mary. Certainly many pre-modern writings, including many of the texts considered in this study, confirm the medieval origins of traditions emphasizing Mary's obedience, humility, virginity and purity. Yet other more constructive aspects of her medieval cult have been largely forgotten. Georgianna Donavin issues a vital corrective when she writes that 'Mary's reign over scriptural exegesis and devotional expression has been too long underplayed in analyses confusing virginity and subordination with vacuity.'[65] My exploration builds on recent research such as Donavin's to highlight lesser-known medieval Marian traditions that have not survived continuously through to the modern day: Mary's divine maternity as a source of authority; her breasts and body as positive and fecund, not eroticized and dangerous; her

---

[61] K. Theweleit, *Male Fantasies*, trans. S. Conway, C. Turner and E. Carter, 2 vols. (Minneapolis: University of Minnesota Press, 1987–8), vol. 1, 196; quoted in Waller, *A Cultural Study*, 45.
[62] Waller, *A Cultural Study*, 11.
[63] R.S. Sabbath, *Sacred Tropes: Tanakh, New Testament, and Qur'an as Literature and Culture* (New York: Brill, 2009), 231; as quoted in Waller, *A Cultural Study*, 61.
[64] Such as Jane Schaberg, *The Illegitimacy of Jesus: A Feminist Theological Interpretation of the Infancy Narratives* (New York: Harper & Row, 2006) and Sandra Schneiders, *Beyond Patching: Faith and Feminism in the Catholic Church* (New York: Paulist Press, 1991).
[65] Donavin, *Scribit Mater*, 3; see also Boss, *Empress and Handmaid*.

identity as a literate intellectual, even as an expert exegete; her visionary access to God; her power to counteract patriarchal challenges to women's authority. All of these aspects find expression through the motif of her reading at the Annunciation. In many ways the modern hostility towards Mary is taken out on a mythic medieval inheritance that, in reality, is mistakenly viewed through an early modern (or later) lens, coloured by Protestant and reformed misogynies.[66] In other words, if Christians and theologians today want to recuperate Mary, they should not denigrate her medieval cult but rather turn to its forgotten corners for inspiration.

Indeed, modern thinkers have independently come up with many of the same solutions to the Mary problem as medieval thinkers, rediscovering similar conclusions without necessarily being aware of the medieval precedents. If we put them in parallel, I think we can begin to understand just how radical, empowering and 'forward-looking' some particular medieval representations of Mary at the Annunciation could be, especially in the case of women visionaries. In current positive re-readings, the Annunciation 'becomes an affirmation of women's bodies and female autonomy outside the hegemonic power of male authority and male fantasies',[67] closely concurring with Elizabeth of Hungary and Naples, Bridget of Sweden, Julian of Norwich and Margery Kempe. French theorists such as Luce Irigaray and Julia Kristeva reposition Mary's agreement to Christ's conception as a moment when 'a complex new awareness of herself emerges into the woman's existence',[68] an interpretation also realized in the visions of those holy women, who found a validation for their special access to God in Mary. Her response to the angel is more optimistically interpreted by other critics as a liberating act stressing self-affirmation.[69] Mary's role as reader aligns with these modern understandings because it positions her as a subject, instead of an object. With book in hand, she is an independent subject with her own agency, and

---

[66] Donavin, *Scribit Mater*, 3. See also Paul Williams, 'The English Reformers and the Blessed Virgin Mary', in *Mary: The Complete Resource*, 238–55.

[67] As Waller reports in *A Cultural Study*, 12, aptly referring to Julia Kristeva and Catherine Clément, *The Feminine and the Sacred* (New York: Columbia University Press, 2001), 76–7; and Tina Beattie, *God's Mother, Eve's Advocate: A Marian Narrative of Women's Salvation* (London: Continuum, 2002), 74, 175.

[68] K. McDonnell, 'Feminist Mariologies: Heteronomy/Subordination and the Scandal of Christology', *Theological Studies* 66 (2005): 527–67, 534; cited in Waller, *A Cultural Study*, 12. Kristeva articulates much of the power and problems of the Virgin's history in her article 'Stabat Mater', without being quite aware of the visionary woman's take on her: see Laura Saetveit Miles, 'Looking in the Past for a Discourse of Motherhood: Birgitta of Sweden and Julia Kristeva', *Medieval Feminist Forum* 47(1) (2011): 52–76.

[69] Luce Irigaray, 'Christian Mysteries as Graces in the Feminine', *Key Writings* (London: Continuum, 2004), 162; cited in Waller, *A Cultural Study*, 63.

medieval elaborations of this subjectivity often emphasize her own devotion as a holy woman in her own right, not only in relation to her Son.

But is not the Mother of God, the *theotokos*, beyond imitation? Does not her virgin body – miraculously, impossibly pregnant and yet still pure – put her out of reach as a model for normal women? Certainly it can be argued that Mary was sometimes purposefully placed on a pedestal, 'alone of women, without compare' (or more famously, 'alone of all her sex'), as in a fifth-century poem by Caelius Sedulius.[70] In his tract on Marian theology, Guibert of Nogent (d. 1124) describes Mary as unique and perfect, as 'above all creatures' – *super omnes creaturas* – and describes her role in the Incarnation as a passive one.[71] Yet many medieval people resisted those totalizing, inaccessible representations of the Virgin. As perfect as she was, she still functioned as all the saints did, as a model within the Christian mandate of *imitatio*. St Basil writes to Gregory of Nazianzus: 'he who is anxious to make himself perfect in all the kinds of virtue must gaze upon the lives of the saints (and scriptures) as upon statues, so to speak, that move and act, and must make their excellence his own, by imitation'.[72] That is, the lives of the saints and of Mary and Christ possessed an inherent exemplarity which enjoined *imitatio* from all Christians. Female saints' lives, in particular, fostered 'the expectation [...] that women take the legends of female saints as examples for their own ethical and devotional practices'.[73] The same Guibert of Nogent that promoted a distant, perfect Mary out of reach of ordinary people describes, in his autobiography, his mother's dramatically different view as captured in a vision she experienced. In this vision, a huge, oversized Virgin Mary walks down the church aisle, with the visionary as a young girl following directly in her footsteps. Mary proclaims authoritatively that Guibert cannot leave the abbey (as he had wished): '"I brought him here and made him a monk. By no means will I permit him to be taken away." After this the attendant [Guibert's mother] repeated these same words in like

---

[70] Caelius Sedulius, *Paschale carmen*, Book II, line 69, 'sola sine exemplo ... femina'; and well known as the title to Marina Warner's 1976 book, where these verses are also the epigraph, xvii. For the Latin with facing page translation, see Carl P. Springer, ed. and trans., *Sedulius, The Paschal Song and Hymns* (Atlanta, GA: Society of Biblical Literature Press, 2013).

[71] *Liber de laude sanctae Mariae*, PL 156: 537–78 (537b). Quoted in Anneke B. Mulder-Bakker, '*Maria doctrix*: Anchoritic Women, the Mother of God, and the Transmission of Knowledge', in *Seeing and Knowing: Women and Learning in Medieval Europe 1200–1550*, ed. Anneke B. Mulder-Bakker (Turnhout: Brepols, 2004), 186.

[72] *St Basil: The Letters*, ed. and trans. R. J. Deferrari (Cambridge, MA: Harvard University Press, 1961), vol. 1, 15.

[73] Catherine Sanok, *Her Life Historical: Exemplarity and Female Saints' Lives in Late Medieval England* (Philadelphia: University of Pennsylvania Press, 2007), ix.

fashion.'[74] While in this vision Mary is literally *super omnes creaturas* as she looms over them larger than life, at the same time her actions and words are to be directly imitated, and in their repetition Mary's maternal authority is invested in the female visionary, also a mother. The gap between Guibert's perfectly passive Virgin and his mother's active, authoritative Virgin aptly demonstrates how *imitatio Mariae* can often vary between genders.

The types of *imitatio Mariae* I explore in this study position Mary as a model to be imitated, whether that is in her solitude, her enclosure, her silence, her speech, her reading, her interpretation, her understanding, her singing, her praying, her meditation, her contemplation, her ecstasy, her desire – all of which take on metaphorical meaning in reference to her conception of Christ. Even if the image of Mary's book originated, or was intended as, a purely symbolic representation of the Word made flesh, nothing would prevent a reader or viewer from seeking to imitate literally Mary's reading. Or, in the case of some female visionaries, Mary's bold assertion of authority over mortal men. Again, not that men could not or did not imitate Mary (indeed, I examine several instances), but the evidence of my study insists that the power dynamic inherent to a literary, exegetical *imitatio Mariae* functioned differently for women. Not only did Mary exert a special mimetic power for women strengthened by their shared gender, for this reason could an *imitatio Mariae* sometimes overshadow *imitatio Christi* for some holy women, for instance Elizabeth. This finding provides a helpful counter-balance to the predominant understanding of medieval women as *more* drawn to Christ (than men even were), for instance as heavenly bridegroom, or as endorsing bodily weakness like Christ crucified. These are the ways in which suffering and food control, according to Caroline Walker Bynum, seem to have functioned for most female saints: 'there is still little reason to feel that these distinctive themes of women's religiosity were primarily an effort by women to counter the notion that they were lustful and weak. The immediate religious motive was, as it was for men, desire to imitate Jesus.'[75] In contrast, the female visionaries I analyse suggest that the Annunciation demonstrates how an *imitatio Mariae* could be a stronger religious motive than an *imitatio Christi* for many medieval holy women, and often to satisfy directly an urgent need to counter the notion that they were lustful and weak. The power of this *imitatio Mariae* was in no small part due to distinctive themes of women's religiosity quite different from asceticism and anorexia, and sometimes neglected by modern critics: transformative reading, interpretation, contemplation and revelation.

[74] Guibert of Nogent, *De vita sua*, translated by John F. Benton, *Self and Society in Medieval France: The Memoirs of Abbot Guibert of Nogent* (New York: Harper & Row, 1970), 76; also quoted and discussed in Mulder-Bakker, '*Maria doctrix*', 185.
[75] Caroline Walker Bynum, *Fragmentation and Redemption: Essays on Gender and the Human Body in Medieval Religion* (New York: Zone Books, 1992), 155.

A vital point about the nature of this *imitatio Mariae* is that as opposed to mimicry as a kind of mindless copying, the Annunciation offers a moment for *mimesis*, which includes, significantly, 'both an *active* and a *cognitive* component', as Gunter Gebauer and Christoph Wulf point out in their influential study *Mimesis: Culture-Art-Society*.[76] They specify that 'mimesis in reference to others represents a productive intervention into modes of thinking and speaking that are other than one's own'.[77] Mimesis here is creative and transformative, far beyond 'mere' mimicry. The Annunciation's *imitatio Mariae* not only opens up Mary's posture, actions and speech for mimesis, but also her 'mode of thinking', her cognition and her devotion, elaborated on in these texts far beyond Luke's Gospel passage. When she reads the Old Testament, many medieval authors posited, she imagines herself as part of the story; shaped by her reading, her thinking becomes imaginative, interpellative, self-aware, even self-creating, in a way that its imitation could radically change how the reader's own reading and cognitive processes function. She sees history's overlapping patterns; she interprets meaning beyond the literal; she opens up the way for figuration to function, as enabled by Christ's Incarnation. For the spiritual guidance texts examined in the following chapters, this crucial mimetic moment re-forms the reader to prepare them for the spiritual journey of the rest of the text – to be ready to be transformed. Thus the Annunciation demonstrates one way in which devotional treatises and lives of Christ could be literally life-changing, not just behaviour-changing, for medieval readers. Once they read the Virgin reading, they will never read the same again; indeed, they will never see themselves the same way again.

---

[76] Gunter Gebauer and Christoph Wulf, *Mimesis: Culture-Art-Society*, trans. Don Reneau (Berkeley: University of California Press, 1995), 5.
[77] Gebauer and Wulf, *Mimesis*, 4.

2

Performing the Psalms: The Annunciation in the Anchorhold

From its earliest elaborations the scene of Mary at the Annunciation has been defined by her enclosure. In the fourth century, Ambrose insisted that the Virgin was inside alone when Gabriel arrived; by the twelfth century, this aspect of the story had strongly shaped what the scene meant, and how and in what ways the Annunciation scene facilitated devotion. Much more was at stake than simply setting the stage: Mary's enclosure came to symbolize the necessary intactness of her womb, her unassailable virginity. The miraculously sealed room and womb merge to help prove the miraculousness of God made man. Simultaneously, however, the room must be porous to angels, her womb porous to the Holy Spirit and the whole event porous to the imaginative prayers of devout Christians. No longer private at all, the space of her room-womb is so public as to be the business of God and all humankind; it is the site of the Incarnation, the moment when the hope of salvation opens to the world. The concurrent containment and porosity of the Annunciation straddle the same paradoxical ambivalence as God and man in Christ.

The ambivalent sacred space of the Annunciation room and the historical spaces with which it metaphorically overlaps in medieval texts can be productively theorized by means of Foucault's idea of the heterotopia, discussed in a 1967 lecture and subsequently published posthumously.[1] As a kind of heterotopia the space of the Annunciation can be seen to 'presuppose a system of opening and closing that both isolates [it] and makes [it] penetrable' (Foucault's

---

[1] Michel Foucault, 'Of Other Spaces', trans. Jay Miskowiec, Diacritics 16(1) (1986): 22–7. See Laura Saetveit Miles on the heterotopia in 'Space and Enclosure in Julian of Norwich's *A Revelation of Love*', in *A Companion to Julian of Norwich*, ed. Liz Herbert McAvoy (Cambridge: D.S. Brewer, 2008), 154–65.

fifth principle).[2] Mary's private room can be inhabited by God and the angel, approaching from heaven, and yet also inhabited by the meditant, approaching from the future. Its contained penetrability extends across time, as does its relevance to Foucault's third principle of the heterotopia: 'The heterotopia is capable of juxtaposing in a single real place several spaces, several sites that are in themselves incompatible.' The texts I examine in this chapter combine together the historical space of the Annunciation room with the very real historical spaces of enclosed female readers – Mary's room merges with the anchorhold or the recluse's room. Early medieval sources consistently describe Mary as praying alone and enclosed when Gabriel arrives, and often they identify her as following a religious life. She becomes an anchoress, and the anchoress becomes her. Each 'single real place' of Annunciation room and anchorhold transforms, meanwhile, into an idealized site of prayer, a kind of symbolic state of spiritual being represented in the imagination by the image of these rooms. Precisely how all these heterotopic layers interact, however, is one of the most compelling questions about this corner of medieval religious culture.

Focusing on the late eleventh and early twelfth centuries, this chapter surveys texts written by men for and about enclosed holy women, particularly anchoresses, to argue that these texts present Mary's enclosure, prayer and reading at the Annunciation as a paradigmatic model of contemplative devotion. When these texts depict Mary as a recluse, they enable their female recluse readers to imagine themselves as Mary. Anchoritic writings develop the idea of enclosure into a metaphorical model based ultimately on the enclosure of Mary's womb. Enclosure offered the Virgin and the holy woman a refuge of sanctified concentration powered by both silence and sound: in fact, as I will demonstrate, enclosure functioned as a kind of echo chamber that amplified and empowered a woman's vocalized prayer, whether spoken or sung. In this contemplative moment prior to Gabriel's arrival, the *Logos* is made present in the uttered words of prayer as a foreshadowing of the fleshly presence of the *Logos* about to happen.

The authors of these anchoritic texts of the long twelfth century link the Virgin Mary with the psalms – by nature a performative text, meant to be prayed, sung, chanted, vocalized, engaged and interiorized in ways different to any other part of the Bible. Throughout the Middle Ages the psalms were both the foundation of the monastic Divine Office, sung communally in monastic institutions, and also recited or read by lay and religious individuals as part of personal devotion. Few modern scholars are familiar with the early medieval tradition of Mary engaging the psalms at the Annunciation, because Isaiah becomes the more prominent text featured from the thirteenth century onwards. In this chapter I examine how, in the eleventh and twelfth centuries,

[2] Foucault, 'Of Other Spaces', 26.

the Annunciation scene evolved to mirror the experience of the enclosed solitary woman, and what it means when texts connect Mary with the psalms at the moment of Christ's Incarnation. First we follow the tradition linking the Virgin's room with the contemplative's cell, and then explore how two female anchoritic readers encountered Mary at the Annunciation as suggested by their devotional materials. Eva, for whom Goscelin of St Bertin wrote his *Liber Confortatorius*, would have encountered in that text a monasticized Mary whose confident psalm-singing both facilitates and expostulates the Incarnation. Christina of Markyate's *Vita* (c. 1150), meanwhile, describes a scene where the holy woman reacts to a supernatural visit not of an angel, but of demonic toads. She defeats them with her loud, devout chanting of the Psalter in her lap – a kind of perversion of the Annunciation illumination found in the beautiful St Albans Psalter, likely made for Christina herself. In the anchoritic textual tradition of this chapter, Mary both reflects the newly idealized holy woman of the anchoress and encourages anchoritic readers to imitate her devotions. When Mary's text shifts from the Book of Psalms to Isaiah's prophecies, as it does in the texts considered in the next chapter, her song ends and a different kind of reading begins.

Eva, Christina and Aelred's sister were part of the fast-growing trend of women seeking a religious life in post-Conquest England. As one historian puts it,

> Whether one characterizes the twelfth century as a period of intellectual and cultural renaissance, of emerging scholastic and monastic cultures, or of ecclesiastical reformation in both secular and monastic institutions, it is clear that the century saw a tenfold increase in the number of, if not in the relative status of, women's institutions.[3]

Like this growth in women's monastic houses, another option for a holy life apart from the world was also becoming much more popular: the vocation of an anchoress. Anchoresses, or urban recluses, led a life of solitary prayer, typically living alone (or with a maid) within a cell (or cells) attached to the side of a parish church. Daily life for an anchoress consisted in private performance of the Divine Office, prayers, readings and meditations, punctuated by watching or hearing the church's celebration of services and mass through a squint

---

[3] William T. Flynn, 'Ductus figuratus et subtilis: Rhetorical Interventions for Women in Two Twelfth-Century Liturgies', in *Rhetoric Beyond Words: Delight and Persuasion in the Arts of the Middle Ages*, ed. Mary Carruthers (Cambridge: Cambridge University Press, 2010), 250. For an historical examination of this movement see Sharon K. Elkins, *Holy Women of Twelfth-Century England* (Chapel Hill: University of North Carolina Press, 1988). See also B.L. Venarde, *Women's Monasticism and Medieval Society: Nunneries in France and England, 890–1215* (Ithaca, NY: Cornell University Press, 1997), 52–88.

or small window.[4] She also offered her prayers and guidance to the people of the outside world; most famously, for example, Margery Kempe's *Book* describes her visit to the anchorhold of Julian of Norwich and the counsel she received from the anchoress. The vocation was popular from the eleventh century through the Reformation, and though both men and women could be enclosed in anchorholds, more than twice as many women are recorded over these several hundred years. Almost all the surviving anchoritic guides seem to have been written for women by men in various clerical positions.[5]

In part because it is in these women-oriented texts that the Marian and Annunciation motives dominate – and that the female implied reader motivates the majority of the spiritual texts connected with the anchoritic vocation – I focus on anchoresses and the texts written for them.[6] Yet at the same time the very fact that these texts were written for women *by men* demonstrates the broad power of Mary as a model for both genders. Both men and women venerated and emulated the Virgin, as Carolyn Walker Bynum and Rachel Fulton Brown's work has long established.[7] Male authors' intimate knowledge

---

[4] Ann Warren, *Anchorites and Their Patrons* (Berkeley: University of California Press, 1985) remains the dominant source of historical statistics and information about anchoritism. Among recent scholarship on anchoritism, Mari Hughes-Edwards helpfully examines many of the anchoritic guides describing these practices in her book *Reading Medieval Anchoritism: Ideology and Spiritual Practices* (Cardiff: University of Wales Press, 2012), while Liz Herbert McAvoy explores the more theoretical gender dynamics of anchoritic enclosure in *Medieval Anchoritism: Gender, Space and the Solitary Life* (Cambridge: D.S. Brewer, 2011).

[5] Warren's table counts 414 female solitaries, 201 male solitaries and 165 of current unknown gender. The gender gap was larger in the earlier centuries; for instance, the thirteenth century shows about three female anchoresses to every male anchorite. See Warren, *Anchorites and Their Patrons*, 18–29, esp. 20, Table 1. A recent book compiles a comprehensive array of sources that provides some context for these numbers: *Hermits and Anchorites in England, 1200–1550*, trans. and ed. E.A. Jones (Manchester: Manchester University Press, 2019).

[6] Some of the earliest of the few rules for male anchorites, for instance the so-called *Dublin Rule*, do not emphasize the Annunciation; the later *Speculum Inclusorum*, an early fifteenth-century 'rule' for male anchorites, passes over the Annunciation and Incarnation as a contemplative scene to focus on the crucifixion (as does its Middle English translation for women anchorites, *A Mirror for Recluses*). See E.A. Jones, ed., *Speculum Inclusorum: A Mirror for Recluses: A Late-Medieval Guide for Anchorites and its Middle English Translation* (Liverpool: Liverpool University Press, 2013), xxi, esp. 52–7 of the texts. For the *Dublin Rule* see the edition by Livarius Oliger, ed., 'Regulae tres reclusorum et ermitarum angliae saec. Xiii–xiv', *Antonianum* 3 (1928). Later in this book I will consider how Annunciation motifs play out in other genres for male or mixed readerships.

[7] Bynum, *Fragmentation and Redemption*, 153 ff.; Rachel Fulton, *From Judgment to Passion: Devotion to Christ and the Virgin Mary, 800–1200* (New York: Columbia University Press, 2002), 195. While Bynum describes how 'the woman herself

of Marian devotion displays both their own practices and what they deemed appropriate for religious women.[8] However, while the relationships between Mary and men and women could be equally strong, they are inevitably different, because Mary has a gender herself: people's connections to her vary both between the genders and within the genders, and of course over time and space. In the eleventh and twelfth century in England things were changing dramatically for religious women in a way that they were not for men. At this key period of evolution in the literary and cultural force of women, how did the image of Mary at the Incarnation function for those female readers in particular? Whether she is reading or singing or praying aloud, how does Mary's textually engaged female body make a difference to those who textually engage with their own female bodies?

Not only did the number of women following an enclosed religious life dramatically increase over the long twelfth century, the period also 'saw the emergence of the anchoress as a figure of idealized interiority, and thus an ideal reader', as Barbara Newman points out.[9] I argue that Mary at the Annunciation offered a paradigmatic model of this idealized anchoritic reader. The texts I discuss in the following two chapters encourage their readers to replicate, and enter into, Mary's room as an imagined space constructed within the act of prayer. This imagined space, however, finds a supportive parallel in the enclosed rooms within which readers pray. Both of these enclosed spaces – Mary's imagined Annunciation room, and the recluse's cell – parallel the Virgin's enclosed womb, intact and yet full with the Word made flesh. When Mary reads at the Annunciation, her physical and physiological containment become an even more critical aspect of the scene. Contemplation parallels gestation; spiritual conception parallels physical conception: in this chiasmic framework, the female body offers more than just concrete imagery for

---

    tended to ignore the female model to discuss instead the imitation of Christ', the sources I consider demonstrate that though this may be so, Mary did emerge as a female model of meditation, reading and interpretation that was both promoted for women and embraced by them.

[8] The widespread phenomenon of men writing religious texts for women is considered by Joan M. Ferrante, *To the Glory of Her Sex: Women's Roles in the Composition of Medieval Texts* (Bloomington: Indiana University Press, 1997), ch. 2, 'Religious Texts'.

[9] Barbara Newman, 'Liminalities: Literate Women in the Long Twelfth Century', in *European Transformations: The Long Twelfth Century*, ed. Thomas F.X. Noble and John Van Engen (Notre Dame, IN: University of Notre Dame Press, 2012), 354. Anneke B. Mulder-Bakker also points out how because of Mary's earlier time in the temple 'nuns could therefore easily recognize in her a proto-nun, and recluses a proto-recluse', as part of her exploration of how women recluses of the Low Countries developed an 'intimate relationship' with Mary as *doctrix* (focusing on aspects other than Mary as reader); '*Maria doctrix*', 195.

abstract devotion. Devotion *originates* in the female body – specifically, Mary's body – since, after all, she is the first person to pray with the knowledge of Christ. What these anchoritic writings demonstrate is how stasis, solitude and stillness precipitate the profound rush of God into man, whether in Christ or in each Christian soul. According to these texts solitary enclosure enables the concentration necessary for reading, utterance and interpretation, and thus conception of the divine.

Indeed, the parallel of an inviolable inner self and an inviolable outer enclosure emerges as one of the main tropes for expressing inwardness in medieval England, according to Jennifer Bryan's taxonomy of the 'inward man'. And this trope is gendered, with the enclosed female religious at its centre. The nun or anchoress, her heart, her very subjectivity, 'becomes a locked space, a privy chamber or a *hortus conclusus*' where 'sealed off from the temptations and distractions of the outside world, she can await her spouse', that is, Christ.[10] Bridal metaphors dominate many representations of the nun as 'a private space inaccessible to others', Roberta Gilchrist points out.[11] Descriptions of the Annunciation scene, however, tend to lean away from such spousal imagery and instead towards a more contemplative, literary frame for enclosure. It is text and *Logos* that does the penetrating, not the metaphorical spiritual bridegroom, the manly Christ. At the moment no man, not even the metaphorical shadow of one, violates the symbolic power of Mary's room and womb. In contrast to the Passion and its open spaces, its public nature, no other meditative scene offered such a resonant parallel to the enclosed contemplative life as the Annunciation, defined by the complex associations with reading, solitude and spiritual conception.

'That secret chamber of your prayers'

Perhaps the earliest text to emphasize Mary's reading in relation to the Annunciation closely connects her literary devotion to enclosed solitude. In *De Virginibus ad Marcellinam*, written around 377 at the request of his sister Marcellina, Ambrose speculates on the circumstances of the Annunciation:

> Haec ad ipsos ingressus angeli inventa domi in penetralibus, sine comite, ne quis intentionem abrumperet, ne quis obstreperet; neque enim comites feminas desiderabat, quae bonas cogitationes comites habebat. Quin etiam

---

[10] Jennifer Bryan, *Looking Inward: Devotional Reading and the Private Self in Late Medieval England* (Philadelphia: University of Pennsylvania Press, 2008), 46.

[11] Roberta Gilchrist, *Gender and Material Culture: The Archeology of Medieval Women* (London: Routledge, 1994), 5. Also quoted in Bryan, *Looking Inward*, 46. See also Jeffrey Hamburger, *Nuns as Artists: The Visual Culture of a Medieval Convent* (Berkeley: University of California Press, 1997), 157–9.

tum sibi minus sola videbatur, cum sola esset. Nam quemadmodum sola, cui tot libri adessent; tot archangeli, tot prophetae?[12]

(She, at the actual approaches of the angel, was found at home in the innermost places, without a companion, so that none might interrupt her concentration, none might disturb her; neither, moreover, did she desire female companions, she who had good thoughts as friends. Indeed, to herself she seemed less alone, when she was alone. For in what way was she alone, for whom so many books would have been present; so many archangels, so many prophets?)

Solitude and study define Mary's debut. No longer in the temple but in the innermost places (*in penetralibus*) of her domestic home, her secure seclusion parallels her virginal unpenetrated body. Her solitude, vital to the development of the Annunciation tradition in the coming centuries, facilitates both focused reading and angelic visits. And not light reading: this scholarly Mary conjures up more the image of St Jerome immersed in his library than the humble girl of the apocrypha's temple.[13] *De Virginibus* was composed for an audience of a congregation of both male and female virgins: where better than *domi in penetralibus*, the inmost recesses of a house, to protect one's chastity? Because of its isolation from the world, Mary's heterotopic room, like her body, remains simultaneously impenetrable by sin and penetrable by Gabriel and the divine.

When the Annunciation is invoked in the medium of prayer itself, Mary's solitude parallels both the physical privacy of an individual at prayer and the imperturbability of her soul. Around 1080-2, when Goscelin was writing his *Liber Confortatorius* for the recluse Eva, Saint Anselm of Lucca the Younger (*c.* 1036–1086) was composing a series of prayers for the Countess Matilda of Tuscany (1046–1115). In one of the two prayers directed to the Virgin Mary, Anselm of Lucca traces the life of the Virgin as a topic of meditation. His words, addressing Mary, draw Matilda in to join her at the Annunciation: 'Sed expecto tempore quo Gabriel ingreditur ad salutandum, ut post illum secretum cubiculum orationum tuarum temeraria ingrediar' (And yet, I look to the time when Gabriel enters to greet you, that after him I may enter boldly into that secret chamber of your prayers).[14] In the imagined world created by her own prayer, Matilda sees Mary at prayer, like her. Matilda follows the angel

---

[12] *De Virginibus ad Marcellinam*, Book II, 2:10–11; PL 16: 210A. See also Chapter 1.
[13] In the iconographic tradition, Ambrose's emphasis on Mary's indoor solitude would almost completely replace the apocryphal suggestion of Gabriel's initial visitation at the public well, as it is described in the *Protoevangelium*. For more detailed readings of Ambrose and Otfrid, as well as other related evidence, see Miles, 'The Origins and Development'.
[14] *Orationes venerabilis Anselmi Episcopi ad Sanctam Mariam*, III, Henri Barré, ed., *Prieres Anciennes de l'Occident a la Mere du Sauveur, Des origines a saint Anselme*

into the 'secret chamber' where, if not for this scene taking place imaginatively, as a human she would be barred from entry. Gabriel's voice works its power in the devotee's soul as it does in Mary's chamber. Though footsteps of the 'I' of the meditant's voice follow Gabriel's steps, and it is Gabriel's voice that she hears, Mary is the addressee throughout. It is her *secretum cubiculum* that merges with the meditant's room. Fulton considers this instance in Anselm of Lucca's prayer perhaps 'the first time in the Christian devotion – certainly the first time in the tradition of Marian prayer – a prayer instructs the meditant not only to contemplate her sinfulness and her need for Mary's intercession but to do so *through the life of the Virgin itself*. She continues, comparing the *Liber Confortatorius* passage on consecrating the hours of the day to Christ, stopping just short of the Annunciation anecdote to claim that 'Goscelin did not, however, recommend that Eve perform the same type of meditation on Mary or her co-sufferings.'[15] In contrast, I would suggest that Anselm and Goscelin concurrently (and independently) constitute perhaps the earliest suggestions for prayer 'through the life of the Virgin itself'. The example of Countess Matilda, as a laywoman, shows how the praying like Mary and the Marian *secretum cubiculum* motif was offered to lay readers as well as recluses and monastics, while being based upon vowed seclusion as a paradigm that could be understood by others. In other words, that Mary's body, Mary's cell and the monastic cell all offered accessible modes of thinking about the enclosure of prayer – both concrete and spiritual.

Indeed, the soul was often envisaged as a *cubiculum*, an inner chamber to which only God had entry, as with Saint Anselm of Canterbury (*c.* 1033–1109) in his *Prosologion*: 'Intra in cubiculum mentis tuae, exclude omnia praeter deum et quae te iuvent ad quaerendum eum, et clauso ostio quaere eum' (Enter the inner chamber of your soul, shut out everything except God and that which can help you in seeking him, and when you have shut the door, seek him).[16] This made metaphorical the practical advice found in the gospel of Matthew 6:6: 'Tu autem cum oraveris, intra in cubiculum tuum, et clauso ostio, ora Patrem tuum in abscondito' (But thou when thou shalt pray, enter into thy chamber, and having shut the door, pray to thy Father in secret). Written in 1078 for a monastic audience, Anselm's theological treatise offers an ontological argument for the existence of God – an attempt to put understanding behind faith. Embarking on such a challenging philosophical quest for the divine necessitates closing out the noisy world both physically and mentally.

(Paris: Lethielleuz, 1963), 230; translation from Fulton, *From Judgment to Passion*, 226.

[15] Fulton, *From Judgment to Passion*, 225–6.

[16] *Anselmi Opera Omnia*, ed. F.S. Schmitt (Edinburgh, 1946–61), tomus I, vol. I, 97. Sister Benedicta Ward, trans., *The Prayers and Meditations of St Anselm* (Harmondsworth: Penguin, 1973), 239.

The heterotopic space of the *cubiculum* parallels its physical manifestation of the cell or chamber with the metaphorical space of the soul; in Mary's case, her womb also matches this paradigm. Each must close out the outside world in order to become open to God.

Bernard of Clairvaux (1090–1153) even more explicitly linked Mary's virginity and holiness to the enclosure of the Annunciation site. Perhaps the most extensive eleventh- or twelfth-century elaboration of Mary's solitude at the Annunciation can be found in Bernard's famous *Homiliae Quatour de Laudibus Virginis Matris, super verba Evangelii 'Missus est angelus Gabriel'*. [17] In the third sermon he considers the line from Luke 2:27, 'Et ingressus Angelus ad eam' (And the angel went into her):

> Quo ingressus ad eam? Puto in secretarium pudici cubiculi, ubi fortassis illa, clauso super se ostio, orabat Patrem suum in abscondito . . . Nec fuit difficile Angelo per clausum ostium penetrare ad abdita Virginis . . . Suspicandum igitur non est, quod apertum invenerit Angelus ostiolum Virginis, cui nimirum in proposito erat hominum fugere frequentias, vitare colloquia, ne vel orantis perturbaretur silentium, vel continentis castitas tentaretur. Clauserat itaque etiam illa hora suum super se habitaculum Virgo prudentissima, sed hominibus, non angelis.[18]

> ('Went in' where? Into the private chamber of her modest room where, I suppose, having shut the door she was praying to the Father in secret . . . It was not hard for the angel to enter the Virgin's private room through a closed door . . . There is no reason to suspect that the angel found the Virgin's little door ajar. She clearly had it in mind to flee human company, to avoid conversation lest the silence of one given to prayer should be disturbed and the purity of one given to chastity assailed. Surely then the most prudent virgin had at that time closed the door of her private room to men, but not to angels.)

Here the space of the Annunciation, as a kind of sanctified heterotopia, functions as a system simultaneously isolated from the worldly and yet penetrable by the heavenly. The virginity of her body is what is at stake here: her *cubiculum* comes to metaphorically stand in for her *uterus*. Both body and building must be *pudici*, or modest, and closed. Bernard cites reasons similar

---

[17] A synopsis of Bernard's mariology can be found in H. Barré, 'Saint Bernard, docteur marial' in *Saint Bernard théologien*, Analecta S.O.C. IX, 3–4 (1953), 92–113; on Bernard and the feminine in terms of Mary see also Jean Leclerq, *Women and Saint Bernard of Clairvaux*, trans. Marie-Bernard Saïd OSB (Kalamazoo, MI: Cistercian, 1989).

[18] *Homiliae* III:1; Jean Leclerq and H. Rochais, eds, *Sancti Bernardi Opera*, IV (Rome: Editiones cistercienses, 1966), 13–58 (36); translation Saïd, *Homilies*, 33–4.

to Ambrose's: 'lest the silence of one given to prayer should be disturbed and the purity of one given to chastity assailed'. Disrupted concentration precedes the disrupted body. Written for Bernard's fellow monks around 1115, these sermons achieved a wide readership and deeply influenced Marian devotion through the thirteenth century and beyond, especially in England (including Aelred of Rievaulx).

For one author, Bernard's emphasis on Mary's 'private chamber of her modest room' strongly suggested the space of the anchorhold. The thirteenth-century early Middle English *Ancrene Wisse*, a guide to living for anchoresses, extensively borrows from Bernard's sermons in order to situate Mary as a model solitary. This lengthy work was part of a coherent programme of spiritual reading written between c. 1200 and 1230 for a number of anchoresses, 'in English prose whose quality of style and of thought was not to be equaled for over a century', according to one critic.[19] In the Corpus text (Cambridge, Corpus Christi College MS 402) written c. 1225–40, one of the most interesting and complete vernacular versions of the *Ancrene Wisse*, the influence of Bernard's presentation of the Annunciation shapes the author's approach to the idea of solitude.[20] Elsewhere the *Ancrene Wisse* acknowledges his debt to Bernard explicitly, yet the close parallels between the framing of this exact verse from Luke strongly suggests Bernard's influence here despite the *Ancrene Wisse* author's silence on his source. In a section on the importance of the solitary life, we find the sentiment, if not the exact words, of the passage above, creatively recast for an audience of enclosed holy women:

> Vre leoue Leafdi, ne leadde ha anlich lif? Ne fond te engel hire in anli stude al ane? Nes ha no-wher ute, ah wes biloken feste. For swa we i-findeð: *Ingressus angelus ad eam dixit. Ave Maria, gratia plene, Dominus tecum, benedicta tu in mulieribus.* Þet is, 'Þe engel wende in to hire.' Þenne wes heo inne in anli stude hire ane. Engel to mon i þrung ne edeawede neauer ofte.[21]

---

[19] Anne Savage and Nicholas Watson, eds, *Anchoritic Spirituality: Ancrene Wisse and Associated Works* (New York: Paulist Press, 1991), 9. For a clear and concise introduction to the anchoritic life as framed by the *Ancrene Wisse* see also the Introduction to Robert Hasenfratz, ed., *Ancrene Wisse* (Kalamazoo, MI: Western Michigan University, Medieval Institute Publications, 2000).

[20] On the Corpus text, its dating and its relationship to the other extant *Ancrene Wisse* texts, see the Introduction to the edition by Bella Millett with Richard Dance, *Ancrene Wisse: A Corrected Edition of the Text in Cambridge, Corpus Christi College, MS 402 with variants from other manuscripts*, 2 vols, EETS e.s. 325 and 326 (Oxford, 2005, 2006), as well as Savage and Watson, *Anchoritic Spirituality*, 41–6.

[21] Original from Millett, *Ancrene Wisse*; translation from Savage and Watson, *Anchoritic Spirituality*. Citations are identified by part and paragraph number, page

(Our dear Lady, did she not live a solitary life? Did not the angel find her all alone in a solitary place? She was not outside, but was closely shut in. For so we find, *Ingressus angelus*, that is, 'The angel went in to her.' Then she was inside, in a solitary place, on her own. An angel has very seldom appeared to someone in a crowd [or throng].)

Under Bernard's influence here, the *Ancrene Wisse* author extrapolates from the phrase *ingressus angelus* that Mary was alone at the Annunciation; he goes one step further to propose that in fact Mary led a reclusive life, like his readers.[22] Mary's envisaged vocation as solitary holy woman recasts her as much more than the exemplary virgin – an exemplary anchoress. 'Engel to mon i þrung ne edeawede neaver ofte' impresses upon the anchoritic reader what she has to gain from her solitude: heavenly company as Mary enjoyed at the Annunciation. Or as Bernard explains it, 'Solent angeli astare orantibus, et delectari in his quos vident levare puras manus in oratione' (Angels are accustomed to taking their stand beside those who pray, and they delight in those whom they see lifting pure hands in prayer).[23] By mimicking Mary's prayerful posture, anchoresses can invite angelic visitors or, even better, divine intercession.

Sealed enclosures layer over one another – Mary's room, Mary's body, the anchoress's room, the anchoress's body, the soul – and at their symbolic centre, Christ's dwelling in Mary's womb, the Incarnation itself. The *Ancrene Wisse* author extends the metaphor of recluse to include Christ in both birth and death:

> Ant new he him seolf reclus i Maries wombe? Þeos twa þing limpeð to ancre, nearowðe ant bitternesse; for wombe is nearow wununge, þer ure Lauerd wes reclus, ant tis word 'Marie', as Ich ofte habbe iseid, spealeð 'bitternesse'. Ȝef ȝe þenne I nearow stude þolieð bitternesse, ȝe beoð his feolahes, reclus as he wes i Marie wombe. Beo ȝe ibunden inwið fowr large wahes? ... Marie wombe ant þis þruh weren his ancre-huses.[24]

(And was he not himself a recluse in Mary's womb? These two things belong to the anchorhold: narrowness and bitterness. For the womb is a narrow dwelling, where the Lord was a recluse; and this word 'Mary', as I have often

---

and line number of the original, and translation page number in parentheses; here, *Ancrene Wisse*, Part III.21, 62, l. 575–80 (Savage and Watson, 108).

[22] Modern editors, including Millett and Hasenfratz, have not acknowledged Bernard as a probable source for this passage.

[23] *Homiliae* III:1; Leclerq and Rochais, *Sancti Bernardi Opera*, 36; Said, *Homilies in Praise of the Virgin Mary*, 34.

[24] *Ancrene Wisse*, Part VI.13, 142, l. 417–25 (Savage and Watson, 186).

said, means 'bitterness'.[25] If you then suffer bitterness in a narrow place, you are his fellows, recluse as he was in Mary's womb. Are you imprisoned within four wide walls? ... Mary's womb and this tomb were his anchorhouses.)

First Mary is a recluse, as in the earlier quote; now Christ, inside Mary, is also a recluse. The layers multiply as the Incarnation takes on the whole signifying weight of reclusion.[26] Where Christ took flesh, there the anchoress finds her identity; Mary makes of herself a dwelling for both God and the individual female recluse. The parallel between womb and tomb has been recognized before: Goscelin, in his *Liber*, notes how 'ibi egreditur de clauso utero, hic de clauso mausoleo' (this time he emerged from a closed womb, that time from a closed tomb).[27] Just as we never see Mary's womb open to birth Christ, so we never see the tomb's stone moving to release Christ. The spaces of womb and tomb paradoxically release their inmate – Christ – while remaining sealed, and without revealing their mysteries to mankind. Liz Herbert McAvoy explores the relationship between womb and tomb in anchoritic writings, claiming that:

> for the anchoress then, the movement into the tomb of the anchorhold, as well as constituting a figurative death, could also be seen in terms of a return to the womb, a rejection of the past and the announcement of the beginning of a new life, a passion which would be enacted until the moment of her physical death.[28]

This womb-tomb coupling corroborates the importance of Mary's room at the Annunciation as a productive parallel for the anchorhold. Mary's room echoes Mary's womb; Mary's womb echoes Christ's tomb – thus the anchorhold (as well as the anchoress's contained body) possesses the potential to echo any of these enclosures.

Despite – or because of – their 'bitternesse', these metaphorical and physical enclosures can offer a kind of freedom for their inmates. From the 'nearowðe' womb comes birth, the life of and in Christ; from the tomb comes rebirth, the risen Christ and salvation in heaven. In the anchorhold, for the anchoress, such seemingly narrow and bitter enclosures open up the power of the divine, far preferable to the empty, bustling power of the world outside. In the enclosed

---

[25] The author picks up on the traditional orthographical connection between 'Maria' and the Latin word *amara*, meaning 'bitter'.
[26] Janet Grayson provides a clarifying chart of these metaphors, in *Structure and Imagery in* Ancrene Wisse (Hanover, NH: University of New Hampshire, 1974), 168–9. Linda Georgianna also discusses this passage in *The Solitary Self: Individuality in the Ancrene Wisse* (Cambridge, MA: Harvard University Press, 1981).
[27] Book III, Talbot, 83; Otter, 100–1.
[28] Liz Herbert McAvoy, *Authority and the Female Body in the Writings of Julian of Norwich and Margery Kempe*, Studies in Medieval Mysticism 5 (Cambridge: D.S. Brewer, 2004), 72.

cell a kind of direct portal between earth and heaven can be unlocked – in Mary's case, resulting in the Incarnation, and in the anchoress's case, resulting in a privileged access to God's mercy and the possibility of rebirth in Christ. In the enclosed cell a woman can pray, sing and read undisturbed, and find Christ as *Logos* in the words she utters. With the secular world silenced, the stillness of the enclosed cell does not silence its inhabitant, but rather allows her voice to be heard all the better by herself and God. Those 'fowr large wahes' amplify the anchoress's voice. Yet the kind of privacy allowed by religious reclusion does not necessitate complete solitude: the anchoress, for instance, might live with servants who hear her praying, creating a more communal experience that is still private.

In this way, for both Mary and the anchoress such enclosures – and their proximity to the divine – enable an authoritative, validated female voice. Some critics have generalized the *Ancrene Wisse* as quite the opposite:

> Women are taught to control their bodies. They are to be silent, repress anger, and, most of all, control their senses. The cackling Eve must be transformed into the passive, silent Mary rather than into an active, abstract thinker. If women have a voice, it is the constructed querulous female voice the author uses in his text. More often, because of their sexuality, women are denied any voice at all.[29]

Here 'the passive, silent Mary' refers to the sister of Martha, the Mary who sits silently at Christ's feet while Martha bustles with activity (Luke 10:38–42). In medieval culture Mary came to represent the silent, contemplative life and Martha the active life. While it is true that women's talking is disparaged elsewhere in the text, the female voice does find its worth in another Mary, the Virgin Mary, mother of God, whose body enables the transformation of both text and divinity. The *Ancrene Wisse* author uses Mary's incarnation of Christ, and specifically her role in the Annunciation episode, as an opportunity to redeem the female voice.

Such gendered redemption can be seen elsewhere in the text. An excerpt from Bernard's fourth sermon *Super missus est* precedes the *Ancrene Wisse*'s unexpected interpretation of Mary's speech at the Annunciation and is worth quoting at length:

> Vre deorewurðe Leafdi, Seinte Marie, þe ah to alle wummen to beo forbisne, wes of se lutel speche þet nohwer in Hali Writ ne finde we þet ha spec bute fowr siðen; ah for se selt speche hire wordes weren heuie ant hefden muche mihte. Bernardus ad Mariam: *In sempiterno Dei verbo facti sumus omnes et ecce morimur. In tuo brevi responso refitiendi sumus ut ad vitam revocemur.*

---

[29] Elizabeth Robertson, *Early English Devotional Prose and the Female Audience* (Knoxville: University of Tennessee Press, 1990), 74.

Responde verbum et suscipe verbum; profer tuum et concipe divinum. Hire forme wordes þet we redeð of weren þa ha ondswerede Gabriel þen engel; ant teo weren se mihtie, þet wið þet ha seide, *Ecce, ancilla Domini; fiat michi secundum verbum tuum* – ed tis word Godes sune ant soð Godd bicom mon, ant te Lauerd þet al þe world ne mahte nawt bifon bitunde him inwið hire meidnes wombe ... Neomeð nu her ȝeme, ant leorniað ȝeorne her-bi hu selt-sene speche haveð muche strengðe.[30]

(Our precious St Mary, who ought to be an example for all women, was of such short speech, that nowhere in Holy Writ do we find that she spoke, except four times; but because of this rarity of speech, her words were heavy and full of power. Bernard to Mary: *In the eternal Word of God were we all made, and behold, we are dying. In your short answer we shall be restored and so recalled to life. Answer with the word and receive the word; offer up yours, and conceive the divine.* Her first words that we read of were those she answered to the angel Gabriel. And they were so powerful that as she said them – *Behold the handmaid of the Lord, let it happen to me according to your word* – at these words God's Son and true God became man, and the Lord whom all the world might not contain, enclosed himself in her maiden's womb . . . Take a lesson from this and learn it ardently, that sparse speech has much strength.)

In keeping with the rest of the work's emphasis on silence and the dangers of the female voice, Mary is cited for her 'lutel speche'.[31] The pattern of speech and silence, presence and absence, gives speech 'muche strengðe'. Thus Mary's example sanctions the reader to partake in her power, in her voice, and not be bridled; the text insists that the female voice can not only be heard by God, but invite God into her. Bernard's eloquent entreaty of the Virgin at the Annunciation, his affirmation that her spoken consent is necessary for Christ's conception to move forward, is connected to the *Ancrene Wisse* author's rhe-torical about-face: speech – when sparse – possesses 'muche strengðe'. The passage acknowledges the undeniably positive relationship between a woman's words and the incarnation of the Word, *Verbum*. The *Ancrene Wisse* author

---

[30] *Ancrene Wisse*, Part II.21, 31–2, ll. 442–52, 463–4 (Savage and Watson, 76–7). The list of Mary's four speech instances is based on Bernard's *Sermo in dominica infra octauam assumptionis B. Mariae, Opera*, 5.270. The quoted excerpt is from *Homiliae de Laudibus Virginis Mariae*, IV:8; Leclerq and Rochais, 51–2 (Saïd, 53). Millett in her note suggests this quotation originated as a marginal comment in an earlier version and was subsequently incorporated into the body of the text in Corpus. This would explain why the Latin is not translated for the reader, as is the case with almost all other Latin quotations.

[31] Georgianna briefly discusses this passage, noting that Mary is the 'ideal anchor-ess because she spoke so rarely'; *The Solitary Self*, 74. But she does speak, and this speech is also part of her idealization by male writers.

has opted for the theological interpretation that identifies Mary's words, not Gabriel's words, as the cue for the conception. 'Heuie' and with 'muche mihte', Mary's voice shares in the power of the Scripture and the power of the *Logos*, the eternal Word. Yet this authorized female voice is not restricted only to the Mother of God. Rather, it is offered as a lesson to be learned and emulated by the anchoress. Mary is 'to alle wummen to beo forbisne', an example for all women, even at the moment at which she is theologically elevated above them. While Bernard's original sermon may have been intended for an audience of Cistercian monks, who could also look to Mary as an example, this anchoritic text insists on Mary as a model for 'wummen', and so uses the legitimacy of Mary's speech to counteract directly the negligence of Eve's speech (nearly an obsession throughout the rest of the *Ancrene Wisse*). Thus the Annunciation scene functions as an important opportunity for specifically female readers to claim the efficacy of their voice.

The tradition of portraying Mary as an enclosed contemplative at the Annunciation emerges from the early Middle Ages to capture the imagination of twelfth-century authors writing for an anchoritic audience. Mary's intact womb functions as the metaphorical centre of layers and layers of enclosures, reaching from womb to tomb to anchorhold. Kept pure from the world, however, their confined spaces allow these women a privileged, intimate access to God. At the Annunciation, Mary's active voice – 'heavy and full of power' – provided an empowering model for enclosed women. The Virgin's voice was not only heard through Luke's passage and her responses to the angel. The Virgin's voice was heard in her recitation of the psalms as imagined by Goscelin in his work written for a female recluse named Eva; the Virgin's voice was implied, perhaps, by her open book in the Annunciation illumination in the St Albans' Psalter, likely created for a female recluse named Christina. Note that in Bernard's sermons and the *Ancrene Wisse* Mary's book never appears; the point is not the means of her prayer, but its private location. Her mode of prayer, left unspecified in those sources, takes on the particular form of psalm-singing in Goscelin's *Liber Confortatorius* and the *vita* and Psalter of Christina of Markyate. While Bernard and the *Ancrene Wisse* author establish Mary's solitude and an anchoritic-like vocation, Eva and Christina encounter the Mother of God as a more detailed reflection of their singing and reading recluse selves. They see their books in her hands. They hear her voice echoing in theirs.

Goscelin of St Bertin's *Liber Confortatorius*

Goscelin of St Bertin (*c.* 1040–1114) emigrated to England from France at the age of twenty, with the court of Herman, newly appointed bishop of Ramsbury. He soon became affiliated with the royal nunnery at Wilton, probably serving as a chaplain, and began mentoring and tutoring the nun Eva (*c.* 1058–1120) while she was still a child. Sometime between 1080 and 1083, he wrote the long, letter-like *Liber Confortatorius* for her. The work was a response to some startling news: after over fifteen years of mentorship and tutoring under Goscelin, Eva had suddenly left England to become an anchoress at the church of St Laurent at Angers, France, without informing him.[32] As one of the most extensive and detailed guides to living the enclosed life unfolds, Goscelin's fondness and concern for his disciple cannot be concealed; Liz Herbert McAvoy describes the text as 'a letter of unrequited passion by a man struggling to come to terms with the enormity of its implications', and explores the complex gender reversals and metaphors.[33] His *Liber Confortatorius* employs biblical, patristic and contemporary sources to offer advice on the prayer, reading and meditation that he hoped would shape Eva's life. Whether or not Eva actually received, welcomed or read the book written for her, we may never know.

In Book III Goscelin has been discussing the virtues of reading the scriptures when he segues into an exploration of the day of Christ's redemption and how its hours can be mapped onto the hours of the Divine Office. Riffing on the topic of Christ's conception, he then describes a practice of Mary's when she was a virgin in the temple, conflating it with the moment of the Annunciation:

> Audiui a quodam monacho non indocto, cum illa singularis omnium uirgo Deum paritura media nocte sancta assuetudine ad diuinos hymnos, surgeret et Canticum graduum inter surgendum timpanizaret, ad hunc uersum ubi dixit: *Dominus custodiat introitum tuum et exitum tuum*, ingressum fuisse Gabrielem archangelum cum celesti splendore, adeo ut uirgo uideretur hunc tali salutatione excipere, immo illum quem nuntius ferebat nasciturum ex se, cuius Dominus custodiret introitum in conceptione, et exitum in natiuitate; atque ita de angelico nuntio exultante spiritu in Deo salutari suo, sinagogam intrasse cum sequentis psalmi cantico. *Letatus sum im his que dicta sunt michi. In domum Domini ibimus.* (III: 83 [166])[34]

---

[32] For more biographical background on Goscelin and Eva, see C.H. Talbot, 'The Liber Confortatorius of Goscelin of Saint Bertin', *Studia Anselmiana* 37 (1955): 1–117 (5–22). Mari Hughes-Edwards discusses Goscelin's narrative relationship with Eva in her essay 'The Role of the Anchoritic Guidance Writer', in *Anchoritism in the Middle Ages: Texts and Transitions*, , ed. Catherine Innes-Parker and Naoe Kukita Yoshikawa (Cardiff: University of Wales Press, 2013), 31–46.

[33] McAvoy, *Medieval Anchoritisms*, 87.

[34] The Latin is edited by Talbot, 'The Liber Confortatorius' (which is the same citation as M.M. Lebreton, J. Leclerq and C.H. Talbot, *Analecta monastica: Textes et études sur la vie des moines au moyen age*, 3rd ser. (Rome, 1955), 1–117. I will be citing the translation by W.R. Barnes and Rebecca Hayward, available in *Writing the Wilton Women: Goscelin's Legend of Edith and Liber Confortatorius*, ed. Stephanie Hollis et al (Turnhout: Brepols, 2004), 97–212. The work is also translated by Monica Otter, *The Book of Encouragement and Consolation [Liber Confortatorius]: The Letter of Goscelin to the Recluse Eva* (Cambridge: D.S. Brewer, 2004). Excerpts from the *Liber*

(Here is something I heard from a learned monk: the Virgin, unique among all others, who would give birth to God, once rose in the middle of the night, as was her sacred custom, to sing divine hymns. As she rose [she] intoned the gradual psalm; and when she arrived at the verse where it says, 'May the Lord watch over your comings in and goings out' [Psalm 120:8] – at that very moment the Archangel Gabriel entered with heavenly splendour, so that the Virgin appeared to be receiving him with this greeting. More importantly, she received the one who the messenger said would be born of her, and the Lord would be watching over his 'going in', in his conception, and over his 'going out', in his birth. Thus, her spirit rejoicing from this angelic message in God her saviour, she entered the Synagogue chanting the following psalm: 'I was glad when they said to me, let us go into the house of the Lord.' [Psalm 121:1])

The Annunciation is imaginatively re-crafted as an anecdote of hermeneutics. Goscelin plays with the flexible potential of the Annunciation by conflating Mary's earlier service in the temple with the later Incarnation scene, thus combining a monastic, liturgical performance of the psalms with the tradition of her reading the psalms at Gabriel's visit.[35] The psalm verse at which Gabriel enters, 'May the Lord watch over your comings in and goings out', is one of the 'gradual psalms' (Psalms 120–34), imagined by the Gospel of Pseudo-Matthew to have been recited by Mary as she ascended the fifteen steps to the altar of the temple where she was dedicated as a young virgin (as young as three years old in some versions of the scene).[36] This act of recitation found new life in medi-

---

are identified by book, page numbers from Talbot's edition and translation page numbers in brackets.

[35] Otter describes the Annunciation as 'somewhat confusingly' connected to the Virgin's temple service. She notes that 'the association between psalm prayer and the Annunciation goes back to the Apocrypha, which describe Mary's designed program of daily prayer'. However, the Apocryphal Gospels never make any connection between Mary's temple prayers and the Annunciation (that I know of). Monica Otter, 'Entrances and Exits: Performing the Psalms in Goscelin's *Liber Confortatorius*', *Speculum* 83 (2008): 286, n. 24.

[36] *Gospel of Pseudo-Matthew*, chapter 4, where Joachim and Anna drop her off at the temple, 'Quae cum posita esset ante foras templi, ita veloci cursi ascendit quindecim gradus' (And when she was put down before the doors of the temple, she went up the fifteen steps so swiftly). Constantinus Tischendorf, ed., *Evangelia apocrypha*, 2nd ed. (Leipzig, 1876, 60, Caput IV); trans. Alexander Walker, *Apocryphal Gospels, Act, and Revelations* (Edinburgh, 1870), 23. Walker notes that the fifteen steps correspond with the fifteen 'Songs of Degrees', Psalms 120–34 in the Vulgate numbering. Mary's ascent of the fifteen steps featured in the two surviving medieval plays on the Presentation of the Virgin, a late medieval feast day. Philippe de Mézières (1327–1405), regarding his *Presentation Play*, writes in a letter about the 'matura ascensio Marie quindecim graduum, de quibus non immerito ecclesia quindecim psalmos graduales in memoriam ascensionis prelibate sibi assumpsit' (Mary's

eval monasteries, where the gradual psalms were often recited by the monks as they processed from their dormitories and entered the night office of Matins.[37] Goscelin's anecdote utilizes these traditions in order to depict a praying Mary perfectly positioned for emulation by both Eva and himself. While this passage has received some attention – Monica Otter offers an elegant analysis and I build on many of her points – it has not yet been fully contextualized in the traditions surrounding the Annunciation scene itself, one of the central discourses here.[38] I will work through this passage from several angles: the depiction of space and solitude; liturgical engagement with the psalms as an interpretive act; the shadowy yet insistent presence of the physical Psalter; the history of the psalms as Mary's reading material; and, finally, the anecdote's position at the intersection of regional traditions of women's monastic practice with contemporary Annunciation iconography. At the centre of this exploration lies the proposal that the Virgin Mary's vocalized devotion acts as a kind of hermeneutic key, unlocking the meaning of the psalm verse, enabling its words to come alive – the *Logos* to take flesh – through its performance.

Goscelin begins by inviting us right into the most intimate space of Mary's night prayers. Though he does not describe her precise surroundings – communal dormitory? single room? – the narrative silence suggests the quietness of a private cell, much like Eva's anchorhold. The Annunciation tradition leading up to the twelfth century, as we have seen, consistently represents Mary alone in an enclosed space – a private space that Goscelin reconfigures as connected to a main worship space, a 'synogogue', evoking the Jewish temple where the apocryphal gospels described her living before her betrothal. This maps onto a medieval monastic set-up: according to their 'sacred custom', the monk or nun rises from bed to prepare him- or herself for Matins, before joining the

---

mature ascent of the fifteen steps, for which reason, the church has adopted not inappropriately the fifteen Gradual Psalms in memory of the aforesaid ascension); see Philip de Mézières, *Figurative Representation of the Presentation of the Virgin Mary in the Temple*, trans. and ed. Robert S. Haller, intro. M. Catherine Rupp OSM (Lincoln: University of Nebraska Press, 1971), 64, 57; also xxiii–xxiv. In the *Mary Play* of the N-Town Manuscript, when Mary is presented in the temple by her parents, Episcopus proclaims to her that 'þu xalt be þe dowtere of God eternall / If þe fyftene grees þu may ascende' and also that 'Every man þat thynk his lyff to amende, / Þe fyftene psalmys in memorye of þis mayde say', at which point Mary recites the introits to the psalms along with short explications. *The Mary Play from the N. Town Manuscript*, ed. Peter Meredith (London: Longman, 1987), 43, 16. Elizabeth of Hungary also features Mary's ascent of the steps in her *Revelations*, a scene I discuss in Chapter 4.

[37] A connection made by Otter, *The Book*, fn. 86; see also Henri Leclerq, 'Office divin', *Dictionnaire d'archéologie chrétienne et de liturgie*, 12 (Paris, 1935), cols 1962–2017 (col. 2006).

[38] Otter, 'Entrances and Exits'.

rest of the community in chapel for the main liturgy. Like Eva as anchoress, Mary seems to be practising a kind of religious, solitary life; the Virgin's room comes to mirror Eva's cell. Their solitude merges. Hayward and Hollis point out that for Goscelin, 'an anchorite's cell is an ideal site for devotional literary activity'.[39] As Goscelin writes to Eva, if you read 'delectabit te solitudo tuo' (your solitude will delight you) (III: 81 [164]); as Ambrose describes Mary to his congregation of virgins, 'Indeed, to herself she seemed less alone. For in what was she alone, for whom so many books would have been present; so many archangels, so many prophets?' (quoted above). McAvoy also points out that Goscelin repeatedly emphasizes both the security of Eva's cell and its permeability only by books – the influence of the Fathers and himself.[40] This is precisely the tension captured in this Annunciation scene. In Goscelin's story, we see Mary begin her singing in the privacy of her own room or cell, when she receives the angel and the *Logos* (only after that does she proceed to the synogogue, continuing her psalm chant).[41] Mary remains in the privacy of her room where she first recites the psalms to receive both Gabriel and the incarnate Christ. Room intact, womb intact, both serve as echo chambers for her singing – resounding up to God.

When Mary lifts her voice, Goscelin carefully describes how two simultaneous new meanings for the psalm text are born. *Introitum tuum*, 'your comings in', now applies to both Gabriel's entrance to Mary's room and Christ's entrance to Mary's womb. Her words enable a typological interpretation of the Old Testament psalm verse in terms of these New Testament events, the Annunciation and Incarnation. Instead of stressing the divine plan or even quoting Gabriel's announcement, Goscelin focuses on the ability of Mary's voice to align with, even precipitate, the conception of Christ. The implication, I argue, is that Eva, too, can use her voice to invoke God's grace by reciting the psalms. Eva's semi-liturgical performance can unlock Christ's presence in her soul. Elsewhere Goscelin explicitly endorses this concept for Eva, encouraging her to conceive Christ spiritually: 'Tam amabilem unice diligendo, concipe, parturi, gigne, enutri. A paruo nasci et in plenitudinem caritatis crescere dignetur tibi' (In loving uniquely one so worthy of love conceive him, carry him, give birth to him, feed him. Let him deign in you from infancy to be born and to grow to the fullness of love) (IV: 107 [194]). The metaphor roots its power in Mary's conception of Christ. In the Annunciation anecdote, Eva is invited to share the

---

[39] Hayward and Hollis, 'The Female Reader in the *Liber Confortatorius*', 386.
[40] McAvoy, *Medieval Anchoritisms*, 91.
[41] Otter reads the passage differently when she writes 'the monk would take his seat in the choir every night saying his gradual psalms, picturing the Virgin doing the same – and being impregnated by Gabriel's greeting at that very moment'. I would posit the text depicts Mary moving to the choir *after* Gabriel's greeting. See Otter, 'Entrances and Exits', 286.

interpretation of the psalm verse and understand Christ as coming into her own soul as he came into Mary's womb.

Just as Gabriel and Christ come to inhabit the 'you' of the psalm verse, so can Eva (as well as Goscelin himself) come to inhabit the role of Mary. Monica Otter contends that this exercise constitutes a semi-theatrical 'performance' of the psalms and, like Goscelin's other devotional usages and his reflections on them, invites and helps construct 'a kind of heightened, quite self-conscious first person, an "I" that is and is not the speaker's personally, that can be inhabited by the meditator to variable degrees and in fluid ways'.[42] In Otter's reading, both Goscelin and Eva are implicitly invited to echo Mary's recitation and interpretation of the psalms. This is part of a larger devotional practice: 'The keying of Office psalms to events in salvation history is a kind of polyphony, a kind of performative intertextuality that makes it possible to run several texts in one's head simultaneously for their mutual enrichment.'[43] In this case, we have the parallel playing of Luke 1:26–38 and Psalm 120:8. But Goscelin also cues other scriptural tunes with his choice of the rather obscure verb *timpanizare* to describe Mary's utterance of the gradual psalm: 'surgeret et Canticum graduum inter surgendum timpanizaret' (as she rose [she] intoned the gradual psalm). This rare word, not found in most historical dictionaries, has been variously rendered as 'to intone, to chant' by modern translators of the *Liber*; its root is *tympanum*, the timbrel or drum recurring throughout the Old Testament at moments of musical merrymaking or praise. The Psalms themselves define their own purpose of lauding God in terms of this instrument: both the well-known verses Psalm 149:3, 'Laudent nomen ejus in choro, in tympano et psalterio psallant ei' (Let them praise his name in choir: let them sing to him with the timbrel and the psaltery) and Psalm 150:4, 'laudate eum in tympano et choro (praise him with timbrel and choir). So in one way the Virgin performs the Psalms as they demand: if not sung with a drum, sung like a drum, clearly and confidently. In addition *timpanizare* also links Mary's singing in this Annunciation scene with another, earlier Mary, as Miriam was known, the Israelite prophetess who plays the *tympanum* as the Red Sea parts in Exodus 15:20–1: 'Sumpsit ergo Maria prophetis soror Aaron, tympanum in manu: egressaeque sunt omnes mulieres post eam cum tympanis et choris: Quibus praecinebat dicens: Cantemus Domino, gloriose enim magnificatus est' (So Mary the prophetess, the sister of Aaron, took a timbrel in her hand: and all the women went forth after her with timbrels and with dances: And she began the song to them, saying: Let us sing to the Lord, for he is gloriously magnified). Just as Mary's role can be foretold by the prophecies and psalms, so can her active voice be foreshadowed by Miriam's song of praise. Eleventh-century

---

[42] Otter, 'Entrances and Exits', 284.
[43] Otter, 'Entrances and Exits', 287.

continental commentator, Odilo of Cluny (d. 1049), had also connected the Virgin Mary's Magnificat at the Visitation with the jubilation of the *tympani*: 'Quomodo orabat? Canticum quod cecinit tympanizans, exclamat: Magnificat anima mea Dominum' (In what way was she praying? She exclaimed the song which sounds the tympani: My soul doth magnify the Lord).[44] For Odilo, praying is singing is exclaiming. Behind Goscelin's chanting Virgin Mary and his unusual choice of *tympanizare* we hear the joyous call to praise of the Psalms themselves; we hear the distant drumming of a female prophet who shares her name; we see the first scene of the New Testament illumined by an Old Testament text still vivid for the readers of the *Liber Confortatorius*.[45] With this word *tympanizaret*, Goscelin invites Eva to perform the same typological, interpretive reading as demonstrated by the Virgin herself.

This engagement of the psalms, with their interpretation centred on the reader's self as a reflection of the Virgin, also aligns with the sophisticated reading practices Goscelin supports in Eva. He encourages her to become an independent reader and interpreter of scripture.[46] The rewards of sensitive reading include being filled with the spirit of wisdom, as Mary was filled with the *Logos*, the Son:

> Nec uero refugias sicubi sensu hereas, sed occupa, reuolue, relege, donec affatim capias, quia nil tam difficile est quin possit querendo inueniri, et labor omnia uincit improbus, et querenti et pulsanti aperiet Dominus, et intrabit ad te benignus sapientie spiritus. (III: 81 [164])

> (Nor indeed should you give up if anywhere you cannot follow the sense, but take hold, return, read again, until you understand abundantly, because nothing is so difficult that it cannot be found by seeking, and persistent effort conquers all, and the Lord will open to one seeking and knocking, and the gracious spirit of wisdom will enter into you.)

---

[44] PL 142: 1024b.

[45] About a century after Goscelin, hagiographer Jacques de Vitry similarly calls up these semiotic resonances when he describes Marie d'Oignies (d. 1213), a holy woman and beguine of Liège in the Low Countries, as a *tympanistria*, or drummer, when she sings to God. For more analysis of this rich word, see Bruce Holsinger, *Music, Body, and Desire in Medieval Culture: Hildegard of Bingen to Chaucer* (Stanford, CA: Stanford University Press, 2001), 216, as well as Jennifer N. Brown, 'The Chaste Erotics of Marie d'Oignies and Jacques de Vitry', *Journal of the History of Sexuality* 19(1) (2010): 77.

[46] Hayward and Hollis, 'The Female Reader in the *Liber Confortatorius*', in *Writing the Wilton Women*, 387. For another discussion see Gopa Roy, 'Sharpen Your Mind with the Whetstone of Books: The Female Recluse as Reader in Goscelin's *Liber Confortatorius*, Aelred of Rievaulx's *De Institutione Inclusarum* and the *Ancrene Wisse*', in *Women, the Book and the Godly: Selected Proceedings of the St Hilda's Conference, 1993*, vol. 1, ed. Lesley Smith and Jane H.M. Taylor (Cambridge: D.S. Brewer, 1995).

Goscelin writes this exhortation in the chapter just before the anecdote related by the 'learned monk'. By anticipating that devotional exercise with this description of reading, he primes the reader to have the necessary tools to effect her own spiritual incarnation of Christ in imitative parallel to Christ's physical incarnation in Mary. The abundant capacity of 'sense' referred to here echoes the added layers of understanding reached by an interpretative approach like that of Mary at the Annunciation. 'If then you choose to have Christ born in you,' writes Aelred of Rievaulx in a later sermon, 'fill yourself with the begettings of Wisdom – that is, of Christ.'[47] Word is made flesh, in the reader as in Mary. Goscelin carefully sets up the acts of reading or singing the psalms as a generative devotional process: 'When you weave anew the web of the Psalter, sing as if you were in the sight of the angels' (III: 82 [165]). There is the sense that, like Christ's 'going in' or conception at the utterance of the psalm verse, reading or singing the text constitutes a tangible creation: she weaves the web of the Psalter like she weaves the Word with her flesh.

So where is Mary's book in this scene? Goscelin does not mention any physical psalter, not in the same explicit way that we will soon see the *Vita* author describe Christina of Markyate with a psalter in her lap. As a reflection of a medieval nun or monk, this Mary could easily be singing her gradual psalms from memory, still in the dark, or eyes closed. What becomes important in this scene is not the codex itself but the same symbolic power represented by the physical psalter as by its performance: the power of the psalm text to interpret the present moment of the Incarnation, to act as a way of using the Old Testament to understand the opening event of the New Testament. Yet whether she was reciting the psalms by memory or reading the words from a book, her words originated in a written text. That is, as this fictionalized Mary might reflect the actual practices of a nun or anchoress like Eva, she would have originally memorized them by reading or singing them from a page.[48] The *Ancrene Wisse* implies an anchoress based her performance of the Divine Office, or

---

[47] Sermon 22:17, *The Liturgical Sermons: The First Clairvaux Collection*, 312.

[48] The relationship between the written text and memorized utterance in the liturgy of the Middle Ages is discussed by Tom Elich, 'Using Liturgical Texts in the Middle Ages', in Gerard Austin, ed., *Fountain of Life: In Memory of Niels K. Rasmussen OP* (Washington, DC: Pastoral Press, 1991), 69–83, where he points out that though a liturgical text or chant may be memorized the written text often remained as an aide-memoire, and that during the twelfth century 'the liturgy is increasingly regulated by writings and is conceived of in those terms' (79). By the fourteenth and fifteenth centuries, private prayer would shift to reading silently from a book such as a Book of Hours; see Paul Saenger, 'Books of Hours and the Reading Habits of the Later Middle Ages', in *The Culture of Print: Power and Uses of Print in Early Modern Europe*, ed. Roger Chartier (Princeton, NJ: Princeton University Press, 2014), 141–73; and 'Silent Reading: Its Impact on Late Medieval Script and Society', *Viator* 13 (1982): 367–414.

hours (which include psalms) on an immediate written source: 'Euch-an segge hire ures as ha haveth i-writen ham' (Let each one say her hours as she has written them).[49] Christina of Markyate and her Psalter – and the ambivalence which clouds their relationship – offer a prime example of a holy woman's inscribed psalms. Goscelin's anecdote leaves it open to the reader to picture Mary with or without a book; in this way, the description can flex to reflect the reader's own practice. But if we set this version of the Annunciation back into a history of the scene, we can see how prominent the psalter book was in representations of Mary, and how its presence should be felt in Goscelin's scene as well. Goscelin's *Liber* is one of the first texts to transform Mary's textual prayer in the Annunciation episode into a mimetic opportunity for a female reader. In the medieval literary and iconography tradition in which this anecdote should be read the Virgin's role as Mother of God becomes wrapped up inextricably with her role as reader; her reading, as much as her virginal body, becomes a site of devotion and hermeneutic fecundity.

In the fourth century, Ambrose first suggested Mary might have been reading before Gabriel arrived – reading not the Psalms, but Isaiah's prophecy foretelling the Incarnation. Perhaps the earliest surviving example of Mary specifically reading the psalms is the ninth-century *Evangelienbuch* by Otfrid von Weissenburg (*c*. 800–after 871). In this Old High German versification of the Gospels, Gabriel finds Mary 'fand sia drurenta, / mit salteru in henti, then sang si unz in enti' (praising God/ With her psalter in her hands, singing it through to the end).[50] Also in the mid-ninth century, select Carolingian ivory carvings of the Annunciation begin to show Mary with a book on a lectern. The *Liber Confortatorius* appears to be the next known textual instance of connecting Mary with the psalms at the Annunciation, placing it just at the forefront of the twelfth-century surge of the iconography of the 'reading Annunciate'. Goscelin was an early adopter of the motif; in addition, his significant innovation is to turn Mary's engagement with the psalms into an interpretive and spiritually transformative act that the reader is exhorted to imitate. Otter writes that Goscelin 'tends to anticipate ideas and practices that are familiar to us from the later Middle Ages, and it is often surprising to find them here in the 1080s.'[51] His mimetic representation of Mary singing the psalms should definitely be considered among one of his most forward-looking moments. As outlined elsewhere, we can pinpoint the meteoric rise in popularity of the 'reading Annunciate' to the late eleventh century – a rise concurrent with a

[49] Hasenfratz, *Ancrene Wisse*, Part 1, 74.
[50] *Otfrids Evangelienbuch*, ed. Oskar Erdmann, 6th ed., by Ludwig Wolff. Altdeutsche Textbibliothek 49 (Tübingen: Niemeyer, 1962); Book 1, part 5, lines 11–12 (20–1). See Miles, 'The Origins and Development' for extensive discussion of this early tradition.
[51] Otter, 'Entrances and Exits', 283.

dramatic growth in the cult of the Virgin, the expansion of women's religious life and an increase in women's overall literacy and access to books.[52] While representations of Mary's solitary reading were initially directed towards male clerics and monks, in the long twelfth century the use of the motif shifted to include its prominent use as a mimetic devotional moment for enclosed religious women. By positioning this passage within an iconographical history of Mary's book, we can see how Goscelin participated in timely, regional trends connecting the Virgin at the Annunciation with women readers.

Goscelin describes an Annunciation scene that undoubtedly relies upon the established literary and artistic tradition of Mary with a book, and yet pushes beyond it. He presents a sophisticated narrative version of the Reading Annunciate iconography that might have been familiar to Eva; how else, after all, to visually represent psalm-singing but with a psalter? His familiarity with that Annunciation iconography makes sense: in fact, Goscelin's travels overlap closely with the places of origin of two of the earliest extant manuscript illuminations of the Annunciation, each of which focuses exclusively on the figures of Gabriel and Mary with her book: from the Benedictional of Æthelwold (c. 973) (Figure 5) and the Boulogne Gospels (c. 990–1007).[53] The earlier Benedictional seems to have inspired, or at least have some connection to, the later Boulogne Gospels, which were created by an Anglo-Saxon visitor at the Abbey of St Bertin. That is the same Franco-Flemish monastery where, a few decades later, Goscelin spent time as a monk before leaving for England sometime around 1053–8.[54] Indeed, Goscelin's travels map both these illuminated manuscripts very closely. If the Anglo-Saxon artist responsible for the Boulogne Gospels was familiar with (or even responsible for) the Benedictional of Æthelwold, he would have spent time in the Winchester area, where the Benedictional was created for the Bishop Æthelwold. Winchester is about forty miles from the convent of Wilton. Goscelin, therefore, dwelled at or near the two religious centres that produced the earliest extant insular Annunciation illuminations featuring Mary's book.

A further connection ties Wilton to Bishop Æthelwold, the man behind the Benedictional. Just before penning the *Liber Confortatorius*, Goscelin wrote a life of St Edith, *Vita Edithae*, as a commission by the house of Wilton. Edith,

---

[52] Miles, 'The Origins and Development', 657–8.

[53] The Benedictional of Æthelwold, London, British Library, Additional MS 49598 (full-page Annunciation, fol. 5v); the Boulogne Gospels, Boulogne-sur-mer, Bibliothèque Municipale, MS 11 (Annunciation, fol. 11v). Further discussion of these illuminations can be found in Miles, 'The Origins and Development', which includes a reproduction of the Boulogne Gospels illumination.

[54] William of Malmsbury describes Goscelin as 'monachus de Sancto Bertino'; William of Malmesbury, *De Gestis Regum Anglorum*, ed. William Stubbs (London, 1889), vol. II, 389; cited by Talbot, 'The Liber Confortatorius', 5.

Figure 5. Annunciation. Benedictional of St Æthelwold (971–84, c. 973). London, British Library, Additional 49598, fol. 5v

daughter of Abbess Wulfthryth (former wife of King Edgar), was born in 961 and was a member of the Wilton convent until her death at the age of 23 (c. 984). Goscelin's *Vita Edithae* specifies that Bishop Æthelwold's intervention precipitated Edith's first taking of the veil.[55] Æthelwold clearly involved himself in life at Wilton. Was the Annunciation featured in his commissioned Benedictional (perhaps the earliest extant illumination of Mary and her book) inspired by the well-educated women Æthelwold knew at the convent? Edith, like Eva, could read and write Latin with fluency. Goscelin lauds Edith's 'generosum et ad omnia capax ingenium, legendi intellectuosa flagrantia; manus pingendi, scriptitandi, dictitandi tam decentes' (noble intellect capable of all kinds of thought, perceptive ardour in reading, hands as elegant as they were accomplished in painting and writing as scribe or as author) (4: 42 [26]).[56] One of her books, 'orationalis eius pugil memorabili pignore ... uirginea eius manu cum subscriptis' (a manual of her devotions as a token of her memory ... written in her virginal hand) (11: 68 [38]), was still cherished by the monastery when Eva lived there.[57] Perhaps the inclusion of Mary's book in this Annunciation scene should be understood not only as symptomatic of a larger monastic reform movement emphasizing the importance of scripture, as I have previously argued, but also as a more local reflection of the community of literate women at Wilton, who must have often resembled Mary, at prayer, book open.

Conversely, we should ask: could Goscelin have been inspired by this regional iconographic tradition, captured in the two illuminations, to depict Mary engaging the psalms at Gabriel's arrival? It is not necessary for Goscelin to have seen either the Boulogne Gospels or the Benedictional and their illuminations of Mary reading at the Annunciation, but enough to suggest that he and they flourished in the same devotional climate where such an image – visual or textual – would have been promoted. This climate seems to have been present in both the East Anglian and Northern Franco-Flemish traditions; cross-pollination between the two, in the movement of both people and artefacts, raises the chances Goscelin knew the iconography. While Goscelin

---

[55] 'Interueniente quippe sancto Uuintonie pontifice Adeluuoldo ... de mundiali regno et thalamo, uirginali sancte Dei genitricis *Uuiltonie* successit monasterio' (With the intervention of Æthelwold, the holy bishop of Winchester ... she left an earthly kingdom and bridal and came to the monastery [of Wilton] of the virginal mother of God). The Latin is edited by A. Wilmart, 'La légende de Ste Édith en prose et vers par le moine Goscelin', *Analecta Bollandiana* 56 (1938), 5–101, 265–307. From the translation of *The Vita of Edith* by Michael Wright and Kathleen Loncar, in *Writing the Wilton Women*, 23–67. As with the *Liber*, references to the *Vita Edithae* are by chapter, Latin page number and translation page number in brackets.

[56] On the education of Edith and Eva, see Stephanie Hollis, 'Wilton as a Center of Learning', in *Writing the Wilton Women*, 307–38. In the *Liber*, Goscelin exhorts Eva to turn to texts by Augustine, Orosius, Boethius and others.

[57] *Vita Edithae*, Chapter 8; Wilmart, 55 (Wright and Loncar, 34).

was doubtless familiar with the apocryphal story of Mary singing the psalms as a young virgin in the temple, perhaps it was an artistic representation of the Annunciation that motivated him to conflate the two scenes and imagine how Mary's understanding of a text could parallel the Incarnation.

Christina of Markyate and the St Albans Psalter

On the sixth of November, c. 1096–8, about fifteen years after Goscelin completed the *Liber* for Eva, an infant was born in Huntingdon, near Cambridge, and christened Theodora – at least that is what we read in the Latin *Vita* of Christina of Markyate, the holy woman Theodora was to become. Christina spent much of her youth trying to resist the sexual advances of various men including her 'husband' Burthred. In order to preserve her chastity and live a pious life she rebelled and escaped. Hiding for two years first with the recluse Alfwen at Flamsted, and then for four years with the hermit Roger at Markyate, Christina built up a reputation for her holiness and asceticism. Around 1131 she made a monastic profession at St Albans and began her professional relationship with its abbot, Geoffrey de Gorran. Although Christina's *Vita* breaks off around 1142, we know that by 1145 she had successfully founded a priory at Markyate. She passed away around 1155.[58]

The Virgin Mary at the Annunciation – her enclosure, her voice and her book – both modelled and defined Christina's sanctity as a holy woman. I will connect two key pieces of evidence that link Christina's sanctity to the Annunciation: a kind of inverted, nightmare Annunciation scene of toad infestation in the *Vita*, and the full-page Annunciation illumination in the St Albans Psalter (Hildesheim, Dombibliothek, MS St Godehard 1). This huge and beautiful tome of 209 pages and 40 full-page illuminations was created at St Albans in a complex fashion over a number of years; the details of its creation, who it was intended for and who actually used it all remain under debate. Many scholars believe that the manuscript was created for Christina's use between

---

[58] For the Latin and a facing-page translation of the *Vita*, see C.H. Talbot, ed. and trans., *The Life of Christina of Markyate: A Twelfth Century Recluse* (Toronto: University of Toronto Press, 1998) (1st ed., Oxford, 1959); cited by page number, with any amendments to his translation bracketed. Without its prologue, the *Vita*'s author, intended audience and date of composition all remain open to speculation. The work survives in a single manuscript, London, BL, MS Cotton Tiberius E.I., written in the second quarter of the fourteenth century, and seems to have been prepared for St Albans. Talbot reconstructs a chronology of Christina's life, *Life*, 14–15, among a broader biographical introduction; see also the helpful article by Henrietta Leyser, 'Christina of Markyate: An Introduction', in *Christina of Markyate: A Twelfth-Century Holy Woman*, ed. Samuel Fanous and Henrietta Leyser (Routledge: London, 2005), 1–12.

c.1119–*c*.1136/9.⁵⁹ Whether or not it was used by Christina, its pictorial programme still strongly suggests a close association with the idea and idealization of a holy woman. The full-page miniature of the Annunciation on p. 19 features Mary seated under a baldachin and holding an open (but blank) book in her lap (Figure 6).⁶⁰ This illumination is one of the earliest insular depictions of Mary with a book. Analysing the *Vita* text and the Psalter image together gives us a fresh insight into how Christina modelled her new identity of holy woman on the figure of Mary. As with Mary and the other anchoresses considered in this chapter, enclosure defines Christina's sanctity when she first embarks on her new life – but it is how she *prays* like the Virgin that legitimates her status as holy woman. When considered together, the illumination and the *Vita* 'toad scene' connect the St Albans Psalter to Mary's book at the Annunciation, and highlight how reading and singing of the psalms offered medieval holy women an opportunity for self-reflection and self-knowledge – an opportunity validated by the precedent of the Virgin's prayer at the Annunciation.

Christina's life as a holy woman began dramatically. Dressed in men's clothes and riding a stolen horse, Christina escaped from her parents' house to stay with the 'venerable anchoress' Alfwen in Flamstead. Here she hides in a small room: 'Necnon in secretissimam amarissimamque camaram vix illi pre angustia sufficientem detrusa, [sed] delectata pro Christo, multo tempore diligenter occultata delituit' (Hidden out of sight in a most secret and bitter chamber hardly large enough, on account of its size, to house her, she remained carefully

---

[59] Significant studies of the St Albans Psalter include Otto Pächt, C.R. Dodwell and F. Wormald, *The S. Albans Psalter (Albani Psalter)* (London: Warburg Institute, 1960); Kristine L. Haney, *The St Albans Psalter: An Anglo-Norman Song of Faith* (New York: Peter Lang, 2002); Jane Geddes, *The St Albans Psalter: A Book for Christina of Markyate* (London: British Library, 2005); and *The St Albans Psalter: Painting and Prayer in Medieval England*, ed. Kristen Collins, Peter Kidd and Nancy Turner (Los Angeles: J. Paul Getty Museum, 2013); *St Albans and the Markyate Psalter: Seeing and Reading in Twelfth-Century England*, ed. Kristen Collins and Matthew Fisher (Kalamazoo, MI: Medieval Institute, 2017). Essential articles include Morgan Powell, 'Making the Psalter of Christina of Markyate (the St Albans Psalter)', *Viator* 36 (2005): 293–335; and Kathryn Gerry, 'The Alexis Quire and the Cult of Saints at St Albans', *Historical Research* 82 (2009): 593–612, where she presents a sceptical reading of the connection between Christina and the psalter, arguing that it was more likely made for the monastic community at St Albans than for an individual. There is a printed facsimile by Johann Bepler and Jane Geddes with codicological commentary by Peter Kidd, *The St Albans Psalter* (Simbach am Inn, Germany: Müller und Schindler, 2008); the manuscript is also online at http://www.abdn.ac.uk/stalbanspsalter (accessed 17 August 2019).

[60] For more on this image and its history in Annunciation iconography, see Miles, 'The Origins and Development', 664.

Figure 6. Annunciation. St Albans Psalter (c. 1140–6). Hildesheim, Dombibliothek, MS St Godehard 1, p. 19.

concealed there for a long time, finding great joy in Christ) (92–3).[61] Like her new mentor, the anchoress Alfwen, Christina isolates herself in an enclosed space in order both to keep out the world and to cultivate her relationship with Christ. It is a kind of impromptu anchorhold for an impromptu anchoress. The *Vita* author describes the enclosure as *secretissimam amarissimamque*, most secret and most bitter, echoing the two characteristics of the anchorhold identified by the *Ancrene Wisse* author: 'nearowðe ant bitternesse', narrowness and bitterness. The *Ancrene Wisse* author plays with the Latin word for 'bitter', *amara*, and its orthographical similarity to 'Maria', when he connects Mary's womb to the narrow and bitter anchorhold. Behind the *Vita*'s diction, then, we read the shadows of other spaces: the formal anchorhold, Mary's womb, Mary's room, Christ's tomb. In fact, the extreme constriction of her *camarae* – just large enough to fit her body – evokes the constriction of the womb and the tomb, and becomes a kind of second skin, a shell safeguarding her virginity and concentrating her holiness. Christina's room is mysteriously porous to the supernatural, like Mary's room at the Annunciation, as we will soon see. Now that her body and soul are protected within this secure space, Christina's correspondence with the Virgin at the Annunciation can begin.

Through the textual devotions she follows *in secretissimam amarissimamque camaram*, Christina mimics both the idealized anchoress and the Virgin Mary. The narrator continues in the next sentence to describe her activity in this enclosure: 'Statimque eadem die cepit de tricesimo psalmo septimo leccionem quinque versus, quorum primus est: Domine ante te omne desiderium meum. Apta quidem lectio conveniensque fortune legentis' (And on that very day she took for her reading five verses from the thirty-seventh psalm, of which the first runs: 'Lord, all my desire is before thee' [Ps. 37:10]. A very suitable passage and one that described the situation of the reader) (82–3). Like the Mary of Ambrose and Bernard, Christina can pray most effectively when enclosed and alone. In the view of the narrator, the psalms functioned as a mirror in which Christina saw herself and came to understand her spiritual life, just as in Goscelin's passage Mary understands the psalms as a parallel to Christ's Incarnation (and in turn, the reader Eva does the same). The psalms are personal, their meaning flexible: their verses are to be interpreted as a reflection of the reader's particular situation.

In the next scene Christina's enclosure and her reading of the psalms combine to form a shocking inversion of Annunciation episode. A series of visions deepen Christina's desire to live a holy life and resist the intimidations of her family and those who want her to marry. The culminating incident leaves the realm of vision and becomes a terrifying reality:

---

[61] Talbot elides *secretissimam* and translates *amarissimam* as 'dark'; I have amended the translation to more closely represent these words.

Interim latebre sue vitaque tranquillla diabolum exacerbabant. lecciones ac psalmodia die noctuque cruciabant. Quanquam enim occultat lateret homines: nequaquam latebat et demones. Qui ad deterrendam reverendam ancillam Christi: bufones irrumpebant in carcerem: eo quod averterent virginis obtutum. specie illa per omnem deformitatem. Apparebant subito teterrima. terribilibus ac spaciosis orbibus oculorum. sedebant hinc et hinc: psalterio vendicantes medium locum in gremio virginis quod propemodum omnibus horis iacebat expansum in usum sponse Christi. At cum illa nec se moveret nec psalmodiam dimitteret: iterum abibant. Under magis credendum est eos fuisse demones. presertim quia deformita te tales apparentes et insperate comparentes videri non potuit unde venerint vel quo devenerint vel quo exierint: adeo carcer ille clauses erat et obstructus undique. (98–9)

(In the meantime her concealment and her peaceful existence irritated the devil: her reading and singing of the psalms by day and night were a torment to him. For although in her hiding-place she was hidden from men, she could never escape the notice of the demons. And so to terrify the reverend handmaid of Christ toads invaded her cell to distract her attention by all kinds of ugliness from God's beauty. Their sudden appearance, with their big and terrible eyes, was most frightening, for they squatted here and there, arrogating the middle of the psalter which lay open on the lap [of the virgin] all hours of the day for [the use of the bride of Christ]. But when she refused to move and would not give up her singing of the psalms, they went away, which makes one think that they were devils, especially as they appeared unexpectedly; and as the cell was closed and locked on all sides it was not possible to see where they came from, or how they got in or out.)

This is the Annunciation gone wrong. Christina, enclosed and at prayer just like Mary, invites in not angels but demonic toads. For both women, their heterotopias are closed to men yet mysteriously porous to supernatural powers; for both women, these unearthly visitors validate their chastity and sanctity – though Christina admittedly gets a tougher test. Rather than being silently and mysteriously impregnated by the Holy Spirit, Christina suddenly finds the toads attempting to molest her *gremium* – a word with a semantic range including lap, bosom, womb, interior, female genital part – but both body and soul are protected by the book covering her lap.[62] Her psalter operates as a physical protection against the lechery symbolized by the toads; as a moral protection, it keeps her concentration on Christ and away from the distractions of the devil. Her steadfast concentration manifests inner and outer virginity. Inaccessible to men, yet porous to either the Devil or Christ: Mary's

---

[62] Lewis and Short, *gremium*, *ii*, n.

room and the recluse's enclosure blur together as emblematic spaces defining the woman's soul within.

The precise details in the episode with the toads suggest the degree to which a recluse's physical containment determines, in some measure, her holiness. 'Surely then the most prudent virgin had at that time closed the door of her private room to men, but not to angels,' Bernard of Clairvaux explained about Mary in his sermon. Substitute 'angels' with 'devils': no earthly doors resist the supernatural. Like Bernard, the *Vita* narrator makes it very clear that Christina's small space cannot be entered by men; if it could, it would be a worldly bedroom where earthly lust, not heavenly glory, rules. It would become that bedroom she fled when she refused the advances of the lecherous suitors who plagued her prior life. Those suitors return again, their sin symbolically present as toads, ubiquitous as sinful thoughts. Toads, identified as demons, often appear to holy men and women; 'though not sought after, these attacks serve to exemplify a person's holiness', notes Renate Blumenfeld-Kosinksi. A similar episode to Christina of Markyate's happened to Christina of Stommeln: she was praying before bed, heard the sounds of toads and felt the presence of demons.[63] Like all enclosed holy women, Christina of Markyate's *carcer*, or cell, like her virgin body, must be closed to men: yet both will always be penetrable by the evil that can tempt her and the good that can reward her.

Christina was not an anchoress by vocation, like Julian of Norwich. Rather, she was more or less forced into reclusion by a lack of other options – a situation which was to change dramatically by the end of her lifetime, during which many female religious communities came into being, among them her own priory. Regardless, seclusion comes to define Christina's existence and her devotion. Linda Georgianna, in her examination of the nature of Christina's reclusion in terms of twelfth-century attitudes towards the solitary life, seems to overlook Christina's use of the Psalter in this passage when she writes, 'it is especially noticeable in an otherwise highly dramatic and vividly descriptive work that so little is said about what Christina *does* in her cell, except that she finds "delect [ationem] pro Christi".[64] I think that Christina's secluded psalm reading, and its rich connections to the model of the Virgin Mary as recluse,

---

[63] 'The Strange Case of Ermine de Reims (*c.* 1347–1396): A Medieval Woman between Demons and Saints', *Speculum* 85 (2010), 347. For more on toads, see Mary E. Robbins, 'The Truculent Toad in the Middle Ages', in Nona C. Flores, ed., *Animals in the Middle Ages: A Book of Essays* (New York: Garland, 1986), 25–47; on animal attacks on saints see William Short, *Saints in the World of Nature: The Animal Story as Spiritual Parable in Medieval Hagiography (900–1200)* (Rome: Pontificia Universitas Gregoriana, 1983).

[64] Georgianna, *The Solitary Self*, 39.

counter the claim that 'Christina's sanctity, then, is achieved almost in spite of, and certainly not because of, her solitary life.'[65] In fact, her virginity, literate devotion and seclusion all combine to achieve a sanctity magnified by its prototype in Mary. We should understand Christina's identity as a holy woman as formed by the dual models of the anchoress and the Virgin – in the twelfth century, overlapping figures of sanctified enclosure marked by vocal, powerful praying of the psalms.

Initially, the psalter book on her lap together with her insistent reading and singing the psalms protect Christina from the toads. Yet Christina's book also represents Mary's book: the full significance of the *Vita*'s inverted Annunciation scene emerges only when we analyse it alongside the St Albans Psalter and its representation of Mary's book in its Annunciation illumination. The two women mirror each other: Mary holds an open book in her lap, just as Christina is described in the toad scene (Figure 6).[66] The correspondence is especially startling when we realize that almost all earlier Annunciation images featured Mary's book on a stand or lectern, not placed on her body and symbolically guarding her womb in the same way (as in the Benedictional illumination, Figure 5). Its placement matches the *vita*, where the toads were 'arrogating the middle of the psalter which lay open on the lap [of the virgin] all hours of the day for [the use of the bride of Christ]'. Just as the psalms offered Christina a meditative opportunity for self-reflection and self-knowledge, so the Annunciation image would have presented a particularly powerful and relevant model of female literacy. The St Albans Psalter does not contain Luke's text (or any textual version) of the Annunciation; although Christina surely had been made familiar with the story, as a recluse this illumination was perhaps her primary mode of contemplating the moment of the Incarnation of Christ. Indeed, the entire prefatory cycle leads the viewer through the life of Christ in lieu of the Gospel texts themselves. What the images present becomes the 'gospel truth' for Christina.

At the end of the manuscript we find a letter by St Gregory (copied in both Latin and French) commending the use of religious pictures for learning. As Michael Camille suggests, this excerpt shows how its inclusion helps to justify the dozens of full-page illuminations that follow it:[67]

> Aliud est picturam adorare aliud per picture historiam quid sit adorandum addiscere. Nam quod legentibus scriptura hoc ignotis prestat pictura qua in

---

[65] Georgianna, *The Solitary Self*, 42.
[66] For relevant examples, see Miles, 'The Origins and Development'.
[67] Michael Camille, 'Seeing and Reading: Some Visual Implications of Medieval Literacy and Illiteracy', *Art History* 8 (1985): 26.

ipsa ignorantes vident quid sequi debeant. In ipsa legunt qui litteras nesciunt. Unde & precipue gentibus pro lectione pictura est.[68]

(It is one thing to worship a picture; another to learn, through the story of a picture, what is to be worshipped. For the thing that writing conveys to those who read, that is what a picture shows to the illiterate; in the picture itself those who are ignorant see what they ought to follow. In [the picture] itself those who are unacquainted with letters [are able to] read. Whence, and particularly among common folk, a picture serves in place of reading.)

This letter points to the blurry idea we have of Christina's literacy. She could 'read' the psalms, in as much as she likely had them mostly memorized and the text provided cues to memory; hers was a predominantly oral religious experience. But there is no evidence she was as learned as an Eva or Edith of the previous generations – no evidence she read the New Testament or the commentaries on it. What Christina learns from this Annunciation image is not limited to the story of Gabriel's arrival and Christ's conception. She also learns that the angel found Mary, the Mother of God, in solitude with a book: that a virgin, like her, prayed by reading and earned the presence of Christ in her womb. Facing outwards towards the viewer, the book in Mary's hands reflexively stands in for the St Albans Psalter itself in which it is painted. The book on her lap is ruled, but blank: on its empty page the viewer can project the text of her own imagining.[69] Perhaps it is Psalm 120:8, 'May the Lord watch over your comings in and goings out,' as the 'learned monk' told Goscelin that Mary was reading when Gabriel arrived. Or perhaps it is the Old Testament prophecy of Isaiah, as Aelred of Rievaulx suggests to his female readers (discussed in the next chapter). Or perhaps its ruled lines empty of text imply the Luke gospel being performed at that very moment, as Mary fulfils the Old by writing the New with the flesh of her body. Whatever text Christina may have imagined Mary to have read – or sung – that portrait of the Virgin invited an act of self-reflection.

---

[68] Page 68 of the Psalter; from the transcription and translation published on the St Albans Project site, https://www.abdn.ac.uk/stalbanspsalter/english/translation/trans068.shtml (accessed 17 August 2019). An edition of the full text of Gregory's letter can be found in Caecilia Davis-Weyer, *Early Medieval Art, 300–1150: Sources and Documents* (Toronto: University of Toronto Press, 1986), 47–9. Much work has been done on the implications of Gregory's argument; see, for instance, L.G. Duggan, 'Was Art Really the "Book of the Illiterate"?', *Word and Image* V (1989): 227–51; and C.M. Chazelle, 'Pictures, Books, and the Illiterate: Pope Gregory I's Letters to Serenus of Marseilles', *Word and Image* VI (1990): 138–53.

[69] Also in the miniature of the three kings before Herod, page 23, Herod's book is blank.

Christina's 'reading and singing of the psalms by day and night' recalls Goscelin's description of Mary rising 'in the middle of the night, as was her sacred custom, to sing divine hymns'. In Goscelin's *Liber*, Mary chanted (*timpanizaret*) the psalms as part of a private celebration of the monastic hours, but he doesn't mention a book; in Christina's *Vita*, we both hear her chanting or singing of the psalms (*psalmodia*) and see a psalm book on her lap. The *Vita*'s close correlation of Christina's reading and singing (*lecciones ac psalmodia*) reinforces the idea that prayer in these instances was as much text-based contemplation as semi-liturgical performance and, indeed, that these modes of devotion blur together. After all, the St Albans Psalter Annunciation illumination completely sidesteps this question: Mary's mouth is decorously closed as she regards Gabriel. What she was doing with her book before his arrival – silently contemplating its message, quietly uttering its words under her breath, chanting aloud its verses – the viewer is left to imagine. Neither do we know what psalm verse Christina was singing in her inverted amphibianized Annunciation. We do know, however, that her words have 'muche strengðe' just like Mary's (to borrow the words of the *Ancrene Wisse* author): the power to discourage the devil and to delight God. Christina's chanting aloud of the psalms, her performance of the written word, succeeds not only in warding off the toads, but also in validating her identity as a holy woman for the reading audience.

'With a loud clear voice'

These examples demonstrate how closely eleventh- and twelfth-century representations of Mary mirrored the medieval recluse or anchoress, and some of the understudied ways that enclosed holy women were encouraged to mirror themselves on Mary. In anchoritic writings, Mary becomes an anchoress: her physical enclosure at the Annunciation aligns with the recluse's enclosure; her chaste body aligns with the recluse's chaste body; her singular focus on prayer aligns with the recluse's prayer. At the centre of these representations was the Incarnation: when Mary's womb becomes the anchorhold and Christ the recluse, when the Word of God takes flesh. Foucault's heterotopia principles highlight the unexpected paradoxes that define such a special space: it can be both contained and penetrable; it works to accumulate time (biblical time, liturgical time, the reader's time); and 'it has a function in relation to all the space that remains'. Significantly, both the Annunciation room and anchorhold offer 'a space that is other, another real space, as perfect, as meticulous, as well arranged as ours is messy, ill constructed, and jumbled'.[70] Most importantly, the Annunciation heterotopia's function in relation to all

---

[70] Foucault, *Of Other Spaces*, 27.

the space that remains is that it contains the God-man that will save all mankind. Perhaps this particular space points out another principle at work in heterotopias: that in them can be heard voices, or sounds, otherwise silenced, ignored, overpowered, or an impossibility in the normal world. From out of these medieval texts ring the voices of anchoritic readers, of Eva, of Christina, of Mary herself, singing the Word made flesh. Not that women's voices aren't heard elsewhere – or can't speak to God outside the anchorhold – but rather that the premise of the Annunciation space sanctions the woman's voice to pray aloud in a way uniquely connected to the presence of God in the world: the moment of Christ's conception. The tradition of Mary performing the psalms at the Incarnation offered medieval holy women a model of active prayer, with Mary's 'exultante spiritu in Deo' (spirit rejoicing in God), in Goscelin's words. Psalter book in the hand or in the head – the distinction fades as the psalm words find life in performance, uttered and interpreted simultaneously. As in Goscelin's *Liber*, when Mary *timpanizaret* (chanted, sung, intoned) the psalms, those verses achieve a new meaning that helps to explain the Incarnation itself as a typological foreshadowing of the Old Testament. When Christ comes alive, the psalm text also comes alive through its performance, its reading or singing aloud – a bodily engagement that comes to parallel Mary's bodily engagement of the divine in Christ's conception. (Of course, being written by men, these medieval writings do not actually bring sound to women's voices, but only demonstrate how that could be so; in a later chapter, we will read women's own accounts where they speak through the Annunciation scene, sanctioned by their visionary vocation.)

The full significance of Mary's confident voice for these enclosed female readers becomes more clear when we understand the environment outside the anchorhold, 'all that space that remains'. One short anecdote from Christina of Markyate's life shows how the model of a singing Virgin could, in a sense, answer the prayers of women called to a holy life. Christina's *Vita*, like many hagiographies, gives us a vivid account of her childhood. When still a girl, she developed an early relationship with Christ wherein

> in noctibus et lectulo suo loquebatur ad ipsum quasi ad hominem quem videret. et hoc alta voce et clara. ut audiretur et intelligeretur ab hiis qui in eadem domo iacebant. estimans cum Deo loquentem non posse audiri ab homine. At illis deridentibus eam morem mutavit. (36–7)

> (she used to talk to Him on her bed at night just as if she were speaking to a man she could see; and this she did with a loud clear voice, so that all who were resting in the same house could hear and understand her. She thought that if she were speaking to God, she could not be heard by man. But when they made fun of her, she changed this mode of acting.)

Young, precocious, full of love for God, not a little naive, Christina learns the hard way how her family will receive her spiritual vocation. This episode helps to provide some background context for her later desires for complete, solitary isolation, where she could pray and chant her psalms as loudly as she wanted, with risk of being teased (or worse). Finding a space outside the lay home in which to pray aloud – an enclosed, solitary, private space, an echo chamber for the voice – turns out to be a necessary reaction to a domestic world that often silences the female voice. In her *Vita*, Christina's 'loud, clear voice' draws the attention of the devil-toads, just as it drew the attention of her judgemental family members many years before. Both threats are defeated by her persistence. In Goscelin's *Liber*, Mary's singing at the Annunciation acts as a celebratory greeting for both Gabriel and Christ, and rings out from the page in a discourse that otherwise tempers the female voice. For the female anchoritic reader, performing the psalms may be a bodily, aural manifestation of the spiritual conception of Christ facilitated by such semi-liturgical prayer – in direct reflection of the bodily, visual manifestation of the physical conception of Christ by the Virgin Mary. Otherwise often fleshly and weak, in these incarnational moments a woman's body brings her closer to God, not exclusively through Christ's humanity but rather more through the woman's body that gave him that humanity.

3
Reading the Prophecies: Meditation and Female Literacy in Lives of Christ Texts

Mary's voice rings out from the eleventh- and twelfth-century texts of the anchorhold. She sings the psalms and hears in them the Incarnation, all in concert with enclosed women readers. Within this Annunciation imaginary, contained space (whether the concrete cell or the abstract soul) both protect and liberate devotion to God. The previous chapter explored how male authors set up Mary's containment at the Annunciation to offer a paradigm for female readers, particularly anchoresses, to engage with the psalms like the Virgin: speaking or singing psalms aloud so as to conceive Christ spiritually just as Mary conceived him physically. Their voices are validated as they interpret the psalm verses in relation to themselves and Mary, inhabiting the lyrical 'I', connecting the typological power of the Psalter with the transformative power of the Incarnation.

Yet also in the twelfth century, a rival tradition came to dominate representations of the Annunciation from the medieval period to the present: Mary engages not the psalms, but rather reads the Old Testament prophecies foretelling the Annunciation, specifically Isaiah 7:14, 'Ecce virgo in utero concipiet et pariet filium' (Behold a virgin shall conceive in her womb and bear a son). This apocryphal tradition probably originated with Ambrose of Milan (c. 337–97), who first claimed about Isaiah that 'legerat hoc Maria' (Mary had read this) in his commentary on Luke. Three centuries later, Bede (c. 672–735) adopted Ambrose's theme in his own commentary on the gospel; around the turn of the millennium, Fulbert of Chartres and Odilo of Cluny likewise refer to Mary reading Isaiah's prophecy in their sermons.[1] The verse had long been

---

[1] Quotations and details on these texts can be found in Miles, 'The Origins and Development'.

linked to the Annunciation through the liturgy; in England the Sarum Mass for the Feast of the Annunciation, 25 March, featured Isaiah 7:14 in the Introit, the Epistle and the Communion chant.[2] But the belief that Mary was *reading* this Old Testament prophecy only truly took off when it became a part of the widespread late medieval genre of 'lives of Christ', or 'gospel meditations', prose narrative biographies of Christ and his family – many featuring the Annunciation as a prominent scene, as the moment of Christ's conception.

Lives of Christ, in Latin and many European vernaculars, utilized the power of the imagination to lead the reader on an interiorized journey following the life of Christ. Inviting readers to reconstruct mentally biblical and apocryphal scenes and even participate in the events offered a vivid and emotional spiritual experience that helped catapult these texts to great popularity. From the twelfth century on, the genre shaped religious culture for both lay and clerical Christians, propelling the pervasive tradition of affective meditation on the Passion, 'the staple of the religious practice of the devout and the religious élite of late medieval England and Europe in general'.[3] One of the earliest examples, the anchoritic guide *De Institutione Inclusarum* by Aelred of Rievaulx (*c.* 1110–1167), was first written in Latin for enclosed female readers and later translated into English twice, for a mixed lay and clerical audience. Like *De Institutione*, the lives of Christ genre quickly shifted from a limited religious audience to include a broader readership, encompassing more of literate society. In the early fourteenth century, the most influential life of Christ text emerged from Italy: the *Meditationes vitae Christi* (*MVC*), thought by medieval readers to have been written by Bonaventure. The *MVC* spawned an entire lineage of lives of Christ in its pseudo-Bonaventuran tradition, with translations throughout Europe and England, including, in Middle English, the fifteenth-century *Mirror of the Blessed Life of Jesus Christ* by Nicholas Love and the anonymous *Speculum Devotorum*. Twenty-four longer and multitudes of shorter vernacular Passion narratives based on the *MVC* circulated in fourteenth- through sixteenth-century England. 'They are a remarkably rich and still largely untapped resource for understanding ...

---

[2] Éamonn Ó Carragáin, *Ritual and the Rood: Liturgical Images and the Old English Poems of the* Dream of the Rood *Tradition* (London: The British Library and University of Toronto Press, 2005), 356, discusses the Sarum Missal's liturgy for the mass on 25 March in terms of its long early medieval history. Bible commentaries such as in the *Glossa Ordinaria* do not mention Mary's reading of the verse.

[3] Eamon Duffy, *The Stripping of the Altars: Traditional Religion in England c. 1400–c. 1580* (New Haven, CT: Yale University Press, 1992), 265. On Passion narratives and devotions, see Denise Despres, *Ghostly Sights: Visual Meditation in Late-Medieval Literature* (Norman, OK: Pilgrim, 1989), esp. chapter 1, 'Franciscan Meditation: Historical and Literary Contexts'; and Thomas Bestul, *Texts of the Passion: Latin Devotional Literature and Medieval Society* (Philadelphia: University of Pennsylvania Press, 1996).

the vibrancy of mainstream later medieval devotional textual culture,' Ian Johnson rightly points out.[4]

How precisely did these meditations work? For example, the *MVC* directs the reader not only to observe the events of Christ's life, but actually to insert themselves in the scene: 'Nunc ergo et hic bene aspice, et tanquam ipso facto presens existens, intellige omnia que dicuntur et fiunt' (20:29–31) (Now then, here too watch closely, as if you were actually present, and take in mentally everything said and done) (13).[5] Imagining with the mind's eye surpasses a passive experience of observation because the reader *ipso facto* participates in the scene by becoming an agent within their own devotional fantasies. Imagination, or *imaginatio*, as a faculty of the soul, was the powerful engine behind this engagement. In her important study, *Imagination, Meditation, and Cognition in the Middle Ages*, Michelle Karnes explains how 'imagination helps the meditant to imagine scenes vividly and feel appropriate emotion, but it also uses the light that shines on it when engaged in the act of knowing in order to lift the meditant to Christ'.[6] In other words, the very act of imagining brought the reader closer to the divine. This ascent relies on Christ's combination of human and divine natures. According to Bonaventure's writings, such as the *Lignum vitae*,

> gospel meditation serves to traverse the distance between Christ's humanity and divinity, a feat it accomplishes in part through imagination. Since Christ functions in the mind to draw understanding out of sense knowledge, the mind that directs itself to Christ uses Christ to proceed from sensory knowledge of his humanity to spiritual understanding of his divinity. Imagining Christ's life accordingly takes advantage of the mind's own cognitive resources to draw the meditant closer to God.[7]

Thus the topic of these meditations has everything to do with their function and efficacy. Christ's life is not merely a good theme, it is *the* theme that can launch the human mind to the heights of divine understanding – and the soul nearer to God.

---

[4] Ian Johnson, *The Middle English Life of Christ: Academic Discourse, Translation, and Vernacular Theology* (Turnhout: Brepols, 2013), 3. Elizabeth Salter surveys Middle English lives of Christ in *Nicholas Love's 'Myrrour of the Blessed Lyf of Jesu Christ'* (Salzburg: Insitut für Anglistik und Amerikanistik, Universität Salzburg, 1974).

[5] M. Stallings-Taney, *Iohannis de Caulibus Meditaciones vite Christi, olim S. Bonaventuro attributae*, CCCM 153 (Turnhout: Brepols, 1997), with the modern English translation, *Meditations on the Life of Christ*, trans. Francis X. Taney Sr, Anne Miller OSF and C. Mary Stallings-Taney (Asheville, NC: Pegasus, 2000). All quotations from the *Meditationes* will be from this edition (identified by page and line number) and translation (identified by page number), respectively.

[6] Karnes, *Imagination, Meditation, and Cognition*, 112.

[7] Karnes, *Imagination, Meditation, and Cognition*, 19–20.

Though *intellige* suggests the reading of meditations was an activity engaging the mind, *intellectus*, it also heavily engaged feelings or *affectus* in several ways: these texts both taught and refined affective compassion. Sarah McNamer argues that affective meditations on the Passion were 'richly emotional, script-like texts that ask their readers ... to perform compassion for that suffering victim in a private drama of the heart'.[8] Through 'iterative affective performance', these texts taught their readers how to feel.[9] Affection also helped to imprint indelibly the imagined events in the memory of the meditant, the *MVC* suggests: 'ipsa rumines et bene delecteris in eis, toto affectu ea memorie commendando, et opere imitando, quia deuotissima sunt' (18:98–100) (Review and take real delight in them by committing them to memory with all your affection; and by imitating them in your own activity, because they are most devotional) (12). Reading a gospel meditation was only the first step; thus stored in the memory, the biblical scenes become places to revisit, to re-view, in order to shape everyday behaviour. Such devotional practice gives the reader two intertwined aspects to imitate in their life: the continual imitation of their own compassionate reactions to the Passion of Christ, and the imitation of actions and behaviours of biblical figures. For instance, imitating Christ's mercy and kindness, his patient suffering, Mary's grief at the foot of the cross – or her meditation at the Annunciation.

The importance of Mary's meditation just before the Incarnation as a model for the reader's own meditation has been overlooked by modern scholars. In their examinations of how these gospel meditations worked and their roles in medieval life, most researchers have focused mainly on the Crucifixion scene and its cultural power. The Annunciation interfaces *imaginatio* and *affectus* in a quite different way from the Passion. While the sorrowful end of Christ's life emphasizes affective compassion as a reaction to meditation on the text, the moment of his conception establishes the basic relationship of meditation *with* the text. It offers the first and only opportunity in the narratives for the reader to see imaginative reading at work – in Mary's reading of the prophecies that she will momentarily fulfil – and to imitate this in their own textual engagement. For medieval readers, Mary's reading models the potential for Christ to be reborn in each Christian's soul by means of text-based meditation. It sets up the entire paradigm of Christ's life *as a book*, the Word made flesh, which undergirds the power of the gospel meditation text itself. 'Meditation is an adjunct to the gift of the Incarnation,' Karnes points out; 'it is how those who were not present for Jesus's historical life can share it. To this extent, Christ's life and passion are intended for mental commemoration.'[10] As a scene, then,

---

[8] McNamer, *Affective Meditation*, 1.
[9] McNamer, *Affective Meditation*, 2.
[10] Karnes, *Imagination, Meditation, and Cognition*, 146.

the Incarnation is the ideal place to set up meditation as a repeatable act, modelled by Mary – sometimes with a book, sometimes not, but always praying devoutly when Gabriel arrives. While the Passion provokes 'iterative affective performance', as McNamer articulates it, the Annunciation provokes what I would call 'iterative meditative performance': the performance of meditation itself. This performance needs a model just as much as affective compassion does, which is why Mary's meditation takes on so much importance for the reader's own formation as a meditant. More importantly, when Mary's own meditative performance includes her book, readers can simultaneously see their literary meditation reflected in her *and* model their literary meditation in her reflection.

Mary's role in the Incarnation – giving flesh to God, encompassing the divine made man in her womb – literally embodies the incarnational leaps these imaginative, meditational texts intend their readers to make. Karnes clarifies the medieval theory linking imagination to the Incarnation:

> It is no coincidence that Bonaventure in fact collapses the two binaries, reading the mind's progress from sense to intellect precisely as one from Christ's human to divine natures. Only the miracle of Christ's joint natures can enable human beings to overcome the materiality of their bodies and their surroundings to know immaterial things. Imagination lies at the nexus of both transitions within the mind, functioning crucially in both cognitive and spiritual capacities.[11]

Thus it is appropriate that the sole example of textual meditation in these narratives (nowhere else does anyone explicitly read in the stories) coincides with the joining of *Logos* and our material body. Mary's reading shows itself as much more than a metaphor for the Incarnation – it is a primary means for each reader to bring Christ into the world. The *MVC* reminds us that through reading, meditation and its attendant joys God shows himself: 'In his ergo meditare, in his delectare et iucundaberis, et forte ostendet tibi Dominus ampliora' (24: 146–8) (Therefore, meditate on these things, take delight in them, and you will be filled with joy, and perhaps the Lord will reveal even more to you) (17). Meditation precipitates revelation; it sets up a conduit between man and God, made possible by the God made man.

Considering all these theological implications, the practical consequences of a literate, Bible-toting Mother of God deserve closer attention. Mary *could* function as this genre's main model of scriptural reading and reading in general – if the author allows her to keep her Old Testament prophecies in hand. But sometimes she was not depicted reading, despite the motif's popularity, despite – or perhaps because of – its metaphorical significance. The full power

---

[11] Karnes, *Imagination, Meditation, and Cognition*, 112.

of her reading act only surfaces when we map it onto historical evidence of actual reading practices. How does Mary's activity at the Annunciation illuminate scriptural reading habits in medieval England? What does it mean when Mary is and isn't reading? If we take this single scene from the main lives of Christ texts read in medieval England, and closely analyse the passages in comparison, an intriguing new story of the intertwined evolution of reading and meditation emerges.

This chapter begins with Aelred's twelfth-century *De Institutione Inclusarum*, the earliest instantiation of the spiritual biography genre, as an ideal case study for tracing the historical evolution of scriptural reading habits in medieval England. He unreservedly encourages his female readers to read like Mary. Yet this image of a woman reading the Bible, without the mediation of a male priest or confessor, or even the textual mediation of a gospel re-telling like these texts themselves, proved controversial enough in later centuries that the two Middle English translations amended or even omitted this key detail. The *MVC* does not specify Mary as reading, only praying, while one of its vernacular translations, Nicholas Love's *Mirror of the Blessed Life of Jesus Christ*, takes care to insert the detail – despite certain censoring legislation restricting exactly that type of reading. Then again the *Mirror of Devout People* depicts Mary praying only – and, overall, discourages any kind of direct contact with the Bible.

Such variation parallels the shifting religious-political environments of twelfth- to fifteenth-century England. The treatment of Mary's reading functions as a kind of barometer of regional, chronological microclimates concerning scriptural engagement. Minute adjustments in the scene's wording sometimes match larger trends of biblical reading and affective piety – and sometimes buck the trend, reminding us of culture's heterogeneity, those bubbles of belief, pockets of progressiveness, or moments of moderation. By tracking the image of Mary's book over several centuries, we can map the shifting landscape of female literacy and the expectations of the men who wrote texts for women (as well as scribes who adapted texts for broader audiences). This is a matter of both representation and audience. Mary, as a female figure in a text meant for imitation, expresses what the authors thought might be appropriate for their women readers to imitate. If it seemed logistically reasonable for women to read the Old Testament, it would be reasonable to present Mary doing so – or vice versa. In that way Mary's activity in the texts can be interpreted as a reflection of historical practices as well as expectations of medieval women's reading, or at least the authors' reflection of those practices and expectations.

In terms of audience, several of these gospel meditations originally targeted a female audience, usually enclosed, including Aelred's *De Institutione Inclusarum* and the *Mirror for Devout People*. The manuscript history of all the texts in this chapter, however, shows they enjoyed wide readerships of both men and women, lay and religious. Yet that doesn't mean that all readers responded the same ways to these texts. In the cases of this chapter, for instance, it is my view that a special gendered identification could operate between Mary as a female reader and historical female readers, that would be different from the identification between a male reader and Mary. Of course, just as women could imitate Christ, men also could imitate the Virgin: in her joy, her tears, her devotion, her reading. But they had many, many other models of meditative reading. In fact, male readers could identify directly with nearly all other models of reading, since they were nearly all men. The default is male. Mary, being perhaps the most iconographically prominent woman reader, proves an exception that would make an impression on women readers.

Aelred's *De Institutione Inclusarum*

'Suster, thou hast ofte axed of me a forme of lyung accordyng to thyn estat, inasmuche as thou art enclosed,' begins his rule of living for a recluse, titled *De Institutione Inclusarum*.[12] Around 1160, Aelred (*c*. 1110–1167), abbot of the Cistercian abbey of Rievaulx in northern England, wrote his only work addressed to a woman.[13] The identity and location of this anchoress are unknown, but it seems likely she was Aelred's biological sister. Like the *Ancrene Wisse*, *De Institutione Inclusarum* is concerned with both the outer, practical life of the recluse and the inner, spiritual life that motivates her day-to-day devotions. In his consideration of this inner life, Aelred presents a specialized programme of threefold meditation: on things past (biblical events), things present (the self and current life) and things to come (death, judgement, heaven and hell). This threefold meditative technique constitutes one of Aelred's most prominent contributions to late medieval spirituality. While he did not invent the technique, through this text he did popularize the practice of imaginatively visualizing Christ's life.[14]

---

[12] *Aelred of Rievaulx's* De Institutione Inclusarum: *Two English Versions*, ed. John Ayto and Alexandra Barratt, EETS o.s. 287 (Oxford: Oxford University Press, 1984), l, ll. 5–6 (MS Bodley 423). Hereafter textual references will be by line number; other references by page number in Ayto and Barratt.

[13] On Aelred, see the twelfth-century life by Walter Daniel, *The Life of Aelred of Rievaulx*, trans. by F.M. Powicke, intro. Marsha Dutton (Kalamazoo, MI: Cistercian, 1994); and two modern books on his life and works: Brian Patrick McGuire, *Brother and Lover: Aelred of Rievaulx* (New York: Crossroads, 1994), and Aelred Squire, *Aelred of Rievaulx: A Study* (London: SPCK 1969).

[14] Ayto and Barratt, *De Institutione Inclusarum*, xiii. See also *Quand Jésus eut douze ans*, ed. Dom A. Hoste OSB (Paris: Cerf, 1958), 7. Further considerations of the content of *de Institutione* include Stephan Borgehammer, 'The Ideal of the Recluse

Aelred's contemplative tour offers as its first stop Mary's *cubiculum*, her little room, in which the reader can witness 'first-hand' Gabriel's Annunciation to the Virgin, based on Luke 1:26-38. Aelred opens his devotional exercise:

> Cum igitur mens tua ab omni fuerit cogitacionum sorde uirtutum exercitatione purgata, iam oculos defecatos ad posteriora retorque, ac primum cum beata Maria, ingressa cubiculum, libros quibus uirginis partus et christi prophetatur aduentus euolue. Ibi aduentum angeli praestolare ut uideas intrantem, audias salutantem, et sic repleta stupore et extasi dulcissimam dominam tuam cum angelo salutante salutes, clamans et dicens: *Aue, gratia plena, dominus te cum, benedicta tu in mulieribus.*[15]

> (When, therefore, your mind has been purged from every uncleanness of thought by the exercise of virtues, now cast back cleansed eyes on what comes next, and first with blessed Mary, entering the bedroom, open [unfold/roll out] the books in which the virgin birth, even the arrival of Christ, is prophesied. There, stand ready for the approach of the angel in order that you may see him entering, listen to his greeting, and so filled with numbness and ecstasy, you may greet with the greeting angel your most sweet lady, crying out and saying, *Hail, full of grace, the Lord is with you, blessed are you among women.*)

Vivid and dramatic, the text draws the reader deep into the scene, where she adopts first the role of Mary, solitary reader. In this performative mode she follows Mary's imagined reading of the Old Testament prophecies foretelling the Incarnation – such as Isaiah 7:14, 'Ecce virgo in utero concipiet et pariet filium' (Behold a virgin shall conceive in her womb and bear a son). Mary emerges from the historical past into an active present where she operates as both companion and model for the anchoritic reader. The Old Testament was often imagined as a scroll, here evoked by the verb *euolue*, 'open, roll out,

---

in Aelred's "De Institutione Inclusarum"', in *In Quest of the Kingdom: Ten Papers on Medieval Monastic Spirituality*, ed. Alf Härdelin (Stockholm: Almqvist & Wiksell International, 1991), 177-202; Marsha Dutton, 'Christ Our Mother: Aelred's Iconography for Contemplative Union', in *Goad and Nail: Studies in Medieval Cistercian History*, X, ed. E. Rozanne Elder (Kalamazoo, MI: Cistercian, 1985), 21-45, and 'Gilding the Lily: The Enhancement of Spiritual Affectivity in a Middle English Translation of Aelred of Rievaulx's De institutione inclusarum', *The Medieval Translator*, Vol. 10, ed. Jacqueline Jenkins and Olivier Bertrand (Turnhout: Brepols, 2007), 109-24.

[15] 'The Latin text of *De Institutione Inclusarum*', ed. C.H. Talbot, in Aelredi Rievallensis, *Opera Omnia, Corpus Christianorum Continuatio Mediaevalis* 1 (Turnhout: Brepols, 1971), 637-82 (ll. 888-96); all citations will be from this edition by line number, with my translations. Talbot also published an earlier edition, 'The "De institutis inclusarum" of Ailred of Rievaulx', *Analecta Sacri Ordinis Cisterciensis* vii (1959), 167-217.

unfold', while the New Testament or Bible as a whole was always a codex. The use of *libros* from *liber*, 'book', suggests a codex format, that is, a bound book that opens on the right. This paradoxical description maintains a historically accurate impression of the Old Testament but simultaneously mirrors the bound book in the contemporary reader's hand, further insisting on Mary's relevant 'otherness' (she does ostensibly belong to a distant past). The reader then follows this rather serious *imitatio Mariae* with an exuberant ventriloquization of Gabriel's words of the New Testament, thus enacting the typological connection which defines the relationship between the two parts of the Christian Bible. 'Repleta stupore et extasi', filled with numbness and ecstasy: the text prescribes the reader's devotional experience as an affective one requiring actual vocalization – 'clamans et dicens' – of the angel's greeting, so close in form to the familiar *Ave Maria*. When Aelred makes available to the reader both performance roles of Mary and Gabriel, he encourages a full inhabitation of the scene, a literary and emotional immersion that facilitates maximum devotion. The reader identifies first and foremost with the Virgin herself, and only after speaks as Gabriel in adoration of the Virgin.

By comparing this passage with an earlier text we can glean a deeper understanding of the meaning of Mary's reading when directed towards a female audience. Aelred's reference in *De Institutione Inclusarum* to the Old Testament prophecies as Mary's reading material likely derived from one of his earlier sermons for his fellow monks, a genre which no doubt frequently anticipates elements of his other prose. In terms similar to those in the later *De Institutione Inclusarum*, Aelred describes the scene in his liturgical sermon for the feast of the Annunciation, sermon 9 from the first Clairvaux collection:

> Ingressa erat in priuatum thalamum suum et clauserat ostium suum et priuatim orabat Patrem suum. Hauriebat sibi aquas in gaudio de fontibus Saluatoris, id est de Scripturis sanctis, ubi legerat et Virginis partum et Saluatoris aduentum. Forte, eo tempore quo angelus uenit, habebat Isaiam in manibus, forte tunc studebat in illa prophetia: *Ecce Virgo concipiet et pariet filium, et uocabitur nomen eius Emmanuel*. Puto quod haec Scriptura in illa hora fecerat quandam pulcherrimam rixam in eius corde.[16]

> (She had gone into her private chamber and closed the door and was praying to her Father in secret (cf. Matthew 6:6). She was drawing waters for herself in joy from the fountain of the Saviour – that is, from the sacred Scriptures

---

[16] From Sermon 9, *On the Annunciation of the Lord*. Latin from *Aelredus Rievallensis Sermones I–XLVI: Collectio Claraevallensis Prima et Secunda*, ed. Gaetano Raciti, CCCM IIA, 21 (Turnhout: Brepols, 1989), 74, ll. 167–72. English from Aelred of Rievaulx, *The Liturgical Sermons: The First Clairvaux Collection*, trans. Theodore Berkeley and M. Basil Pennington (Kalamazoo, MI: Cistercian, 1989).

where she had read about both the virgin's giving birth and of the Saviour's coming. Perhaps at the time the angel came, she was holding [the text of] Isaiah in her hands; perhaps she was then studying the prophecy which declares: *Behold a virgin shall conceive and bear a son and his name will be called Emmanuel* (Isaiah 7:14). I think that at this moment these Scriptures were producing a very appealing conflict in her heart.)

Aelred somewhat tentatively suggests what Mary was doing when Gabriel arrived: *forte*, perhaps, she was holding the book of Isaiah; again, *forte*, perhaps she was reading that exact verse. It is an act of creative imagination rather than historical fact, as the biblical episode mentions no such detail, but it is one that makes sense symbolically and theologically. The general idea of Mary's having read this prophecy at some point in the past can be found in Ambrose's commentary on Luke, while here Aelred dramatizes the action by having it happen *in illa hora*, at this moment of the angel's arrival.[17] His speculation on how the Scriptures made her feel *pulcherrimam rixam in eius corde*, 'that very appealing conflict in her heart', demonstrates how Aelred depicts Mary as responding reflectively to her reading, setting her up as an exemplary reader of the Word. Her reading habits and reading space offer a resonant echo of the monks' *lectio divina* and cells – an echo shared by many texts presenting the Reading Annunciate to an enclosed, religious audience, as I discussed in Chapter 2.

Yet the sermon passage does not invoke the listener's response or otherwise shape the audience's devotional relationship to the Virgin. Rhetorically, Aelred himself is the subject of the last sentence most focused on Mary's inner state – what he thinks that she feels – while in *De Institutione* the narrator disappears completely in exchange for the reader ('you') taking the subject position both rhetorically and physically. In exchanging an emphasis on Mary's response to the text with an emphasis on the reader's inhabitation of her role, Aelred much more explicitly encourages the reader to experience Mary's feelings *as* their feelings. He does not so much dictate that his audience feels a particular kind of *pulcherrimam rixam in corde* but rather, when addressing enclosed female readers with the *De Institutione Inclusarum*, he encourages and approves being 'filled with numbness and ecstasy', *repleta stupore et exstasi*. Another significant change between the earlier sermon and the later anchoritic guide: Aelred drops the direct quotation of Isaiah and instead only refers to the general *libros* which prophesy Christ's incarnation. Thus in *De Institutione Inclusarum* we know he has in mind prophesies like Isaiah 7:14, yet he leaves the reading options more open than in the sermon.

---

[17] See Miles, 'The Origins and Development', 640–1.

These changes suggest the significance of the new context for the scene, in a devotional text written for enclosed women. By identifying the book with the Old Testament prophets, and by specifically encouraging a female reader to participate in that same reading, in *De Institutione Inclusarum* Aelred transforms Ambrose's glancing reference to Mary's reading into an endorsement of women's literacy as a spiritually transformative endeavour – as transformative as it could be for men. Perhaps most importantly, Aelred does not present the Virgin as an unapproachable role model. She is certainly *beata*, blessed, but the reader just as clearly opens the book *cum beata Maria*, with the blessed Mary. The reader mimes Mary's every move at the beginning of the devotion: 'ac primum cum beata Maria, ingressa cubiculum, libros quibus uirginis partus et christi prophetatur aduentus euolue' (and first with blessed Mary, entering the bedroom, open [unfold/roll out] the books in which the virgin birth, even the arrival of Christ, is prophesied). In this way the reader is implicitly invited to see her own reading mirrored in the Virgin's. The revolutionary implications of this accessibility will become more apparent when we move forward in time to see how this small detail – *cum* blessed Mary – disappears from the passage in the Middle English translations.

Just as Mary opens the books of the prophets and sees herself in their words, so Aelred's anchoritic reader can open *De Institutione* and see herself in *his* words – mimetically mirroring Mary's interpretive act by imaginatively placing herself in the biblical scenes he describes. With cleansed eyes and a purged mind, the female reader has the potential to read as Mary does: so that the words come true. Mary opens the Old Testament as the first reader who truly understands the fulfilment of the prophecies concerning her. When the anchoress opens it with her, she not only sees herself in Mary's position physically, but like Mary, learns to see herself spiritually through the lens of a text and thus more perfectly practice the imaginative devotional technique advocated by Aelred. In other words, the reader's *imitatio Mariae* extends beyond mirroring Mary's open book to mirroring the interpretive act of seeing one's self reflected in the book. Now, when the anchoress reads the Bible or other devotional text she may recall Mary's model and practice a more profound kind of tropological or moral reading: that is, understanding the text as it relates to her moral self.

One might wonder, however, how such a literary model for anchoresses reconciles with historical evidence of actual women's literacy. Literacy, or reading ability, operated on a spectrum in the Middle Ages. In addition to the layered literacies of Middle English and French (Anglo-Norman), the idea of literacy first and foremost concerned *Latin* literacy on a number of levels as delineated by David Bell:

> The first and simplest level is the ability to read a text without understanding it ... the second level is to read and understand a common liturgical text; the third level involves reading and understanding non-liturgical texts or less common texts from the liturgy; and the fourth level is the ability to compose and write a text of one's own.[18]

Here I am concerned with this third level, which would cover reading the Old Testament prophecies, some of which might be included in the liturgy but the majority of which would require fairly sophisticated familiarity with Latin to read and understand. How realistic would it be for a twelfth-century recluse to read the Vulgate Old Testament, to read Isaiah's prophecies, as Mary does?

First of all, Aelred clearly assumed his sister's ability to read the Latin of the text he wrote for her. He also prescribes a regimen of Latin reading, including 'aliquam lectionem de Vitis Patrum, uel Institutis, uel miraculis eorum (some reading from the lives of the Fathers, their Institutes, or their miracles) (ll. 293–5). He poignantly describes the immediacy and constancy which should characterize her engagement with the Bible itself:

> Cogitanti de Scripturis somnus obrepat, euigilanti primum aliquid de Scripturis occurrat, dormientis somnia haerens memoriae aliqua de Scripturis sententia condiat.
>
> (Let sleep come upon you while pondering the Scriptures, let something from Scriptures occur first to you in waking, let some quotation from the Scriptures, clinging in your memory, flavour your dreams while sleeping.) (ll. 613–15)

Although liturgical texts such as the Psalter would have been the most likely Latin reading material for the literate anchoress, she might also have encountered whole Bible codices, or the books of the prophets, as they circulated independently.[19] Other Old Testament books have been linked to early medieval female readers. For instance, at the learned convent of Barking the nuns

---

[18] David Bell, *What Nuns Read: Books and Libraries in Medieval English Nunneries* (Kalamazoo, MI: Cistercian, 1995), 60. On the complex topic of medieval literacy, M.T. Clanchy, *From Memory to Written Record: England 1066–1307*, 2nd ed. (Oxford: Blackwell, 1993), especially chapter 7, 'Literate and Illiterate'; Katherine Zieman, *Singing the New Song: Literacy and Liturgy in Late Medieval England* (Philadelphia: University of Pennsylvania Press, 2008), 49–56, 118–41; and D.H. Green, *Women Readers in the Middle Ages* (Cambridge: Cambridge University Press, 2007), 30–2.

[19] David Lawton, 'The Bible', *The Oxford History of Literary Translation in English: Volume 1 to 1550*, ed. Roger Ellis (Oxford: Oxford University Press, 2008), 233.

possessed a twelfth-century copy of the Song of Songs and the Lamentations of Jeremiah (Oxford, Bodleian Library, MS Laud Lat. 19).[20]

External evidence suggests that Aelred's sister was not exceptional in her advanced literacy and her engagement of the Scriptures.[21] When Goscelin of St Bertin wrote his *Liber Confortatorius* for the recluse Eva in the late eleventh century, he urged her to read the Latin scriptures and the commentaries, as well as Augustine's *Confessions* and *City of God*, and Boethius' *Consolation of Philosophy*, among others.[22] Aelred's life of St Edward, the *Vita Aedwardi*, was translated from Latin into Anglo-Norman by a twelfth-century nun at the convent of Barking, that bastion of female learning in medieval England.[23] Examples such as these support the suggestion that Aelred's sister 'would not have been exceptional in her ability to read Latin in the mid-twelfth century', as Alexandra Barratt concludes in her consideration of the Latin literacy of post-conquest English women.[24]

Yet Mary's reading – and women's reading – were not static throughout the medieval period. These historical observations of female literacy come into

[20] See Alexandra Barratt, 'Small Latin? The Post-Conquest Learning of English Religious Women', in *Anglo-Latin and its Heritage: Essays in Honour of A.G. Rigg on his 64th Birthday*, ed. Siân Echard and Gernot R. Wieland (Turnhout: Brepols, 2001), 58–64, for this and other examples of Latin manuscripts traced to English convents. More recently, Stephanie Hollis explores Barking's traditions of literacy in 'Barking's Monastic School, Late Seventh to Twelfth Century: History, Saint Making, and Literary Culture', in *Barking Abbey and Medieval Literary Culture: Authorship and Authority in a Female Community*, ed. Jennifer N. Brown and Donna Alfano Bussell (York: York University Press, 2012), 33–55.

[21] On the literacy of enclosed women in medieval England, see Bella Millett, 'Women in No Man's Land: English Recluses and the Development of Vernacular Literature in the Twelfth and Thirteenth Centuries', in *Women and Literature in Britain, 1150-1500*, ed. Carol M. Meale (Cambridge: Cambridge University Press, 1993), 86–103; Barratt, 'Small Latin?'; and Green, *Women Readers*, esp. 129–65. Bell, *What Nuns Read*, in addition to informative introductions, provides an excellent list of manuscripts and printed books from medieval English nunneries.

[22] Talbot, 'The Liber Confortatorius', 80–1. For discussion of Goscelin's reading programme see the previous chapter, as well as Millett, 'English recluses', 88; Green, *Women Readers*, 152; and Hayward and Hollis, 'The Female Reader in the *Liber Confortatorius*'.

[23] Aelred's *Vie d'Édouard* is edited in *La vie d'Édouard le Confesseur: poème anglo-normand du XIIe siècle*, ed. Ölsten Södergård (Uppsala: Almqvist & Wiksells, 1948); see also Green, *Women Readers*, 136, 138; and M.D. Legge, *Anglo-Norman Literature and its background* (Oxford: Oxford University Press, 1963), 60–6.

[24] 'Small Latin?', 65. Aelred does qualify his assumptions of Latin literacy in recognition of the wider audience his text will achieve, an aural audience which may include women who cannot read Latin (nor, perhaps, English): 'illa sane quae litteras non intelligit, operi manuum diligentius insistat' (she who cannot read, let her pursue manual work diligently) (ll. 298–9).

stark relief when we see how their future can be seen reflected in changes to that small textual detail by the Middle English translators of Aelred's *De Institutione Inclusarum*. Almost 250 years later, the first translator edited the scene in quite surprising ways.

The Vernon translation of *De Institutione*

The earlier of the two translations is found in the so-called Vernon manuscript (Oxford, Bodleian Library, MS Bodley Eng. Poet. A.1), dated between 1382 and 1400. Titled *Salus anime* or *Sowlehele*, the book is a deluxe collection of religious prose and verse, including the *Ancrene Riwle*, the A text of *Piers Plowman* and various works of Richard Rolle alongside Aelred's text. The manuscript's origins are not known, but its contents strongly suggest ownership by a convent or a wealthy laywoman. Blake suggests that 'the non-liturgical nature of the volume and the absence of anything connected specifically with an enclosed masculine order may indicate that the intended audience was a house of nuns or of women who had banded together to establish a small community of a semi-religious nature'.[25] The manuscript's large size (each leaf measuring 544 x 393 mm and the manuscript weighing 22 kilograms or 48¾ lbs) suggests it was written primarily to be read aloud, possibly to a court or community.[26] The translation of Aelred's *Rule* preserved in the Vernon manuscript omits the first part of the treatise, on the external forms and practical aspects of anchoritic enclosure, limiting its focus to the internal life alone, and making it more appropriate for an anthology of devotional works and for use by a community of non-anchoresses. Its modern editors posit that the translation existed in earlier versions before its inclusion in Vernon.[27] In other words, the compiler or scribe of the manuscript was not likely responsible for the act of translation itself, but rather found this translation in another source and thought to place the text among others with shared devotional goals. In general, the person

---

[25] N.F. Blake, 'The Vernon Manuscript: Contents and Organization', in *Studies in the Vernon Manuscript*, ed. Derek Pearsall (Cambridge: D.S. Brewer, 1990), 58. For more details, see A.I. Doyle, 'Codicology, Paleography, and Provenance', in *The Making of the Vernon Manuscript: The Production and Contents of Oxford, Bodleian Library, MS Eng. poet. a. 1*, ed. Wendy Scase (Turnhout: Brepols, 2013).

[26] Ayto and Barratt, xviii; P.R. Robinson, 'The Vernon Manuscript as a "Coucher Book"', in *Studies in the Vernon Manuscript*, 15. For more on the Vernon manuscript, see the essays in *Studies in the Vernon Manuscript*, as well as *The Vernon Manuscript: A Facsimile of Bodleian Library, Oxford, MS. Eng. poet. a.1.*, introduction by A.I. Doyle (Cambridge: D.S. Brewer, 1987), now complemented by the digital DVD facsimile, *A Facsimile Edition of the Vernon Manuscript: A Literary Hoard from Medieval England*, ed. Wendy Scase with software by Nick Kennedy (Oxford: Bodleian Library, 2011).

[27] Ayto and Barratt, xviii.

who did translate Aelred's Latin work (the Vernon translator, as I will call him) does not drastically depart from the Latin; his many mostly small additions outnumber the few omissions.[28]

Yet few other omissions change the meaning of the text as much as the one concerning Mary in the Annunciation scene:

> And ferst goo in-to þe pryue chaumbre wit oure lady Marie, wher schee abood þe angel message, and þer, suster, abyd þe angel comyngge, þat þu mowe isee whanne he comeþ in, and hou graciously he grette þilke gracious mayde; and soo þu, as it were irauesched of al þy wittes, whanne þe angel begynþ is salutacioun to þilke blessede mayde and modur, cry þu as lowde as þu my3t grede to þy lady and sey: *Aue maria, gratia plena, dominus tecum; benedicta tu in mulieribus et benedictus fructus ventris tui Ihesus, amen.* (555–61)

The translator simultaneously weakens the description of the Virgin and strengthens the description of the reader's affective response. Mary's reading disappears. Compare the first part of the passage as Aelred wrote it (to repeat from above): 'and first with blessed Mary, enter the bedroom, open [unfold/roll out] the books in which the virgin birth, even the arrival of Christ, is prophesied. There, stand ready for the approach of the angel.' Instead of actively opening the books to read the prophecies, Mary – and the reader – passively 'abyd' the angel's message. In light of the otherwise inclusive – indeed, expansionist – tendencies of the Vernon text, the excision of the reference to Mary reading the Old Testament at the Annunciation is a significant change. Mary sits passively. She silently waits. She becomes a woman with no independent action prior to the prompting of the angel. With her entire literary persona stripped away, the scene shifts its attention to the angel and *his* text. This change dramatically alters the reader's engagement with the text of De Institutione. When the book is taken out of the hands of Mary, the reader is no longer encouraged to engage the scriptures (or any other text) in an interpretive exercise echoing that of the Virgin. The Middle English translation turns inward to the exclusion of other textual experiences instead of placing itself in the context of a wider matrix of reading; the reader no longer imagines her interaction with this narrative as one within a larger literary, interpretive programme.

Perhaps this fits with the translator's rendering of Aelred's 'repleta stupore et extasi' as 'irauesched of al þy wittes'. Instead of being filled with numbness, in this version the reader's prayer specifically involves an emptying

---

[28] See the notes to MS Vernon in Ayto and Barratt. I am indebted to Alexandra Barratt and Marsha Dutton for their helpful conversations with me concerning *De Institutione* and its two vernacular translations (The Medieval Translator Conference, Padua, Italy, July 2010).

or ravishing of her 'wits' or intellect, exchanged for an even more intensely affective outpouring of emotive oral expression. For Aelred, of course, literary prayer and affective prayer were not mutually exclusive in this scene, but the Vernon translator's choices seem to imply that view. When the translator inflates Aelred's 'clamans' into 'cry þu as lowde as þu myȝt', the reader's voice in effect magnifies the angel's presence to become the dominant example of prayer in this entire passage – now that the Virgin's prayer has been rendered invisible and inaudible.

As the editors note, this set of changes 'seems to be a conscious choice' by either the translator or a later copier, as it cannot be traced to any of the Latin exemplars: 'as a result the recluse is not invited to meditate on any subject from the Old Testament'.[29] While it is impossible to identify the particular Latin exemplar of this translation, all the existing Latin copies demonstrate a high level of textual consistency, suggesting that a major omission such as this did not originate in the Latin exemplar but in the initial translation. Marsha Dutton concludes that overall, the Vernon translator 'adapted it toward great affectivity but less passion, so providing a case study of the development of affectivity in medieval English spirituality'.[30] Indeed, the Annunciation scene itself is a case study of how the development of affectivity intertwines with the development of literacy in late medieval England. In this fourteenth-century Middle English version of *De Institutione* an increase in affective response seems to replace the more intellectual act of reading. Dutton observes that the Vernon translator recognized the spiritual value of *De Institutione*, yet:

> he also seems to have found it inadequate for the needs and taste of his audience, whom he apparently envisaged as a woman or women less familiar with biblical characters and stories than Aelred's anchoress had been and accustomed to highly affective devotion to the humanity of Christ.[31]

I think the Annunciation scene provides a good demonstration of the dynamic Dutton suggests: where expressive, emotional prayer enters at the expense of book learning. Not to say that this was the only dynamic at play in fourteenth-century religious culture, but rather that this example shows a particular devotional trend which devalued reading while it promoted affective piety.

---

[29] Ayto and Barratt, 124, n. 555.
[30] Perhaps her distinction between 'affectivity' and 'passion' does not relate here; Dutton, 'Gilding the Lily', 109–24. Domenico Pezzini likewise notes that expansions by the Vernon translator 'are normally used to inflate the text emotionally', especially in the Passion sequence; see 'Two Middle English Translations of Aelred of Rievaulx's *De Institutione Inclusarum*: An Essay on the Varieties of Medieval Translational Practices', in *Atti del VII Convegno Nazionale di Storia della Lingua Inglese*, ed. Giovanni Iamartino, (Rome, 1998), 91.
[31] Dutton, 'Gilding the Lily', 111.

In taking the prophecies out of Mary's hands, and thus (by implication) out of the hands of its female readers, the Vernon version of *De Institutione* reflects two hundred years of widespread cultural shifts in female literacy since Aelred's era. Between the twelfth century and the late fourteenth century, for both lay and religious women, Latin literacy generally declined while vernacular literacy increased.[32] Aelred was probably on the cusp of the beginning of this shift: the twelfth century has been described by M.B. Parkes as the 'turning-point in the history of lay literacy'.[33] In reality the continuum of reading ability for different sectors of society, both lay and religious, proves to be subtle and complex, and focused reference points such as this passage help to fill in our understanding of this continuum. It should also be pointed out that the Latin of the prophets is in a different league from Gabriel's words from the New Testament as preserved in the vernacular *De Institutione* passage: his words form the basis of the *Ave Maria* prayer, one late medieval Christians knew by heart. Repeating these words implies neither Latin reading skills nor understanding.[34]

If in the 1380s a female reader of the Vernon manuscript was unable to read Latin, neither would she necessarily have access to a Middle English version of the prophets. Vernacular translations of the Bible were not widely available, the Wycliffite translation not yet as widespread as it would be by the early fifteenth century. Translations of the Psalter were available, such as Richard Rolle's *English Psalter and Commentary*, but the Old Testament prophets were for the most part left untranslated.[35] The New Testament was well represented in gospel retellings or lives of Christ. Also very accessible was a plethora of religious reading material written in English in the previous century or so, such as the *Ancrene Wisse, Pore Caitiff, The Abbey of the Holy Ghost, A Ladder*

---

[32] Bell, 'Medieval Women Book Owners', 758–9, where she cites the late-medieval examples of Christine de Pizan and Lady Margaret Beaufort as scholarly women who knew minimum Latin.

[33] M.B. Parkes, 'The Literary of the Laity', in *Scribes, Scripts and Readers: Studies in the Communication, Presentation, and Dissemination of Medieval Texts*, ed. M.B. Parkes, (London: Hambledon Press, 1991), 276. Quoted in Bell, *What Nuns Read*, 64.

[34] Zieman explores such 'phonetic literacy' in her chapter 'Extragrammatical Literacies and the Latinity of the Laity' in *Singing the New Song*, 118 ff.

[35] See Laurence Muir, 'IV. Translations and Paraphrases of the Bible, and Commentaries', in *A Manual of the Writings in Middle English, 1050–1500*, ed. J. Burke Severs, vol. 2, 381–409 (New Haven: The Connecticut Academy of Arts and Sciences, 1970); Ralph Hanna, 'English Biblical Texts before Lollardy and their Fate', in *Lollards and Their Influence in Late Medieval England*, ed. Fiona Somerset, Jill C. Haven and Derrick G. Pitard (Woodbridge: Boydell Press, 2003), 141–53; Christina van Nolcken, 'Lay Literacy, the Democratization of God's Law, and the Lollards', in *The Bible as Book: The Manuscript Tradition*, ed. John L. Sharpe III and Kimberly van Kampe (London: British Library, 1998), 177–95.

of Four Rungs and *Handlyng Synne*. These works may excerpt at length from the scriptures, but they do not necessarily advocate reading the Bible directly. In fact, they operate as substitutions that could help make biblical reading unnecessary. Margaret Deanesly notes that in the pre-Wycliffite period, for lay people there was surprisingly little in spiritual manuals about reading the Bible itself. The manuals offered a 'skeleton of theology and the moral virtues and vices, and certainly did not inculcate a personal appeal to the literary sources on which the system of theology and ethics was founded'.[36]

In the Vernon manuscript one such text, another guide to living for a recluse, can be found: *The Scale of Perfection*, by Walter Hilton (*c.* 1343–1396). In Book I of the *Scale* Hilton explains to his female reader the traditional approaches to contemplation: 'Thre meenys there ben whiche men most comonli use that gyven hem to contemplacioun: redynge of Holi Writ and of hooli techynge, goosteli meditacion, and besi praeris with devocioun. Redynge of Holi Writ mai thu not wel use, and therfore thee bihoveth more occupye thee in prayer and in meditacioun.'[37] Hilton does not explain why he so summarily cuts off the anchoress from Holy Writ. As Book I of the *Scale* was most likely written between *c.* 1375 and 1385, maybe we can avoid placing the blame for Hilton's skittishness on the shoulders of Wyclif and the so-called Lollards, a heresy that was still only a nascent anxiety for the Church at that time. Rather, a myriad of localized concerns focused on access to the Bible in the late 1370s and early 1380s when the Vernon manuscript was compiled and Hilton wrote Book I.[38] Considering standards of literacy for enclosed women, perhaps Hilton did not expect his intended female reader to possess sufficient Latin fluency to approach scripture, much less to 'wel use' it. Or perhaps he considered the Bible inappropriate reading material for a woman regardless of her literacy, because it demanded a literary or theological sophistication not met by the typical education of a female anchoress. Hilton either reflects the limits of the actual abilities of his reader, or impresses a limit upon her abilities. The same may be said for the Vernon translator. Perhaps Mary's exemplar had to be amended to fit a reality in which the prophets were simply not a reading option, or to avoid presenting a model which might trouble the reader by encouraging an 'inap-

---

[36] *The Lollard Bible and Other Medieval Biblical Versions* (Cambridge: Cambridge University Press, 1920), 217. For more on the religious literature available in this period see Vincent Gillespie, 'Anonymous Devotional Writings', in *A Companion to Middle English Prose*, ed. A.S.G. Edwards (Cambridge: D.S. Brewer, 2004), 127–50.

[37] Walter Hilton, *The Scale of Perfection*, ed. Thomas Bestul, TEAMS edition (Kalamazoo, MI: Medieval Institute, 2000), Book 1, chapter 15, ll. 332–5.

[38] I would like to thank Michael Sargent for his discussions with me concerning the dating of Book I and contemporary, localized concern with Bible translation. See also J.A.F. Thomson, 'Orthodox Religion and the Origins of Lollardy', *History* 74 (1989): 39–55.

propriate' interest in a restricted or unobtainable text. Either way, this passage in Vernon helps detail the changing landscape of women's reading habits in medieval England: by 1400, this translator actively avoided using his text to present Mary as a model for reading the Old Testament as a type of the New. Rather, he shifts the emphasis away from meditation on the scriptures and onto vocalized affective prayer – away from a woman's solitary *lectio* and onto Gabriel's ventriloquized voice.

The Bodley translation of *De Institutione*

In the period following the copying of the Vernon manuscript, Latin literacy continued its gradual decline among both lay and enclosed readers, as a rich body of vernacular religious writing flourished in its wake. Meanwhile, scriptural reading, especially in the vernacular, had become a very sensitive topic in England. Perhaps the Vernon translator's hesitancy to feature a woman reading the Old Testament belied a growing concern about immediate access to the Bible by non-clerical readers in the years building up to the censoring legislation of the early fifteenth century. About a decade after the *terminus ante quem* of the Vernon manuscript, English literary culture was influenced by Archbishop Thomas Arundel's Constitutions of 1409, 'a series of articles that lay down new regulations for various aspects of the preaching and teaching life of the Church in general and the University of Oxford in particular'.[39] Arundel's Constitutions seem to have been in large part a reaction to John Wyclif's endorsement of vernacular Bible translation and his criticisms of the Church, as well as the Wycliffite (sometimes known as Lollard) movement that grew up around him and his works. Article 7 of the Constitutions stipulates that 'it is a dangerous thing … to translate the text of the holy Scripture out of the tongue into another; for in the translation the same sense is not always easily kept' and that therefore 'no man, hereafter, by his own authority translate any text of the Scripture into English or any other tongue, by way of a book, libel or treatise' unless it received official ecclesiastical approval.[40] Despite these restrictions, over 250 vernacular Bibles survive in one form or another from this era, and some scholars now argue the Oxford translation project was in fact quite

---

[39] Nicholas Watson, 'Censorship and Cultural Change in Late-Medieval England: Vernacular Theology, the Oxford Translation Debate, and Arundel's Constitutions of 1409', *Speculum* 70 (1995): 827. On the Constitutions and Lollardy, see Anne Hudson, *The Premature Reformation: Wycliffite Texts and Lollard History* (Oxford: Oxford University Press, 1988) and *Lollards and Their Books* (London: Hambleton Continuum, 1985), as well as Kantik Ghosh, *The Wycliffite Heresy: Authority and the Interpretation of Texts* (Cambridge: Cambridge University Press, 2002).

[40] From the sixteenth-century translation by John Foxe, *Acts and Monuments*, 3 vols (New York: AMS Press, 1965), vol. 3, 245.

orthodox.[41] Clearly the Constitutions did not entirely dissuade lay engagement with the Scripture in its new, accessible English form. Moreover, it appears that certain monastic audiences enjoyed near immunity from censoring control – an argument supported by the following example.[42]

Between thirty and a hundred years after the Vernon manuscript, a quite different rendering of the scene was found by the readers of the next Middle English translation of Aelred's work. A second, independent translation of *De Institutione Inclusarum* was included in a manuscript now bound as Sections B and C of the composite manuscript Oxford, Bodleian Library, MS Bodley 423.[43] Likely copied between 1430 and 1480, these sections of Bodley stand as a typical devotional miscellany containing various other vernacular devotional works including *Fervor Amoris* (*Contemplations of the Dread and Love of God*), excerpts from St Birgitta's *Revelaciones*, a verse *Salve Regina* and an *Ars Moriendi*.[44] The part of the manuscript containing *De Institutione* (ff. 178–92) was written by the prolific scribe Stephen Dodesham (d. 1482), Carthusian monk of Witham Charterhouse and later of Sheen.[45] Dodesham's long and prolific career as a scribe spanned both his professional days before retreating from the world, and his time as a monk. While possibly copied by Dodesham in a Carthusian charterhouse, the manuscript could have been commissioned for other readers: conversely, while its devotional texts (not unlike those in Vernon) are addressed to women, that does not preclude a mixed readership.[46] The Bodley Middle

[41] As according to Henry Ansgar Kelly, *The Middle English Bible: A Reassessment* (Philadelphia: University of Pennsylvania Press, 2016).

[42] Kathryn Kerby-Fulton argues for a more mitigated impact of the Constitutions on vernacular literature than commonly thought, in *Books Under Suspicion: Censorship and Tolerance of Revelatory Writing in Late Medieval England* (Notre Dame, IN: University of Notre Dame Press, 2006), throughout, but esp. 399–401. The articles of *After Arundel: Religious Writing in Fifteenth-Century England*, ed. Vincent Gillespie and Kantik Ghosh (Turnhout: Brepols, 2011), deal with the complexities of the issue from many angles.

[43] For further analysis on literary differences between the two Middle English translations of *De Institutione*, see Anne Clark Bartlett, *Male Authors, Female Readers: Representation and Subjectivity in Middle English Devotional Literature* (Ithaca, NY: Cornell University Press, 1995), 40–55.

[44] Ayto and Barratt, xxvi.

[45] Ayto and Barratt, xxix–xxxi. On Dodesham's scribal work, see M.B. Parkes, *Their Hands Before Our Eyes: A Closer Look at Scribes. The Lyell Lectures Delivered at the University of Oxford, 1999* (London: Routledge, 2008), 122–3, and especially, A.I. Doyle, 'Stephen Dodesham of Witham and Sheen', in *Of the Making of Books: Medieval Manuscripts, their Scribes and Readers: Essays Presented to M.B. Parkes*, ed. P.R. Robinson and Rivkah Zim (Aldershot: Scolar Press, 1997), 94–115.

[46] See the editors' note to lines 274–5 of Bodley 423 for a suggestive clue that links the translation to the Birgittine monastery Syon Abbey.

English translation features extensive abbreviation, conflation and omission of the original Latin.[47]

Now nearly three hundred years after Aelred's original composition, in this translation the Virgin and the reader find themselves in yet another new balance of agency and passivity. This translator places the Old Testament prophecies firmly in Mary's hand, yet deprives the reader of almost all devotional agency:

> As touchinge to the first, when thy soule is purged clerly from alle vnclene thoughtes, than entre in-to that pryue chambre where our blessed Lady praide deuoutly vnto the tyme the aungel grette hir, beholdyng bisely hou she was occupied with redynge of suche prophecies in the whiche weren profecyed Cristis comynge thorugh a maydens birthe. Abyde there awhile and thou shalt se hou the aungel cometh and gretith hir, seieng thus: *Aue Maria gracia plena, dominus tecum.* (696–702)

Here, unlike in the Vernon version, the detail of Mary reading the prophecies is preserved from Aelred's Latin, and one addition is made: that Mary 'praide deuoutly vnto the tyme the aungel grette hir'. While the reader beholds busily, Mary likewise assiduously occupies herself with reading; everyone focused and quiet. The reader abides. One other subtle omission is important to note: Aelred's *cum beata Maria* also disappears, meaning that the text does not explicitly invite the reader to open the book *with* Mary, to mimic Mary's reading. The reader *beholds*: she is now fully a spectator instead of a participant, a listener instead of a speaker. Then the only voice to break the silence is that of Gabriel: the devotee watches the angel arrive and greet the Virgin, but only listens to what he says, not uttering his words aloud with him like the readers of Aelred's Latin or the Vernon translation. Numbness, ecstasy, ravishment, crying aloud, *clamans* – none of these affective outbursts of prayer are offered to the reader. Mary's modelling of literary prayer now dominates the scene at the expense of the modelling of affective devotion.

In these post-Arundelian decades of complex political and theological controversies surrounding biblical reading it makes sense that the Bodley translator would tread a middle ground: without altogether ignoring Mary's powerful model of reading the Scriptures, he does not risk expressly promoting her act as suitable for the reader to imitate. Better to read less dangerous devotional texts like those in this manuscript, perhaps. Yet still the representation of a woman reading the Bible remains, testifying to its hardiness even in a post-Constitutions censoring situation. Possibly the motif's preservation can be linked to its audience. One likely audience for the Bodley manuscript – enclosed religious women – seems to have been functionally exempt from

---

[47] Ayto and Barratt, xiii.

investigation for violating the Constitutions.[48] Whatever their devout reading, it was carefully overseen by a confessor, and presumably appropriate for their spiritual vocation. David Bell has traced a handful of late medieval Latin and vernacular Bibles to medieval convents.[49] The Old Testament prophecies foretelling the Incarnation would also have been aurally familiar to most church-going medieval Englishwomen, vowed or not, by means of the liturgy: the Sarum Use, for instance, prominently features Isaiah 7:14 in both the feast of the Annunciation and Advent services. But this is not the same as holding the books of the prophets and reading them in private or semi-private – that is, without an accompanying priest. Such unmediated access to the word of God, and its possible misinterpretation, was precisely the cause for concern in fifteenth-century England.

The Annunciation scene is not the only place the Bodley translator side-steps direct promotion of scriptural reading for his female audience. Earlier the text suggests what devout exercises best fend off the devil:

> for there is no thinge that ouercometh so sone the fende as doth redynge of deuoute thinge and prayer and meditacyon of Christys passyon. A mayde should so be occupied vpon oon of these thre, prayer, meditacion, or redynge, that though she were stured to do vnlauful thinges, she should not be suffred for remors of conscience. (ll. 469–71)

The same passage in the Latin *De Institutione* reads as follows:

> Nihil enim magis cogitationes excludit inutiles, uel compescit lascivas quam meditatio uerbi Dei, cui sic animum suum uirgo debet assuecere, ut aliud uolens, non possit aliud meditari. (ll. 610–11)

> (Indeed, nothing better shuts out harmful thoughts, or quenches lust than meditation on the word of God, to which thus the maiden ought to devote her mind, so that though she might be willing another thing, that other thing cannot be meditated upon.)

When the translator replaces 'meditatio uerbi Dei' (meditation on the word of God) with 'redynge of deuoute thinge and prayer and meditacyon of Christys passyon', he essentially replaces official Scripture with devotional works and spiritual biography like *De Institutione* itself. The addition of 'prayer, meditacion, or redynge' in the last sentence amplifies the singular emphasis upon 'meditatio' found in the Latin. This trio of 'prayer, meditacion, or redynge' closely parallels the reference in the *Scale of Perfection* to 'redynge of Holi Writ and of hooli techynge, goosteli meditacion, and besi praeris with devocioun' available to men (quoted above). Hilton explicitly notes his hesitancy

---

[48] Kerby-Fulton, *Books Under Suspicion*, 278 ff.
[49] See Bell, *What Nuns Read*, 245 ff.

over this use of Scripture by his female readers: 'redynge of Holi Writ mai thu not wel use'. The Bodley translator seems to share this hesitancy. By excising the Latin's indisputable reference to the Bible – 'uerbi Dei' – and replacing it with the more vague 'redynge of deuoute thinge and prayer and meditacyon of Christys passyon', he reflects, according to the modern editors, 'the late medieval ambivalence towards recommending the reading of the Bible in a vernacular treatise'.[50] Exactly as we have seen in the Annunciation scene, the translator hesitates to promote Scriptural reading overtly. Simultaneously, he also endorses a popular genre of vernacular literature of which Aelred's *De Institutione Inclusarum* was an early and influential example: lives of Christ or Gospel meditations which offer a 'meditacyon of Christys passyon' as an alternative to the Gospel accounts, such as the pseudo-Bonaventuran *MVC* and related texts, to which I will soon turn.[51]

Thus the Bodley translation represents a kind of open ambivalence towards Mary's reading, and perhaps women's reading practices in general. To return to using the Annunciation scene to map the relationship between literacy and reading habits, and the development of affectivity: what does this nexus reveal? Here in this mid-fifteenth-century text we find no partiality towards affective prayer practice: it is deliberately excised. Mary's reading remains, emphasizing the intellectual aspect of her devotions. Does this represent the individual translator's taste or some broader trend away from more emotional outpourings of devotion? While the style of affective piety seen in the other versions of the scene was undoubtedly still shaping medieval devotional texts, that does not mean that all authors advocated it, or that all audiences desired it. But regardless, offering up unmediated scripture reading for imitation did not seem to be so controversial, suggesting that Arundel's Constitutions were somewhat limited in their impact.

The *Meditationes vitae Christi* and Nicholas Love's *Mirror of the Blessed Life of Jesus Christ*

As the 'single most influential devotional text written in the later Middle Ages', in its several versions of the pseudo-Bonaventuran *MVC* survives in Latin and many vernaculars in hundreds of manuscripts.[52] It reflects the widespread late medieval devotional tradition promoted by St Francis (1181–1226) and his followers, based on the inward imitation of events in Christ's life accomplished

---

[50] Ayto and Barratt, 82, note to 469–70. See also Deanesly, *The Lollard Bible*, 211–20.
[51] Bestul, *Texts of the Passion*, especially chapter 2, 'Medieval Narratives of the Passion of Christ'.
[52] McNamer, 'The Origins of the *Meditationes Vitae Christi*', 905.

through their interiorized, imaginative re-creation.[53] Aelred's *De Institutione Inclusarum* anticipated this tradition of 'spiritual biography' of Christ as it was later advanced by the Franciscans. Erroneously attributed to the Franciscan theologian Bonaventure by medieval scribes, the *MVC* in its various short and long versions has eluded easy authorial identification and dating.[54] The latest and most convincing argument comes from Sarah McNamer, who suggests that the short Italian version (which she calls the *testo breve*) was composed first by a Poor Clare nun from Pisa, sometime between about 1300 and 1325. Then between about 1325 and 1340 a Franciscan friar expanded the text by glossing it with additional sources and citations and 'correcting' certain passages, producing two longer Italian versions and finally the 100-chapter Latin *MVC* which was to achieve renown across Europe.[55]

This long Latin version was used as the basis for many vernacular translations including the Middle English *Mirror of the Blessed Life of Christ* by Nicholas Love, and the *Speculum Devotorum* by an anonymous Carthusian monk, the two texts I will be analysing here (as well as another vernacular life of Christ I discuss in Chapter 5, *Meditationes domini nostri*). We know little about Nicholas Love beyond the fact that he was prior of the Yorkshire Carthusian house of Mount Grace from 1410 to about 1417; his death is recorded in 1424.[56] Apparently the *Mirror* constitutes his main, if not only, composition.

[53] On Franciscan spirituality and its influence, see John Moorman, *A History of the Franciscan Order from its Origins to the Year 1517* (Oxford: Clarendon Press, 1968); John Fleming, *An Introduction to the Franciscan Literature of the Middle Ages* (Chicago: Franciscan Herald Press, 1977); and Denise Despres, *Ghostly Sights: Visual Meditation in Late-Medieval Literature* (Norman, OK: Pilgrim, 1989), esp. chapter 1; Michael Sargent, ed. *Nicholas Love's 'Mirror of the Blessed Life of Jesus Christ': A Full Critical Edition Based on Cambridge University Library Additional MSS 6578 and 6686* (Liverpool: Liverpool University Press, 2005), 'Introduction'; and *Medieval Franciscan Approaches to the Virgin Mary: Mater Sanctissima, Misericordia, et Dolorosa*, ed. Steven McMichael and Katie Wrisley Shelby (Leiden: Brill, 2019).

[54] Sarah McNamer lays out these arguments in *Meditations on the Life of Christ: The Short Italian Text* (Notre Dame, IN: University of Notre Dame Press, 2018), following up on her earlier article 'The Origins of the *Meditationes Vitae Christi*'. The previous argument for Johannes Caulibus can be found in M. Stallings-Taney, *Iohannis de Caulibus Meditaciones vite Christi, olim S. Bonaventuro attributae*, CCCM 153 (Turnhout: Brepols, 1997); and arguing for Jacobus de Sancto Geminiano, Peter Tóth and Dávid Falvay, 'New Light on Date and Authorship of the *Meditationes vitae Christi*', in *Devotional Culture in Late Medieval England and Europe: Diverse Imaginations of Christ's Life*, ed. Stephen Kelly and Ryan Perry (Turnhout: Brepols, 2014), 17–106. In my view McNamer's recent work convincingly overrides these other identifications; see my further discussion in Chapter 4 in reference to Elizabeth of Hungary and Naples.

[55] McNamer, *Meditations on the Life of Christ*, xxii; on dating, see cxix–cxlvi.

[56] On Love and the Carthusians, see Sargent, *A Full Critical Edition*, 'Introduction'. Other critical discussions include Salter, *Nicholas Love's 'Myrrour of the Blessed Lyf*

That the *Mirror* successfully fulfilled a devotional need for a broad spectrum of the English reading public is demonstrated by its large number of surviving manuscripts: among Middle English texts, only the Wycliffite Bible, the *Prick of Conscience* and Chaucer's *Canterbury Tales* outnumber the *Mirror*'s 64 manuscript witnesses.[57] Beyond its general popularity, the *Mirror* also enjoyed the Church's official approval according to the new examination and licensing requirements stipulated by Arundel's Constitutions of 1409.[58] Seventeen manuscript copies append a 'Memorandum' to the *Mirror* which explains how Love presented his book to Archbishop Arundel,

> who after examining it for several days, returning it to the abovementioned author, commended and approved it personally, and further decreed and commanded by his metropolitan authority that it rather be published universally for the edification of the faithful and the confutation of heretics or lollards.[59]

Indeed, according to the *Mirror*'s editor Michael Sargent, Love's addition of 'a good deal of material commenting directly on Wycliffite positions' heavily emphasizes obedience to the ecclesiastical hierarchy as it simultaneously refutes Lollard doctrinal positions.[60]

Overall, Love dramatically reshapes the face of the *MVC* while maintaining its underlying skeleton of meditations on the life of Christ spread out over the seven days of the week. By omitting over thirty chapters, reordering much of the remaining text and adding other material, Love created a fundamentally

---

of Jesu Christ',; David J. Falls, 'The Carthusian Milieu of Nicholas Love's *Mirror of the Blessed Life of Jesus Christ*', in *The Pseudo-Bonaventuran Lives of Christ: Exploring the Middle English Tradition*, ed. Ian Johnson and Allen F. Westphal, MCS 24 (Turnhout: Brepols, 2013), 311–39. On the *Mirror* in general, see Ian Johnson, 'Prologue and Practice: Middle English Lives of Christ', in *The Medieval Translator: The Theory and Practice of Translation in the Middle Ages*, ed. Roger Ellis et al. (Cambridge: D.S. Brewer, 1989), pp. 69–85; and the contributions to *Nicholas Love at Waseda*, ed. Shoichi Ogura, Richard Beadle and Michael G. Sargent (Cambridge: D.S. Brewer, 1997).

[57] Michael Sargent, ed., *The Mirror of the Blessed Life of Jesus Christ: A Reading Text* (Exeter: Exeter University Press, 2004), ix.

[58] On the Constitutions and Love's *Mirror*, see Nicholas Watson, 'Censorship and Cultural Change in Late-Medieval England: Vernacular Theology, the Oxford Translation Debate, and Arundel's Constitutions of 1409', *Speculum* 70 (1995): 852–6.

[59] Sargent, *Mirror: A Reading Text*, xlv; 7, for the original Latin.

[60] Sargent, *Mirror: A Reading Text*, xlvi. See also Michael Sargent, *The Mirror: Full Critical Edition*, 'The Anti-Wycliffite Stance of the *Mirror*', introduction 54–75; and Sargent, 'Nicholas Love's *Mirror of the Blessed Life of Jesus Christ* and the Politics of Vernacular Translations in Late Medieval England', in *The Medieval Translator: Vol. 12, Lost in Translation*, ed. Denis Renevey and Christiania Whitehead (Turnhout: Brepols, 2009), 205–23.

new work.[61] To supplement the foundational *MVC*, Love turned to several other texts when he wrote the *Mirror*, among them the *Revelations* of St Elizabeth of Hungary and Naples, and Bernard of Clairvaux's *Homiliae de Laudibus Virginis Matris*. He either directly interweaves passages from these sources into his text or finds inspiration for interpolations.

Significantly, the *MVC* – one of the most probable and potentially influential vehicles for the motif of Mary reading – makes absolutely no mention of it. For the opening of the Annunciation scene, the male Franciscan behind the long *MVC* focuses more on representing the theological issues concerning the Incarnation and the Trinity than on Mary's actions. Only her location is mentioned:

> Surgen igitur Gabriel iucundus et gaudens uolitauit ab alto, et in humana specie in momento fuit coram uirgine, in thalamo domuncule sue manente. Sed nec sic cito uolauit quin preueniretur a Domino et sanctam ibi Trinitatem inuenit que preuenit nuncium suum. (20: 22–6)

> (Rising up joyful and exulting, Gabriel flew down from on high, and was in an instant in human form and face to face with the Virgin, who was then in the bedroom of her little house. But swift as he was, the Lord arrived first, and Gabriel found there the blessed Trinity, who preceded its messenger.) (13)

No details about Mary until her response to Gabriel's greeting, and no suggestion that the reader echo the angel's words – in other words, no specifically literary or affective models of prayer (though the text otherwise frequently encourages affective response). The narrator continues to guide the reader's engagement with the text, but in a more distanced and intellectual way: 'Nunc ergo et hic bene aspice, et tanquam ipso facto presens existens, *intellige* omnia que dicuntur et fiunt' (20:29–31) (Now then, here too watch closely, as if you were actually present, and take in *mentally* everything said and done) (13; my italics). Perhaps this *intellige* is because the chapter displays a concern with properly explaining the theological relationship of the Trinity to the Incarnation event; only later in the chapter does Mary's modesty and humility in her response to Gabriel receive mention as imitable virtues. Yet continental manuscript copies of the *MVC* show that even if the text does not mention it, Mary's book was an assumed necessity in the scene: an important manuscript

---

[61] On Love's reworking and new sources, see Sargent, *Mirror: Full Critical Edition*, 'Introduction', as well as Michelle Karnes, 'Nicholas Love and Medieval Meditations on Christ', *Speculum* 82 (2007): 380–408; Ian Johnson's extended consideration of how Love relies on *auctors*, in *The Middle English Life of Christ*, esp. ch. 3; and David J. Falls, *Nicholas Love's Mirror and Late Medieval Devotio-Literary Culture* (London: Routledge, 2015), esp. ch. 1.

witness, an Italian, mid-fourteenth-century copy of the Latin *MVC* (Oxford, Corpus Christi College, MS 410), features a miniature of the Annunciation in which Mary kneels in front of a book on a lectern; Paris, BnF, MS Ital. 115 also features an Annunciation.[62] Indeed, generally speaking, by the fourteenth century one has difficulty finding an artistic representation of the Annunciation scene in which Mary does *not* look upon a book.

When the *MVC* was imported to England, Nicholas Love added the motif of Mary's reading to his dramatically altered version of the text, *The Mirror*, in its Annunciation scene of the *Die Lune* (Monday) reading. Like many of the other life of Christ narratives, he encourages his readers to imagine themselves right in the scene: 'take hede & haue in mynde as þou were present in þe pryue chaumbur of our lady where þe holi trinyte is present with his angele Gabriel' (24.5–7). In the description of Mary, Love mostly retains the language of the *MVC*, but inserts an important detail (my emphasis):

> And so anone Gabriel risyng vp glad & iocunde, toke his fliȝt fro þe hye heuen to erþe, & in a moment he was in mannus liknes before þe virgine Marie, þat was in hire pryue chaumbure þat tyme closed *& in hir prayeres, or in hire meditaciones perauentur redyng þe prophecie of ysaie, touchyng þe Incarnacion*. And ȝit also swiftly as he flewe, his lord was come before & þer he fonde al þe holy Trinite comen or his messagere. (21.35–22.3)[63]

Love's passage matches the Latin *MVC* in many respects. He closely translates *in thalamo domuncule* as 'in hire pryue chaumbure', but then adds extra emphasis on the enclosed solitude of the space, 'þat tyme closed' and, most notably, Love adds the detail of Mary's state, 'in hir prayeres, or in hire meditaciones perauentur redyng þe prophecie of ysaie, touchyng þe Incarnacion'. Love incorporates the now widespread motif of Mary reading not the Psalms but Isaiah's prophecy.

As I explained at the beginning of this chapter, Mary's reading of Isaiah 7:14 was a longstanding textual tradition passed down from Ambrose, through Bede, Fulbert of Chartres, Odilo of Cluny and into the fifteenth century through a multitude of sources – including Aelred's *De Institutione Inclusarum*, the spiritual biography at the root of the tradition in which Love was working. Love parallels both Aelred's emphasis on Mary's enclosure in an inner room, and her reading material as the Old Testament prophecies. Perhaps Love, a

---

[62] For a description of the manuscript, see Stallings-Taney, *Meditaciones vite Christi*, xiii–xiv; and McNamer, *Meditations on the Life of Christ*, cxxx. On illustrated copies of the *MVC*, see Holly Flora, *The Devout Belief of the Imagination: The Paris 'Meditationes vitae Christi' and Female Franciscan Spirituality in Trecento Italy* (Turnhout: Brepols, 2009), 96–8.

[63] All citations are from Sargent's Liverpool full critical edition, *The Mirror: Full Critical Edition* (2005), by page and line number.

106 *The Virgin Mary's Book at the Annunciation*

Carthusian prior, was familiar with the text through a Carthusian connection. MS Bodley 423, the later Middle English translation of *De Institutione*, appears to have Carthusian connections through its scribe, Stephen Dodesham. Perceived Carthusian connections must be approached with caution, however, as some of their members had scribal careers before their enclosure – as was the case with Dodesham. However, Aelred as an author was generally known to Love. Sargent notes that Love uses Aelred's *Vita Edwardi Regis*.

Yet the manuscript tradition of the *Mirror of the Blessed Life* suggests a different source: at this passage the usual apparatus of marginal notations notes 'Bernardus'. This authorial notation, part of an extensive system of annotations, is meant to identify the source of this addition as the writings of Bernard of Clairvaux, the author whom Love cites most often in his additions. Love was familiar with Bernard's sermons *Super Missus est*, or *Homiliae de Laudibus Virginis Matris*, perhaps the most influential of Bernard's contributions to the tradition of Annunciation commentary, as discussed in the previous chapter. While these sermons did provide material for other parts of Love's consideration of the Annunciation and Incarnation, his sermons could not have supplied this detail as the note implies, for nowhere does Bernard mention Mary's reading. Rather the marginal notation represents more the 'principle of security through *auctoritas*': the translator's explicit reliance on *auctors* such as Bernard in order to authorize his text.[64]

In his explanatory notes, Sargent turns away from Bernard to the *Revelations* of Elizabeth of Hungary and Naples as a source.[65] Examined at length in the next chapter on visionary women's texts, Elizabeth's *Revelations* were read in England in both Latin and in Middle English; two distinct translations survive, at least one of which pre-dates Nicholas Love's *Mirror*.[66] As Sargent notes, the problem with that source is that this exact detail – Mary reading *when* Gabriel arrives – does not exist in Elizabeth's *Revelations*. Elizabeth's series of fascinating Annunciation-centred visions instead offers a differing narrative. In a vision to Elizabeth, Mary explains one scene in which she reads Isaiah's prophecy foretelling the Incarnation:

> And sche answerde, 'Sothly, on a day qwanne I adde a confort of God and so wondyrfully þat I adde neuer felth swych before, and qwanne I was coum aȝen to myself, I began to þynke wyt most brennyng herte and to wish þat Y mite sumwhat doon & han in me wherfore God schulde neuere suffre me

---

[64] Johnson, *The Middle English Life of Christ*, 15.
[65] Sargent, *Full Critical Edition*, 354, note to 23.15. *De Institutione Inclusarum* is not noted as a possible source.
[66] Sarah McNamer, ed., *The Two Middle English Translations of the Revelations of St Elizabeth of Hungary* (Heidelberg: Universitatsverlag C. Winter, 1996), also includes the Latin text.

departe fro hym. And qwanne I adde þowt þys, I ros vp and wente to a bok and redde. And in þe ferste opnyng of þe bok cam to myn eyin þys word of Ysaye þe prophete: *Loo, a maydyn schal conceyve and bere a chyld &c.* (V, 72)[67]

The next night, Mary tells Elizabeth, she has a vision in which a voice tells her that she will be that maiden that will bear the Son of God. After that Mary experiences the traditional biblical episode of the Incarnation:

> Þerfore qwanne I was all brennyngg in þe loue of God and so mich swetnesse felte of hym þat for hym al þe world was vanyte to me, I stode wyt a deuowt sowle alone in a priuy chambere; and sodeynly þe angyl Gabriel apperede to me and, as þe gospel seyth, grette me seying '*Heyl, ful of grace, Owr Lord ys wyt þe. Blessyd be þou among all wommen.*' (VI, 80)

Mary is definitely in a 'priuy chambere' ('in secreto thalamo' in the Latin), in a close parallel to the *MVC*, Love's *Mirror* and Bernard's *Homilia IV* – and picking up on the tradition of portraying Mary as a solitary holy woman explained in the first chapter. What also binds together the *Revelations* and the *Mirror* is that Mary reads the prophecy of Isaiah. Nonetheless, Elizabeth's visionary version of Mary's Annunciation does not formally include a book in the scene when Gabriel enters. Instead the Virgin's act of reading is relocated to an earlier scene of Mary's generalized meditation.

In a way, it does not matter where Love sourced the detail of Mary's reading Isaiah. By the turn of the fifteenth century the identification was standard, and maybe Love added it because he thought the detail would have been expected by his contemporary English audience. Like the Bodley translation of Aelred's *De Institutione Inclusarum*, perhaps the most interesting aspect of its inclusion is that Love betrays no concern that this depiction of unmediated contact with the Bible *by a woman* should be a problem.[68] It is notable that the authorities who approved Love's text in accordance with the 1409 Constitutions regulating reading and translation of Scripture do not seem to have taken any issue with this image of a woman reading the Old Testament. Not that Mary herself should *not* be imagined as reading the prophecies, but that in this capacity within Love's text she stands as a potential incentive for female readers to partake in this same activity of reading and interpreting the prophecies of the Bible on one's own without a priest's

---

[67] All quotations are cited by chapter and page number from Cambridge University Library Hh.i.11, the earlier of the two Middle English translations edited by McNamer.
[68] Indeed, McNamer suggests that the *Mirror* presents a coherent platform of conflating the practice of affective meditation with gendered feminine performance; *Affective Meditation*, 120–33.

mediation (or the intermediary of a paraphrase like Love's text). Soon after this passage Love encourages his reader to pray alone like Mary: 'Here þan maiȝt þou take ensaumple of Marie, first to loue solitary praiere & departyng fro men þat þou mowe be worþi angeles presence' (24.40–1). Perhaps, like the Bodley translator's choice to keep the book, Mary's reading here supports the view that the Constitutions were not so strictly interpreted or enforced as we sometimes think.[69]

Of course, the ubiquity of the motif in late medieval iconography could have somewhat inured the authorities to its latent influence; yet for the individual female reader, its power remains, as Mary reaches out from the text to encourage her devotees in their biblical literary devotion. This contradicts the general *modus operandi* of Love's work, as described by Kantik Ghosh:

> What it conspicuously does not offer are the exact words of scripture. Instead, the biblical words and the author's meditations on them are welded into a near-inseparable unity, the emphasis falling on an imaginative emotional participation ... rather than on the reader's ability to assess the validity or otherwise of particular interpretations (and methodologies of interpretation) of scripture.[70]

In this way, Nicholas Watson has charged, Love visualizes his lay reading audience as characterized by 'ignorance, intellectual simplicity, spiritual childishness and carnality'.[71] While elsewhere the *Mirror* positions its readers as devout children 'in a state of perpetual intellectual disenfranchisement, and therefore entirely dependent on the loving ministrations of Holy Mother Church', at the moment of the Annunciation the reader is allowed to see him or herself reflected in the text as a reader with sanctioned access to the sacred books whose meanings demand interpretation – remarkably in line with Wycliffite views on reading.[72] In fact, recently Ryan Perry has postulated that certain wordings in Love's *Mirror* suggest that Love assumed that 'some readers of his book would have access to an English translated Bible – the Wycliffite Bible'.[73] The image of Mary reading Isaiah supports this position.

---

[69] Kerby-Fulton, *Books Under Suspicion*, 278, 397–8.
[70] Kantik Ghosh, 'Nicholas Love', in *A Companion to Middle English Prose*, ed. A.S.G. Edwards (Cambridge: D.S. Brewer, 2004), 55.
[71] Nicholas Watson, 'Conceptions of the Word: the Mother Tongue and the Incarnation of God', in *New Medieval Literatures* 1, ed. Wendy Scase, Rita Copeland and David Lawton (1997), 95.
[72] On Wycliffite views on reading, see Ghosh, 'Nicholas Love', 55 (although nowhere do Ghosh or Watson address Mary's reading at the Annunciation).
[73] Ryan Perry, '"Some Sprytuall matter of gostly edyfycacion": Readers and Readings of Nicholas Love's *Mirror of the Blessed Life of Jesus Christ*', in *The Pseudo-Bonaventuran Lives of Christ: Exploring the Middle English Tradition*, ed. Ian Johnson and Allen F. Westphal, MCS 24 (Turnhout: Brepols, 2013), 82.

Love's inclusion of her reading should be understood as a concrete symbol of literary empowerment, of self-prescribed Bible reading and individual understanding of the meaning of the Old Testament in terms of the New.

The *Mirror to Devout People*

In the decades after Love wrote his *Mirror of the Blessed Life of Jesus Christ*, another Carthusian, this one anonymous, also set about making an English version of the pseudo-Bonaventuran *MVC* – despite discovering he had been scooped by Love some years earlier.[74] The *Mirror to Devout People*, or *Speculum Devotorum*, was written in the early 1430s by a monk of Sheen Charterhouse for a 'gostly syster' (3, 2) at Syon Abbey, the Birgittine double house across the river from Sheen.[75] Two manuscripts survive, dating from about 1430–70s, the earlier having been copied for a religious audience and the later for a lay audience. The thirty-three chapters of the *Mirror to Devout People* use the structural framework provided by the *MVC*, while interweaving many borrowings from the Vulgate and other scholastic, homiletic, theological and devotional sources, including the revelations of what the author calls 'approued women' (6, 127): Mechtild of Hackeborn, Catherine of Siena and Birgitta of Sweden. Though the author describes how he 'herde telle that a man of oure ordyr of charturhowse had iturnyd the same boke into Englyische' (3, 25–6), he does not seem to exhibit any first-hand knowledge of Nicholas Love's own *Mirror* to which he refers.[76] So we have an author who is working with basically the same material and in the same affective meditation tradition as Love, but likely without sight of Love's text, and shaping all his textual materials towards an audience of first and foremost female readers, though also encompassing the entire community of nuns and brethren at Syon.[77]

---

[74] Johnson, *The Middle English Life of Christ*, considers the rhetorical complexities of the translator's claim regarding Love (151–2).

[75] Paul Patterson, ed., *A Mirror to Devout People (Speculum Devotorum)*, EETS o.s. 346 (Oxford: Oxford University Press, 2016). References to the text will be by page and line numbers.

[76] Vincent Gillespie, 'The Haunted Text: Reflections in *The Mirror to Deuout People*', in *The Text in the Community: Essays on Medieval Works, Manuscripts, Authors, and Readers*, ed. Jill Mann and Maura B. Nolan (Notre Dame, IN: University of Notre Dame Press, 2006), 142, where he differs from Michael Sargent's argument that the author had Love's *Mirror* 'constantly in mind in shaping his own work'; Sargent, 'Versions of the Life of Christ: Nicholas Love's *Mirror* and Related Works', *Poetica* 42 (1994): 65.

[77] On the aesthetic significance of this text for Syon, see Laura Saetveit Miles, '"Syon Gostly": Crafting Aesthetic Imaginaries and Stylistics of Existence in Medieval Devotional Culture', in *Emerging Aesthetic Imaginaries*, ed. Lene Johannessen and Mark Ledbetter (London: Lexington, 2018), 79–92. Rebecca Selman explores the

Critics have noted the strong role Mary plays in the *Mirror to Devout People*. Paul Patterson points out that Mary 'is the key figure in preserving the most valuable narrative to man' – the story of Christ's birth.[78] In Chapter 5, the author expands on Luke 2:19 to make her an authority and co-author with the Apostles: 'But oure lady kepte wel all in here herte haply þat sche mygth the bettyr telle hyt to hem that schulde wryte hyt aftyrwarde' (34, 200–1) thus shaping the resulting narrative a 'female-centric story that could not exist without her perspective'.[79] Likewise, Vincent Gillespie reads her 'as a model contemplative and a paradigm of reflection and meditation on the events that unfolded before her'.[80] This may be true – but curiously the author does not take the opportunity to incorporate the now nearly ubiquitous motif of Mary's reading into his adaptation of the *MVC*'s Annunciation scene, as Love did when he adapted the *MVC*. In the third chapter, the author of the *Mirror to Devout People* describes the Annunciation scene by closely following Luke's language (without ever referring directly to the Gospel source). He encourages the reader to imagine the scene unfolding:

> Now thanne, beholdyth deuoutly how the angil entryth in the forseyde cytee of Naȝareth and into the place þat oure Lady duellyde inne. And hyt ys wel lykly he fond here in here deuout preyerys, for sche was alwey wel ocupyed. And fyrste he knelyth downe reuerently merueylynge the excellence of here that he salutyth. (18, 29–34)

Mary's prayer is generic and not focused on a book or a specific text; she is 'in hir prayers' exactly like Love's Mary, who is found 'in hir prayeres' – but also described meditating on the prophecies. Mary's devotion and especially her humility receive plenteous praise; any possible literary or intellectual leanings receive no mention. Whether or not the *Mirror to Devout People* author knew

---

shaping towards female readers in particular relation to a borrowing from Suso, in 'Spirituality and Sex Change: *Horologium Sapientiae* and *Speculum devotorum*', in *Writing Religious Women: Female Spiritual and Textual Practices in Late Medieval England*, ed. Denis Renevey and Christiania Whitehead (Cardiff: University of Wales Press, 2000), 63–80. Paul Patterson discusses the text's significance for both enclosed and lay women, in 'Female Readers and the Sources of the *Mirror to Devout People*', *Journal of Medieval Religious Cultures* 42(2) (2016): 181–200; while also pointing out the ways in which the text also addresses the larger community including priests, deacons and lay brethren in 'Translating Access and Authority at Syon Abbey', in *Devotional Culture in Late Medieval England and Europe: Diverse Imaginations of Christ's Life*, ed. Stephen Kelly and Ryan Perry, MCS 31 (Turnhout: Brepols, 2014), 443–59.

[78] Patterson, 'Female Readers', 194.
[79] Patterson, 'Female Readers', 195.
[80] Gillespie, 'The Haunted Text', 146. See also Selman, 'Spirituality and Sex Change', 67–8.

of Love's *Mirror*, here he also does not demonstrate any familiarity with the motif as it could have been found in the *Revelations* of Elizabeth or in Aelred's *De Institutione Inclusarum*. Rather his scene more closely resembles that of the Vernon translation of Aelred's *De Institutione Inclusarum*, where Mary's reading is omitted. Without her book, Mary offers a more passive version of the devout woman, and as the tone of the explanatory 'for sche was alwey wel ocupyed' suggests, one worth the imitation of a devout nun. This language echoes a late-fifteenth-century letter to the nuns of Syon Abbey, probably written by their Birgittine brother Thomas Betson, where he exhorts them to be 'never unoccupied as in redyng, studiyng, writyng, suying, wasshyng, delfyng or herbys settyng or sowyng with othere, litle or never seen out of here place'.[81] Yet the *Mirror to Devout People* pointedly omits any explicit representation of Mary as 'redying', passing on the opportunity taken by other lives of Christ authors – 'deuout preyerys' being rather ambiguous as to whether or not books are involved.

Taking the book out of Mary's hands – and putting it into his own – is entirely in keeping with the generally conservative approach taken by the *Mirror to Devout People* author with regards to outside reading. Characteristically, he keeps the reader's eyes on his own text: the Bible and other sources have been properly quoted, paraphrased and referenced so that the reader has no need to extend herself into that foreign territory of the Scriptures. She can stay within his book's safe, orthodox confines. Nowhere does the author encourage the reader to look beyond his book; rather, he repeatedly emphasizes how his own offering of quotations from Scripture and other authoritative sources is more than sufficient for her needs. For example, in the chapter immediately preceding the one on the Annunciation, he spends several folios discussing the various Old Testament foreshadowings of the Incarnation, and concludes by writing:

> These and manye othyr fygurys were ischewde afore in olde tyme þat oure Lorde Ihesu Cryste schulde come to saluacyon of mankynde. But these that I haue shortly tolde 3ow here I hope suffyce as for example. Also hyt was forseyde be prophetys, of the whyche one, Ysaye, that spekyth moste opynly of the Incarnacyon of oure Lorde seyde thus: 'Ecce virgo concipiet et pariet filium et vocabitur nomen eius emanuel.' Thys ys in Englyisch: 'Loo, a mayde schal conseyue and brynge forth a sone and hys name schal be callyd Emanuel', that ys exponed as the Euangelyst seyt, God ys wyth vs. Thys and many othyr were forseyde be the forseyde prophete of the incarnacyon and the

---

[81] A.I. Doyle, 'A Letter Written by Thomas Betson, Brother of Syon Abbey', in *The Medieval Book and A Modern Collector: Essays in Honor of Toshiyuki Takamiya*, ed. T. Matsuda, R. Linenthal and J. Scahill (Cambridge: D.S. Brewer, 2004), 257; see also Gillespie, 'The Haunted Text', 164, n. 41.

byrthe of oure Lorde and also manye othyr propheciys were seyde before [by] the same prophete and othyre of the Incarnacyon, the Byrthe, Passyon, Resurreccyon, and Ascencyon of oure Lorde Ihesu Cryste, and also of the comynge of the Holy Goste, the whyche were to loonge to telle here. But thys that I haue compendyusly seyde I trowe be inowgth as for example, for hyt was worthy and resunyable, as I haue forseyde, þat so excellent werkys schulde be betokenyd and prophecyed afore. (ch. 2; 16–17, 86–103)

Clearly he considers the Old Testament prophecies, especially Isaiah, vital to understanding the Incarnation and indeed all of Christ's life – yet they are best handled directly by him, and not by Mary or the implied female reader. 'These that I haue shortly tolde 30w here,' he writes, 'I hope suffyce as for example' – in other words, be satisfied, gentle reader, it is just more of the same beyond what I give you. He assures the reader that his 'compendious' examples 'be ynough' for her, thus discouraging any further unmediated consultation of the Old Testament; he becomes the authoritative expert controlling the flow of information. By distancing the prophecies across a chapter divide from the later staged scene of the Annunciation, the author avoids the model of Mary's unmediated access to divine Scripture. The Old Testament remains in his hands, not Mary's, and definitely not the readers', whether women or men. The *Mirror to Devout People* shows how conservative strains in the Bible-reading debate persisted through the mid-fifteenth century, even for the highly literate nuns at Syon Abbey.

In this history of an image, Aelred helped to initiate a vital version for the English tradition. Though the relationship of *De Institutione Inclusarum* with later devotional works is often unclear, Love's inclusion of Mary's reading, possibly inspired by Aelred's text, testifies to the detail's vitality through the fifteenth century.[82] The Annunciation scene in *De Institutione* and its detail of Mary's reading, when tracked in its various iterations over time, provides an invaluable window onto the subtle shifts in women's literacy and Bible reading in general in medieval England. Aelred's invocation of Mary's reading the prophecies as a mimetic act for the female reader vaults the Virgin into a considerably more complicated role model position – too complicated for some,

---

[82] Marsha Dutton discusses the prominent role of Aelred's text in the development of the affective spirituality textual tradition in her article 'The Cistercian Source: Aelred, Bonaventure, and Ignatius', in *Goad and Nail: Studies in Medieval Cistercian History, X*, ed. E. Rozanne Elder (Kalamazoo, MI: Cistercian, 1983), 151–78; 'Both Bonaventure's *The Tree of Life* and Ignatius' *Spiritual Exercises* find their ultimate source in Aelred's single treatise on the contemplative life, *De Institutione Inclusarum*' (151). Neither of these texts, however, include the image of Mary reading at the Annunciation.

like the Vernon translator of *De Institutione*, who seemed to have decided the detail was not suitable for his readers. Yet then the Bodley translator retained the book while toning down the affective aspects of Aelred's narrative. The author of the *Mirror to Devout People*, whether or not he knew of Aelred's text, was doubtless familiar with the image of Mary's book from other sources; regardless, he, too, resisted her potential as a model reader and chose to exert tight control over his reader's contact with Scripture. That Love portrayed Mary reading in his *Mirror* despite the prescriptions against reading the Bible demonstrates the power of Mary to offer a model of piety that challenged the general dampening of women's access to Scripture and Latin theological materials. The *Mirror to Devout People*, however, demonstrates this dampening by distancing the Old Testament from his female readers.

As the hesitancy of its later translators testifies, both the motif's vitality and controversy lie in its specificity: Mary is now reading the Old Testament prophecies, such as Isaiah 7:14, not simply the Psalms or generic devotional material. By reading the prophecies, Mary offers not just a model of reading, but a model of interpretive, exegetical reading. She physically embodies the typological understanding of the Old Testament as a prefiguring of the New, in her reading of the Word which is made flesh in her womb: *verbum caro factum est*. For medieval readers, Mary's reading models the potential for Christ to be reborn in each Christian's soul by means of text-based meditation. The Annunciation scene urges in its readers the repetition of an iterative meditative performance where a woman provides the ultimate example of transformative reading. Such a radical moment has no parallel in medieval culture.

McNamer has argued for the importance of *imitatio Mariae* in Middle English meditations that 'cast their readers in feminine subject positions – especially in the roles of spouse, mother, or feminized man – as a core technique for eliciting compassion'.[83] Love's *Mirror* achieves this through a series of female figures, exemplary practitioners of affective prayer, including, of course Mary at the Annunciation.[84] Yet we have seen that some authors, in particular the Bodley translator of Aelred's text, took care to distance Mary from affective compassion and to emphasize her presence as a restrained meditative reader. In the other texts it is Gabriel's words that the readers cry out, not Mary's. The angel provokes the most affective response of the scene, while Mary silently holds her book, waiting her turn. While at some moments gospel meditations may 'feminize the reader by fostering identification with Christ's mother',[85] in

---

[83] McNamer, *Affective Meditation*, 120.
[84] McNamer, *Affective Meditation*, 131–2. McNamer identifies them as 'In addition to Cecilia and to the Poor Clare for whom Bonaventure wrote, we encounter Elizabeth of Hungary, whose relevations are quoted in Chapter 2, and the Virgin Mary', 131.
[85] McNamer, *Affective Meditation*, 126.

fact sometimes Christ's mother is not so definitely feminine at all: she simultaneously resembles a studious monk and a devout anchoress, a scholar and a mystic, at her moment of becoming a mother. Her gender is unambiguous, but its valences resist simplification. In the same way, while as a devotional practice affective meditation may sometimes bear special connections with the feminine subject position, I agree with Karnes that affective meditation is 'at its foundation neither female- nor lay-oriented'.[86] However, as I will explore next, some female visionaries did see in Mary's female body a feminine subject position that enabled a particularly maternal connection to the divine.

---

[86] Karnes, *Imagination, Meditation, and Cognition*, 13.

4
Writing the Book: The Annunciations of Visionary Women

Lives of Christ texts like Aelred's *De Institutione Inclusarum*, the *MVC* and Love's *Mirror* transformed how meditation worked in medieval Europe. Readers were encouraged to respond to the scriptures by imagining themselves as part of scriptural stories, as witnessing first-hand Christ's life, transported there by the power of the imagination – a cognitive power itself enabled by the Word made flesh. Seeing Mary see herself in the psalms or Isaiah's prophecy offered the perfect impetus to this new kind of participatory piety. Just as Mary imagined herself part of a prophetic future, so could readers imagine themselves part of a biblical past. The Annunciation scene likewise appears in some medieval visionary accounts, where instead of the devotee going to a book to read about Mary and the angel, Mary herself often appears to the visionary to relay the miracle of the Incarnation from her point of view. Such immediacy was exactly the goal of the imaginative meditation. The textual genres fed off each other, with visionary accounts influencing devotional treatises and vice versa. Both types of mystical re-visioning of the scriptural story, can, in their own ways, offer 'a kind of direct access to God that sometimes bypasses – or at least supplements – clerical structures, reminding the reader of the extra-liturgical presence of the divine'.[1] Both the visionary and meditation genres take the opportunity to present the Virgin as a powerful authority in her own right, independent of – and sometimes superseding – male authority figures.

While in the previous chapter I argue that the Virgin's role in the Incarnation is formative for the reader of devotional texts, in this chapter I demonstrate how her role is equally formative for the visionary who produces a text to be read. Chosen because of the unique centrality of their representations

---

[1] Jessica Barr, 'Visionary "Staycations": Meeting God at Home in Medieval Women's Visionary Literature', *Medieval Feminist Forum* 52(2) (2016): 75.

of the Annunciation scene, the visionary accounts of four late medieval holy women are the focus of this chapter: Elizabeth of Hungary, the nun of the Dominican house in Naples (*c.* 1260–1322), Birgitta of Sweden (*c.* 1303–1373), Julian of Norwich (*c.* 1342–after 1416) and Margery Kempe (*c.* 1373–after 1438). I explore how these women all participate in an *imitatio Mariae* wherein the Virgin's reception of the Annunciation functions as the primary model for their own reception of the visionary gift, and how they understand their identity as female visionaries. Mary's conception of the Word of God thus becomes the paradigmatic ideal for the presence of Christ in the female visionary's physical heart and spiritual soul. While each visionary experiences a different, idiosyncratic vision or visions of the Annunciation, in every case the scene functions as a kind of mirror in which they are able to see reflected different core aspects of their visionary vocation. Elizabeth's text carefully crafts a literate, contemplative Mary, quite distanced from physical motherhood; Julian finds in Mary a hermeneutic key for interpreting her visions and ultimately construing a maternal Christ; Birgitta and Margery, in their own distinct ways, maximize the scene's potential to validate a maternal authority rooted in channelling the divine, through prophecy. All of them, however, reconfirm their identities as visionaries at the moment that Mary is confirmed as mother and Christ is formed in her womb. By means of the Annunciation scene, these four visionaries witness Mary discovering her own vocation, not only as Mother of God, but as a visionary and prophet, focii of Marian devotion that come to the fore in the fourteenth and fifteenth centuries. Mary's identity solidifies as the events of the Annunciation unfold and are relived by both the Virgin and the visionary, so that the spiritual powers of the two women emerge simultaneously.

The process of embodying the divine presence on parchment likewise found a model in Mary, traditionally depicted with a book open to the prophecy she will engender. By combining textual engagement with the maternal, or maternality, these Marian moments radically re-gender the literary and the interpretive as female. This chapter examines how the inherent 'textuality' of the Annunciation – a textual scripture of the oral exchange which accompanied the Virgin's (in)corporation of the divine Word into the speaking 'text' of the corporal Christ – offered a way of situating the visionary experience of medieval women within literary discourse, usually male-coded. Not all of these women describe visions where Mary actually reads at the Annunciation. In fact, only the earliest considered here, Elizabeth, explicitly describes Mary reading Isaiah 7:14. If the book's absence marks unease with female scriptural engagement in the male-authored texts of the previous chapter, what does its absence mean in these female-authored texts? In one way, these women can be seen to forge their own relationships to the Virgin that do not explicitly rely on her book (and textual culture); but I would argue that, in fact, the book is still present, silently and invisibly, as a locus for their Marian piety and visionary vocation. Remembering Mary's reading helps explain much about these women and their visions. As a symbol, its representation of the Incarnation drives how all four women relate to the Virgin. All their visionary accounts revolve around the link, implicit or explicit, between Incarnation and Word, between womb and text, between vision and book – all bringing Christ into the world through revelation, turning revelation into text and validating that act in a society that habitually denies women literary and theological authority. Maternal fecundity becomes linked to textual production and female textual subjectivity. Likewise, as Alexandra Barratt points out, 'medieval women visionaries, themselves engaged in the activity of spiritual autobiography, are so ready to construct the Virgin as engaged in a similar activity'.[2] The Virgin's narration of her experiences, as in the visions of Elizabeth, Birgitta and Margery, validates their own narration of their experiences, as they, like Mary, channel God to the world. The iconography of Mary's book (not only the theological metaphor it stands for, but also the actual image itself) hovers in the background as an important presence for Birgitta, Julian and Margery's Annunciation scenes.

Witnessing the Annunciation in a vision was not overly common in the Middle Ages. These four particular visionaries have been chosen for this chapter because their accounts feature the most specific, characteristic Annunciation visions in the insular and even continental traditions.[3] I do not claim that this particular kind of *imitatio Mariae* was widespread, but rather that it was significant for certain female visionaries, and that its power and complexity has been overlooked. It is important that Elizabeth, Birgitta, Julian and Margery's uses of the Annunciation are not seen as disconnected anomalies; the first two, after all, were majorly influential in late medieval devotional culture, especially in England, while the latter two reflected major influences of that culture. Margery and Julian are connected by more than just a common devotional tradition – they met in person. By comparing these four visionaries together, we can nuance our understanding of how Mary functioned for medieval holy women, moving beyond Caroline Walker Bynum's claim that

---

[2] Alexandra Barratt, 'The Virgin and the Visionary in *The Revelations* of Saint Elizabeth', *Mystics Quarterly* 42 (1992), 129. See also Kate Greenspan, 'Autohagiography and Medieval Women's Spiritual Autobiography', in *Gender and Text in the Later Middle Ages*, ed. by Jane Chance (Gainesville: University Press of Florida, 1996), 216–36.

[3] As far as I am aware, no such particular Annunciation episodes can be found in the visionary accounts of other major European visionaries, such as Margeurite d'Oingt, Hildegard von Bingen, Mechtild of Magdeburg, Mechtild of Hackeborn, Elizabeth of Schönau, Catherine of Siena, Richard Rolle, Richard Methley, Henry Suso, or Meister Eckhart.

the fullest elaboration of the notion that Mary is a model for women or the notion that women are models for each other was found in biographies written by men (for example, those of Clare of Assisi and Columba of Rieti). Where we can compare the biographer's perspective with that of the subject (as we can in the case of Clare), we find that the woman herself tended to ignore the female model to discuss instead the imitation of Christ.[4]

Of course *imitatio Christi* is important for all medieval saints, to some extent; however, Bynum's position elides how a powerful *imitatio Marie* was developed by certain holy women (and not their male confessors). Elizabeth of Hungary and Naples barely mentions Christ in her visions, for instance. These women also looked to each other as models, even as models of imitating Mary. Before an *imitatio Christi* became possible there was an *imitatio Mariae* in which the visionary saw reflected in the Virgin her own female body and its power to channel the divine, and trusted that precedent enough to trust their own calling. Bynum also argues that 'in fact and in image, suffering (both self-inflicted and involuntary) and food (both eucharist and fasting) were women's most characteristic ways of attaining God'.[5] As this chapter will show, the Annunciation (including but not only the Incarnation), which has nothing to do with either suffering or food, shows how maternality (i.e. expressing or resembling the maternal) should also been seen as a characteristic way for women to attain God. And not just maternality, but maternality as a way of *making female* textual engagement and interpretation – that which is usually marked male. Certainly there were men who embraced the metaphor of maternality as a way to attain God, as Bynum amply demonstrates; but it remained just that – a metaphor. For women it could be literally true because they share their female body with Mary, whether or not they bore children. Contrary to some arguments, this chapter (and this study) demonstrate how Mary's impossible body as both virgin and mother could still make her a possible model to all women, both virgins and mothers, and they did have a special mimetic relationship to her, different than men.

These four texts also come together in a coherent trajectory crossing from the continent to England and showcasing the insular story of the visionary tradition. Continental visionaries like Elizabeth and Birgitta, whose influence was widespread throughout Europe, likewise shaped the English visionary tradition, which can no longer be seen as operating in some kind of 'English mystical vacuum'.[6] Julian and Margery were without a doubt 'inheriting and

---

[4] Bynum, *Fragmentation and Redemption*, 153.
[5] Bynum, *Fragmentation and Redemption*, 172.
[6] Liam Peter Temple, 'Returning the English "Mystics" to their Medieval Milieu: Julian of Norwich, Margery Kempe and Bridget of Sweden', *Women's Writing* 23(2) (2016): 142. Temple is one of the latest in a 'growing body of literature which insists

participating in a rich and diverse movement of female religious experience' transmitted over the Channel from all over Europe.[7] While Margery's *Book* explicitly identifies several continental holy women as influences, including Birgitta and Elizabeth, Julian is more circumspect about all her sources; however, while she was writing the *Revelations* later in her life, she was likely exposed to the late fourteenth- and early fifteenth-century burgeoning of vernacular religious writing of which Birgitta and Elizabeth's texts were a part.[8] The revelations of both continental holy women circulated in England in Latin as well as the vernacular; the English holy women likely would have encountered Middle English versions, which is why they are used in this chapter.[9] While Birgitta knew Elizabeth through her book, and Margery knew both Birgitta and Elizabeth through their books, Margery actually knew Julian in person – though we have no evidence she knew of the anchoress' writings when she visited her anchorhold. This is a community of women who rely on each other's precedents as much as they rely on the Virgin for precedent; all are equally imitable. Not one is an unreachable model, the texts insist. The way the Annunciation operates in these visionary accounts helps to counter the misunderstanding that Mary was primarily a source of subjection and silencing for medieval women.

---

that these "English mystics" did not exist inside an "English mystical vacuum'" (142), including Nicholas Watson, 'The Middle English Mystics', *The Cambridge History of Medieval English Literature*, ed. David Wallace (Cambridge: Cambridge University Press, 1999), 539–65; and Liz Herbert McAvoy and Diane Watt, 'Writing a History of British Women's Writing from 700 to 1500', *The History of British Women's Writing, 700–1500*, ed. Liz Herbert McAvoy and Diane Watt (Basingstoke: Palgrave, 2012), 1–30.

[7] Temple, 'Returning the English "Mystics"', 144. Temple demonstrates how Julian and Margery 'can be seen as part of a transnational tradition of feminized affective piety' by comparing their texts to Birgitta's *Liber Celestis*, focusing only on Christ's crucifixion and the motherly suffering of Mary, but not on the parallels between Annunciation representations.

[8] Nicholas Watson, 'The Composition of Julian of Norwich's *Revelation of Love*', *Speculum* 68 (1993): 682. Denise Baker also argues for the need to look more into Julian's continental influences rather than her insular ones: 'Julian of Norwich and the Varieties of Middle English Mystical Discourse', in *A Companion to Julian of Norwich*, ed. Liz Herbert McAvoy (Cambridge: D.S. Brewer, 2008), 56.

[9] While Elizabeth and Birgitta are of course very international writers, consideration of their engagement with the Annunciation in the context of their impact across Europe (i.e. more than just an English phenomenon) remains outside the scope of this study, as does a more extended engagement with the various Latin and vernacular forms of Birgitta's *Liber* that circulated in England.

The *Revelations* of Elizabeth of Hungary and Naples

The name 'Elizabeth of Hungary' has caused confusion for over seven hundred years and counting. Two Middle English translations of the *Revelations of Saint Elizabeth of Hungary* survive (as well as versions in Italian, Spanish, Catalan and French), and up until Alexandra Barratt's pioneering work on the text, most medieval and modern readers attributed the Latin original to St Elizabeth of Hungary, also known as Elizabeth of Thuringia (1207–1231).[10] Elizabeth of Thuringia was well-known from her life in the *Legenda Aurea* as a widowed mother of three, devoted to poverty and an active life caring for the sick and poor, as a lay member of the Third Order of St Francis – but not, according to any early sources, inclined to mysticism. Moreover, the *Revelations* themselves strongly suggest the visionary was enclosed, living a contemplative life, evidence for which I will examine in this chapter. Then Alexandra Barratt and Sarah McNamer put forth a stronger candidate for the Elizabeth of these visions: her lesser-known great-niece Elizabeth of Töss (1294–1336), a Dominican nun of the Swiss convent of Töss. According to her *vita* written by fellow nun Elsbet Stagel, she fostered a deep devotion to the Virgin Mary and was admired for her extreme piety and her visions. It could have been Stagel who recorded Elizabeth's revelations – as she famously did those of Henry Suso, the Dominican mystic.[11] Peter Tóth and Dávid Falvay dissented from this conclusion, in my view unconvincingly, but their pressure on the assignation led Sarah McNamer to return to the issue in her 2018 edition of the earliest version of the pseudo-Bonaventuran *MVC*.[12] Here she effectively refutes the

---

[10] Alexandra Barratt offers an excellent introductory bibliographical sketch of the text in 'The *Revelations* of Saint Elizabeth of Hungary: Problems of Attribution', *The Library*, Sixth Series, XIV(1) (1992): 1–11. She discusses more of the text's content in 'The Virgin and the Visionary', and excerpts passages in her *Women's Writing in Middle English* (London: Longman, 1992). Sarah McNamer corroborates Barratt's identification in her earlier article, 'Further Evidence for the Date of the Pseudo-Bonaventuran *Meditationes vitae Christi*', *Franciscan Studies* 50 (1990): 235–61; in her side-by-side edition of the two Middle English versions and their closest surviving Latin exemplar, *The Two Middle English Translations of the Revelations of St Elizabeth of Hungary* (Heidelberg: Universitatsverlag C. Winter, 1996); and 'The Origins of the *Meditationes vitae Christi*', *Speculum* 84 (2009): 905–55. (For her recent re-consideration, see below.)

[11] On Suso and Stagel, see Barratt, 'Problems of Attribution', 8, and 'The Virgin and the Visionary', 125; Barbara Newman, *God and the Goddesses: Vision, Poetry, and Belief in the Middle Ages* (Philadelphia: University of Pennsylvania Press, 2003), 12.

[12] Peter Tóth and Dávid Falvay, 'New Light on the Date and Authorship of the *Meditationes Vitae Christi*', in *Devotional Culture in Late Medieval England: Diverse Imaginations of Christ's Life*, ed. Stephen Kelly and Ryan Perry, MCS 11 (Turnhout: Brepols, 2014), 17–104; and also Dávid Falvay, 'St Elizabeth of Hungary in Italian Vernacular Literature: *Vitae*, Miracles, Revelations, and the *Meditations on the Life*

key arguments that diminish the authenticity of the *Revelations* as a genuine visionary account by a woman named Elizabeth, and she puts forth a new candidate for the visionary woman behind the text: the Dominican nun Elizabeth of Hungary (c. 1260–1322), daughter of King Stephen V of Hungary and Elizabeth the Cuman, and prioress of the Dominican Abbey of San Pietro a Castello in Naples.[13] Because of 'this Elizabeth's early years in a Dominican convent, her life as a nun in Italy, and the confluence of Dominican and Franciscan cultures around the Naples court and Santa Maria Donna Regina', she could well prove to be the most viable candidate, according to McNamer.[14] This would mean that it would be quite possible for the *Revelations* to be circulating in Italy soon after her death in 1322 (and thus incorporated into the *MVC* soon after).

McNamer's new hypothesis of the Dominican nun Elizabeth of Hungary and Naples, as I shall dub her for clarity's sake, rings true with the analysis of the *Revelations* I deploy below. Any identification of this Elizabeth with a historical figure must take into account the content of the visions themselves: how the text shapes the Virgin Mary as an enclosed contemplative in a conscious reflection of the visionary herself. The Annunciation, with its long tradition of framing Mary as a contemplative model and mirror for enclosed women, becomes the central axis around which the entire *Revelations* turn.

---

of Christ', in *Promoting the Saints: Cults and the Contexts from Late Antiquity until the Early Modern Period: Essays in Honor of Gábor Klaniczay for his 60th Birthday*, ed. Ottó Gecser et al. (Budapest: CEU Press, 2010), 137-50. Tóth and Falvay dispute Barratt and McNamer's assignation to Elizabeth of Töss because it contradicts their larger argument about the origins of the *MVC*, which borrows a large section on 'the seven petitions to God' directly from the *Revelations*; they reject McNamer's later *terminus post quem* of 1336 (Elizabeth of Töss's death) and revive the option of Elizabeth of Thuringia as the visionary behind the *Revelations*, supporting their earlier *MVC* date of composition at c. 1300, and even suggest there was no historical Elizabeth behind the text at all and that the text is an invented fiction. While the complex details of the *MVC* versions and origins are beyond the scope of this chapter, much of the evidence Tóth and Falvay provide to disprove the later nun's authorship of the *Revelations* remains deeply problematic. For instance, it is unlikely, as they argue, that a corruption in the title meaning *virgo* refers to Mary and not Elizabeth in all three surviving instances (56); it is irrelevant that Hungarian royal origins were sometimes assigned to women in romance literature and unwise to dismiss the label 'Hungarian princess' as merely a literary tool (56–7); it underestimates of the translation efforts and transmission networks of fourteenth-century Dominicans and Franciscans to claim that the *Revelations* could not have made its way to Italy between 1336 or even latest 1360 (Stagel's death) and 1381 (their *terminus ante quem*) (57–8). Much longer texts travelled much greater distances in far less time – such as Catherine of Siena's *Dialogo* and Birgitta of Sweden's *Revelationes*.

[13] Sarah McNamer, ed., *Meditations on the Life of Christ: The Short Italian Text* (Notre Dame, IN: University of Notre Dame Press, 2018), cxxxix–cxlvi. Here she deals with some of the issues I list in the footnote above as well as others.

[14] McNamer, *Meditations on the Life of Christ*, cxliii.

So even if it is not this particular Elizabeth of Hungary, though I suspect it is, it is much more likely to be some other Elizabeth living a contemplative life than the active Elizabeth of Thuringia, whose cult focused not on her private prayer but on her helping the sick and poor. In addition, in comparison to the visions of mothers Birgitta of Sweden and Margery Kempe, where Mary's representations are very much shaped by her motherhood of Christ, the *Revelations* almost completely ignores Mary's maternality in preference for her contemplative lifestyle – suggesting against the visionary's identity as a mother or even acting in a mothering way towards others, as Elizabeth of Thuringia does.

Like many visionary narratives, the *Revelations of Saint Elizabeth* is written in the third person so that 'the authoritative voice of the narrator appears to emanate from a detached position separate from the visionary herself'.[15] While this can sometimes be an extremely complicated issue (as with Margery Kempe) in Elizabeth's case I concur with Barratt's consideration of the text as the written record of 'an originally oral authentic first-person narration' and thus a kind of 'pseudo-third person narrative'.[16] The text gives us little reason to understand the amanuensis as more than scribe and/or editor or Elizabeth as less than author. Both translations into Middle English, the first appearing in manuscript in the second half of the fifteenth century and the second printed by Wykyn de Worde in 1493, likely derive from a common Latin version.[17] Scholars of Middle English visionary literature have given little attention to this text and its focus on the Virgin Mary, although its influence on medieval religious culture in England from Margery Kempe to Love's *Mirror* has been briefly discussed.[18]

The *Revelations* are almost entirely centred around the Virgin Mary; Elizabeth converses with the Virgin in the first nine of thirteen individual visions, and with Christ in the last three. Christ's Passion or any Eucharistic devotion are conspicuously absent from the text, save for the penultimate paragraph containing a brief vision of Christ's side wound. Rather it is the Annunciation event – reconfigured, extended and carefully detailed – that powers Mary's

---

[15] Barratt, 'The Virgin and the Visionary', 125.
[16] Barratt, 'The Virgin and the Visionary', 125, 126.
[17] McNamer, *Two Middle English Translations*, 16–20.
[18] See McNamer, *Two Middle English Translations*, 40–8 on 'The *Revelations* in England'; as well as Alexandra Barratt, 'Margery Kempe and the King's Daughter of Hungary', in *Margery Kempe: A Book of Essays*, ed. Sandra J. McEntire (New York: Garland, 1992), 189–201; and Carol M. Meale, '"oft siþis with grete deuotion I þought what I miȝt do pleysyng to god": The Early Ownership and Readership of Love's *Mirror*, with Special Reference to its Female Audience', in *Nicholas Love at Waseda: Proceedings of the International Conference, 20–22 July 1995*, ed. Shoichi Oguro, Richard Beadle and Michael G. Sargent (Cambridge: D.S. Brewer, 1997), 19–46.

transformation into a model visionary living the life of a contemplative. Practice evokes theology and vice versa: her bodily conception of Christ is contextualized within her spiritual conception of God through prayer and reading, coupled with visionary experiences explicitly parallelling Christ's coming alive in her womb. Essentially Mary mirrors the visionary Elizabeth herself, in a kind of metatextual mimesis that reveals as much about the medieval holy woman as about medieval Marian traditions. In her examination of the *Revelations*, Barratt considers this mimetic reflection a rather conscious manipulation of the narrative, in that 'it is noticeable that the text models the Virgin on Elizabeth rather than vice versa, so that the Virgin, like Elizabeth, is constructed as an ecstatic visionary communicating her spiritual experiences to a third person'.[19] As Mary's paradigmatic moment of channelling God, the Annunciation becomes the main paradigm for expressing the visionary contemplative identity shared by the two women.

The *Revelations* constantly weaves the words and gestures of Mary at the Annunciation throughout the text, so that the moment of the Incarnation is both foreshadowed and recalled as pivotal for Elizabeth's conception of herself as a visionary woman. The first eight chapters prominently feature elements tied to the Annunciation and Incarnation, such as the motif of the handmaiden, or the study and prayer which together prepare Mary for Christ's conception, or the ecstatic experience that marked the Incarnation itself. A brief outline shows the shape of the text and its pervasive Annunciation motives:

ch. 1   Mary invites Elizabeth to be her handmaiden.
ch. 2   Mary encourages Elizabeth to greet her like Gabriel greeted her.
ch. 3   Elizabeth responds to Mary, imitating Mary's response at the Annunciation.
ch. 4   Mary teaches Elizabeth her prayer from the temple (the seven petitions).
ch. 5   Mary describes reading Isaiah and her prayer; vision of God's voice.
ch. 6   Mary describes the Annunciation scene, promoting it as an imitable moment.
ch. 7   Mary challenges Elizabeth to compare herself to saints.
ch. 8   Elizabeth desires to pray like Mary prayed, and Mary explains a detailed allegory for the act of prayer.
ch. 9   God sends St John the Evangelist to be Elizabeth's confessor.
ch. 10 Christ praises her devout prayer on behalf of a wicked woman.
ch. 11 Elizabeth hears a voice urging hope in God, etc.
ch. 12 Christ speaks to Elizabeth of his sacrifice and mercy.
ch. 13 Elizabeth has a vision of Christ's bleeding hand and side.

---

[19] McNamer, *Two Middle English Translations*, 129.

Chapters 1–8 inaugurate Elizabeth into her visionary vocation with Mary as 'mistress' and guide, in effect preparing her for chapters 9–13 where Christ takes over from Mary as the main visionary interlocutor. This pattern parallels Mary's own role in the story of the Bible and apocrypha, where she nurtures her spiritual vocation in preparation for the coming of Christ, whom she ends up bearing herself in her own body. The Annunciation as that transformative moment of vocational and divine conception is woven into the overall structural fabric of the *Revelations*.

From the opening of the text, the recurring motif of 'handmaiden' (*ancilla*) links together Elizabeth and the Virgin by echoing the language of the Gospel itself, where Mary identifies as *ancilla* in her final response to Gabriel in Luke 1:38: 'Behold the handmaid of the Lord; be it done to me according to thy word' (ecce ancilla Domini fiat mihi secundum verbum tuum). In the first paragraph of the first chapter Mary invites Elizabeth to be 'myn handmayden' (*ancilla*), after which, 'Seynt Ely3abeth, fallyng doun to þe erþe, worschepyd here, and stondyng vp a3en, bowhede here knes and puth here hondys and ioynede [hem] to þe hondys of Owre Lady' (I, 58).[20] Facing with their hands clasped together, the two women's bodies mirror each other, establishing their close identification that will shape the rest of the text. Mary then confirms her as 'my dowtyr, my discyple, and myn handmaydyn' and explains that 'qwanne þou art suffysently tawt and reformyd of me, I schal brynge þe to my Sone, þy spouse, þe qwech schal resseyue the into ys hondys as I aue take þe now' (I, 58). By drawing attention to the physical position in which they remain, Mary highlights the symbolic importance of their gesture of joined hands as one Elizabeth will share with both Christ's mother and eventually Christ himself – a triple mirroring. While holding hands in such a way imitates the rite of feudal obedience on one level, as McNamer notes,[21] I would argue that its dominant meaning here is to foreshadow Mary's physical submission as *ancilla* at the Annunciation later on in the *Revelations*.

While the motif of becoming the 'handmaiden to the handmaiden of God' is fairly unusual in the late thirteenth century, it is not without precedent. Over 700 years earlier, the Spanish saint Ildefonsus (*c.* 607–67), Archbishop of Toledo, mentions this kind of *imitatio Mariae* in his influential tract *Liber De*

---

[20] All quotations are taken from McNamer, *Two Middle English Translations*, cited by chapter and page number from Cambridge, CUL MS Hh.i.11, the earlier of the two Middle English translations, compiled around the second half of the fifteenth century. Compared to the later 1493 Wynken de Worde printing, this earlier manuscript is closer to the periods in which the other visionary texts in this chapter were written and circulated. Parenthetical references to the Latin text are from Cambridge, Magdalene College, MS F.4.14 as edited by McNamer.

[21] McNamer, *Two Middle English Translations*, 104.

virginitate perpetua Beatae Mariae. After an extended discussion of the Incarnation, Gabriel and the Annunciation, he prays to the Virgin:

> Ideo ego seruus tuus quia tibi filius Dominus meus. Ideo tu domina mea, quia tu ancilla Domini mei. Ideo ego seruus ancillae Domini mei quia tu domina mea facta es mater Domini tui. Ideo ego factus seruus, quia tu facta es mater factoris mei.[22]

> (Thus, I am thy servant because thy Son is my Lord; thou art my Lady, because thou art the handmaid of my Lord; I am the servant of the handmaid of my Lord, because thou, my Lady, wast made the Mother of thy Lord; I was made servant, because thou wast made the Mother of my Creator.)

Ildefonso repeats Mary's reply to Gabriel, that she is the *ancilla Domini* (handmaid of the Lord), and when he mirrors her own servitude in imitation of hers, he switches to refer to himself as *seruus*, the masculine slave or servant. His emphasis is on his servitude to Christ *through* Mary: 'So that I might be the devoted servant of the begotten Son, I eagerly desire servitude to the mother' (Ut sim deuotus seruus filii generantis, seruitutem fideliter appeto genitricis).[23] Ildefonso had a large influence on the development of the cult of the Virgin in the early Middle Ages, and not just in Spain; *De virginitate* was a well-known text through the thirteenth century, and Latin copies surviving from Spain, France, Italy, Germany and England.[24] He anticipated the more affective devotional trends of those later centuries, and his imitation of Mary in this way was ahead of its time. It is possible that Elizabeth was exposed to this text, though she certainly didn't need a source to have originated the idea herself. Elizabeth takes the motif far beyond Ildefonsus' passing mention, integrating it more pervasively and profoundly into her text as a way of shaping her own identity as a female visionary.

Thus it is important to note that the *Revelations* uses not Ildefonso's masculine word *seruus*, servant, but particularly the feminine *ancilla Christi* (handmaiden of Christ) and *ancilla Dei* (handmaiden of God) to refer to Elizabeth, which highlights the shared gender of Mary and Elizabeth as well as Elizabeth's vocation as a nun. After being established as Mary's handmaiden in

---

[22] Ildefonso of Toledo, *De Virginitate Beatae*, ed. Vicente Blanco García, Textos latinos de la edad medina española – Sección 3 (Madrid: Centro de Estudios Historicos/ Rivadeneya, 1937), 162–3. Translation from Sister Athanasius Braegelmann OSB, *The Life and Writings of Saint Ildefonsus of Toledo* Volume IV (Washington, DC: The Catholic University of America Press, 1942), 152. Robert Deshman discusses this aspect of Ildefonsus' text in 'Servants of the Mother of God in Byzantine and Medieval Art', *Word and Image* 5/1 (1989): 39

[23] *De Virginitate Beatae*, ed. García, 167; translation from Deshman, 'Servants', 39.

[24] See García's edition for a list of manuscripts, 7–30, and Braegelmann, *The Life and Writings*, 133.

the opening scene, the text takes seriously Mary's promise to substitute Christ for herself and refers to Elizabeth as *ancilla Dei* at the beginning of chapter 2, and *ancilla Christi* at the beginning of chapters 3 and 5–13.[25] This insistent repetition draws attention to the epithets' dominant meaning in the Middle Ages: the specific combinations of *ancilla Christi* and *ancilla Dei* denote a nun, according to definitions relevant to the period of the *Revelations*.[26] Elizabeth is not only a metaphorical servant of Christ or God – she is a vowed servant, the text emphasizes; her position as *ancilla Dei* and *ancilla Christi* insists she lives a life of enclosure, contemplation and virginity, just like Mary's life in the temple that she describes in such detail.

While Elizabeth becomes Christ's handmaiden almost right away, some suspense builds within the *Revelations*. In chapter 3 the text offers another allusive moment recalling the Annunciation, before Mary recalls the original scene itself. After Mary offers to make a charter and have St John the Evangelist as her confessor, Elizabeth responds with gesture and words perfectly foreshadowing Mary at the Annunciation: 'Þanne blessyd Eliȝabeth fel down on here kneys, and handes ioned on þe herte, and worchypt here, and seyde, "Of me, my lady, as of yowr andmaydyn, dooth qwat ȝe wyln"' (III, 60). It is not until three chapters later that this moment's importance becomes clear, when we read Mary's response to Gabriel and recognize the rhetoric on which Elizabeth's words are modelled: Mary 'keste myself into the erthe, & knes lowed and handys ioynyd, I worschypt and seyde, "*Lo þe handmaydin of Owr Lord, be yt do to me aftyr þy word*"' (VI, 80). Now the Annunciation scene emerges as the original, with Mary's words translating directly the account in Luke 1:38, and her detailed posture all aligning with Elizabeth's words in the previous two scenes. Elizabeth mimics Mary's physical and spiritual obeisance, taking her handmaiden position in relation to God, now to Mary. This recurring motif of imitating Mary emphasizes her immediate relevance as a model for holy women, in this case, especially related to her role at the Annunciation – to

---

[25] Other examples can be found within the chapters as well, for example V, 70. The earlier Middle English translation does not retain the *ancilla* in the openings of chapters 9, 10 and 11.

[26] See *ancilla* 1.c. '(w. *Dei* or sim.) nun' in *The Dictionary of Medieval Latin in British Sources*, ed. R.E. Latham, D.R. Howlett and R.K. Ashdowne (London: British Academy, 1975--). Also for 'ancillæ Dei', 'monasteriales' in DuCange, et al., *Glossarium mediæ et infimæ latinitatis* (Niort: L. Favre, 1883–7). The entry for *ancilla* in both sources can be found online at http://logeion.uchicago.edu/index.html#ancilla (accessed 17 August 2019). McNamer points out the significance of the word in *Two Middle English Translations*, 14. On the term *ancilla Dei* as referring to the cloistered woman in religious literature, see Michael Goodich, '*Ancilla Dei*: The Servant as Saint in the Late Middle Ages', in *Women of the Medieval World: Essays in Honor of John H. Handy*, edited by Julius Kirshner and Suzanne F. Wemple (Oxford: Basil Blackwell, 1985), 120.

engage with the scriptures as a way of bringing Christ into the world, and to channel him spiritually through visionary experience.

Paradoxically, Mary herself models for Elizabeth how to be a handmaiden to the Mother of God, not only to God or Christ, and at the centre of this service is a particularly literary kind of prayer. The visions present an innovative interpretation of the tradition of the Virgin's reading Isaiah 7:14 in advance of the Incarnation that the verse prophecies. In chapter 5, Mary explains:

> Sothly, on a day qwanne I adde a confort of God and so wondyrfully þat I adde neuer felth swych before, and qwanne I was coum aȝen to myself, I began to þynke wyt most brennyng herte and to wish þat Y mite sumwhat doon & han in me wherfore God schulde neuere suffre me departe fro hym. And qwanne I adde þowt þys, I ros vp and wente to a bok and redde. And in þe ferste opnyng of þe bok cam to myn eyin þys word of Ysaye þe prophete: *Loo, a maydyn schal conceyve and bere a chyld &c.* Qwanne I thowte þat maydynheed schulde mich plese God, for he wolde ys Sone be bore of a maydyn, I purposede þanne in my herte and in my thowt my maydynheed for to kepe in reuerence of here, þat ȝyf yt befeel me for to se here, þat I mayte in maydynheed seruyn here al þe tyme of my lyf and go on pilgrymage wyt here throw al þe world ȝyf yt nede. (V, 72)

Mary describes herself in a mystical state of ecstatic joy – recalling its Latin roots of 'ex-' and 'stasis', standing outside one's self – having to 'coum aȝen to myself' before turning to the scripture for guidance on how to maintain that kind of closeness to God. She is destined, as the commentary tradition suggests, to open the book in an act of sacred prognostication at the exact prophecy which foretells her own conception of Christ, Isaiah 7:14. But this time Mary herself gives insight on her twofold interior response to the prophecy: she will keep her own virginity in reverence of this virgin maiden, and she would serve her and accompany her on pilgrimage (not yet knowing, of course, that she herself will be that woman). Earlier in chapter 4, Mary lists a similar desire as the fifth of her 'seven petitions to God': 'þat he schulde make me to se þat tyme in þe qwech þe blessyd maydyn schulde be born þat aftyr tellingis of prophetis schulde bere ys Sone' (IV, 64). Echoing behind the words *maiden* and *maydynheed* is the word *handmaiden*, highlighting the important element of virginity as part of the service of handmaiden into which both women offer themselves. Mary and Elizabeth become parallel figures: at the opening of her revelations Elizabeth has promised her virginity and her service to Mary the Mother of God, just as Mary does here. Elizabeth becomes what Mary wished to become; the mirroring cycle is complete, with the book itself as the mirror reflecting each woman's new identity back for her to imagine and inhabit.

While the image of Mary reading would seem to cue Gabriel's entrance and the Annunciation scene, what happens next comes as a surprise. The night after she has prayed concerning the maiden who will bear his son, Mary experiences a corporeal vision and locution in which God the Father speaks directly to her:

> After þys in þe nyth folwyng as I preyde wyt a deuowt mende, askende God þat he wolde lete me se þe forseyde maydyn or I deyde, sodeynly beforn my eyin qwanne I was in þe derke swych a syte apperede to me þat in comparisown of þat þe sonne ys noȝth. And fro þat lyth I herde a voyse clerly seying to me, 'Maydyn of Dauit kyn, þou schat bere my Sone.' And he seyde also, 'Certaynly, wyt þou wele that þat honor and þat reuerence þat for loue of me þou desiredyst to do to anoþer maydyn, of oþer schal be do to þe. For I wele þat þu be þat same maydin þat schalt bere my Sone.' (V, 72–4)

Mary's *active* seeking of God's favour, her assiduous reading, devotion and prayer initiates divine contact and the pre-emptive revelation that the woman Mary prays to see is in fact herself: 'þu be þat same maydin þat schalt bere my Sone'. Prayer, with reading, in effect mirrors the self and facilitates Mary's discovery of her true identity as the Mother of God. This echoes a longstanding contemplative tradition wherein, as Gregory the Great explains, reading 'presents a kind of mirror to the eye of the mind' so that we 'transform what we read into our very selves'.[27] Here, the effect is doubled. Mary reads the prophecy *about herself* just as Elizabeth reads *about Mary*. Through reflective acts of reading, both women succeed in creating (or rediscovering) the self in accordance with the text. Mary's seeking out of a mystical experience, and God's validating words, justify Elizabeth's own visionary experiences and the profitable self-discovery which might result from such experiences – she, too, like the Virgin, can discover her true holy purpose through the message of the *visio*. Such powerful reading experiences in turn strengthen the authority of the material book of the *Revelations* itself and its spiritual value for its readers.

God the Father's message to Mary, his first and only recounted by her in this text, functions as a kind of pre-Annunciation announcement of the Incarnation: when Gabriel visits Mary in the next chapter, she already knows the punchline. By pre-empting the biblical Annunciation episode with God's own announcement, Mary circumvents the intermediary role of Gabriel, demonstrating a direct access to the divine not documented by Luke. Mary thus grants Elizabeth a first-hand account of a new narrative of divine communication preceding the Annunciation, supplementing scriptural narrative and

---

[27] From the preface to *Moralia in Job*, Iii and I.xxxiii, translated in Mary Carruthers, *The Craft of Thought: Meditation, Rhetoric, and the Making of Images, 400–1200* (Cambridge: Cambridge University Press, 1998), 159, and quoted in Jennifer Bryan, *Looking Inward: Devotional Reading and the Private Self in Late Medieval England* (Philadelphia: University of Pennsylvania Press, 2008), 79.

the ecclesiastical tradition which privileges its male-authored accounts. For Elizabeth, this vision within a vision of God's pre-Annunciation goes beyond the example of Gabriel's visit as *visio* to reconfirm the primacy of visionary experience for the holy woman's relationship with God. Mary is not only a visionary herself, but moreover a mystic: she receives a divine locution directly from the Father. This passage, I would suggest, demonstrates that Mary's active mysticism is foundational to her successful divine motherhood.

Set structurally and figuratively at the centre of the text, Mary's recounting of the Annunciation establishes the moment as an ideal model of visionary and mystical experience. She describes exactly how it felt, worth quoting here in full:

> Þerfore qwanne I was all brennyngg in þe loue of God and so mich swetnesse felte of hym þat for hym al þe world was vanyte to me, I stode wyt a deuowt sowle alone in a priuy chambere; and sodeynly þe angyl Gabriel apperede to me and, as þe gospel seyth, grette me seying '*Heyl, ful of grace, Owr Lord ys wyt þe. Blessyd be þou among all wommen*.' Qwanne I adde herd þys, I was ferst abascht; buth aftyrward, throw ys lowely and homly spech, I was confortyd and mad sekyr, noþyng dowtyng þat yt was trowthe þat he seyde, and keste myself into the erthe, & knes lowed and handys ioynyd, I worschypt and seyde, '*Lo þe handmaydin of Owr Lord, be yt do to me aftyr þy word.*' And whanne I hadde seyd þys word, I was all takyn owt fro myself, and so gret plente of Godys grace beschynyd me þat I felde all þese comfortes and swetnesses of my sowle. And in þys rafchyng Godys Sone tok flesh and þe clenneste dropys of my blod wytowtyn felyng of me or ony fleshly delite. (VI, 80)

Luke's dialogue has been stripped down to Gabriel's greeting (crucial to the *Ave Maria* prayer) and Mary's final response (crucial to the theme of 'handmaiden-hood' in the *Revelations*). Added details depict the ecstatic nature of Mary's piety: she is 'brennyng in þe loue of God' in her initial devotion, she casts herself onto the ground before speaking, she is taken out of herself and, at the moment of the Incarnation, experiences a ravishing, 'rafchyng' (*raptu*). The fullness of God's grace, 'plente of Godys grace', which marks Christ's conception gives her the same feelings of 'comfortes' and 'swetnesses' which define her mystical experience – and Elizabeth's mystical experience as well. Elizabeth's own feelings of God's mystical ravishing echo this paradigmatic moment, which establishes the legitimacy of the female body to channel God both spiritually and physically.

Another small detail draws our attention: Mary is praying 'alone in a priuy chambere' (*in secreto thalamio*). This no doubt alludes to the idea of Mary in a private room when Gabriel arrives, an element of Annunciation iconography with a long tradition outlined earlier in this study. For example, in Bernard of

Clairvaux's third homily *De Laudibus Virginis Matris*, the angel went 'into the private chamber of her modest room where, I suppose, having shut the door she was praying to the Father in secret'.[28] Throughout Elizabeth's *Revelations* explicit references to physical space or context are sparse: in the fifth revelation 'oon of Eliʒabethys felaws (*socialibus*)' interrupts her prayer (V, 68), implying she is in a place accessible by her fellow nuns, as *socius* is a term often used to refer to a member of a monastic community;[29] but otherwise the only time/space context might be a passing reference to the liturgical feast on which Elizabeth receives a revelation. Yet in the opening sentence of the text there is a significant, though subtle, echo of Mary's 'priuy chambere'. The Latin reads, 'Una dierum cum beata Elizabeth … in secreta oracione' (I, 56). In Cambridge, CUL MS Hh.i.11, the translation has 'On a day as Seynt Elyʒabeth, being in deuwt preyowr', missing the meaning of *secreta*. However, the other surviving Middle English translation, the Wynken de Worde print of *c.* 1493, has 'On a day when Saynt Elisabeth was in preuy prayer', capturing the importance of *secreta* with the more precise translation *preuy*, or private. The Latin draws a clear rhetorical parallel between Mary *in secreto thalamio* and Elizabeth *in secreta oracione*, so that Mary's appearance to Elizabeth becomes an annunciation of its own to an enclosed woman. Elizabeth, like Mary, initiates her special communion with the divine by drawing inward, seeking solitude, withdrawing from the outside world in order to enter the world of Christ and his mother.

Beyond her example of solitude, Mary explicitly presents her speech at the Annunciation as a model of revelatory reception for Elizabeth to emulate. After describing the event, Mary declares to Elizabeth:

> Why dede God þys grace princepaly to me? Yt was faith and mekenesse þat I wyt full feyth trowede to þe angelys seinnges, and al mekede myself, & schop me al to Godys wyl; þerfore deynede he to ʒyue me so mich grace. Ryth so þou, dowtyr, in all þyng þat he behotyth to þe or doth, be nowt vnstable in þys triest, ne aʒenstonde hym nowt, seyhyng, 'Lord, qey dost þou þus to me?', buth be ensawmple of me, say, 'To þe handmaydin of Owr Lord be yt do to me aftyr þy word.' (VI, 82)

As we have seen, Elizabeth heeds Mary's advice: three chapters earlier, Elizabeth has responded to Mary with precisely this posture and rhetoric ('Of me, my lady, as of yowr handmaydyn, dooth qwat ʒe wyln' (III, 60)), putting herself in the same handmaiden position to Mary that Mary herself wished for after

---

[28] *De Laudibus virginis matris*, Homily III, 33; see Chapter 2, 49–50.
[29] McNamer makes this connection, *Two Middle English Translations*, 14; see *socius* (7, b) as 'member of a *collegium* or similar association; b. monk', in R.E. Latham, et al., *The Dictionary of Medieval Latin*; online at http://logeion.uchicago.edu/index.html#socius (accessed 17 August 2019).

reading Isaiah. Ventriloquizing Mary and mimicking her bodily movement are only two of the ways that Elizabeth incorporates the Annunciation scene into her spiritual life: she also learns proper prayer practice from both the Virgin and Gabriel.

Gabriel's greeting to Mary at the Annunciation provides Elizabeth with efficacious words to use in prayer. Mary's recounting of the scene privileges Gabriel's initial greeting, 'Heyl, ful of grace, Owr Lord ys wyt þe. Blessyd be þou among all wommen,' above the rest of his speech, and its power assists Elizabeth in various ways. In the second revelation Mary advises Elizabeth: 'Buth fehth stable aȝen vicys, and sey oones þe gretyng of þe awngyl wiþ þe wech Gabriel, Goddys messager, grette me, & all þy trespassys schal be frely forȝeuyn to þe of my Sone' (II, 60). Elizabeth soon finds out for herself the power of the *Ave Maria* prayer; its recitation has the power to prompt visits from the Virgin: 'Anoþer tyme in þe vygilie of þe berthe of Howre Lord, whylys sche preyde wyt a streght vp mende and seyde þe gretyng of þe Virgine Marye wyt hey voys and mych deuociown and droppyng terys, vysibly Owr Lady aperede to her' (IV, 62). Mary also remarks concerning her petition for the seven gifts of the Holy Spirit from her time in the temple as a young girl: 'Alle þese, my dere dowter, þat I askede wer grauntyd to me, as þou mayst vndirstonde of þe salutacyoun of þe angyl, wyt whech I was gret of Gabriel þe archangyl' (V, 76). Indeed, the discourse of the Annunciation provides for Elizabeth the ultimate key to an *imitatio Mariae*, to understanding and imitating the Virgin's life of prayer, revelation and intimacy with God.

But the model extends beyond personal piety and into realms of earthly power: the main premise of Elizabeth's *Revelations* is based upon Mary's assertion of her superior authority, superior even to priests. At the opening of the first revelation, Elizabeth despairs of the unusual absence of 'here spouse Iesu Cryst' and considers going to a male authority figure for help, when Mary quickly intervenes:

> And as sche dysposyd hyr in here preuy thowt for to gon to sum gostely brothyr for to haue cunsseyl (*consilio*) of þys þyng, Owre Lady Seynte Marye apperede to here and seyde, 'Eliȝabeth, ȝyf þu wyth be my discepele, I schal be þy maystresse; and ȝyf thow wyth be myn handmaydyn, I schal be þy lady.'
>
> To qwom sche sayde, 'What be ȝe, lady, þat woldyn han me to ȝow discyple and andmaydyn?'
>
> And Owr Lady answerde, 'I am þe modyr of Goddys Sone lyuynng, swych þou ast chosyn to þy lord and to þy spouse.' And sche seyde eueremor, 'Þer ys no broþer in þys world þat of þy spouse kan betere enforme þe þan I.'[30] (I, 56)

---

[30] Interestingly, of the two Latin manuscript witnesses which compose 'Group II' from which the English versions are derived, one omits this last sentence entirely;

In the nick of time Mary takes over the position of spiritual authority from the 'gostely brother' (implying a monastic brother rather than a sibling brother). This brother is one of two mentions or (non)appearances of mortal men in the entire text: the second is in chapter 9, when Elizabeth is in 'greth gostly torment' because she did not have frequent enough access to her confessor. These are not especially flattering representations of male authority figures. No other men feature in the narrative; the only other humans are women. Although Christ, God the Father and St John the Evangelist operate as male spiritual guides, they exist outside her priestly sphere which evidently falls short of Elizabeth's needs. Mary most explicitly fills this power vacuum by offering herself as an 'alternative maternal authority … superior to that of the institutional Church' – an authority not only maternal in the sense that she behaves maternally towards Elizabeth, as Barratt suggests, but also maternal in the sense that her authority is granted to her because of her position as Mother of God.[31] When Mary offers herself as 'maystresse' and pointedly explains, 'Þer ys no broþer in þys wor[l]d þat of þy spouse kan betere enforme þe þan I', she claims the role of learned master – in the female form *maystresse* – expert in both *consilio* and *discretio spirituum*. In the visionary realm, there is no doubt of female expertise, and no need for male worldly authority. The setting of the *Revelations*, I suggest, mirrors the visionary's historical environment where such female authority would have been endorsed, such as a convent like the Dominican one Elizabeth of Hungary and Naples belonged to. Bynum makes a similar argument when she points out that 'women sheltered by special religious status, especially those raised in convents, rarely spoke of female weakness as a bar to theological expression or religious practice'.[32] No bars, not to mention woman's weakness, stand in the way of Elizabeth; in contrast, women are powerful, even more powerful than men.

In stark contrast, the *vita* of the lay, widowed Elizabeth of Hungary from the *Legenda Aurea* emphasizes almost the opposite: she constantly obeys a series of confessors who hold full power over her, and there are no women of authority present in the narrative. Mary never counteracts men's power over the holy woman, or even appears as an authoritative figure. In fact, Elizabeth's efforts to find female spiritual company are denied by the powerful men in her life. The *vita* explains a startling scene concerning a confessor named Master Conrad:

> On a time because she went into a cloister of nuns, which prayed her diligently for to visit them, without licence of her master, he beat her so sore therefor that the strokes appeared in her three weeks after, by which she

---

see the textual apparatus, McNamer, *Two Middle English Translations*, 57.
[31] Barratt, 'The Virgin and the Visionary', 133.
[32] Bynum, *Fragmentation and Redemption*, 167.

showed to our Lord that her obedience was more pleasing than the offering of a thousand hosts. Better is obedience than sacrifice.[33]

Such male domination finds no parallels in the *Revelations* text, where in fact the visionary is explicitly encouraged to model herself on the cloistered life, and to obey not male priests but Mary herself. The two examples seem incompatible.

Another important factor in the question of the visionary's identity is the way that throughout the text Mary suggests how Elizabeth may 'be ensawmple of me' and imitate her contemplative customs. Like in the anchoritic and monastic texts of Aelred's *De Institutione Inclusarum* and Goscelin's *Liber confortatorius*, Mary is the ideal contemplative: devout, solitary, focused, literate and studiously following the monastic practices of *lectio*, *meditatio* and *oratio*. An important difference with Elizabeth is that she is a woman proposing Mary as literary contemplative, confirming late medieval shift of this kind of *imitatio Mariae* from men to women.[34] In a vision in chapter 4, the Virgin appears to Elizabeth as she prays during the vigil of the Nativity, declaring herself as the visionary's teacher: 'I am coum to þe to tech þe þe preyowr þe qwech I made qwan I was a maydyn yong in þe temple' (IV, 62). Mary describes how she studied the law and commandments, and regularly rose in the night to pray before the altar, commanding Elizabeth to 'do as I dede in þe begynyng of my ȝoyugþe in þe temple' (IV, 64). Then follow the seven petitions, a motif that found later popularity through the *MVC*. In the next chapter Mary exhibits a more private, literary mode of prayer, when she opens and reads a book in which she finds Isaiah's prophecy of the Incarnation. Finally, in chapter 8 Elizabeth yearns to know 'in what wyse the blyssed Mayde prayed'; Mary responds with an involved allegory of the digging and construction of a new well to explain how she learned to love God by means of 'redyng, thynkyng, and prayeng' – the monastic *lectio*, *meditatio* and *oratio* (VIII, 87). Mary's time as a young virgin in the temple expands to define all of her life; there is no mention of later years outside religious enclosure, as an active mother of Christ, or even at Christ's Passion. Barratt, working with her claim that the Elizabeth behind these visions is the young nun Elizabeth of Töss, argues that 'the picture of the life the Virgin leads in the temple is clearly based on Elizabeth's own life as a

---

[33] From 'The Life of S. Elizabeth', in Jacobus de Voragine, *The Golden Legend: Readings on the Saints*, trans. William Caxton, vol. 6, reprinted (London: J.M. Dent and Co., 1900). Available at the Fordham Medieval Sourcebook: https://sourcebooks.fordham.edu/basis/goldenlegend/GoldenLegend-Volume6.asp#Elizabeth (accessed 17 August 2019).

[34] On this shift of Mary's reading as a model by and for men in the early medieval period to a model by and for women in the later medieval period, see Miles, 'The Origins and Development'.

nun'.[35] With the visionary's identity now under debate again, this contemplative representation of Mary offers compelling evidence in support of the historical visionary also leading a contemplative life, where she pursued this particular *imitatio Mariae* – such as in the Dominican Abbey where Elizabeth of Hungary and Naples was prioress.

In fact, the only act explicitly attributed to the visionary is the act of prayer (with its attendant weeping and crying); and while prayer is obviously an act shared by both lay and enclosed holy women, it is not detailed in the lay woman's *vita* on the same scale as the *Revelations*. The total absence of any of the activities emphasized by the *vita* of Elizabeth of Hungary such as serving the poor and extreme ascetic penance would seem quite unusual if these were her visions. The setting in which the visionary is described bears little resemblence to the outside, secular world so crucial to the shaping of Elizabeth of Thuringia's holiness – there is no interaction with lay people or secular authorities. In contrast, it resembles the secluded convent, as Elizabeth is only described as interacting with women identified as *sociae*, a term used to refer to a member of a monastic community.[36]

Moreover, in the *Revelations*, the Virgin's contemplative, monastic mode completely overshadows the kind of domestic maternality that drives representations of Mary in the visions of lay mothers such as Birgitta of Sweden and Margery Kempe, as we will soon see, and that we might expect to mark any visionary accounts of Elizabeth of Thuringia, wife and mother. Birgitta and Margery gave birth to and raised eight and fourteen children, respectively; each woman engages with Mary in complex ways – but definitely including the nativity of Christ and its practical aspects as resonating with their personal experience. The *Revelations*, however, explores at length the spiritual and visionary aspects of conceiving God, but never moves from the metaphorical to the practical aspects of Mary's motherhood: no pregnant belly, no birthing scene, no swaddling the Christ child. Rather the visions linger on Elizabeth's solitary devotions, Mary's devotional techniques and their profound shared desire to channel Christ through the soul by means of devout 'privy' prayer. Just as Mary's mothering body takes a silent supporting role to her visionary and devotional prowess in the *Revelations*, Elizabeth's body remains unremarked and uninscribed in the text, only a source of tears, invisible and inviolable in its virginity. If we see the Annunciation scene as a mirror in which visionary women can see their visionary vocation reflected, this Elizabeth emerges as an enclosed, literate contemplative, a 'mayde … yonge and beyng in the temple' just like Mary.

[35] Barratt, 'The Virgin and the Visionary', 129.
[36] McNamer, *Two Middle English Translations*, 14.

The *Liber Celestis* of Birgitta of Sweden

Like Elizabeth's *Revelations*, the *Liber Celestis Revelationes* of St Birgitta of Sweden (*c.* 1303–1373) was transmitted to England and met with a public voracious for more visionary accounts by holy women. Bridget, as she was called by English speakers, was born into an influential noble family in the Swedish town of Vadstena, married at thirteen and managed a large and wealthy household of eight children. Within days of her husband's death in 1341 Birgitta received a calling vision in which God stated her role as bride and channel of Christ. By 1350 Birgitta had permanently relocated to Rome, as instructed by Christ in her visions, in order to petition for the Pope's return to the city and await the pontiff and emperor's simultaneous presence there. Over the next twenty-seven years Birgitta worked tirelessly as ecclesial, political and social activist. She undertook several more pilgrimages to both holy sites and royal courts in need of reform, and she succeeded in founding her divinely mandated new monastic order, the Order of St Saviour. Despite some controversy, she was canonized in 1391.[37]

Her record of over seven hundred visions, the *Liber Celestis Revelationes*, was created with the help of several confessors. The *Liber Celestis* achieved wide circulation throughout Europe even during Birgitta's lifetime. Its wide-ranging themes – from vivid descriptions of biblical scenes; to direct discourse from Christ, Mary and a range of saints; to calls for moral reform; to prophecies about the past, present and future – made it popular reading in Latin and many vernaculars.[38] Birgitta's *Liber, Extravagantes, vita, Sermo Anglicus* and various other texts circulated in England in both Latin and Middle English. These works were transmitted as wholes and as excerpts integrated into other compilation texts and manuscript anthologies, thus ensuring a widespread influence on insular vernacular devotional traditions.[39]

---

[37] An excellent biography is Bridget Morris, *St Birgitta of Sweden* (Woodbridge: Boydell Press, 1999); see also Claire L. Sahlin, *Birgitta of Sweden and the Voice of Prophecy* (Woodbridge: Boydell Press, 2001), 13-33, and Païvi Salmesvuori, *Power and Sainthood: The Case of Birgitta of Sweden* (New York: Palgrave, 2014).

[38] On Birgitta's prophetic vocation, see Sahlin, *Birgitta of Sweden*, and Rosalyn Voaden, *God's Words, Women's Voices: The Discernment of Spirits in the Writing of Late-Medieval Women Visionaries* (York: York Medieval Press, 1999).

[39] On Birgitta's influence in England, see Laura Saetveit Miles, 'St Bridget of Sweden', in *History of British Women's Writing, Vol. 1: 700–1500*, ed. Diane Watt and Liz Herbert McAvoy (Basingstoke: Palgrave, 2011), 207–15; Roger Ellis, '"Flores ad Fabricandam ... Coronam": An Investigation into the Uses of the *Revelations* of St Bridget of Sweden in Fifteenth-Century England', *Medium Aevum* 51 (1982), 163–86; Ellis, 'Text and Controversy: In Defence of St. Birgitta of Sweden', in *Text and Controversy from Wyclif to Bale: Essays in Honour of Anne Hudson*, ed. Helen Barr and Ann M. Hutchinson (Turnhout: Brepols, 2005), 303–21; and Julia Bolton Holloway, 'Bridget

While Christ as holy spouse occupies most of Birgitta's revelations, the Virgin Mary introduces herself early in the text as a vital divine voice, and acts as instructor, intercessor and guide in at least a third of the revelations. Birgitta's Marian piety has slowly received more and more attention since Claire Sahlin's 1993 observation that studies of that aspect of her spirituality 'remain in their early stages'. Sahlin's work on Birgitta's *imitatio Mariae* remains the most exhaustive. She examines the prominent devotion to the heart of Mary documented in Birgitta's texts; the many themes used to link Birgitta as Mary's successor, making Christ visible on earth; and the ways that gender relates to prophetic authority.[40] Birgitta's Marian self-identity is tightly linked to Vadstena and her Order, Samuel Fanous explains in an article where he also examines the significance of images of birthing.[41] Børresen argues for Birgitta's 'exemplary feminist intention', though somewhat compromised by the 'androcentric impact' of Birgitta's writings.[42] More recently, Mary Dzon probes the ways in which Birgitta's texts transmit a private female discourse where Mary 'reveals intimate details about the Holy Family to another woman in whom she trusts'.[43] In contrast, Yvonne Bruce sees Mary's role in the *Liber* as part of the Birgitta's 'very indifference' to larger issues of female agency and misogynist patristic doctrine.[44] Mary's role as mother of Christ, and what this means for Birgitta, recurs in Birgittine scholarship as an obvious focus of analysis, but

---

of Sweden's Textual Community in Medieval England', in *Margery Kempe: A Book of Essays*, ed. Sandra McEntire (New York: Garland, 1992), 203–21.

[40] See Claire Sahlin, '"His Heart was My Heart": Birgitta of Sweden's Devotion to the Heart of Mary', in *Heliga Birgitta – budskapet och förebilden*, ed. Alf Härdelin and Mereth Lindgren (Stockholm: Almqvist and Wiksell, 1993), 213–27; 'The Virgin Mary and Birgitta of Sweden's Prophetic Vocation', in *Maria i Sverige under tusen år. Foredrag vid symposiet i Vadstena 6–10 oktober 1994: I*, ed. Sven-Erik Brodd and Alf Härdelin (Skellefteå: Artos, 1996), 227–54; 'Gender and Prophetic Authority in Birgitta of Sweden's *Revelations*', in *Gender and Text in the Later Middle Ages*, ed. Jane Chance (Gainesville: University Press of Florida, 1996), 69–95; and *Birgitta of Sweden*, ch. 3, 'Mystical Pregnancy and Prophecy in the *Revelations*: Birgitta's Identification with the Virgin Mary'.

[41] Samuel Fanous, 'Becoming Theotokos: Birgitta of Sweden and Fulfilment of Salvation History', in *Motherhood, Religion, and Society in Medieval Europe, 400–1400: Essays Presented to Henrietta Leyser*, ed. Conrad Leyser and Lesley Smith (Ashgate, 2011), esp. 274–80.

[42] Kari Elisabeth Børresen, 'Birgitta's Godlanguage: Exemplary Intention, Inapplicable Content', in *Birgitta, hendes værk og hendes klostre i Norden*, ed. Tore Nyberg (Odense: Odense Universitetsforlag, 1991), 23.

[43] Mary Dzon, *The Quest for the Christ Child in the Later Middle Ages* (Philadelphia: University of Pennsylvania Press, 2017), 187.

[44] Yvonne Bruce, '"I am the Creator": Birgitta of Sweden's Feminine Divine', *Comitatus* 32(1) (2001): 20.

where and how exactly this role originates as a major authorizing force in the *Liber* has not yet been scrutinized.

I suggest that the Annunciation and the mystery of the Incarnation provide the foundation for Birgitta's imitative relationship with Mary. In this visionary Annunciation scene, the text depicts a vivid *imitatio Mariae* wherein the Virgin's reception of the divine functions as a major model for Birgitta's own reception of the visionary gift. Twice the Virgin Mary describes the Annunciation scene to Birgitta, the first within the first few pages of the massive collection and the second several hundred pages in. The two narratives are distinguished by an important shift: from humility and obedience, to assertion and authority. The first narrative legitimates her visionary vocation and the obedient humility undergirding the authority it grants her, while the second carries out that authority by assertively exercising her prophetic power in the world – appropriate for the development of her revelatory career. Both representations of the Annunciation parallel Mary's conception of Christ with his presence in Birgitta's visions, but it is a final scene of Birgitta's mystical pregnancy that brings the parallel to its conclusion: that the book of the *Liber Celestis* is Christ physically brought into the world through the same maternal power to channel the divine that Mary models at the Annunciation. Interestingly, nowhere does Mary explicitly read a book in these two versions of the scene; instead, the text positions both Birgitta and Mary outside of traditional book learning so that they can wield a differently powerful, divinely granted wisdom that circumvents the patriarchal hold on intellectual knowledge and simultaneously places them above and beyond that patriarchy. Far from disqualifying or dirtying their spiritual agency, the female body and its generative maternality authenticate Mary and Birgitta's ability to effect transformations between divine body and divine book. Birgitta evokes such a position in one of her early meditations, *Quattour oraciones*, which survives in medieval Swedish. The prayer directly addresses Christ:

> Praise be to you, God's body, for the Virgin who bore you, for all that you did with her, for the word became flesh and blood in her inwards, by her flesh and blood, and by the conception and increase of the holy spirit, with virginity whole and intact and without any kind of contamination.[45]

John 1:14, 'And the Word was made flesh' (et Verbum caro factum est) reverberates in these lines, where flesh – specifically female flesh – is not fallen but fecund. Birgitta is well aware of the scriptural resonances between *verbum* and *virgo*, and the rich potential of the conception of Christ as a metaphorical vehicle for expressing the conception of her revelations.

---

[45] Bridget Morris, 'Four Birgittine Meditations in Medieval Swedish', *Birgittiana* 2 (1996): 184.

Though Mary's virginity is stressed in the Swedish meditation, Birgitta's own non-virginal flesh and blood does not prevent the visionary from mimicking Mary's 'flesh and blood'. The two Annunciation scenes, when closely compared together for the first time, bring new insight to a passage that has been studied by several scholars: Birgitta's mystical pregnancy, where she feels Christ moving within her womb, or heart. Critics agree that this experience suggests that Birgitta 'saw her task of broadcasting God's words to the world as analogous to Mary's motherhood', as Sahlin writes; Børreson likewise describes the mystical pregnancy as manifesting Birgitta's identification as 'revelatory instrument in the sense that she imitates Mary's role in the incarnation of Christ'.[46] However, in these examinations the significance of Mary's *interpretation* of the mystical pregnancy goes unmentioned. For Mary's role in the Incarnation of Christ not only offers a model of revelation to Birgitta, but also a model of authoritative interpretation, both of the revelation itself but also of truth in the world. I argue that because of the way that scriptural prophecy works in the Annunciation scene – its typological fulfilment interpreted by Mary with/in the conception of Christ – we need to see Birgitta's mystical pregnancy as also a demonstration of a maternal *interpretive* power.

Birgitta, very similarly to Elizabeth, first encounters the Annunciation scene through the mediating narrative of the Virgin describing her early life, beginning already in Book 1, chapter 10. In fact the build-up to the two Annunciation scenes presents some fascinating parallels and departures between the two women's visionary accounts. Birgitta's Mary moves quickly over her time in the temple; for Elizabeth's Mary, this period of study, meditation and prayer dominates her life story (reflecting Elizabeth's own vocation as a nun, I believe). While Elizabeth's Mary reads Isaiah directly and then desires to be the handmaiden to that maiden mentioned in the prophecy, Birgitta's Mary does not read Isaiah but rather hears of the prophecy second-hand: 'when I herde þat he, þe same God, suld bi againe þe werld, and suld be born þareto of a maiden, I had so grete a charite to him þat I thoght of noþinge, ne desired noþinge, bot him' (I.X.17; my italics).[47] In Birgitta's visions book learning is not

---

[46] Sahlin, 'The Virgin Mary', 237; Børresen, 'Birgitta's Godlanguage', 38.
[47] Birgitta of Sweden, *Liber Celestis of St Bridget of Sweden: The Middle English Version in British Library MS Claudius B i, together with a life of the saint from the same manuscript*, ed. Roger Ellis, EETS o.s. 291 (Oxford: Oxford University Press, 1987). All references will be to this edition and book, chapter and page number will appear parenthetically in the text. For the standard edition of the Latin, see St Birgitta, *Revelaciones* (Stockholm: Kungl. Vitterhets Historie och Antikvitets Akademien, 1956–2002); *Book I, with Magister Mathias' Prologue*, ed. by Carl-Gustaf Undhagen. Samlingar utgivna av Svenska fornskriftsällskapet, Ser. 2, vol. 7:1 (Uppsala: Svenska fornskriftsällskapet, 1977), online at https://riksarkivet.se/crb (accessed 27 August 2019), Book I, Chapter X, verse 2. Modern English translation: *The Revelations of St Birgitta of Sweden, Volume 1: Liber Cælestis, Books I–III*, trans. by Denis Searby

part of the young Virgin's portfolio of skills.[48] While she is clearly inspired by the prophecy, she is not depicted as encountering it as part of a literate prayer practice. Replacing Mary's unmediated reading of scripture with the generic reference to the prophecy points to how Birgitta's *Liber Celestis* will find the power in the Annunciation scene not through modelling bookish prayer, but rather through modelling a maternal access to divinity, one that authorizes the mothering of a book of visions.

Yet the texts continue on to important similarities. A few sentences later in the *Liber Celestis* Mary proclaims a familiar sounding vicarious aspiration (my italics highlight the parallels): 'þarefore I *desired euir in my herte* þat I mighte leue and se þe time of his birth, if I might *happeli be a worthi handmaiden to seruis* of his modir. Also, I vowed in mi herte euir *to kepe maidenhede if it plesed* and suld be acceptabill *to God*' (I.X.18). This closely echoes the words of Elizabeth's Mary in direct response to Isaiah: 'Qwanne I thowte þat *maydynheed schulde mich plese God*, for he wolde ys Sone be bore of a maydyn, I *purposede þanne in my herte* and in my thowt my maydynheed for to kepe in reuerence of here, þat ȝyf yt befeel me for to se here, þat I mayte *in maydynheed seruyn here* al þe tyme of my lyf' (V, 72). It may be possible that the tight verbal parallels here – especially the purposing or vowing in the heart to keep maidenhead, and that maidenhead pleases God – originate in Birgitta's exposure to Elizabeth's *Revelations* in Rome, since the text did circulate in Italian religious circles in the mid- to late fourteenth century.[49] Though the seven petitions of God that were borrowed from the *Revelations* into the popular *MVC* – undoubtedly read by both Birgitta and Margery – describe Mary's fifth petition to 'se þat tyme in þe qwech þe blessyd maydyn schulde be born þat aftyr tellingis of prophetis schulde bere ys Sone' (IV, 64), the specificity of serving in virginity cannot be gleaned from that excerpt. Regardless, they show how in their early visions both holy women encountered a Mary who imagined herself part of a prophetic future, and whose desires to interact vicariously with the Mother and Son of God could be imitated – or even carried out 'spiritually' – by means of visions. Such an *imitatio Mariae* emphasizes the foundational importance of the Annunciation to the formation of the visionary self.

---

with introductions and notes by Bridget Morris (Oxford: Oxford University Press, 2006), 66. I will note only meaningful departures from the Latin in this Middle English version, the only full translation currently edited.

[48] Nor was it necessarily one of Birgitta's own strengths, as she reportedly struggled to learn Latin as an adult. See Christine Cooper-Rompato, *The Gift of Tongues: Women's Xenoglossia in the Later Middle Ages* (Philadelphia: Pennsylvania State University Press, 2010), 62–4, 94–100.

[49] Falvay demonstrates the influential presence of Elizabeth's *Revelations* in medieval Italy, in 'St Elizabeth of Hungary in Italian Vernacular Literature', 143–4.

Later in the same chapter and just before the Annunciation scene, the *Liber Celestis* carefully sets up Mary as a model visionary whose mystical experiences culminate in the conception of Christ. When she is alone in her devotions, she 'saw thre grete meruails': a star, a light and a sweet smell, all otherworldly. Finally she 'herd a voice, but noȝt of mannes mouthe', immediately after which Gabriel appears (I.X, 18). This vaguely echoes Mary's mystical experience in Elizabeth's *Revelations*, where an extraordinarily bright light appears right before God's voice speaks to her to announce the Incarnation (V, 72). In both cases the parallels between the visionary vocations of the holy woman and the Virgin are explicitly drawn just prior to the Annunciation moment, in order to establish Christ's physical conception as a way of understanding his appearance in the holy woman's visions as a kind of visionary conception. These women channel Christ; his power flows through their bodies and words. The Annunciation and Incarnation provide a crucial framework for legitimating the rest of the visionary text.

In the next paragraphs of Birgitta's *Liber Celestis*, Mary's Annunciation account generally follows Luke's Gospel even as it omits some verses – and supplements scripture with brief first-person, introspective commentaries angled to frame Mary as an authorizing prophetic model for Birgitta. The repeated emphasis on Mary's unworthiness, culminating in the perfect alignment of her will with God's, demonstrates the ideal state of humility for spiritually conceiving the Son in the heart or soul:

> Bot onone þare aperid ane aungell of God, as a man of soueraine bewte, noght clethed, and he said to me, '*Ave gracia plena et cetera*: haile, full of grace, þe lorde is with þe. Þou art more blissed þan all oþir women.' When I had herd þis, I was astoned, merueilinge what þis suld betaken, or whi he profird to me swilke a salutacion. I wist wele and trowed miselfe vnworthi ani swilke, for I held me noȝt worthi ani gude; bot I wiste wele it was noȝt vnpossibill to God for to do what him liked. Þan saide þe aungell againe, 'Þat sall be born of þe is hali, and it sall be called þe son of God; and as it hase plesed him, so it sall be.' Neuirþeles I held me noȝt worthi, ne I asked noȝt of þe aungell, 'Whi or when sall it be?', bot I asked þe maner, 'How it sall be þat I, vnworthi, be þe modir of God, þe whilke fleshli knawes no man.' And þe aungell answerd to me as I saide, 'To God is noþinge vnpossibill, but what he will be done, sall be done.' (I.X, 18–19)

Mary essentially ventriloquizes Luke, speaking scripture in a woman's voice through the voice of a living woman, Birgitta. In this vision the direct discourse of the Vulgate, what Mary says to the angel, returns once more to her own mouth, accompanied by further insights into her state of mind at the moment: consistent humility in the face of great honour. Mary follows Luke closely until she adds the point that 'I wist wele and trowed miselfe vnworthi ani swilke, for I held me noȝt worthi ani gude.' Here she makes clear that humility drives her reaction to the angel's greeting; likewise, throughout the *Liber, vita* and supplementary texts, accentuating humility, passivity and obedience are common verbal justifications for Birgitta's legitimacy as female prophet.[50] Rosalynn Voaden points out that, generally, '*vitae* of women visionaries and accounts of their visions placed enormous emphasis on the humility, obedience, chastity, patience, and prudence of the visionary, and her willing submission to her spiritual director; these qualities, of course, are all important criteria of *discretio spiritum*'.[51] Thus it is entirely appropriate for such an emphasis on humility to occur at the beginning of Mary's introduction to both Birgitta and the reader. Yet the Virgin's next words more boldly foreshadow the words that Gabriel will utter a few lines later: 'bot I wiste wele it was noȝt vnpossibill to God for to do what him liked'. In using this phrase Mary asserts that this knowledge is hers already before Gabriel imparts it to her, and hers to offer to Birgitta – and the reader – first. Though this passage primarily emphasizes Mary's humility, it gives a hint of the later chapter where the Annunciation recurs in order to demonstrate not Mary's humility but her powerful authority.

In fact, the Virgin's explanation of her humility and faith subtly functions to distinguish her response from someone else's failure in the face of divine revelation: Zachariah, husband of Mary's cousin Elizabeth. In Birgitta's vision Mary explains her inner thoughts behind the question, emphasizing her unworthiness, and that humility helps her avoid the wrong questions – 'whi or when sall it be?' – that doomed her relative Zachariah at his angelic visit. Earlier in Luke 1, Gabriel visits Elizabeth's husband in order to announce that she will bear a son named John (Elizabeth already knows). Zachariah questions the angel, 'Whereby shall I know this? for I am an old man, and my wife is advanced in years.' The angel responds unequivocally:

> Et dixit Zaccharias ad angelum unde hoc sciam ego enim sum senex et uxor mea processit in diebus suis. Et respondens angelus dixit ei ego sum Gabrihel qui adsto ante Deum et missus sum loqui ad te et haec tibi evangelizare. Et ecce eris tacens et non poteris loqui usque in diem quo haec fiant pro eo quod non credidisti verbis meis quae implebuntur in tempore suo.

> (I am Gabriel, who stand before God: and am sent to speak to thee, and to bring thee these good tidings. And behold, thou shalt be dumb, and shalt not be able to speak until the day wherein these things shall come to pass, because thou hast not believed my words, which shall be fulfilled in their time.) (Luke 1:18–20)

---

[50] Claire Sahlin, 'Gender and Prophetic Authority', 77.
[51] Voaden, *God's Words, Women's Voices*, 71.

As Bernard of Clairvaux explains in his fourth sermon *De Laudibus Virginis Matris*, 'We read that this same angel punished Zechariah's doubt, but we never read that Mary was blamed for anything.'[52] Mary's two examples of 'whi or when' parallel Gabriel's reprimand that Zacharias 'did not believe my words' (the 'why') 'which will come true at their proper time' (the 'when'). Instead of arrogantly challenging Gabriel's prophecy, Mary recalls her own unworthiness, and her humility averts Gabriel's rebuke. She not only models the correct reply to such an announcement but also warns against the wrong ones, useful guidance for anyone receiving angelic or divine visitations, such as Birgitta herself. Here Birgitta learns from Mary how to respond properly to her visions and ensure her voice is not silenced like Zachariah's.

However, Mary's actual reply to Gabriel in the *Liber* presents a fascinating divergence from scripture:

> Eftir þe whilke worde of þe aungell, I had þe moste feruent will þat might be had to be þe modir of God. And þan spake mi saule þus for lufe: 'Lo, I here redi: þi will be done in me.' At þe whilke worde anone was mi son conceiued in mi wombe with vnspekeabill gladnes of mi saule and of all mi partis. (I.X, 19)

Her response here departs meaningfully from her response in the Vulgate, Luke 1:38: 'Ecce ancilla Domini: fiat mihi secundum verbum tuum' (Behold the handmaid of the Lord; be it done to me according to thy word). Even though earlier in the chapter Mary had picked up the theme of the handmaiden from the prophecy, here the verbal parallel to the *ancilla* or handmaid in Isaiah is omitted, and replaced with a new parallel with the Lord's prayer, derived from Matthew 6:10: 'Fiat voluntas tua sicut in caelo et in terra' (Thy will be done, in heaven as it is in earth). Except now God's will is done not in heaven or in earth but 'in me', the female body now a new site of God's will, which aligns with Mary's own 'moste feruent will'. Also significant is the omission of the Vulgate references to the 'word', *verbum*, in Mary's final response (Luke 1:38, 'fiat mihi secundum verbum tuum'). Through this small change from 'word' to 'will' the text shifts the emphasis from God's incarnate Word onto the efficacy of Mary's uttered words: 'at þe whilke worde anone was mi son conceiued'. It is at the moment of *her* spoken agreement that Christ becomes incarnate by the Holy Ghost. Mary shows herself to be fully in control of the narrative, now *her* gospel, when she pinpoints the moment of Incarnation – after *her* reply to Gabriel. The repetition of the first person insists on the Virgin's agency over her body, her will and her story: 'mi saule', 'I here', 'in me', 'mi son', 'mi wombe', 'mi saule', 'mi partis'. Immediate and personal, these few sentences make the Incarnation become not just about the dramatized humility of this particular

---

[52] Saïd, *Homilies in Praise of the Virgin Mary*, 51.

mother, but also about the mutual willingness of both her corporality and her spirituality to undertake the will of God.

The significance of the Annunciation for Mary and Birgitta is dramatically amplified in its second recurrance much later in the *Liber*, in Book III: this presentation much more explicitly uses the Incarnation to legitimate female access to God, female prophecy and female authority.[53] Birgitta describes a vision in which Mary revisits the Annuciation scene, where the Virgin slightly changes her description of the moment to support a different set of priorities for Birgitta. At this point it seems the visionary no longer needs a model of humility in the face of divine visitation, but a new model of intellectual assertiveness in the face of earthly male authority. Evidently, Birgitta has been challenged by a master of divinity and Mary counsels her on how to respond to him. She subtly, but meaningfully, shifts the tone of her recollection of the Annunciation:

> I was so brenninge in þe lofe of God, and þe fire of God was so feruent in mi hert, þat þare plesed me nothinge bot þe will of God, þat shewed to me his grete charite, insomikill þat he sent to me his messagere to make me knawe þat I suld be þe modir of God. And fro I wist þat þat was þe will of God, I assentid in mi hert, and of a grete charite I spake oute and saide vnto þe messagere, 'Be it done vnto me eftir þi worde.' (III.VIII, 208)

Gabriel's words are completely subsumed here and only Mary's speech is direct discourse. This time she quotes more precisely her response recorded in Luke 1:38, and this time the phrase 'eftir þi worde' (in Luke, *secundum verbum tuum*) is necessary for underscoring the power imbued in her because God's word takes on her flesh. The importance of this renewed emphasis on the *Logos* becomes clear as Mary explains how her conception of Christ changed her:

> And in þat same instans was God within me made man, and Goddes son mi son. And so þe fadir and I had bothe one son, þat was both God and man, and I bothe modir and maiden. Bot fro þe time þat he was conceiued within mi bodi, as he was full of wit, he filled me full of wit, insomikill þat noȝt oneli I vndirstode þe grete wit of maistres, bot also wheþir it come of letterure or elles of þe charete of God. (III.VIII, 208)

The word Mary utters at the Annunciation ('May it be done according to your word') aligns with both the divine Word, the *Logos* (λόγος) or *verbum* of John 1:14, 'And the Word was made flesh and dwelt among us' (*et verbum caro factum est et habitavit in nobis*), and now the 'words' of the scholars. While

---

[53] The following passages are also discussed in relation to the significance of the Virgin Mary for Julia Kristeva in her well-known essay 'Stabat Mater'; Miles, 'Looking in the Past'.

not mentioning the tradition of Mary reading the scripture at Gabriel's arrival, the passage nonetheless taps into its invisible presence, as it thereby underscores the miraculousness of her superiority *above* those who read: her power comes not from book learning but from God himself.[54] Physical conception of the Word grants Mary immediate authority in the scholastic realm of letters, texts and books, otherwise generally closed to women; through her maternal body she becomes exempt from the patriarchical requirements that make 'maistres' out of men. She is impregnated with wit, with understanding, with a doctrinal and theological conception of knowledge that can only come from conception of the Godhead (whether physical or spiritual). With this wisdom Mary instructs Birgitta on what questions to ask the master on her behalf, and tells her how to interpret the master's answers; thus the visionary woman exercises this same maternally sourced authority when she interrogates him and, depending on his responses, may find him 'more like to an asse þan to a maistir' (III.VIII, 208).

Mary's special power is essentially an act of interpretation. She becomes an expert in a kind of *discretio* not of spirits, but of intellectual learning, of 'wit'. This 'grete wit of maistres' stems either *indirectly* from 'letterure' (which would include Latin religious literature, as in the writings of the patristic fathers, biblical commentaries, sermons, etc.) or *directly* from the 'charete of God' – i.e. spiritual gifts. Mary, as mediatrix to Christ, is positioned to distinguish the mediacy or immediacy of human knowledge of spiritual things. Through her proximity to her Son Mary accesses this literate realm, but through these visions she passes it on to a daughter, Birgitta, in effect creating a female lineage outside the male-dominated scholastic or ecclesiastical hierarchy. Birgitta will be Mary's spokeswoman on earth. Birgitta, in turn, by writing her visionary text, passes at least the demonstration of this female power over men's 'wit' on to generations of readers.

It is important to understand that because Mary's interaction with Gabriel and her impregnation with the Word of God were both essentially verbal events, she commands the special ability to discern agreement between what is spoken and what is thought by humans:

> For I, þat bare him þat is verrai treuthe, knawe wele if his mouthe and his hert accorde. I haue asked of þe maistir thre þinges, to þe whilke if he had answerde treuli, I suld haue knawen it: for, eftir þe message was saide to me fro þe mouthe of þe archangell Gabriel, treuthe tuke in me both fleshe and

---

[54] At the same time, illustrations of Birgitta receiving divine revelation via rays of light and simultaneously writing it down clearly mean to evoke images of the Annunciation where Mary also has a book in her lap as she receives the same kind of heavenly rays of the Holy Ghost symbolizing Christ's conception. For discussion and illustrations of this deliberate visual parallel see Miles, 'Looking in the Past', 57–9.

blode, and þe same treuthe, both in godhede and manhede, was born of me. And þarefore I knewe wele wheþir in þe mouthe of men be treuthe or noght. (III.8, 208–9)

Her motherhood, her physical carrying of Christ 'þat is verrai treuthe' inside her womb, enables the Virgin to *read* the inner thoughts of men while judging the truth of their oral utterances. 'Treuthe', incarnate in the Son of God, becomes a standard Mary is specially sanctioned to judge against. When Mary emphasizes, 'For I, þat bare him þat is verrai treuthe, knawe wele [the truth of men]', she connects her experience bearing Christ in her body to her ability to discern theological truths. Through the duty of her womb Mary wields a spiritual perspicacity which sets her (and Birgitta, her mouthpiece on earth) in a unique position of authority over the men of the world, with the power to interpret their textual or oral utterances, and to balance them against the truth of their hearts. According to the *Liber*, the Virgin 'was filled with the wisdom of God and given the gift of prophecy', as Sahlin describes her, and I would argue that Birgitta comes to understand the incarnation of Christ as the moment when that transformation happens.[55] By extension, then, for Birgitta the Annunciation represents the conception of herself as a prophet in Mary's image, able to speak the words of Mary's prophecies because of their shared maternal ability to bring Christ into the world.

The particular emphasis on the Virgin's powers given her as a result of the textual/verbal nature of the Annunciation and Incarnation illuminate the textual implications of Birgitta's own experience of mystical pregnancy. This is a fascinating episode that has attracted considerably more critical attention than the dual Annunciation scenes, which have gone mostly unremarked, but all three passages should be read together as a cohesive programme of Mary as model, connecting the Word of God to the maternal female body in order to authorize Birgitta's power. At nearly the end of the *Liber Celestis*, the entirety of chapter 76 in Book VI explains what happened to the visionary on the eve of Christ's nativity one year, in a rare focus on Birgitta's physical body:

> It fell on þe Cristemas night þat þe spouse, with one passing gladsomnes of hir hert, felid as it had bene a whike childe sterringe in hir herte. And at þe hye mes, þe modir of merci apperid to hir and saide, 'Doghtir, right as þou wote noȝt how þat gladnes and stirynge com so sodanli to þe bi þe sone of Gode, so þe comminge of mi son to me was wondirfull and sodaine. And also sone as I assentid to þe aungels message, I felid in me a wondirfull whilke stering child, with a gladnes þat mai noȝt be saide. And þerfore haue comforthe, for þis gladfull stiringe sall laste with þe and incres in þe, for it

---

[55] Sahlin, *Voice of Prophecy*, 96; also 97–8 on the tradition of Mary as 'prophetess'.

is þe comminge of mi son into þi herte, and þou sall shewe to mi sonnes frenndes, and mine, oure will.' (VI.76, 460)

At the time of the liturgical celebration of Christ's birth, Birgitta becomes seemingly physically pregnant in a modelling of Mary's maternity. This impregnation corporally manifests itself as if a living child were moving 'in hir herte' with 'passing gladsomnes of hir hert' – fitting with the medieval understanding of a physiological conflation of womb and heart.[56] In a fascinating mirroring of Luke's Annunciation scene, Mary then appears to Birgitta to announce the parallel between her sensations of pregnancy and the Virgin's own pregnancy with the Son of God. Mary interprets, or 'reads', Birgitta's impregnation as a 'sign' of her son's coming. Through her previous visionary narratives of the Annunciation scene, Mary has carefully prepared Birgitta for the unique feelings that signal conception of the divine: sudden, unspeakable joy; gladness of heart, soul and body; complete absence of pain. Now the 'modir of merci' arrives as the messenger, bypassing Gabriel and passing on a kind of holy women's lore of mystical pregnancy, becoming a mother to a mother, both bearing the same Son. Just as the Virgin became pregnant with the Word made flesh so Birgitta finds herself pregnant not with a child but with the Word of God, with Christ present in her visions and speaking again to the world.

Several critics have picked up on the importance of Birgitta's mystical pregnancy for her prophetic vocation.[57] Sahlin considers at length the phenomenon of the mystical pregnancy and its function in Birgitta's life, arguing that Birgitta does intend to claim that she truly somatically experienced the stirring feeling of a child (it was not simply metaphorical or 'felt' within a vision) and that she considered this as a physical correlation to her visionary incarnation of Christ. Birgitta, of course, was well acquainted with pregnancy, having had

---

[56] On the conceptual conflation of womb and heart in medieval religious literature, see Caroline Walker Bynum, *Wonderful Blood: Theology and Practice in Late Medieval Northern Germany and Beyond* (Philadelphia: University of Pennsylvania Press, 2006), esp. 158–61; Jacqueline E. Jung, 'Chrystalline Wombs and Pregnant Hearts: The Exuberant Bodies of the Katherinenthal Visitation Group', in *History in the Comic Mode: Medieval Communities and the Matter of Person*, ed. Bruce Holsinger and Rachel Fulton (New York: Columbia University Press, 2007), esp. 227–8; and Margaret Bridges, 'Ubi est thesaurus tuus, ibi est cor tuum: Towards a History of the Displaced Heart in Medieval English', in *The Heart*, ed. Agostino Paravicini Bagliani, *Micrologus* 11 (Turnhout: Brepols, 2003), 501–18.

[57] See Sahlin, *Voice of Prophecy*, 78–107; Salmesvuori, *Power and Sainthood*, 81–90; Bruce, '"I am the Creator": Birgitta of Sweden's Feminine Divine', esp. 38–40; Børresen, 'Birgitta's Godlanguage', esp. 38–9; and Joan Bechtold, 'St Birgitta: The Disjunction Between Women and Ecclesiastical Male Power', in *Equally in God's Image: Women in the Middle Ages*, ed. Julia Bolton Holloway, et al. (New York: Peter Lang, 1990), 88–102.

eight children, although when she received this vision she had been widowed and celibate for several decades. Sahlin convincingly suggests that Birgitta was not at all expressing a 'longing to return to the time when she gave birth to her physical children' as presumed by some critics but rather that she 'felt authorized through the maternal role to serve as an outspoken prophet and vehicle of divine revelation'.[58] Samuel Fanous pushes beyond these conclusions to argue that this passage presents Birgitta as a new *theotokos*:

> While Birgitta's spiritual pregnancy appears to be a sign of contemplative union, a formula reiterated by Christ, it is limiting to confine her mystical pregnancy to the level of signification. For *imitatio* is not merely a matter of exciting the affections through signification, but of union with the sign through prolonged contemplation, of becoming. Birgitta therefore does not merely *identify* with Mary, in a real sense she *becomes* the God Bearer.[59]

Directly equating Birgitta as a kind of new Mary suggests the profound power of Birgitta's *imitatio Mariae* to surpass metaphor and radically form her visionary vocation. This interpretation finds echoes in a medieval discussion of Birgitta's sanctity, a Latin treatise by an unknown continental Franciscan friar, written sometime between 1391 and 1409.[60] A defence of the authenticity of Birgitta's revelations, the text contends that 'it was theologically necessary for God to have used a woman as a medium of divine revelation', in part because both Birgitta and the Virgin Mary 'fulfill similar functions in salvation history as mediators of spiritual life'.[61] God returns to earth, again through a woman, and not coincidentally. Such an explanation was an uncommon defence of Birgitta's authenticity.[62]

Indeed, mystical pregnancy such as this was not unusual in the later Middle Ages, but Birgitta's experience stands out as exceptional for several reasons.[63] Not only is it unlikely she was aware of or heavily influenced by other vision-

---

[58] Sahlin, *The Voice of Prophecy*, 84.
[59] Fanous, 'Becoming Theotokos', 276–7.
[60] Sahlin discusses this little-known text in her article 'The Virgin Mary', 228–32. It is found in Lincoln, Lincoln Cathedral Chapter Library, MS 114, fols 18vb–24va, and remains unedited.
[61] Sahlin, 'The Virgin Mary', 229.
[62] Sahlin, 'The Virgin Mary', 231.
[63] Sahlin elaborates on Birgitta's exceptionalism; see Sahlin, *Voice of Prophecy*, 86–8. On other examples of medieval priests, nuns and holy women experiencing mystical pregnancies, see Sahlin, *Voice of Prophecy*, 86–8; Dyan Elliott, *The Bride of Christ Goes to Hell* (Philadelphia: University of Pennsylvania Press, 2012), 225–7; Caroline Walker-Bynum, *Holy Feast and Holy Fast: The Religious Significance of Food to Medieval Women* (Berkeley: University of California Press, 1987), 203–4, 256–8; and Rosemary Drage Hale, 'Imitatio Mariae: Motherhood Motifs in Late Medieval German Spirituality', in *Medieval German Literature: Proceedings from the*

aries' similar experiences, she stood out from them as a mother among female virgins or celibate men. Significantly, the pregnancy physically manifested Birgitta's prophetic voice, authenticating her words through a bodily sign – a meaning unique to this saint. Most significantly, however, is the unusual situation where the meaning of her mystical pregnancy was explained to her by Mary herself, the figure of imitation. Salmesvuori proposes that Mary's interpretation and authorization of the phenomenon from within the context of the vision itself would have encouraged Birgitta and assuaged her confessors in the face of the danger that it was in fact diabolical and not holy, 'since she had felt that Peter's and Mathias's [her confessors] first reactions to her belly's movements were indeed somehow skeptical'.[64] This is another example of how Mary provides the proper interpretation, superceding men's understandings, endorsing Christ's presence in the world not simply as a mother but as the mother whose body fulfilled – interpreted – scriptural prophecies. Mary's comforting words to Birgitta at the time of the mystical pregnancy validate the *maternality* of the role of outspoken prophet, which, I would add to Sahlin's argument, also extends to the maternal role of author – of textual creator.

Just as the result of the conception of the Word of God is the body of the living Christ, so the result of Birgitta's channelling of God's word is the body of written revelations, the *Liber Celestis* text itself.[65] Writing offers embodiment to her transitory visionary experiences, giving a material codex body to the transmission of the divine through her fleshly body. Fanous also makes this connection, extending it beyond the visionary text: 'As Mary gave birth to the Word, Birgitta becomes the Theotokos, re-birthing the *Logos* through her revelations, begetting spiritual children through her personal witness, and bringing forth Vadstena and the Order.'[66] The last line of the mystical pregnancy passage, I think, unlocks the full convergence between Annunciation, Incarnation and Birgitta's visionary vocation: as Mary explains, the mystical pregnancy – indeed all the visions – are 'þe comminge of mi son into þi herte'. Birgitta has a divine mandate to promulgate them because by their means 'þou sall shewe to mi sonnes frenndes, and mine, oure will'. The

---

23rd International Congress on Medieval Studies, Kalamazoo, Michigan, May 5–8, 1988, ed. Albrecht Classen (Göppingen: Kümmerle, 1989), 129–45.

[64] Salmesvuori, *Power and Sainthood*, 84.

[65] Sahlin, *The Voice of Prophecy*, 84. Similarly, the *Offenbarungen* (*Revelations*) of German Dominican nun Margaretha Ebner (1291–1351) records her mystical pregnancy and 'giving birth' to a speech in great pain, as well as feeling a strong desire to suckle the baby Jesus when in the material presence of her own book; see Philipp Strauch, ed., *Margaretha Ebner und Heinrich von Nördlingen. Ein Beitrag zur Geschichte der deutschen Mystik* (Freiburg/Tübingen, 1882), 59 and 120. (My thanks to Ricarda Wagner for this reference.)

[66] Fanous, 'Becoming the Theotokos', 277.

mystical pregnancy functions as a sign for the world of Christ's true presence in Birgitta's visions, and it also entails the birth of a book to bring to term these signs. Thus Birgitta will fulfil Mary's command not just by passively receiving the revelations, but by actively transforming them into texts to be shown to 'frenndes' of Christ and Mary: fellow readers. Birgitta's progeny are now prophecies; her children are her books; her incarnate Christ is captured on the page for all the world to read.

Julian of Norwich and her texts

A few years after Birgitta's death at sixty-eight, a thirty-year-old English woman rested in her sickbed waiting to die. Surrounded by her mother, priest and others, she suddenly received a divine revelation which she would spend the next four decades contemplating, interpreting and writing. We know little about Julian of Norwich (*c.* 1342–after 1416) except the testimony of her own texts, the shorter *A Vision Showed to a Devout Woman* and the longer *A Revelation of Love*, and some sparse evidence of surviving wills. She became the anchoress in the church of St Julian's, Norwich, no later than 1393/4, about the age of fifty, and was still enclosed until at least 1416, into her seventies. Julian's life before her anchoritic enclosure remains a mystery: the current consensus leans towards her enclosure as a nun at Carrow, but there remains the possibility she was a laywoman – possibly married with children – before she became an anchoress.[67] In any case most critics agree with Nicholas Watson's argument that her initial account of her visionary experience, *A Vision* (aka the Short Text), was written sometime in the middle of the 1380s, while its extensive rewriting and expansion as *A Revelation* (aka the Long Text) was probably begun in the 1390s and concluded some time between then and her death.[68] Unlike Elizabeth and Birgitta, Julian does not appear to have had any intermediary in the production of her texts, and their use of the first-person point of view gives them an unusual autobiographical immediacy. They are tightly structured, delicately crafted works that operate as cohesive wholes, far from episodic or fragmented. In content, style and tenor, Julian's visionary accounts differ dramatically from Elizabeth and Birgitta's: she painstakingly describes a series of striking visual images and aural messages received during

---

[67] On Julian's life and writings, for a current introductory overview see Nicholas Watson and Jacqueline Jenkins, eds, *The Writings of Julian of Norwich: A Vision Showed to a Devout Woman and A Revelation of Love* (Philadelphia: Pennsylvania State University Press, 2006), 1–10; Grace Jantzen's *Julian of Norwich: Mystic and Theologian* (New York: The Paulist Press, 1987; new ed., 2000); and Christopher Abbott, *Julian of Norwich: Autobiography and Theology* (Cambridge: D.S. Brewer, 1999).

[68] See Watson, 'The Composition', 666–7, 678.

her visionary experiences, from which she spins out abstract, conceptually sophisticated theological meanings. But at the same time, this anchoress and her writings are clearly part of the broader English movement in women's spirituality that brought Elizabeth and Birgitta's texts to England, and it is entirely possible that Julian knew of them, as Margery Kempe did. And like the other three holy women examined in this chapter, Julian also relies heavily on Mary as a formative figure who appears in her visions in order to affirm Julian's authority *as a woman*, not only as a visionary.

Critics have given enormous attention to Julian's innovative presentation of God as Mother, and less attention to the Mother of God and her presentation. In *A Revelation*, Julian writes that Christ showed her the Virgin Mary three times: 'the furst was as she conceived; the secunde was as she was in her sorowes under the crosse; and the thurde was as she is now, in likinge, worship and joy' (*Rev.* 25: 31–3).[69] The first view of Mary, when she conceived Christ, is part of the first revelation in both texts, located in section four in *A Vision* and in the fourth chapter in *A Revelation* (which will be the initial focus here).[70] Julian presents the Annunciation scene stripped of all its usual iconographical decorations: no study, no open scripture, no books, no ray of light, not even Gabriel himself:

> In this, he brought our lady Saint Mary to my understanding. I saw her ghostly in bodily likenes, a simple maiden and a meeke, yong of age, a little waxen above a childe, in the stature as she was when she conceivede. Also God shewed me in part the wisdom and the truth of her soule, wherin I understood the reverent beholding that she beheld her God, that is her maker, marvayling with great reverence that he would be borne of her that was a simple creature of his making. For this was her marvayling: that he that was her maker would be borne of her that was made. And this wisdome and truth, knowing the greatnes of her maker and the littlehead of herselfe that is made, made her to say full mekely to Gabriel: 'Lo me here, Gods handmaiden.' In this sight I did understand sothly that she is more then all that God made beneth her in worthines and in fullhead. For above her is nothing that is made but the blessed manhood of Christ, as to my sight. (*Rev.* 4:24–35)

The scene is stripped down to the solitary figure of Mary, newly pregnant with God – and pregnant with wonder about this event. Only her final response to

---

[69] Quotations from Julian's writings are identified as either from *Vis.* (*A Vision Showed to a Devout Woman*, the Short Text) or *Rev.* (*A Revelation of Love*, the Long Text) and cited by chapter and line number from the edition by Watson and Jenkins, *The Writings of Julian of Norwich*.

[70] The relationship between the Short and Long Text's versions of this vision will be discussed below.

Gabriel remains from the biblical version: *Ecce, ancilla domini* (Luke 1:38). In Julian's texts, the moment of the Incarnation is not about modelling female literacy, or practical prayer habits, nor is it even a 'crude claim for the orthodoxy and authority of her vision.'[71] Rather, this Annunciation scene draws on what Mary's book, here implicit, otherwise represents: the transformation of Old Testament to New, the interpretive act of the Incarnation itself, transforming Word into flesh. She witnesses Mary's reverent beholding at the moment of the Incarnation, and sees in it a model of how to see, conceive, interpret and thus transform into text her own revelations. The visionary moment supplies a necessary paradigm of *how* to interpret the visions themselves, and indeed how to process all things ineffably divine into human comprehension: an incarnational hermeneutics. Julian utilizes the metaphor of Christ as God made man (the ultimate joining of signified and sign) as a hermeneutic tool with which to understand the theological meanings behind her visions (the signification behind the sign). With Mary as interpretive key, I would argue, Julian was able take *A Vision* and 'unlock' its fuller, deeper meanings, to interpret their theological significances and present them in the radically expanded *A Revelation*. This understanding of Mary in Julian's texts positions the Mother of God as very literally embodying a mode of seeing, reading and writing the divine, a mode necessary to the comprehension of the divine on earth.

While such a claim has not been made directly before, several critics have briefly acknowledged the importance of the Annunciation scene and its relevance to Julian's reception and understanding of her visions. Maud Burnett McInerney suggests that Mary's 'pregnancy is still invisible, latent, known only to Mary herself – and to Julian. The emphasis is not therefore on the visible pregnancy but on the experience of wonder and joy at the conception of Christ, which at this moment unites Julian and Mary in secret knowledge.'[72] Elisabeth Dutton also distinguishes the Virgin's body from her behaviour: 'It is not Mary's motherhood *per se* which interests Julian, but rather her responses to God, which Julian appropriates as models for devotional response.'[73] Yet, I would argue, the Annunciation scene does underscore the vital connection between Mary's motherhood and her responses to God: the physical conception of Christ coincides with spiritual and intellectual conception of God. In their notes to their edition of *A Revelation*, Nicholas Watson and Jacqueline

---

[71] Vincent Gillespie and Maggie Ross, 'The Apophatic Image: The Poetics of Effacement in Julian of Norwich', in *The Medieval Mystical Tradition in England*, V, ed. Marion Glasscoe (Cambridge: D.S. Brewer, 1992), 64.

[72] Maud Burnett McInerney, '"In the Meydens Womb": Julian of Norwich and the Poetics of Enclosure', in John Carmi Parsons and Bonnie Wheeler, eds, *Medieval Mothering* (London: Garland, 1996), 166.

[73] Elisabeth Dutton, *Julian of Norwich: The Influence of Late-Medieval Devotional Compilations* (Cambridge: D.S. Brewer, 2008), 154.

Jenkins support this claim when they point out that 'Mary's reverent marveling parallels Julian's "wonder and marvayle" ... suggesting a wider parallel between Annunciation and revelation, as both in different senses bring Christ to birth in the world'.[74] Mary undoubtedly serves as a model for receiving the divine, but also as a model specifically for the centrality of obedience and humility in devotion in general, Vincent Gillespie and Maggie Ross have argued. They describe how 'her exploration of a traditional image allows, and indeed requires, the reader to make the connections and parallels between the acts of obedience and humility that bind together Christ, Mary and Julian in a trinity of homely reverence and self-emptying humility'.[75] In a later article Gillespie and Ross shift to emphasize the broader methodological potential of this obedience and humility:

> Julian's re-enactment in ch. 4 of Mary's yielding of control and self-will in the Annunciation was the key to her own openness to the showings, and her willingness to 'conceive' of their truth (the gynecological pun is Julian's, not ours), and that readers of her text needed to aspire to the same condition, which Julian calls 'mekenes': 'Lo me, Gods handmayd.' In modern terms, this translated into a willingness to listen to the text without preconceptions and without a pre-formed interpretive agenda.[76]

Thus obedience and humility become a prerequisite for successful interpretation of the text not only by herself but also by us, its readers and critics. Such a metatextual function begins to point to the expansive importance of the Virgin as hermeneutic key.

Yet there is a missing link in scholarly understanding thus far of the Annunciation scene, a link that ties together these individual points to reveal the profundity of Julian's *imitatio Mariae*: the present absence of Mary's book. I suggest that here Julian silently draws upon the tradition of the Virgin's transformative reading of the Old Testament into a conception of the New in her womb. Fully developed by the late fourteenth century, this tradition would have surrounded her, and was prevalent in visual art, in the liturgy, in devotional texts and in anchoritic texts Julian likely read: Aelred's *De Institutione Inclusarum* and *Ancrene Wisse*.[77] Both before and even after her reclusion she would have encountered Mary as a reader in some form

---

[74] Watson and Jenkins, 136, note to *Revelation* ch 4, ll. 28–9.
[75] Gillespie and Ross, 'Apophatic Image', 64. Also, 'the individual soul longing for the incarnation of meaning must take as its paradigm the humble obedience of Mary at the Annunciation in yielding control and self-will, in submitting to the imperatives of becoming God's meaning' (55).
[76] Vincent Gillespie and Maggie Ross, '"With mekenes aske perseverantly": On Reading Julian of Norwich', *Mystics Quarterly* 30 (2004): 131.
[77] On how these texts deal with the Annunciation, see chapters 1 and 2 of this book.

or another, such was its ubiquity; yet even without her book, the Virgin still functioned as an interpreter of texts. The textuality of the Incarnation, the Word made flesh, lingers behind Mary's stripped-down representation as a 'simple maiden' in *A Revelation*. Christ is in many ways an interpretation of and into language and so, to use that as a methodological impetus, in pursuing these questions I advance with Gillespie's caution in mind that 'Julian's Long Text always requires us to attend deeply and suspiciously to the texture of the writing.'[78] Mapping out the paradigmatic power of this scene requires our own attention to be focused (like Julian's) simultaneously on the micro-level of syntax and diction and on the macro-level of abstract theological conclusions – two levels woven together not unlike the fleshly letter and the spiritual Word that come together in Christ. Only very close reading can reveal the depth of Julian's careful, innovative construction of her text's 'tone of seeing', the linguistic framework which defines the prime spiritual, intellectual and physical state for receiving revelation – and understanding its full meaning. The Annunciation passage, I suggest, establishes the significance of the key verbs *to behold*, *to conceive* and *to marvel*. These words function throughout her writing as 'word-knots', wherein Julian 'takes a nucleus word and winds around it strands of homonyms, grammatical variants, near-puns and half-rhymes that constitute the genetic code of her theology'.[79] I will, as much as it is possible, disentangle these word-knots – not with the goal of deciphering, but rather of mapping. Only then can we see the structure of how Julian connects Mary's pregnant body with her soul's beholding and marvelling, building a zeugmatic bridge between visionary experience and its (re)vision on the page through the creation of a text.

Something significant has been overlooked: that the verb *to behold* and its gerund *beholding* appear for the first time in *A Revelation* with reference to Mary at the Annunciation, when Julian is granted a view of Mary's soul wherein Julian 'understood the reverent *beholding* that she [Mary] beheld her God' (my italics). Thus the Virgin's reception of the divine operates as the paradigmatic model of *beholding*, what many critics agree is, in Gillespie's words, 'the core work of Julian's response to her showings'.[80] Gillespie, McNamer and Michael Raby, among others, underscore the importance of *beholding* and its web of meanings for not only the devotion portrayed in Julian's texts but also for late medieval English devotion in general. 'To behold', from OE *bihaldan*, 'to give regard to, hold in view', retains the etymological sense of understanding

---

[78] Vincent Gillespie, '"[S]he do the police in different voices": Pastiche, Ventriloquism and Parody in Julian of Norwich', in *A Companion to Julian of Norwich*, ed. Liz Herbert McAvoy (Cambridge: D.S. Brewer, 2008), 195.
[79] Gillespie and Ross, '"With mekenes aske perseverantly"', 135.
[80] Gillespie, 'Pastiche', 194.

'by' means of 'holding' in the sight or mind (from *healdan*, to hold); thus the Middle English *biholding*, 'the act of looking', as well as 'the act of applying one's mind'.[81] As with Mary's example, it is both seeing visually and comprehending intellectually. In addition, however, a specifically spiritual connotation pertains; Gillespie explains how in Julian's texts 'beholding' 'emerges as a transactional state in which God constantly beholds and comprehends us and we struggle fitfully to behold him, but fail to comprehend in him this life'.[82] The exception to this mortal failure is, of course, Mary, the only one of all humans fully able to comprehend – behold – conceive – God himself, by means of carrying Christ in her womb. She models the most complete beholding that the rest of Christianity could strive for, Julian included. The bidirectional exchange that Gillespie refers to, beholding both by and of God, likewise first occurs in the text as the object of Mary's own marvelling: 'that he that was her maker would be borne of her that was made'. The mutual indwelling theme that drives nearly all of *A Revelation* emerges originally at this moment and elegantly concretizes the abstraction of 'beholding'.[83]

'Beholding', Gillespie asserts, 'is also a viable critical methodology for reading Julian's account of that work.'[84] Julian herself uses Mary as a hermeneutic model to behold first her own visions and, second, to behold the Short Text itself in order to produce the more advanced interpretations contained in the Long Text. We, as readers, likewise must use this interpretive tool of beholding in order to fully engage the depth of meaning in Julian's texts; or, rather, to allow the texts to guide us into their meaning. In his discussion of how attention and beholding works in *A Revelation*, Raby comments that there is only one explicit imperative of *behold* directed at the reader; 'instead, Julian engages readers by aligning their sight with her own, and, in doing so, helps them to see as she saw'.[85] But how is beholding truly different from the normal acts of 'seeing' and 'understanding', beyond being marked by obedience and humility?

The trick is in the polysemy of the Annunciation itself, demonstrated by Mary holding God in sight, mind – *and* womb. Beholding is comprehending

---

[81] MED entry for *biholding*, (ger.)1, and 2. As McNamer points out, the MED fails to consult Julian's texts for examples of usage; Sarah McNamer, *Affective Meditation and the Invention of Medieval Compassion* (Philadelphia: University of Pennsylvania Press, 2010), 136.

[82] Gillespie, 'Pastiche', 194; see also Gillespie and Ross, '"With mekenes aske perseverantly"', 137.

[83] For more on mutual indwelling and motifs of space, see Miles, 'Space and Enclosure'.

[84] Gillespie, 'Pastiche', 194.

[85] Michael Raby, 'The Phenomenology of Attention in Julian of Norwich's *A Revelation of Love*', *Exemplaria* 26(4) (2014): 358.

corporally as well as intellectually. McNamer discusses this physical aspect of the term in other Middle English devotional works:

> In its original context, this Middle English term may have functioned as a mechanism for generating sensory perception itself: for generating a specific way of seeing, in other words, that had the potential for producing – in the body, as well as in the mind – an impulse toward a particular form of compassion: the protective and ameliorative action of holding.[86]

She pushes beyond the definitions offered in the MED to suggest that beholding functions 'as a distinct, Middle English way of seeing' where it is not just a synonym for 'to see' or 'to look at' but 'the sense of seeing empathetically'.[87] In gospel meditation narratives, the physicality of (imaginative) devotion generates an emotional response: 'the repeated practice of holding Jesus (as infant, child, then grown man) in a protective or loving way is what produces the perceptive habit of "beholding" him, which in turn produces an impulse to hold in an ameliorative embrace'.[88] In making this important and interesting point McNamer nevertheless overlooks how in all these vernacular representations, including Julian's texts, the first holding of Christ is *not* as an infant in arms, but as a fetus *in utero*, held within a female body. Mary's womb enveloping God made man functions as the ultimate ameliorative embrace – or rather, generative embrace. The physical compassion of Mary's motherhood, so frequently cited in reference to her gaze or weeping at the Passion, should be seen as deeply rooted in her womb's beholding at the moment of the Incarnation, where she – and the readers – first learn how to see, feel and embrace compassionately through a polysemous conception of Christ.[89]

Crucial to Julian's spinning of the word-knot *behold* is that it carries the same punning doubleness as the Middle English verb *conceiven*, 'to conceive', and indeed the metaphorical potential of both words work in tandem in the texts. Julian deliberately uses the Latinate verb for its parallel meanings 'to become pregnant' and 'to form in the mind', both inherent in its Latin cognate, the verb *concipere* (pp. *conceptus*), to take in and hold (*con-*, with + *capere*, to take); she stands at the forefront of these vernacular usages, which according to the examples from the MED emerged in the last quarter of the fifteenth century, when she is actively writing.[90] Before the vision of Mary, Julian has

---

[86] McNamer, *Affective Meditation*, 135.
[87] McNamer, *Affective Meditation*, 135.
[88] McNamer, *Affective Meditation*, 137.
[89] McNamer, *Affective Meditation*, 138; 'In Love's *Mirror*, the Virgin's gaze is specifically maternal and empathetic, holding with her eyes much as she bodily holds her son at his death.'
[90] Lewis and Short, *concipere*, v. (1); MED, *conceiven* (v. 1, 5, 6) (through Middle French *concevoir*).

already used the verb *to conceive* in its conceptual meaning twice in *A Revelation*, first in the second chapter to describe the development of her wish to receive three wounds (*Rev.* 2:33–4, 'I conceived a mighty desire to receive thre woundes in my life') and later at the opening of the fourth chapter to describe her understanding of the validity of her vision of Christ's bleeding head (*Rev.* 4:4–5, 'I conceived truly and mightly that it was himselfe that shewed it me').[91] Then we have the first – and only – instance of the word used in its concrete sense: Mary appearing 'in the stature as she was when she conceivede' (*Rev.* 4:25). What might at first seem like a default word choice actually reveals itself as a core syntactic strategy for highlighting the Virgin's role as hermeneutic key. She embodies the dual meanings of *conceive* in the pattern of the Incarnation. Using the polysemous power present in 'to behold' and 'to conceive' parallels the acts of mental understanding and physical pregnancy, so that when Julian receives visions 'in her sight' she becomes like Mary receiving Christ in her womb. Thus even on the etymological level, Barr's claim holds that 'physicality is inextricable from the cognitive processes that are nonetheless necessary for her attainment of transcendent knowledge. For Julian, analytic reflection and interpretation, the cognitive work that gives rise to the fullest understanding of her visions, are interdependent with physicality.'[92] With each word Julian carefully builds the parallel between Annunciation and revelation; or rather, the parallel permeates every level of her visionary experience and the texts it engenders.

The Annunciation passage utilizes another word-knot that motivates the text in much the same way as *to behold*: the verb *to marvel* and its gerund *marvayling*. Julian comprehends Mary's '*marvayling* with great reverence that he would be borne of her', continuing on to elaborate that 'this was her *marvayling*: that he that was her maker would be borne of her that was made' (*Rev.* 4:28–31; my italics). 'Marvelling' is as core to Julian's critical vocabulary as the term 'beholding', and indeed both terms, when used in the Short Text,

---

[91] The pun on 'conceive' takes on startling force when we also realize that this Middle English word 'meane' ('without any meane') denotes 'sexual intercourse' (from OE *gemaene*) as well as 'an intermediary' (from OF *mëain*); see MED *mene*, n.(1) a, and n.(2), b. Like the Incarnation, sex is missing from this conception. On the polysemy of the word 'mean' in Julian's writings see also Gillespie and Ross, '"With mekenes aske perseverantly"', 137–8; 'Apophatic Image', 61–2, fn. 28: 'Julian's lexical exploration of the word *mene*, as a noun, adjective, and verb, is one of the most dazzling illustrations of her verbal dexterity in creating semantic clusters of "word-knots"... Julian's exploitation of the polysemousness of this word means that it becomes the meeting place for many of her key ideas, perceptions, responses and expressions.' See also Dutton, *Julian of Norwich*, 70–5, especially about its relation to the Dutch *minnen*, to love.

[92] Jessica Barr, *Willing to Know God: Dreamers and Visionaries in the Later Middle Ages* (Athans, OH: Ohio University Press, 2010), 118.

consistently survive unchanged in the Long Text. The force of this word is again illuminated by its non-English cognates. Etymologically speaking, Mary marvels twice-over here: the Middle English verb *merveillen*, 'to marvel', and the noun *merveille*, 'marvel' came through the Anglo-French *merveille*, from the Latin adjective *mirabilis* which derived from the Latin deponent verb *mirari*, to wonder, marvel at, admire (ultimately from Greek μειδάω).[93] This is the same origin as the English word 'mirror' (again through Anglo-French), and the same, too, for our word 'miracle', from the Latin noun *miraculum*, also from *mirari*.[94] Thus as a word-knot Julian's 'marvel' offers a rich semantic cluster: it is an act of wonder, admiration, miraculousness, reflection, self-reflection, sight and insight. It is not only awe, but also appreciation; it is not only perceiving the other, but conceiving the self. Mary's marvelling acts like a mirror for Julian, enabling her to see herself in the Mother of God, and to mimick Mary's model of reverent reflection. Emerging out of this word *marvel* is the mirroring function of Julian's *imitatio Mariae*, where in the Annunciation she can conceive of her identity as visionary and interpreter of visions.

Moving forward in *A Revelation* reveals the full force of the Annunciation passage and its undergirding of these terms, *behold, conceive* and *marvel*. Once Mary has modelled them through her response to God, Julian returns to them again and again as ways of defining the ideal reader response to both her text and to God's presence in the reader's own life. The words which first describe Mary's reaction at the Annunciation – beholding, marvelling – become linguistic signals for proper devotion, driving the prose itself. Julian goes so far as to explicitly point out this connection when she returns to expand upon the interpretation of her showings in the sixth and seventh chapters of *A Revelation*, long passages that are not present in *A Vision*. Towards the end of the sixth chapter she sums up one overriding lesson from her interpretation thus far of her revelations: 'And therefore we may, with his grace and his helpe, stande in gostly *beholding*, with everlasting *marveling* in this high, overpassing, unmesurable love that oure lorde hath to us of his goodnes' (*Rev.* 6:46–8; my italics). Here 'we' encompasses Julian and all of her 'even-cristen', fellow Christians, towards whom she directs her book. So for both author and reader, proper devotion is actually simply standing and paying attention to the divine in two specific ways: beholding and marvelling, so clearly modelled by the Virgin at the Annunciation, and explicitly linked linguistically by the repetitions of these key word-knots. In a typically circular fashion, Mary as

---

[93] See Lewis and Short, entries for *mirari, miraculum, mirabilis*; OED entries for 'to marvel' (v.) and 'mirror' (n.); MED entries for *merveillen* and *merveille*.

[94] On mirrors in literature and mirror-titled texts, increasingly popular in England from about 1200 on, see Bryan, *Looking Inward*, 80–3, and more generally, Herbert Grabes, *The Mutable Glass: Mirror-Imagery in Titles and Texts of the Middle Ages and English Renaissance* (New York: Cambridge University Press, 1982).

hermeneutic key enables Julian to reach this conclusion that Mary is hermeneutic key – enabling interpretion of all of her visions in order to draw out 'this lesson of love shewed' as she describes it at the end of the sixth chapter.

Julian utilizes the natural breath of the break between the sixth and seventh chapters to shift focus from the 'lesson' back to its visionary origin.[95] The seventh chapter immediately picks up to explain the source of this proper devotional attending; in its opening reproduced below, **this** refers especially to the recent guidance to 'stande in gostly beholding, with everlasting marveling', but also all the interpretations of the sixth chapter the reader has just absorbed:

> And to lerne us **this**, as to my understanding, our good lorde shewed our lady, Sent Mary, in the same time: that is to meane, the highe wisdom and truth that she had in *beholding* of her maker. This wisdom and truth made her to beholde her God so gret, so high, so mighty and so good. This gretnesse and this nobilnesse of her *beholding* of God fulfilled her of reverent dred. And with this she sawe herselfe so little and so lowe, so simple and so poor in regard of her God, that this reverent drede fulfilled her of meknes. And thus by this grounde she was fulfilled of grace, and of alle maner of vertues and overpasseth alle creatours. (*Rev.* 7:1–8; my emphasis and italics)

The Annunciation becomes a tool for teaching, for learning, for re-vision – and also, in itself, a model of devotion. The specificity of the words 'to lerne *us* this' underscores how Mary's example of beholding now extends outwards as a demonstration for the inclusive we: Julian herself, the individual reading or hearing the text and all Christians. Beholding not only characterizes a correct response to revelation and divine visitation but also extends to all worship of God, a position that unites her 'even-cristen'. In this reinterpretation of her previous vision Julian logically outlines the process of reverent beholding as Mary demonstrates it: wisdom and truth prompt beholding of God; beholding of God fills her with reverent dread; reverent dread fills her with meekness; meekness fills her with grace. Thus Julian's interpretation fulfils Gabriel's greeting to Mary from Luke 1:28, 'Ave, gratia plena' (Hail, full of grace). Verbal parallels intimately connect the original description of the showing and its interpretation several chapters later, providing a hermeneutic guide to each shared word that earns new, deeper meaning through the Long Text reflection.

The impact of the Annunciation as an interpretive paradigm helps explain some significant changes between the earlier Short Text, *A Vision*, and the later Long Text, *A Revelation*.[96] Mary's example of beholding teaches Julian how to

---

[95] Dutton convincingly argues that the chapter divisions in *A Revelation* are the author's and not later scribal additions; *Julian of Norwich*, ch. 1.

[96] On *A Revelation* and its differences from *A Vision*, see Barry Windeatt, 'Julian's Second Thoughts: The Long Text Tradition', in *A Companion*, 101–15; and Nicholas

behold her own textual production – the Short Text – and conceive the Long Text. Annunciation parallels revelation; incarnation of the Word of God parallels textual creation, that generative mothering of books. Proof of this ranges from minute edits to larger structural rearrangements. For example, it can be as subtle as the change of one word, the only word substantially altered (as opposed to added) between the Short and Long Text in the Annunciation passage. Mary responds to Gabriel, 'Lo me here, Gods handmaiden', and Julian's narrative voice continues on:

    A Vision   'In this sight I *sawe* sothfastlye' (*Vis.* 4:30)
    A Revelation   'In this sight I *did understand* sothly' (*Rev.* 4:33)

In the intervening years between the texts it is Mary's exemplary beholding that has drawn Julian to examine the difference between 'seeing' and 'understanding,' and to reflect this hermeneutical advance in this targeted edit. From first to second version Julian has advanced from passive observation to active comprehension – parallelling Mary's transformation from reader to interpreter of God's word when she conceives it.

Most dramatically, however, Julian shifts the entire structural location of the Annunciation scene between *A Vision* and *A Revelation*, suggesting its central importance as hermeneutic key for the deeper interpretation of the visions in the Long Text. The modified order of the visual images in the first revelation, when charted side by side, reveals the shift's magnitude:

A Vision
(1) Blood trickling down Christ's forehead (section 3, ll. 10–17)
(2) Little thing the quantity of a hazelnut (section 4, ll. 6–20)
(3) Mary at the Annunciation (section 4, ll. 21–32)

A Revelation
(1) Blood trickling down Christ's forehead (ch. 4, ll. 1–5)
(2) Mary at the Annunciation (ch. 4, ll. 24–35)
(3) Little thing the quantity of a hazelnut (ch. 5, ll. 7–13)

Placing the Annunciation closer to the beginning of the text perhaps expresses a realization on Julian's part that she needs to witness Mary's reverent beholding as a demonstration of how to receive her own revelations, and that this demonstration is so foundational to her interpretational model that it must be set as early as possible in the text – especially before the vision of the hazelnut, that bears so much signification and elicits so much interpretation on Julian's part. Similarly, the reader must be shown this correct way of reading her text before further visions are presented. Another edit proves how careful and

---

Watson, 'The Composition of Julian of Norwich's *Revelation of Love*'.

deliberate this change is in the ordering of the visions in the two texts (deleted words in bold, following Watson and Jenkins' editorial practice):

> *A Vision* 'This litille thinge that es made **that es benethe oure ladye Saint Marye, God shewed it unto me als litille as it hadde been a haselle notte.** Methought it might hafe fallene for litille.' (*Vis.* 4:33–4; my emphasis)

> *A Revelation* 'This little thing that is made, methought it might have fallen to nought for littlenes.' (*Rev.* 5:19–20)

It seems like Julian realized that if 'this litille thinge' is in fact beneath Mary epistomologically, it should be so textually, later in the document itself. Only then can Mary's beholding supply the necessary model for Julian's (and our) beholding of the hazelnut, and facilitate the extensive, detailed interpretation that follows in *A Revelation*, chapters six and seven.

Not only hermeneutically, but also theologically, the re-ordering clarifies the role of the Virgin. Both the Short and the Long Text conclude the Annunciation scene with the statement that 'For above her is nothing that is made but the blessed manhood of Christ' (*Vis.* 4:31–2; *Rev.* 4:34–5).[97] Applying that hierarchy to the structure of the text, it makes sense that Julian would re-order the visions in *A Revelation* to present 1) Christ in his manhood as bleeding crucifix; 2) Mary; 3) the hazelnut, representing everything 'that is made'. Thus that statement can also self-reflexively refer back to the text itself, offering a cue to the rightful order of the showings: *above her* (the first showing of Mary) *is nothing that is made* (written) *but the blessed manhood of Christ* (the opening crucifix showing). 'Made', in that reading, would include the act of writing, of making a text come alive – exactly like Christ, the Word of God, coming alive in Mary's womb. Julian is mother to the text of the revelation. In this passage I think we see her succeed in what McAvoy suggests she aims towards throughout her writing: 'Julian is striving to construct a female body which functions as both metatext and semiotic framework and which, in its doubleness, will eventually overlay *and* integrate traditional "paternal" narratives and interpretations.'[98] Mary provides that model female body. The narrative bends to the pull of her power. The Virgin's womb (re)makes the text.

---

[97] *A Revelation* adds 'as to my sight'.
[98] Liz Herbert McAvoy, '"For we be doubel of God's making": Writing, Gender and the Body in Julian of Norwich', in *A Companion to Julian of Norwich*, ed. McAvoy, 172. McAvoy also writes, 'just as modern feminist commentators such as Kristeva and Cixous have seen the bodily impact of mothers as a powerfully subversive tool in the struggle to oppose the phallogocentric discourse of traditional western thought, so Julian also recognised and exploited its potential as exegetical tool and means towards establishing her own authority as interpreter of the ineffable love of God',

Making as writing, making as creating, making as mothering: the Annunciation scene provides a powerful and flexible base from which Julian can explore and exercise her own textual activity as a woman. Like the elasticity of the word-knots *to behold* and *to conceive*, the multiplicity of meanings behind the verb *to make* is central to Julian's understanding of the Incarnation and Mary's role in it. Julian plays on a three-way pun: *maiden* (young woman, virgin)/ *made* (created)/*made* (led to do something). Italicization reveals the subtle but insistent repetition of the related words in the Annunciation passage:

> I saw her ghostly in bodily likenes, a simple *maiden* and a meeke, yong of age, a little waxen above a childe, in the stature as she was when she conceivede. Also God shewed me in part the wisdom and the truth of her soule, wherin I understood the reverent beholding that she beheld her God, that is her *maker*, marvayling with great reverence that he would be borne of her that was a simple creature of his *making*. For this was her marvayling: that he that was her *maker* would be borne of her that was *made*. And this wisdome and truth, knowing the greatnes of her *maker* and the littlehead of herselfe that is *made*, *made* her to say full mekely to Gabriel: 'Lo me here, Gods hand*maiden*.' In this sight I did understand sothly that she is more then all that God *made* beneth her in worthines and in fullhead. (*Rev.* 4:24–34)

What Mary marvels over is the fact that Christ/God 'that was her *maker* would be borne of her that was *made*'; what Julian marvels over is the fact that Mary 'is more than all that God *made* beneth her in worthines and in fullhead'. God is the ultimate creator, the maker, and yet it is a creature that must help Christ become 'created' by giving him his flesh; the comprehension of this contradiction 'made' Mary (that is, led or compelled her) to offer herself as 'Gods handmaiden'. Mary's servanthood is implicit in her creaturelyness; because she is made, she is a maiden to her maker (not to say that Julian necessarily intends this alternate meaning for the word 'maiden', but that this punning semantic overlap spins out from artful proximity to its homonyms).[99] While being 'made' to do something or acquiesce may seem like a passive mode, Julian complicates any simplication of the moment by emphasizing that Mary's active beholding creates in her the will to accept God's will; it is an active obedience and an active humility, not an apathy. For Julian, and Mary at the Annunciation, beholding *is* making: it is a mirroring of the creation of God, and in that reflection something of God may be held, and reflected again in the creation of the text. Interpretation comes from the

---

in *Authority and the Female Body in the Writings of Julian of Norwich and Margery Kempe* (Cambridge: D.S. Brewer, 2004), 95.

[99] Likewise, *maiden* (OE *maegden*) and *to make* (OE *macian*) do not share any etymological relation.

Incarnation, and the Incarnation's reliance on the female body makes the womb a powerful interpretive mechanism.

The Annunciation's construction of the womb as a powerful interpretive mechanism corresponds with interpretations of both the hazelnut motif and the motif of God as Mother, in conjunction with the Lord and Servant parable. Liz Herbert McAvoy contextualizes how the hazelnut image functions in terms of a feminized mutual indwelling:

> When examined in association with Julian's other use of gynaecentric imagery, the hazelnut encompasses perfectly all the patterns which we have seen emerge so far. Like the womb (and like Mary and all women generally) this 'litill thing' is small and intact and yet it is capable of housing within its walls future promise and growth. ... Such was the womb of Mary which housed the world's salvation within it and such is the womb of those women who will give birth to future generations of 'evencristen'.[100]

While Julian develops the womb as a metaphor, in our assessment of her works it is quite important to return to the concrete womb of Mary and 'those women who will give birth', something the Virgin's pregnant body does quite effectively in the text, returning as it does in the seventh chapter expansion. It unfurls into metaphor again as Julian discusses Christ or God as mother, describing the Trinity in similar ways. This Trinitarian work of creating can be understood as 'womb-work', described by Julian as keeping, enclosing, increasing, knitting and oneing.[101] This is one way of linking the hazelnut vision with the development of the understanding of God as mother:

> The locus of this double enclosing is the maiden Mary who simultaneously encloses and is enclosed by God. As a surrogate mother, Mary provides the physical womb in which the divine mother knits and births his incarnate self. Mary's 'poor flesh' enables the divine mother to do her motherly work ... So, the incarnation is complexly the womb-work of two mothers, one the incarnate divine mother, the other the maiden Mary. In fact, all womb-work is the co-working of two mothers, since Julian sees the generation and nurturing of all human life in the wombs of all mothers as the works of both a human mother and the divine mother.[102]

We might also conclude, thinking in a Julian way, that the importance of Mary as mother (specifically at the Annunciation), both generates and is generated by the idea of Christ as Mother. Mary's maternality, of course, does more than

---

[100] McAvoy, *Authority and the Female Body*, 84.
[101] Patricia Donohue-White, 'Reading Divine Maternity in Julian of Norwich', *Spiritus* 5(1) (2005): 27.
[102] Donohue-White, 'Reading Divine Maternity', 28.

underlie the profound development of an unusual (but not unique) metaphor of a maternal God: it also transforms how gender works in general.

Several scholars have articulated this effect in *A Revelation*. In his article on 'remaking "woman"' in the Long Text Watson argues, in sum, that 'to be "woman" in this sense is, for Julian, simply to be human; it is the inevitable, the proper metaphor for all life that is lived as flesh'.[103] This constitutes a simple yet disruptive claim for a woman to make in the patriarchical Middle Ages. Catherine Innes Parker explains this idea's roots in the God as Mother motif:

> By applying the imagery of motherhood to the incarnate Christ, Julian makes the feminine normative for the Word made Flesh, and thus all flesh. By fundamentally redefining, in feminine terms, who God is, Julian thus also redefines what it means to be created in the image of God. The human ideal, therefore, becomes feminine.[104]

By giving the Annunciation vision its due attention, we can better understand how Julian reaches such a radical conclusion through decades of beholding and marvelling; through imitating the woman who bore God; through conceiving with soul and body, despite the fallenness and femininity of that body – indeed, because of it. In turn, our critical capacity to interpret her interpretations would, in Julian's paradigm, be likewise facilitated by the very act that made God man: the conception of conception *as a cognitive process* can be located in Mary's conception of Christ. And while she never says so explicitly, Julian's *imitatio Mariae* extends to her putting quill to parchment (as we believe she did): bringing Christ alive in the world just as Mary's reading paralleled the inscription of the living Word in her womb.

These arguments about the Annunciation's significance for Julian expand considerably on many of the important arguments about the maternality of the motifs of the hazelnut and Jesus as Mother that have been made by other scholars, particularly Liz Herbert McAvoy and Nicholas Watson. Such analyses have already pushed far beyond the foundational work on Julian's development of Jesus as Mother by Caroline Walker Bynum and Sarah McNamer, and put a new broader emphasis on 'the concept of motherhood as a literal truth, metaphorical tool, textual matrix, religious ideology and philosophy'.[105] This kind

---

[103] Nicholas Watson, '"Yf wommen be double naturelly": Remaking 'Woman' in Julian of Norwich's *Revelation of Love*', *Exemplaria* 8(1) (1996): 25.

[104] Catherine Innes-Parker, 'Subversion and Conformity in Julian's *Revelation*: Authority, Vision and the Motherhood of God', *Mystics Quarterly* 23(2) (1997): 22.

[105] McAvoy, *Authority and the Female Body*, 75; see Caroline Walker Bynum, *Jesus as Mother: Studies in the Spirituality of the High Middle Ages* (Berkeley: University of California Press, 1982); Sarah McNamer, 'The Exploratory Image: God as Mother in Julian of Norwich's *Revelations of Divine Love*', *Mystics Quarterly* 15(1) (1989): 21–8; these are among the earliest and most influential of many publications on this topic.

of research has effectively rendered outdated any critical position that might assume that 'Julian actively resists aligning herself with the feminine, nor does she exploit any sense of female subjectivity for hermeneutical or authoritative purposes.'[106] The Virgin, in fact, does exactly that in Julian's texts; and yet even in the recent scholarly progress, Mary's power continues to be underestimated. This is in part because, I think, the absence of her book – her reading – in Julian's Annunciation scene occludes the crucial link between Word made flesh and vision made word (i.e. written text), that lies implicit behind Julian's understanding of the showing. Although Julian does not describe Mary with scriptures in hand, her texts bear out the assumption that she saw herself as a reading and writing woman reflecting the image of a literate Mary likewise conceiving the divine.

The *Book* of Margery Kempe

About 1393, as Julian entered the anchorhold in which she would spend the rest of her life, Margery Kempe of Lynn (*c.* 1373–after 1438) married and embarked on twenty years of childbearing. Fourteen pregnancies later, she convinced her husband to break off sexual relations so she could fulfil the spiritual life to which she converted some time before. What followed was a series of visions, roarings and cryings, pilgrimages, court trials and visits with prominent ecclesiastics and holy people, filling the pages of what many consider the first autobiography in English. *The Book of Margery Kempe* was written in stages by several amanuenses taking dictation from Margery.[107] She purportedly did not know how to write and acquired most of her extensive knowledge of con-

---

[106] David Aers, 'The Humanity of Christ: Reflections on Julian of Norwich's *Revelation of Love*', in David Aers and Lynn Staley, eds, *The Powers of the Holy: Religion, Politics, and Gender in Late Medieval English Culture* (Philadelphia: University of Pennsylvania Press, 1996), 92; as summarized by McAvoy, *Authority and the Female Body*, 167.

[107] A long, ongoing critical tradition explores issues of the textual production of the *Book*, including: Anthony Bale, 'Richard Salthouse of Norwich and the Scribe of *The Book of Margery Kempe*', *The Chaucer Review*, 52(2) (2017): 173–87; Sebastian Sobecki, '"The writyng of this tretys": Margery Kempe's Son and the Authorship of Her *Book*', *Studies in the Age of Chaucer* 37 (2015): 257–83; Nicholas Watson, 'The Making of *The Book of Margery Kempe*', in Linda Olson and Kathryn Kerby-Fulton, eds, *Voices in Dialogue: Reading Women in the Middle Ages* (Notre Dame, IN: University of Notre Dame Press, 2005), 395–434; and Lynn Staley, *Margery Kempe's Dissenting Fictions* (Philadelphia: Pennsylvania State University Press, 1994), especially the first chapter, 'Authorship and Authority'. While Staley's distinction between the character Margery and the controlling author Kempe continues to be influential if debated, for the purposes of my discussion I simply refer to the single 'Margery' as simultaneously the character, main author of the text and historical figure.

temporary devotional literature by hearing it read aloud. Her book reflects a myriad of genres, most strongly the hagiographical discourse of the virgin martyrs with which she was clearly familiar. Throughout the narrative of her book, Christ continually visits and comforts Margery in her visions, as does the Virgin Mary. While it is her 'mystical marriage to the Lord which defines and endorses her vocation as visionary and prophet',[108] Margery feeds off the persecution and humiliation she earns by living according to God's command, challenging the authority of the Church on earth and refusing to limit herself to the social expectations of wife and mother. As Windeatt explains, 'behind this is the notion that in enduring slander and abuse Kempe is re-enacting in her own experience a kind of crucifixion'.[109] Ultimately, recording these trials in a text offers a consolation to complement the consolation offered by Christ, to both Margery and her readers.[110]

Though many scholars have studied the *imitatio Christi* at work in *The Book of Margery Kempe*, its *imitatio Mariae* has received only sporadic attention. For instance, according to Gail McMurray Gibson, Margery exercises an *imitatio Mariae* inspired by the devotional model of the *MVC*, and her emulation of Mary is 'deliberate and self-conscious'.[111] In Tara Williams' ground-breaking article on the *Book*'s maternal and textual authority, she goes so far as to argue that compared to *imitatio Christi*, 'the more significant devotional model in the *Book* is the lesser-known *imitatio Mariae*' and that Margery uses motherhood, the common ground of her identification with Mary, as a source for spiritual authority.[112] Similarly, Georgiana Donavin emphasizes that while Margery's access to Mary is not through the Latinate liturgies, she nonetheless 'understands the Virgin's power over language in physical terms and according to maternal performances' especially with the multi-valent idea of 'labowr'.[113]

---

[108] Barry Windeatt, ed., 'Introduction', *The Book of Margery Kempe* (Cambridge: D.S. Brewer, 2000), 13.

[109] Windeatt, *The Book*, 'Introduction', 23.

[110] As argued by Rebecca Krug, *Margery Kempe and the Lonely Reader* (Ithaca, NY: Cornell University Press, 2017).

[111] Gail McMurray Gibson, *The Theater of Devotion: East Anglian Drama and Society in the Late Middle Ages* (Chicago: University of Chicago Press, 1989), 50.

[112] Tara Williams, 'Manipulating Mary: Maternal, Sexual, and Textual Authority in The Book of Margery Kempe', *Modern Philology: Critical and Historical Studies in Literature, Medieval through Contemporary*, 107(4) (2010): 531, 543.

[113] Georgiana Donavin, *Scribit Mater: Mary and the Language Arts in the Literature of Medieval England* (Washington, DC: Catholic University of America Press, 2012), 286. Other substantive discussions of Margery's *imitatio Mariae* include Liz Herbert McAvoy, *Authority and the Female Body*, chapter 1, 'Motherhood and Margery Kempe'; Nanda Hopenwasser and Signe Wegener, '*Vox Matris*: The Influence of St Birgitta's *Revelations* on *The Book of Margery Kempe*: St Birgitta and Margery Kempe as Wives and Mothers', in *Crossing the Bridge: Comparative Essays on Medieval European and Heian Japanese Women Writers*, ed. Barbara Stevenson and Cynthia

These important studies demonstrate how Mary is important to Margery in a complex web of ways that still need further mapping.

Margery, like Elizabeth, Birgitta and Julian, receives a vision based on the Annunciation episode in Luke, which I would suggest is far more central to understanding this powerful *imitatio Mariae* than has been yet recognized. But hers is not a momentary glimpse of the profundity of the moment, or a recollection offered by the Virgin herself; rather, as usual in the *Book*, Margery participates actively in re-enacting, and rewriting, the scriptural story. One day as Margery is engaged in her meditation she enquires of Christ, 'Jhesu, what schal I thynke?', and at his reply, 'Dowtyr, thynke on my modyr, for sche is cause of all the grace that thow hast,' Margery experiences her first vision of the Virgin:

> And than anoon sche saw Seynt Anne gret wyth chylde, and than sche preyed Seynt Anne to be hir mayden and hir servawnt. And anon ower Lady was born, and than sche besyde hir to take the chyld to hir and kepe it tyl it wer twelve yer of age, wyth good mete and drynke, wyth fayr whyte clothys and whyte kerchys. And than sche seyd to the blyssed chyld: 'Lady, ye schal be the modyr of God.' The blyssed chyld answeryd and seyd: 'I wold I wer worthy to be the handmayden of hir that schuld conseive the sone of God.' The creatur seyd: 'I pray yow, Lady, yyf that grace falle yow, forsake not my servyse.' The blysful chyld passyd awey for a certeyn tyme, the creatur being stylle in contemplacyon, and sythen cam ageyn and seyd: 'Dowtyr, now am I bekome the modyr of God.' And than the creatur fel down on hir kneys wyth gret reverns and gret wepyng and seyd: 'I am not worthy, Lady, to do yow servyse.' 'Yys, dowtyr,' sche seyde, 'folwe thow me, thi servyse lykyth me wel.' (6: 541–65)[114]

Three generations of the holy family appear in the short span of this passage, where time flexes to include all of Mary's childhood as well as two short conversations between visionary and Virgin. Though Margery reports asking Anne to be her maiden and servant, we do not hear Anne agree before Margery whisks off the newborn Mary, a startling reversal where the Mother of God is mothered by Margery. Such a maternal position is not to be underestimated:

Ho (New York: Palgrave, 2000); and Hope Phyllis Weissman, 'Margery Kempe in Jerusalem: *Hysterica Compassio* in the Late Middle Ages', in *Acts of Interpretation: The Text in Its Contexts, 700–1600*, ed. Mary J. Carruthers and Elizabeth D. Kirk (Norman, OK: Pilgrim, 1982), 201–17. On Margery's *imitatio Christi*, see, for example, Sarah Beckwith, 'A Very Medieval Mysticism: The Medieval Mysticism of Margery Kempe', in *Gender and Text in the Later Middle Ages*, ed. Jane Chance (Gainesville: University Press of Florida, 1996), 195–215.

[114] All quotations are by chapter and line number from *The Book of Margery Kempe*, ed. Windeatt.

'the domestic and housewifely services which Margery Kempe repeatedly performs for the Virgin Mary and the Christ Child in her visionary life are not naïve or childish attempts at mysticism, as they have so often been interpreted, but rather deliberate and self-conscious emulation of the Marian model'.[115] Margery dresses her adoptive daughter like herself, in white, and also projects herself onto Gabriel by making his Annunciation announcement for him seemingly before he gets a chance. Though Margery speaks first in this passage ('Lady, ye schal be the modyr of God'), her message is not her own: she announces to Mary the essence of the Gabriel's words in the Luke episode. She has become Mary's mother and, now, her angel; there is no room for other voices but Mary's and her own.

In a way, Margery does not pass up the opportunity to replace both the angel *and* the book Mary is always depicted reading at his visit: she substitutes her own body and voice for the Bible, rewriting the foreshadowing prophecy of Isaiah, cutting right through the verse's implication to its direct interpretation with Mary as the virgin that shall conceive and bear a son (Isaiah 7:14). Her statement takes on more than the power of prophecy, as she inserts herself as the Old Testament in its transformation of the *Logos* into the Word made flesh of the New Testament – her utterance takes on the power of the Word of God. By speaking as scripture itself in its typological role in the Incarnation, Margery positions herself to become 'the voys of God', where her voice and Christ's are rhetorically conflated. Barbara Zimbalist has probed the radical ways in which Margery speaks for and as the visionary Christ, and how 'Margery presents her words as the manifestation of the Word, and her *Book* purports to legitimize her aspirations to holy speech through textual representation of that Word.'[116] This argument is key for understanding the significance of this scene and the absent presence of Mary's book. While Margery's *Book* can be seen generally to supplement and indeed equal scripture in its representation of Christ's speech, at the Annunciation we see Margery physically taking the place of scripture: Mary does not hold a book in her hands, but stands alone with Margery; she does not read Isaiah, but hears the prophecy from the mouth of her visionary interlocutor from the future. Margery utters the word that will become the Word, the body of Christ, in Mary's womb.

It is predictable, then, that the scriptural account of the actual Annunciation is also silently bypassed in Margery's vision. The Incarnation moment happens outside the frame of the narrative, when Mary 'passyd awey for a certeyn tyme' while Margery continues 'stylle in contemplacyon'. Off-stage, as it were, Gabriel and the Holy Spirit do their work, work that receives no record

---

[115] Gibson, *The Theater of Devotion*, 50.
[116] Barbara Zimbalist, 'Christ, Creature, and Reader: Verbal Devotion in *The Book of Margery Kempe*', *Journal of Medieval Religious Cultures* 41(1) (2015): 3.

168   *The Virgin Mary's Book at the Annunciation*

in Margery's *Book*. Excluding Luke's account, Isaiah's prophecy and Gabriel's role in the Annunciation leaves the entire scene to women's voices (really only one – Margery and Margery's voice relaying Mary's). No non-female textual or divine mediation – even that of God – presents itself in this reckoning of the Incarnation of Christ.[117] It is only mothers and their wombs that we witness.

The calculated removal of all resonances of male-authored scripture from the scene is counter-balanced by some additions that firmly place it in a textual tradition of women's visionary accounts. Not only does Margery superimpose her own voice on that of Luke, the scriptural author of the Annunciation, she also ventriloquizes the visionary accounts of the Annunciation documented by Birgitta and Elizabeth, generating for herself a matrilineal succession of visionary models. Margery's complex relationship with these figures and their texts is well documented in the *Book* and mapped by modern researchers.[118]

---

[117] Because Gabriel, as an angel, is sexless.
[118] For discussions of Birgitta and Elizabeth and their connections to Margery, see Windeatt, 'Introduction', 9–18; Janette Dillon, 'Holy Women and their Confessors or Confessors and their Holy Women? Margery Kempe and Continental Tradition', in *Prophets Abroad: The Reception of Continental Holy Women in Late-Medieval England*, ed. Rosalyn Voaden (Cambridge: D.S. Brewer, 1996), 115–40; and Madeleine Jeay and Kathleen Garay, '"To Promote God's Praise and Her Neighbour's Salvation": Strategies of Authorship and Readership Among Mystic Women in the Later Middle Ages', in Anke Gillier, Alicia Montoya and Suzan van Dijk, eds, *Women Writing Back/Writing Women Back: Transnational Perspectives from the Late Middle Ages to the Dawn of the Modern Era* (Leiden: Brill, 2010), 38–47, on Margery and Elizabeth and Birgitta. McAvoy discusses the influence of Elizabeth and Birgitta on Margery in *Authority and the Female Body*, 44–7, as does Donavin, *Scribit Mater*, 268–71. On Birgitta and Margery in particular, see especially M. Hoppenwasser, 'The Human Burden of the Prophet: St Birgitta's Revelations and *The Book of Margery Kempe*', *Medieval Perspectives* VIII (1993): 153–62; Hopenwasser and Signe Wegener, '*Vox Matris*;' Liz Herbert McAvoy, *Authority and the Female Body*, 45–7; Julia Bolton Holloway, 'Bride, Margery, Julian, and Alice: Bridget of Sweden's Textual Community in Medieval England', in *Margery Kempe: A Book of Essays*, ed. S.J. McEntire (New York: Taylor & Francis, 1992), 203–22; S. Schein, 'Bridget of Sweden, Margery Kempe and Women's Jerusalem Pilgrimages in the Middle Ages', *Mediterranean Historical Review* 14 (1999): 44–58; G. Cleve, 'Margery Kempe: A Scandinavian Influence in Medieval England?', in *The Medieval Mystical Tradition in England V*, ed. M. Glasscoe (Cambridge: D.S. Brewer, 1992), 163–78; and Einat Klafter, 'The Feminine Mystic: Margery Kempe's Pilgrimage to Rome as an *imitatio Birgitta*', in *Gender in Medieval Places, Spaces and Thresholds*, ed. Victoria Blud, Diane Heath and Einat Klafter (London: School of Advanced Study, University of London, 2018), 123–36. There is ongoing debate about how Margery would have encountered Birgitta's visions, whether by one of the extant Middle English translations, one that does not survive, or any of the numerous Latin manuscripts; here I pick up on possible connections with the Claudius version, but further work is needed. Roger Ellis confirms that Elizabeth of Hungary's 'tretys' that Margery was exposed to was probably the *Revelations* text, as edited by McNamer; 'Margery Kempe's Scribe and

One of her priest-scribes 'red to hir many a good boke of hy contemplacyon and other bodys, as the Bybyl wyth doctowrys therupon, Seynt Brydys [Birgitta's] boke, [Walter] Hyltons boke, Boneventur, *Stimulus Amoris*, *Incendium Amoris*, and swech other' (58.4818–21), and we later read that, like Margery, 'Elizabeth of Hungary cryed wyth lowde voys, as is wretyn in hir tretys' (62:5173–4). Holy women mentioned in the *Book* such as Birgitta, Elizabeth and Marie d'Oignies each function simultaneously to legitimate Margery's status as a female visionary that was married and a mother, as well as to provide precedents for Margery's exuberant expressions of holiness, particularly her raving and weeping. She imitates them but also seeks to surpass them in sanctity; as Jessica Rosenfeld articulates this dynamic, her 'competitive relationship to other female saints thus allows her to borrow their authority while also asserting her own difference'.[119] For instance, when Christ says to Margery, 'My dowtyr, Bryde, say me nevyr in this wyse' (20:1517–33) we should understand that 'Margery's desire to supersede Birgitta in the love shown to her by Christ is entirely typical and constitutes another strategy used by her to achieve authority in the *Book*,' McAvoy explains.[120] The *Book* performs this tension both through explicitly mentioning the holy women and by implicitly parallelling their texts through rhetorical or thematic similarities.

The influence of Elizabeth and Birgitta's visionary texts on Margery's Annunciation passage, a scene so crucial for the development of the identity of all three visionaries, stands out as a significant, and under-studied, example of her relationship to other holy women. Mary's non-scriptural response to Margery, 'I wold I wer worthy to be the handmayden of hir that schuld conseive the sone of God,' closely echoes her words in Elizabeth's *Revelations* and Birgitta's *Liber Celestis* – two of the most influential books for Margery. Similarly, Margery's wish to serve Mary puts her in the footsteps of the visionaries themselves. For each woman, Mary's wish to be a part of the prophecy provides a model of the visionary's own desire to interact with the holy family – and Mary's subsequent identification as the Mother of God likewise parallels the visionary's promotion to be Mary's handmaiden. In other words, Mary shows them what participatory piety sounds and looks like. In Elizabeth's *Revelations*, as discussed earlier in this chapter, Mary explains her response to

---

the Miraculous Books', in *Langland, the Mystics and the Medieval English Religious Tradition*, ed. Helen Phillips (Cambridge: D.S. Brewer, 1990), 161–75, esp. 164–8. Barratt explores in great depth 'echoes of Elizabeth's treatise in Kempe's book' (not including the Annunciation passage) and argues that it was 'Kempe herself rather than her amanuensis who was influenced by this little-known though fascinating text' in her article 'Margery Kempe and the King's Daughter of Hungary', 190.

[119] Jessica Rosenfeld, 'Envy and Exemplarity in The Book of Margery Kempe', *Exemplaria: A Journal of Theory in Medieval and Renaissance Studies* 26 (2014): 107.
[120] McAvoy, *Authority and the Female Body*, 46.

reading Isaiah, how she desires to preserve her own maidenhood so that she may serve the maiden who bears the Son of God:

> And in þe ferste opnyng of þe bok cam to myn eyin þys word of Ysaye þe prophete: *Loo, a maydyn schal conceyve and bere a chyld &c.* Qwanne I thowte þat maydynheed schulde mich plese God, for he wolde ys Sone be bore of a maydyn, I purposede þanne in my herte and in my thowt my maydynheed for to kepe in reuerence of here, þat 3yf yt befeel me for to se here, þat I mayte in maydynheed seruyn here al þe tyme of my lyf. (V, 72)

I argue above that this sentiment, in fact almost the exact words, are echoed in Birgitta's revelation of Mary recollecting her response to the prophecy: 'I desired euir in mi herte þat I might leue and se þe time of his birth, if I might happeli be a worthi handmaiden to seruis of his modir' (I.10:18). The words of Margery's Mary closely echo both texts: 'I wold I wer worthy to be the handmayden of hir that schuld conseive the sone of God.' A fascinating contrast is how Elizabeth's text emphasizes *maidenhead*, virginity, which fits the possibility of the visionary being Elizabeth of Hungary and Naples, chaste nun. Margery omits any reference to virginity, only emphasizing the act of serving as handmaiden, fitting with her status as mother. Margery's response, 'I pray yow, Lady, yyf that grace falle yow, forsake not my servyse,' likewise parallels Elizabeth's request to serve Mary. Earlier in Elizabeth's visions, Mary offers the role of handmaiden to Elizabeth several times, saying '3yf thou wyth be myn handmaydyn, I schal be þy lady' (I, 56) and again, 'Yf þou wyth be my dowtyr, my discyple, and myn handmaydyn, I schal be þy moder, þy lady, and þy maystresse' (I, 58). Mary similarly affirms Margery's privileged position of personal service, replying, 'folwe thow me, thi servyse lykyth me wel.'[121] Citing the other parallels of this motif of handmaiden in *The Book of Margery Kempe* and Elizabeth's *Revelations*, Alexandra Barratt has also argued that 'the idea of the Virgin as a teacher or "maystresse," and of the visionary as her disciple, clearly derives from Elizabeth.'[122] The Annunciation scene, I suggest, establishes these parallels between visionary and virgin Mary, and in both cases the relationship undergirds the visionary's identity as authentic visionary and claim to spiritual authority through Mary's role in the Incarnation.

Of course, all of these iterations of the role of handmaiden, *ancilla*, recall Mary's concluding words in Luke's Annunciation, *Ecce ancilla domini*, 'Behold the handmaiden of the Lord.' Thus Margery folds the Virgin's gesture back on her self, so that she can be in the position of making the same request to serve

---

[121] The motif of Margery as handmaiden to Mary recurs many times after this initial 'hiring'. See lines 1606–08, 2802, 3037–8, 6386–7, 6560–1, 6841–2, as Windeatt notes (*Book*, 77). See also McAvoy, *Authority and the Female Body*, 51.
[122] Barratt, 'Margery Kempe and the King's Daughter of Hungary', 196.

the Mother of God – in essence, echoing Mary, Elizabeth and Birgitta concurrently. The Mary who appears to Margery is not simply Luke's young maiden but also the Mary that appears to Birgitta, and the Mary that appears to Elizabeth. *Imitatio Mariae* here becomes channelled through a ventriloquization of a shared female visionary *imitatio Mariae*, wherein prophetic authority becomes a power rooted in motherhood, whether physical or spiritual.

From generation to generation, Margery's insinuation of herself into the female lineage behind Christ echoes her insinuation into a line of female visionary foremothers, medieval holy women whom she saw as sharing her spiritual vocation. Likewise, Margery's presumptuous borrowing of the child Mary from Anne aptly parallels the series of textual and verbal borrowings which subtly connect almost every line of this passage to the Annunciation revelations of those female visionary foremothers. A kind of matrilineal succession of handmaidens, originating in the Virgin, manifests itself in Margery. Such close textual parallels create an authoritative continuum between the two recognized visionaries' experiences and Margery's visions, and through this continuum Margery's text is able to share in the authority granted to the texts of Elizabeth and Birgitta.

Yet does Margery *herself* share? She does not seem to share with Anne her rearing of the Virgin; nor does she share with Gabriel his announcement. Birgitta, Elizabeth and Luke's text may play supporting roles in Margery's Annunciation episode, as scripture and other texts frequently do throughout the *Book*. Their reverberations might be heard by the attentive reader. But Margery's voice, ventriloquizing their words without citation, dominates. Her rhetorical competition with these women can be framed as part of a structural logic of envy, as construed by Rosenfeld, where Margery is 'performing exemplary singularity, constructing a notion of exemplarity that preserves the singularity and integrity of both imitator and imitated'.[123] To push Rosenfeld's argument further, another important facet of the ethos of competition seen in the Annunciation passage and throughout the *Book* is the competitive edge to Margery's *imitatio Mariae*. Mary, as exemplar of exemplars, has a singular position within the text. I argue that Margery sets up the same motif of competition with Mary, only to cede her dominance at the last moment, in order to maintain the Virgin as a higher authority upon which she can build her own claims to spiritual authority. In other words, Margery competes with Mary, but she knows Mary must win; Mary stands as the authority that must be authoritative for Margery's power structure to hold up. We see this play out neatly in the Annunciation passage. Margery takes over as Mary's mother; she boldly prophesies to the Mother of God her future as Mother of God ('Lady, ye

---

[123] Rosenfeld, 'Envy and Exemplarity', 111.

schal be the modyr of God').[124] Then, in a satisfying power shift, Mary returns *as* the Mother of God to claim her position of power over Margery through a pointed echoing of her words: 'Dowtyr, *now* am *I* bekome the modyr of God' (my italics). Mary makes clear that *now* Margery is the daughter and no longer the mother – and that while Margery's words have come true, *now* Mary is the only one with the authority to be proclaiming the Incarnation. Margery's *imitatio Mariae* holds the competitive forces of envy in tension with the vital need for an unassailable model of holy motherhood.

This tension captured in the Annunciation scene, among the web of tensions woven throughout the text, holds together the complex narrative of the *Book*. Reading between the lines of the Annunciation scene reveals the other narratives lying hidden beneath, and emphasizes the meaningful lack of Mary's own book at an Incarnation moment that is completely elided. Without any book to compete with Mary's attention, we are left with Margery's *Book*, singular and exemplary; her textual offspring, like Mary's Christ, stands alone above all others. Donavin points towards this conclusion when she herself concludes that 'in all, *The Book of Margery Kempe* is conceived through Kempe's *imitatio Mariae*, and as the Word of Christ, offers the fruit of the Virgin Birth'.[125] Perhaps we should think of the *Book*, Margery's immortal child, as much a conception conceived in that slight moment of the visionary being 'stylle in contemplacyon' as Mary's conception of the Son of God. Perhaps we should think of Gabriel's arrival to Mary as passed over in silence because it intersects with Margery's (pro)creative envisioning of the text – being read at that exact moment by the reader. Mary's time, Margery's vision-time, her writing time and the reader's time collide and collapse together.

Conclusion

Mary emerges as prophet, visionary, contemplative, imaginative reader, interpreter and pregnant mother. For these holy women the scene of the Annunciation opened up a rich variety of aspects of Mary, most completely distinct from those aspects developed at the Passion and having little to do with her roles as queen of heaven and intercessor. This kind of *imitatio Mariae* encouraged an approach to the divine not through the body of Christ itself but through the body that bore Christ, a woman's flesh. Bynum extensively explores the gendered implications of the Incarnation for medieval Christians,

---

[124] On Margery as operating within a tradition of medieval women prophets, such as Christina of Markyate and of course Birgitta of Sweden, see Diane Watt, *Secretaries of God: Women Prophets in Late Medieval and Early Modern England* (Cambridge: D.S. Brewer, 1997), 27–37.
[125] Donavin, *Scribit Mater*, 286.

ultimately emphasizing the dominance of *imitatio Christi* over any *imitatio Mariae* performed by holy women.[126] Women, she argues, were by and large not overly concerned with their female bodies that they shared with Mary; 'in fact, religious women paid surprisingly little attention to their supposed incapacity'.[127] While true, this claim overlooks how in fact, religious women did pay quite a lot of attention to the powerful *capacity* of the female body as exemplified by the Virgin, as these Annunciation episodes insist. In other words, because of Mary at the Incarnation, they came to see the female body as not only fecund, but as multivalently generative, as transformative, even as intellectual and literary. Physical motherhood was no longer exclusively an embarrassment or irreversible step away from virginity.

Such a self-conception nuances Bynum's later statement that 'women reached God not by reversing what they were but by sinking more fully into it', a female identity and approach to the divine which she qualifies as most characterized by 'suffering (both self-inflicted and involuntary) and food (both eucharist and fasting)'.[128] When Gabriel arrives to announce the coming of Christ, there is no suffering, no food, neither wails nor weeping nor silence. Mary's mouth is neither full nor empty nor parched, but uttering the words that vocalize the transformation of Old Testament into New, of *Logos* into flesh, of the signification behind the sign of the eucharist itself. The Virgin becomes the foremost paradigm for channelling the divine, whether through visions, prophecy, or interpretation. To Elizabeth, Mary narrates her book-based prayer practice as it intersected with her emergent visionary vocation, with the Annunciation scene broken down and spread throughout the *Revelations* in order to become a kind of structural foundation for the text. With Birgitta, the Annunciation likewise appears in multiple places in her text, with significant shifts in Mary's narration that parallel Birgitta's growing confidence as a prophet committed to reform and challenging male systems of power. Through her mystical pregnancy Birgitta shares in Mary's physical conception of Christ in order to gain her powers of intellectual conception, of interpreting the truth of what men say and superceding their scholastic authority via her maternal body. Julian maximizes Mary's interpretive power by positioning her as a hermeneutic key necessary for understanding the full meaning of her own visions. While the Virgin utters her responses to Gabriel at the Annunciation, the emphasis is not on her physical motherhood, but on her metaphorical

---

[126] Bynum, *Fragmentation and Redemption*, 155: 'But there is still little reason to feel that these distinctive themes of women's religiosity were primarily an effort by women to counter the notion that they were lustful and weak. The immediate religious motive was, as it was for men, desire to imitate Jesus.'
[127] Bynum, *Fragmentation and Redemption*, 154.
[128] Bynum, *Fragmentation and Redemption*, 172, also quoted above at the beginning of the chapter.

conception of the relation between all of creation and the divine. She models how to behold, for Julian the only way for humans to effectively approach God. Margery utilizes the Annunciation scene as the first opportunity to become intimately involved in the holy family, to mimic Mary's maternal position in it, to exercise her new-found prophetic voice and ultimately to establish Mary as the imitable female authority of the *Book*.

This chapter should put to rest any assumption that Mary, 'alone of all her sex', was too unique for medieval women to emulate. After the opening of the *Liber* Christ himself insists on her imitability for Birgitta: 'take ensampill at mi moder, þe whilke, fro þe biginninge of hir life to þi ende, wald noþinge bot þat I wilde' (I.1l.24–5). In Elizabeth's *Revelations*, the Virgin herself commands an *imitatio Mariae* with the literal ventriloquization of her words: 'be ensawmple of me, say, "*To þe handmaydin of Owr Lord be yt do to me aftyr þy word*"' (VI, 82). The handmaiden emerges as a common mimetic mode for these four visionary women. While Julian more subtly draws attention to the motif by citing Mary's response to Gabriel, 'Lo me here, Gods handmaiden,' as the only direct discourse of the vision, Elizabeth, Birgitta and Margery all explicitly invoke the motif of Mary desiring to be the handmaiden to the virgin mentioned by Isaiah 7:14. At that moment when Mary steps up to become that virgin, the handmaiden of the Lord, it opens up an endlessly replicable 'understudy' handmaiden role for these holy women to step into. This shared position brings the holy women together in a female literary tradition motivated by Mary, as it simultaneously creates a new kind of virtual textual community. Though she is alone at Gabriel's announcement, when Mary shares her 'private female discourse'[129] with the visionary she offers divinely sanctioned female companionship and mentorship. When the Virgin's voice is heard through the texts of other visionary women – as when Margery reads of Mary's revelations to Birgitta and Elizabeth – this female companionship widens into female community. Margery reminds us that the positive reinforcement of such a community can be complicated by feelings of competition and envy. Nonetheless, before the male body of Christ becomes visible, it is Mary's body that brings together these holy women across time and space at her side in her solitary room. It is her channelling of the Word that legitimates their written words, rendering superfluous male authorities – at least in the sacred visionary sphere. As Mary explains to Elizabeth, 'Þer ys no broþer in þys world þat of þy spouse kan betere enforme þe þan I' (I, 56).

---

[129] Dzon, *The Quest for the Christ Child*, 187.

5

Imagining the Book:
Of Three Workings in Man's Soul and Books of Hours

The Annunciation has always been a story of suspense. In the pacing of most narrative tellings like the ones we have examined so far, the author may briefly describe what Mary is doing before Gabriel's arrival, before moving on to the real action – their conversation and the Incarnation itself. Bernard of Clairvaux introduced the tradition of dramatic suspense in the moment between Gabriel's final words, 'quia non erit impossibile apud Deum omne verbum' (because no word shall be impossible with God), and Mary's acquiescent acceptance, 'Ecce ancilla Domini: fiat mihi secundum verbum tuum' (Behold, the handmaid of the Lord; be it done to me according to thy word) (Luke 2:37–8), the whole event's climax. His Sermon IV *Super missus est* addresses the Virgin directly:

> Exspectat angelus responsum … Hoc totus mundus tuis genibus provolutus exspectat. Nec immerito quando ex ore tuo pendet consolatio miserorum, redemptio captivorum, liberatio damnatorum: salus denique universorum filiorum Adam, totius generis tui. Da, Virgo, responsum festinanter. O Domina, responde verbum, quod terra, quod inferi, quod exspectant et superi.[1]

> (The angel is waiting for your reply … For the whole world is waiting, bowed down at your feet. And rightly so, because on your answer depends the comfort of the afflicted, the redemption of captives, the deliverance of the damned; the salvation of all the sons of Adam, your whole race. Give your

---

[1] Bernard of Clairvaux, *Sermones Super missus est* from *Homilia De Laudibus Virginis Matris*, Sermon IV.8, PL 183: 83; translation, Said, *Homilies*, 53.

answer quickly, Virgin. My lady, say this word which earth and hell and heaven are waiting for.)

Bernard elaborates at length on – and thus himself effectively extends – this expectant pause. It can only be resolved by the free will of Mary to accept that 'tu es cui hoc promissum est' (you are the one who was promised) in the prophecies, and he implores her to 'responde verbum, et suscipe Verbum: profer tuum, et concipe divinum' (say the word and receive the Word: give yours and conceive God's).[2] Her 'Ecce' relieves the wait and ensures Christendom's salvation.

The appeal of Bernard's dramatic interpretation was not lost on later devotional authors. The longer *MVC* directs its readers to use the Bernardine suspension of time as a contemplative opportunity: 'Intuere hic pro Deo, et meditare, qualiter tota Trinitas est ibi exspectans responsionem et consensum hujus suae filiae singularis, amanter et delectabiliter aspiciens verecundiam ejus, et mores et verba' (Consider this for God's sake, contemplate how the whole Trinity is here, awaiting the answer and the consent of this unique maiden, considering her modesty and her manner and words with love and delight).[3] Nicholas Love then adapted the moment from the *MVC* for his *Mirror of the Blessed Life of Christ*, where he describes the Holy Trinity 'abydyng a finale answere & assent of his blessed douhtere Marie'; also waiting are Gabriel, all the spirits of heaven and all the righteous men of earth.[4] In turn the author of the late fifteenth-century N-Town *Mary Play* draws directly on Love, developing the moment of anticipation into what Richard Beadle describes as 'perhaps the first ... outstandingly effective use of stage silence'.[5] In the Salutation scene a stage direction interrupts Gabriel's long speech: 'Here þe aungel makyth a lytyl restynge and Mary beholdyth hym,' after which Gabriel gives voice to Bernard's imploring of the Virgin: 'Mary, come of and haste the, / And take hede in thyn entent.'[6] Beadle interprets this staged pause in light of the N-Town play's overall enabling of *deuote imagination*, so that 'the Virgin's silence suspends the action for a moment of contemplation on the mystery of the Incarnation'.[7]

---

[2] Sermon IV.8, PL 183: 84; translation, Said, *Homilies*, 54.
[3] M. Stallings-Taney, *Iohannis de Caulibus*, 24; trans. Taney, et al., *Meditations on the Life of Christ*, 13.
[4] Sargent, *Mirror: Full Critical Edition*, 26, l. 30.
[5] Richard Beadle, '"Devoute ymaginacioun" and the Dramatic Sense in Love's *Mirror* and the N-Town Plays', in *Nicholas Love at Waseda: Proceedings of the International Conference, 20–22 July 1995*, ed. Shoichi Oguro, Richard Beadle and Michael G. Sargent (Cambridge: D.S. Brewer, 1995), 3.
[6] Peter Meredith, ed., *The Mary Play from the N. Town Manuscript* (London: Longman, 1987), 74, ll. 1323-5.
[7] Beadle, '"Deuoute Ymaginacioun"', 5.

Suspense in Annunciation narratives, then, not only functions to dramatize the momentous happening of the Incarnation itself, but also to allow the space and time for contemplation *on* the Incarnation – that very act of imaginative prayer drawing us closer to God, a cognitive act made possible by God's drawing closer to us through Christ's humanity, as we explored in Chapter 3. Yet neither Bernard, nor the *MVC*, the *Mirror*, nor the N-Town play suspend time in the Annunciation episode quite so radically as an obscure vernacular prose work almost completely overlooked by modern scholars: *Of Three Workings in Man's Soul* (or *O3W*).[8] After a didactic section on the hierarchy of thought, meditation and contemplation, this fourteenth-century Middle English treatise expands with such detail and dwells so languorously on Mary's contemplation in the moment *prior* to Gabriel's arrival that the Annunciation scene itself begins *after* the text itself ends: his 'Hail' is the last line. Time slows as the narrator painstakingly describes how the Virgin reads and imagines herself participating in Isaiah's prophecy, all as an example for the reader. Mary's mimetic power enables the author not only to encourage devotion *to* Mary, but also to practice devotion *as* Mary, *like* Mary, the ideal contemplative. Though it is not long (only about two thousand words), *O3W* survives as the most detailed, imaginative textual consideration of the Annunciation in Middle English. The treatise testifies to the vitality of the devotional tradition centred on a literate, contemplative Mary figure. Its full examination has much to offer to our understanding of late medieval Marian devotion and the English contemplative tradition.

O3W's iteration of the scene contains many of the Annunciation motifs accumulated over the centuries and analysed in the previous chapters: she prays alone in her room; she reads Isaiah 7:14; she desires to participate on the Old Testament prophecy; she contemplates and experiences a mystical rapture. But perhaps more significantly, *O3W* combines a multiplicity of genres in order to position Mary as expert contemplative and perfect model for devotees new to meditation, both men and women. Theoretical contemplative treatise, devotional instruction, gospel meditation or life of Christ and visionary account tinged by hagiography come together for a strikingly original composition. In this way this text stands as proof of the centrality of the Virgin as a model of reading, interpretation and devotion in medieval England. *O3W* demonstrates how *imitatio Mariae* initiates the Annunciation scene reader – and viewer – into devotional practice as a way of transforming the self through the Word just as Mary was transformed by the Word. Conceiving Christ in

---

[8] The text is item M.5, O.15 in P.S. Joliffe, *A Check-list of Middle English Prose Writings of Spiritual Guidance* (Toronto: Pontifical Institute of Mediaeval Studies, 1974); and no. 5 in R.E. Lewis, N.F. Blake and A.S.G. Edwards, *Index of Printed Middle English Prose* (New York: Garland, 1985).

the soul could only happen through *imitatio Mariae* – and only then could an *imitatio Christi* become possible. One must learn how to read, think, meditate and contemplate like the Virgin first.

In the first half, *O3W* educates an inexperienced reader about the basics theory of thought, meditation and contemplation by discussing *The Mystical Ark*, commonly known today as *Benjamin major*, by Richard of St Victor (d. 1173), a Scotsman who joined the pre-eminent Cistercian Abbey of St Victor in Paris and became 'an experienced contemplative, an exceedingly skilled theologian and preacher and an unusually sensitive guide along the spiritual journey'.[9] The second half offers Mary before the Annunciation as a scene on which to practise meditating, where Mary also models the proper intellectual, emotional and physiological aspects of meditation the reader is supposed to aim towards. Such a representation builds on the long tradition of presenting Mary as the ideal contemplative, developing out of eleventh- and twelfth-century anchoritic literature, and continued in the lives of Christ genre of the twelfth through fifteenth centuries – a history examined in Chapters 2 and 3. As with guided meditations on the life of Christ like the *MVC*, readers of *O3W* are meant to use their imagination to re-create the scene in their mind and to participate in it, with the narrator teaching them about Mary's contemplative practice through his frequent insights into her thoughts and feelings. *O3W*, however, in its detailed focus on Mary's successfully ecstatic contemplation, also echoes hagiographic descriptions of visionary women and as well as their visionary accounts of Mary – in particular, Elizabeth's *Revelations* (discussed in the previous chapter). Gospel meditation and visionary text blur together; imaginative visualization and divine vision combine to bring devotees closer to God. Barbara Newman describes texts like these as 'scripted visions ... meant to help readers visualize the life of Christ so vividly that *pious imagination would shade into visionary experience*'.[10] The transferable power of *O3W*'s rendering of Mary meditating with her book can be seen in its interpolation into the Annunciation scene of a little-known fifteenth-century life of Christ called *Meditationes domini nostri*. Its afterlife demonstrates the fluidity between devotional genres that also shapes its creation, and the centrality of the literate Mary for the formation of the devotional subject in late medieval England.

This chapter will probe the possibility that *O3W* could have been originally composed by the English mystic and author Richard Rolle (*c.* 1300–1349) for a female religious reader – but that it was definitely later revised for male readers. Male readership brings us full circle to the origins of the motif of Mary's

---

[9] Grover A. Zinn, trans. and intro., *Richard of St Victor: The Twelve Patriarchs, The Mystical Ark, Book Three of the Trinity* (New York: Paulist Press, 1979), 1.
[10] Barbara Newman, 'What Does it Mean to Say "I saw"? The Clash between Theory and Practice in Medieval Visionary Culture', *Speculum* 80 (2005): 25.

reading: first developed by monks in the ninth and tenth century, then shifting in the eleventh century to be predominantly a model for enclosed women, now the image of a literate Mother of God emerges again as an exemplar for men as well as women. Or rather, male monastics have always been reading and praying like Mary, but the evidence of this particular text emphasizes how accessible this female exemplar could be to men. Mary's room was a 'gendered and potentially gendering sanctum' that male readers could enter only at the expense of their masculinity: they have to *feel* like a woman, in Sarah McNamer's words, in order to achieve the height of contemplation achieved by Mary.[11] *Imitatio Mariae* could sometimes be about compassion, as McNamer convincingly argues, while this chapter will demonstrate how *O3W*'s primary objective was to offer Mary as a model of reading, interpretation and imagination as part of meditative practice.

Finally, I examine how *O3W*'s meditation needs to be contextualized within established lay/monastic crossover devotional routines like the rosary (since *O3W* introduces its Marian meditation as part of a rosary prayer) and Books of Hours. In all these routines Mary was not merely the object, she was also the mode of devotion, an aspect that has been undervalued by many scholars. The Annunciation as one of the opening illuminations of illustrated Books of Hours prepares the devotee in the proper Marian mode of receiving and conceiving the divine, much as she functions at the beginning of lives of Christ, as well as at the start of Julian's *Revelations* where she prepares Julian to interpret her visions. This idea is made explicit by a series of striking Books of Hours' Annunciation illuminations where Mary reads and Gabriel has not yet entered, or the patron's portrait is given precedent over the angel, who hovers in the background. The Annunciation becomes about modelling meditation, with Christ's Incarnation postponed. The visual representation of the same suspended moment captured in *O3W* suggests that both authors and artists recognized the importance of Mary as model of literate devotion.

Virtually undiscussed in recent scholarship, *O3W* has received little attention since the Middle Ages. This neglect needs to be rectified, especially because of its ties to Rolle. Of the four manuscript witnesses (discussed below), one identifies 'Richard hermyte' as author, and another survives in an important Rolle anthology. *O3W* was first mentioned by C. Horstmann in *Yorkshire Writers* in 1895–6, and subsequently by Hope Emily Allen in her 1927 *Writings Ascribed to Richard Rolle*, where she dismisses the work as 'a somewhat dilute work of mysticism' and rejects its ascription to Rolle. *O3W* was first critically edited in 1995 by Stephen B. Hayes in an edited collection chapter that has

---

[11] McNamer, *Affective Meditation*, 132, where she discusses Mary in terms of compassion, but not touching on Mary's literate or interpretive modelling.

gone unremarked.[12] Hayes takes the treatise seriously, exploring its sources and parallels in English religious culture, though shying away from affirming its author's identity as Rolle or not. Regardless, the text remained ignored by Rollean scholars throughout the surge of critical interest beginning in the 1990s and continuing today.[13]

More recent work, however, has re-opened the door to its consideration. The text's next editor, Ralph Hanna, raises again the prospect of Rollean roots by including a critical edition in his volume *Richard Rolle: Uncollected Prose and Verse with related Northern Texts* (2007), where he supports the identification of Rolle as author.[14] His reasoning: Richard of St Victor is Rolle's 'favoured theorist'; the treatise's Marian devotion aligns with Rolle's presentations of Mary elsewhere (sparse though they might be) – for example, the *imitatio Mariae* in *The Commandment*; and its 'considerable rhetorical cleverness' would be worthy of the early fourteenth-century's star contemplative author.[15] The Northern language of two of the O3W witnesses, as well as its possible intended audience of enclosed women, also might be added to this list, as I will soon explain. As yet I have found no strong evidence *against* his authorship, even though it is always possible that Rolle's name was simply attached to elevate the authority of the tract.[16] Beyond Hanna's initial observations and my discussion below, much work still remains to be done to set O3W more securely in Rolle's approved canon, and to explore its ramifications for our

---

[12] C. Horstmann, ed., *Yorkshire Writers: Richard Rolle of Hampole and His Followers*, 2 vols (London: Swan Sonnenschein, 1896), 1: 82; H.E. Allen, ed., *Writings Ascribed to Richard Rolle, Hermit of Hampole, and Materials for His Biography* (New York: MLA, 1927), 364–6; Stephen B. Hayes, 'Of Three Workings in Man's Soul: A Middle English Prose Meditation on the Annunciation', in *Vox Mystica: Essays for Valerie M. Lagorio*, ed. Anne Clark Bartlett, et al. (Cambridge: D.S. Brewer, 1995), 177–99.

[13] One brief mention can be found in Bryan, *Looking Inward*, 55, fn. 72. A passage from O3W is quoted, without being named and without further analysis, in Roger Ellis and Samuel Fanous, '1349–1412: Texts', in *Cambridge Companion to Medieval English Mysticism*, ed. Samuel Fanous and Vincent Gillespie (Cambridge: Cambridge University Press, 2011), 157.

[14] EETS o.s. 329 (Oxford: Oxford University Press, 2007). This edition does not refer to Hayes' earlier edition. Other recent research on Rolle encourages a broader understanding of Rolle's authorial efforts, which would help to understand O3W as part of his corpus: Andrew Kraebel, 'Rolle Reassembled: Booklet Production, Single-Author Anthologies, and the Making of Bodley 861', *Speculum* 94(4) (2019): 959–1005; and *Biblical Commentary and Translation in Later Medieval England: Experiments in Interpretation* (Cambridge: Cambridge University Press, 2020), especially ch. 3, 'Richard Rolle's Scholarly Devotion'.

[15] Hanna, *Uncollected Prose*, lxix. *The Commandment*, esp. lines 86–96, in S.J. Ogilvie-Thomson, *Richard Rolle: Prose and Verse*, EETS o.s. 293 (Oxford: Oxford University Press, 1988), 34–9.

[16] On this phenomenon see Claire Elizabeth McIlroy, *English Prose Treatises of Richard Rolle* (Cambridge: D.S. Brewer, 2004), 10–12.

understanding of that canon. My main purpose here is to analyse the treatise as part of a Marian devotional tradition, an analysis I hope other scholars will take up again in relation to Rolle's possible authorship.

Connecting *O3W* to Rolle has many significant implications, including the dating of the text. It sets its *terminus post quem* to sometime after 1322, when Rolle's earliest works can be dated, and its *terminus ante quem* before his death in 1349. The piece contains no explicit information about its original intended audience that could help date it.[17] On the one hand, the earliest surviving manuscript of *O3W* dates to the last quarter of the fourteenth century, when the earliest surviving Rolle manuscripts tend to have been produced,[18] and which fits with the growing popularity of vernacular religious treatises in those later decades; if it was not authored by Rolle, it could have been composed later in the fourteenth century. On the other hand, if Rolle wrote it, any sources used by the text must be circulating in England and accessible to Rolle by the end of the 1340s at the latest. This *terminus ante quem* relates directly to one possible source I propose below: the *Revelations* by a nun named Elizabeth, from Hungary and living in Naples, whose visionary account was likely completed soon after her death in Italy in 1322 and would have had to make it to England within the next twenty-five years – *if* indeed it is a source for *O3W*, and *if* indeed it was Rolle who wrote *O3W*. Such indeterminancy still represents progress from our minimal knowledge of the text up to now.

Audiences, reception, manuscripts

An argument for a possible original intended audience of religious women is supported by the possibility of Rolle's authorship. He appears to have written almost all his known vernacular works for enclosed female religious readers, and later in his life. Could a nun or anchoress have been the original intended audience of *O3W* as well? Manuscript rubrics link four of Rolle's vernacular works to enclosed women: *Ego Dormio* to a nun of Yedingham, *The Commandment* to a nun of Hampole and *The Form of Living* to the anchoress Margaret Kirkby, also the recipient of the *English Psalter* (purportedly).[19] No such rubric explicitly identifying a female addressee survives with *O3W*. Only once does the narrator address an ongoing connection between himself and the intended

---

[17] Hanna does not identify any borrowings from his other works that may set it in the known order of his corpus. For a chronology of Rolle's other writings see 'Excursus I', in Nicholas Watson, *Richard Rolle and the Invention of Authority* (Cambridge: Cambridge University Press, 1991), 273–94.

[18] See Ralph Hanna, 'The Oldest Manuscript of Richard Rolle's Writings', *Scriptorium* 70 (2016): 105–15.

[19] Watson, *Richard Rolle*, 32.

reader, when he introduces the Marian meditation, 'qwylke þow hase prayed me of before tyme' (221–4). Justifying a text as requested by a (female) reader was a typical explanation given by a mentoring male confessor; its formulation here resembles the same in other texts written for enclosed women, such as Aelred's *De Institutione*. The fact that the phrase was omitted from one copy of *O3W*, Cambridge, Magdalene College, Pepys Library MS 2125 (or from its source), suggests that later readers reacted to that moment as anomalous and perhaps recalling its origins with a specific, individual intended reader, or perhaps evoking that recipient as a woman.

There is much in the treatise's content and rhetoric to suggest the idea of a religious woman as recipient. Like Rolle's English works, *O3W* is an accessible vernacular text aiming to support a spiritual life, particularly for one just embarking on it, by educating the reader and providing an opportunity to practice what she has learned. More like *The Commandment*, *O3W* adopts a mostly distant, impersonal voice and lacks the intimate tone of personal guidance found in the epistles *The Form of Living* and *Ego Dormio*. There is a defined 'I' of the narrator, who speaks directly to the reader ('you') quite frequently with directions and guidance, but the impression of a close relationship does not emerge here as it does in *The Form of Living*, for example. Thus while we do not see in *O3W* precisely the same 'expression of intimacy' as Nicholas Watson identifies in the other Rollean English writings, *O3W* could still fit with 'what Rolle considers to be his divinely appointed function as a teacher of women' and his 'special role to play in persuading them to the life of perfection'.[20] However, this treatise does demonstrate an intimate, tender elaboration of a female figure perfectly parallelled to those enclosed women he felt so drawn to direct: the reading Virgin Mary, here a devout contemplative protected from the distractions – and temptations – of the world. Imitating the Virgin in *O3W* fits into the way that Rolle positions his readers elsewhere as women, a gendered position, Sarah McNamer argues, that best enables them to feel compassion. Like many of the texts dubiously attributed or misattributed to Rolle, the treatise's connection to him demonstrates how 'the name Rolle functioned as an important cultural signature in late medieval England' in the mode that McNamer suggests: 'What Rolle authorized was a practice embedded in affective meditation as a genre as it developed in England among a broad array of readers – male as well as female, lay as well as religious: the practice of feeling like a woman.'[21] While Rolle's female intended reader accomplishes much of this gendering in his other works, Mary also briefly appears as an exemplar of compassion in the Passion meditations attributed to Rolle. In *Meditation*

---

[20] Watson, *Richard Rolle*, 232, 225.
[21] McNamer, *The Invention of Compassion*, 119. See also McIlroy, *The English Prose Treatises*, 18–20, on the gender of Rolle's initial audience for the vernacular works.

B, for example, Rolle 'presents an exercise in which, through the process of reading, the engaged meditator directly recovers the sacred space and time of the Passion' – an exercise guided by the grieving Virgin Mary.[22] Adding *O3W* to Rolle's oeuvre expands that gendered modelling beyond the Passion to the Annunciation, beyond compassionate feeling to include the mechanisms of devotion itself: Mary's reading, interpreting, and imagining forms the basis of the reader's training in meditation and contemplation. Meditation on the Passion is possible because of the reading of the Annunciation. No longer the purview of male monastics – like Richard of St Victor, who is an *auctor* as a theorist and not necessarily as a practitioner – contemplation is best done like a woman, and like a mother.

But like many texts in this study, Mary as a female model of meditation does not limit her relevance to female readers. In contrast, the manuscript history of *O3W* suggests a male audience. Four surviving copies have been identified:

(1) Cambridge, Trinity College, MS O.8.26, fols 73v–78v
(2) Cambridge, Magdalene College, Pepys Library MS 2125, fols 80v–82v
(3) London, BL, MS Sloane 1009 (vol. 1), fols 25v–26v (abbreviated)
(4) Cambridge, CUL, MS Dd.5.64, part 3, fol. 42v (first few lines only)

The most complete witness is found in Cambridge, Trinity College O.8.26, fols 73v–78v, appearing in the first part of a manuscript created from four originally separate booklets/fascicles.[23] The relevant section dates from the middle or the third quarter of the fifteenth century, and is surrounded by almost all Latin texts, some of which suggest a Carthusian provenance.[24] *O3W* opens with a rubric containing title and author: 'Off thre wyrknyges in mannes saule. Richard hermyte,' with a prominent 'IHC' monogram in the top margin by the same hand, in typical Rollean fashion. The manuscript is in a Northern

---

[22] McIlroy, *The English Prose Treatises*, 45; see also W. Hodapp, 'Sacred Time and Space Within: Drama and Ritual in Late Medieval Affective Passion Meditations', *Downside Review* 115(4) (1997): 240.

[23] M.R. James, *The Western Manuscripts in the Library of Trinity College, Cambridge: A Descriptive Catalogue*, 4 vols (Cambridge: Cambridge University Press, 1900–4), 3: 418–20 (item 1401). Linne R. Mooney, *Index of Middle English Prose Handlist XI: Manuscripts of the Library of Trinity College, Cambridge* (Cambridge: D.S. Brewer, 1995), 130. See also manuscript description in Hanna, *Uncollected Prose and Verse*, liii–liv. Note that Hayes and some other sources mistakenly print 'MS 0.8.26' whereas the correct shelfmark is with the letter 'O': 'MS O.8.26'.

[24] For instance, Alcuin's *Speculum*, a *Meditatio passionis Cristi* ascribed to Bernard and, most tellingly, a document concerning the foundation of the Carthusian order ('Confirmacio Ordinis Carthusiensis'). On the last folios of the Trinity manuscript a second vernacular text can be found, a short note titled 'Richardus Hampole de contricione', edited for the first time by Hanna, *Uncollected Prose and Verse*, 89.

English dialect and placed near Lincolnshire.[25] Trinity thus presents a reliable copy (used as a base text by both Hayes and Hanna), ascribed to Richard Rolle, copied in the north and thus geographically linked to Rolle, and probably created by and for (male) Carthusian readers.

Another version closely related to Trinity also links *O3W* to Rolle: CUL, MS Dd.5.64, fol. 42v, the last folio of the last of the three manuscripts that were combined together into this single codex.[26] The earliest surviving copy of *O3W*, CUL Dd.5.64 dates to the end of the fourteenth century and has unknown provenance and readership, though its Northern language links it geographically to Rolle's corpus. Unfortunately only the first few sentences have been preserved before the entire volume cuts off abruptly at the end of the quire; probably once a full copy of the text, now it is incomplete due to the loss of a quire. CUL Dd.5.64 represents 'one of the most important manuscripts conveying Rolle's English texts'.[27] Though the scribe does not explicitly attribute *O3W* to Rolle, its inclusion in such an anthology suggests it was strongly connected to if not assumed to be authored by him.

The other two witnesses do not name an author, but do suggest male readership like the Trinity manuscript. A full copy of *O3W* can be found in Cambridge, Magdalene College, Pepys Library MS 2125, fols 80v–82v (booklet 2 of the second manuscript section combined to create this book).[28] Also found in this booklet, dated to the end of the fourteenth or beginning of the fifteenth century, are many other relevant vernacular religious texts: several by Rolle, including two copies of *The Form of Living* and *The Commandment*, and *Ego Dormio*, and texts related to the Virgin, such as the item directly following *O3W*, 'The rule of the life of our lady' (IPMEP 22). Hayes suggests a connection to the Birgittines of Syon Abbey based on the inclusion of a commonly excerpted chapter of Birgitta of Sweden's *Revelationes*, VI:65, on the contemplative and active life, but the other three surviving copies bear no clear connection to Syon so that claim must remain speculative – and indeed, I think it unlikely, since Birgitta's name has been removed from this

---

[25] Angus McIntosh, M.L. Samuels and Michael Benskin, *A Linguistic Atlas of Late Mediaeval English*, 4 vols (Aberdeen: Aberdeen University Press, 1986), vol. 1, 65.

[26] Hanna, *Uncollected Prose and Verse*, xxvii–xxix, for manuscript description.

[27] Hanna, *Uncollected Prose and Verse*, xxix. It contains seven other confirmed Rolle compositions, such as *Incendium Amoris* and *Ego Dormio*, alongside various lyrics. See also Ralph Hanna, *The English Manuscripts of Richard Rolle: A Descriptive Catalogue* (Exeter: Exeter University Press, 2010), 8–12;. Andrew Kraebel discusses how the way the lyrics were copied into CUL Dd.5.64 with the name 'Ricardus Hampole' affirms 'the importance of this *auctor* as an authorizing figure'; 'Modes of Authorship and the Making of Medieval English Literature', in *The Cambridge Handbook of Literary Authorship*, ed. Ingo Berensmeyer, Gert Buelens and Marysa Demoor (Cambridge: Cambridge University Press, 2019), 109.

[28] Hanna, *Uncollected Prose and Verse*, xliv–xlviii, for manuscript description.

copy.[29] However, Hayes does note an interesting trend by the scribes of Pepys MS 2125: changing the presumed gender of the reader from female to male in several of the texts, such as *The Chastising of God's Children* (fols 1r–28r), suggesting a male intended audience for the volume as a whole.[30] That evidence is qualified with a few small but telling changes at the beginning of *O3W*, where the generic 'he' is changed to 'þu' in a few places, suggesting an expected female or mixed audience.

An even more aggressive kind of re-gendering occurs in the final witness of *O3W*, London, British Library, MS Sloane 1009 (vol. 1), fols 25v–26v (printed in parallel to Trinity by Hayes).[31] This is the latest copy, dating from the end of the fifteenth century (possibly 1477–96, based on internal evidence[32]). Other items in the manuscript are religious, and it includes Chaucer's *Tale of Melibee*. Titled 'De contemplacione' here, this copy of *O3W* has been dramatically adapted in two ways. First, many parts have been cut out and other parts condensed so that it is about half of the full length; anything not related to Richard of St Victor's quotation is omitted, as is the final elaboration of Mary's imaginative prayer. Second, the prominent addition of four invocations to 'my sone' insists on a male audience. It has been rewritten as an epistle from a more senior male contemplative to a kind of mentee.

While the context of Rolle's oeuvre posits a female religious intended reader, and the later manuscript evidence points towards a male, monastic audience (though without ruling out female and/or lay readers), the treatise itself generically targets beginners in contemplative practice, whether male or female, enclosed or possibly leading a 'mixed life'. It was in this period of the mid-fourteenth century when 'the art of contemplation had begun to be practised outside the monastic life, *de cella in seculum*',[33] and the reception of *O3W* could be an important witness to that trend. The first half of *O3W* simplifies quite advanced monastic contemplative theory. The narrator patiently explains to his readers the theory behind contemplative practice just as he later, in the second half, patiently explains Mary's own contemplative practice. While the Virgin herself is the expert in contemplative practice, the expert

---

[29] Hayes, 'Of Three Workings in Man's Soul', 186.
[30] Hayes, 'Of Three Workings in Man's Soul', 186.
[31] Hanna, *Uncollected Prose and Verse*, l–lii, for manuscript description; also described in detail as part of the online database *Manuscripts of the West Midlands*: https://www.dhi.ac.uk/mwm/browse?type=ms&id=81 (accessed 17 August 2019).
[32] John M. Manly and Edith Rickert, eds, *The Text of the Canterbury Tales: Studied on the Basis of All Known Manuscripts*, 8 vols (Chicago: University of Chicago Press, 1940), vol. 1, 517.
[33] Jeremy Catto, '1349–1412: Culture and History', in *Cambridge Companion to Medieval English Mysticism*, ed. Samuel Fanous and Vincent Gillespie (Cambridge: Cambridge University Press, 2011), 128.

in contemplative theory is Richard of St Victor. Richard's Latin writings were well known in medieval England, and the work at issue here, *The Mystical Ark* (*Arca Moysis*), often referred to today as *Benjamin major*, was one of his most popular, especially among monastic elite readers. *O3W* opens by immediately establishing its basis in Richard's authority: 'A grett clerke þat men calles Richard of Saynt Victoures settes in a boke þat he made of contemplacion thre wyrkynes of crystyn mans saule, qwylke are þise: thoght, thynkyng, and contemplacyon' (1–10).[34] Introducing Richard as 'a grett clerke' seems to assume that readers would not have heard of him, new as they were to the corpus of mystical theology. The book in question is *Benjamin major*, though its title is left unmentioned here as if to suggest it would not mean anything for this reader. Drawn from *Benjamin major*'s chapter 3, titled 'De contemplationis proprietate, vel in quo differat a meditatione, vel cogitatione' (Concerning the particular nature of contemplation, or how it differs from meditation and thinking), a single line provides the focus for the *O3W* author: 'Cogitatio est sine labore et fructu. In meditatione est labor cum fructu. Contemplatio permanet sine labore cum fructu' (Thinking is without labour and fruit; in meditation there is labour with fruit; contemplation continues without labour but with fruit).[35] He translates it fairly closely, taking care to clarify the English translation of *meditatione* as 'thinking': 'He [Richard] says þat thoght is wyth-owtyn trauell & wyth-owtyn frute. And thynking is wyth trauell & wyth frute. Þow schal wytt þat thynkyng & meditacyon is bothe one. And also contemplacyon is wythowtyn trauell & wyth grett frute' (15–23). Over the proceeding paragraphs, it quickly becomes clear that the author is endeavouring to explain this hierarchy in the most accessible fashion possible, to an audience that has very little familiarity with contemplative theory or even with its most basic Latin terminology: 'Bot Thynkyng is propyr Inglysch þerof, for Meditacyon is noon Inglysch, bot it is a worde feyned lyke to Lattyn' (74–8). He assumes either that this reader might not be familiar with the word *meditatio* as a Latinate word, or that if he does know it, it is not be preferred over the English option. Indeed, the 'paraphrasal and popularising nature of the tract' means that the precision of Richard's quite scholarly text is blunted in order to accommodate the introductory level.[36]

Insofar as the vernacular treatise's intended readers are beginning at the very bottom of the contemplative ladder, the concrete images of Christ's life are appropriate for their skills. To exemplify 'thinking' or *meditatio*, the narrator

---

[34] Citations are by line number to Hayes, 'Of Three Workings in Man's Soul'.
[35] PL 196: 66D–67A; translation from McGinn, *Richard of St Victor*, 155–6. Karnes also considers Richard of St Victor's approaches to imagination: *Imagination, Meditation, and Cognition*, 28–31.
[36] Hanna, *Uncollected Prose and Verse*, commentary on the text, 195.

mentions 'þe Passyon of Ihesu Criste, or of þine awne wretchednessse, or of þe ioyses of owre blyssed lady, or of the ioy of awngels' as only a few examples: 'Many maners of thynkynges þer are; I may noght tell all' (90–1). (We soon learn that he chooses one of the joys of Mary over the Passion of Christ for his own lesson.) These topics for meditation are facilitated by *imaginatio*, a facility which Richard of St Victor reserves not for the second level of meditation but for the lower level of thought or *cogitatio*: 'Ex imaginatione cogitatio, ex ratione meditatio, ex intelligentia contemplatio' (Thinking is from imagination; meditation, from reason; contemplation, from understanding).[37] Rather than misunderstanding his source, I see here that the O3W author adapts the source material to the needs of his readers. By elevating *imaginatio* and eliminating *ratio* he reflects their literary reality where meditation is primarily described in terms of 'ymaginacyon'. Later in their devotional careers, when they become more advanced, these practitioners can make more fine distinctions in contemplative theory. This elevation of imagination also fits in with Rolle's general tendency to offer a 'prominent position to imagination within his mystical schema', as Claire Elizabeth McIlroy claims, as part of his affinity with the Franciscan devotional tradition.[38] In this strain of spirituality the individual can 'realise absolute truth by means of *imaginatio* on the life and Passion of Christ', as opposed to the more apophatic mysticism of writers such as the *Cloud*-author, where *imaginatio* cannot bring one to the heights of spiritual perfection.[39] But this applies more to the advanced practitioner: for the beginner, clearly the intended audience of O3W, imagistic meditations are indispensable, the O3W author would agree.

After elaborating on the Victorine contemplative hierarchy, the author departs from *The Mystical Ark* as he transitions away from theoretical concerns about how meditation can be understood and moves towards the practical progression and pitfalls of meditative practice itself. Even 'grett trauell in meditacyon' (120–1) as well as 'souereyn swetenesse' is 'þe swete gyfte of þe grace of godd' (123) and should be gratefully acknowledged as such. The reader should also guard against pride and sloth as expressed in envy of others' contemplative progress: 'þou arte prowde & slawe' (173) if you compare yourself

---

[37] Richard of St Victor, *De Gratia Contemplationis Libri Quinque Occasione Accepta Ab Arca Moysis Et Ob Eam Rem Hactenus Dictum Benjamin Major*, PL 196: 63–202 (67). Translation from Zinn, *Richard of St Victor*, 156. See also Hanna, *Uncollected Prose and Verse*, note to l. 92, 195.

[38] McIlroy, *The English Prose Treatises*, 30.

[39] McIlroy, *The English Prose Treatises*, 30; discussed more generally, 28–40. The complexities of *intellectus*, *affectus* and *imaginatio* as the human faculties employed in the ascent to God are explored in Alastair Minnis, 'Affection and Imagination in *The Cloud of Unknowing* and Hilton's *Scale of Perfection*', Traditio 39 (1983): 350–1; and Karnes, *Imagination, Meditation, and Cognition*.

in a haughty way. Failure to progress to the heights of contemplation might also trigger the 'enmy' or devil to introduce doubting thoughts, bringing to mind 'all þi synnes' (206) or bringing one 'in-to dyspare of swylke swetnesse' (209–10) and thus causing the reader to cease in their meditative work. 'Putt vndyr fute' all these concerns, the narrator exhorts the reader, and pray steadfastly (211–12). Now that the reader has been fully prepared with a crash course in contemplative theory, its divine origins, its challenges and its rewards, next would be to learn about the actual steps involved in meditative practice, its habits, its mental acts, its bodily experience. Far better than telling, however, is showing – with a sacred figure worthy of meditation who happens to be an expert in meditation, the Virgin herself: 'And yf þow wyll vse þe in thynkyng, I wyll tell þe a maner of thynkyng, qwylke þow hase prayed me of before tyme. And it is bothe thynkynge & prayer, & it is of þe ioyes of owre blyssed lady saynt Mary' (219–26).

Meditation on/as Mary: blurring devotional and visionary genres

The Marian meditation then offered by the author can be, for the sake of convenience, mapped out in five sections, though not identified as such in the text itself: 1) description of Mary reading Isaiah's prophecy and meditating on it; 2) description of her body when ravished in contemplation; 3) encouragement to dispose one's soul like Mary's; 4) description of the disposition of Mary's soul, with meekness and desire; 5) continued description of Mary's meditation on Isaiah, directly quoting her thoughts, with reference to her meekness and desire. Thus Mary's reading bookends the passage, providing a model for the reader on every level: intellectual, devotional, physiological, emotional. The reader learns how to read Scripture or vernacular versions of its stories and imaginatively participate in its scenes, an image-based participative piety – but the reader also witnesses how such devotion could segue into the higher level of ecstatic contemplation experienced by Mary which approaches the kind of mystical union with God more closely associated with elites than beginners. Though she can be an inspiration for those just starting out in meditative practice, the Mother of God is nonetheless an advanced contemplative, like the holiest of medieval solitary women. Mary's combination of imagistic and ecstatic spiritual skills in *O3W* captures how the medieval tradition adapted the reading Mary as an exemplar for lay and monastic readers, for men and women, for beginners and advanced meditators – she was the key for anyone to access Christ through prayer.

O3W's opening scene taps into an established tradition of presenting Mary as a reading contemplative in a room, blurred between cell and bedroom, simultaneously isolated from the world but spiritually accessible by the reader, a room metaphorically in parallel with the soul. The reader uses *imaginatio* to visualize, within their soul, Mary's room: 'Fyrst þow schall ymagyn in þi saule a fayre chawmbyr. & in þat chawmbyr þow schall see sitting at a wyndowe, redande on a boke, owre lady saynte Mary. And þow schall sett þi selfe in sum cornere of þis chawmbyr, besyly behaldand hyre qwhere sche syttes' (229–38). From the eleventh century, Mary's Annunciation chamber or *cubiculum* was a way of envisioning one's own soul as a protected place reserved for seeking God, as explored in Chapters 2 and 3 including the following examples. In a Marian prayer that Anselm of Lucca wrote for the Countess Matilda of Tuscany around 1080–2, he encouraged her to imagine herself following Gabriel into the room of the Annunciation, bidding Mary that she might 'secretum cubiculum orationem tuarum temeraria ingrediar' (enter boldly into that secret chamber of your prayers).[40] Anselm of Canterbury likewise describes the mind or soul as a *cubiculum* to be entered in order to shut out the world. Aelred of Rievaulx's *De Institutione inclusarum* (c. 1160) goes into more detail for the Annunciation scene, directing his female reader to enter with Mary into her bedroom, *cubiculum*, and to open with her the books of the prophecy.

Later lives of Christ like the *MVC* and Love's *Mirror* encourage their readers to visualize Mary's reading, but none so specifically invite the reader to imaginatively *inhabit* the room as Aelred and the *O3W* author, who could well have been inspired by Aelred's anchoritic guide. *De Institutione* circulated in England in Latin and in two independent Middle English translations, discussed in Chapter 3. The later of these translations, in Oxford, Bodleian Library, MS Bodley 423, retains some of the Latin's vividness – and Mary's book – lost in the earlier translation, with language closely paralleled by *O3W*. Bodley reads: 'than entre in-to that pryue chambre where our blessed Lady praide deuoutly vnto the tyme the aungel grette hir, beholdyng bisely hou she was occupied with redynge of suche prophecies' (696–702). Both the Bodley translation and *O3W* direct the reader to enter her chamber and then to 'busily behold' her – a key phrase for that active state of devotional image-based imagining so characteristic of late medieval spirituality, and added to Aelred's original Latin. Whether or not he was directly inspired by Aelred's foundational contribution to the lives of Christ genre, the *O3W* author clearly steps into that textual tradition in his portrayal of the Annunciation, creatively expanding the scene to maximize its potential as a learning opportunity for the reader. As I discuss in relation to Julian of Norwich's prose in the previous chapter, 'beholding' functions as

---

[40] Anselm of Lucca, *Orationes venerabilis Anselmi Episcopi ad Sanctam Mariam*, III Henri Barré, *Prieres Anciennes de l'Occident a la Mere du Sauveur, Des origines a saint Anselme* (Paris: Lethielleuz, 1963), 230; translation from Fulton, *From Judgment to Passion*, 226.

a semantically rich word that evokes Mary's conception of Christ as a kind of spiritual comprehending that can be emulated metaphorically by the reader when they 'behold' Christ in meditation. While such a web of meanings might not have been fully realized by the newest of meditants, this rhetorical *imitatio Mariae* was nonetheless already woven into their most introductory devotional literature through the repetition of this 'besyly behaldand'.

Every aspect of Mary just before the Annunciation becomes imitable by means of busy beholding in *O3W*. The narrator takes care to describe not just that she is reading, as mentioned in other texts, but also her posture, her method of reading, the actual text she reads and her imagining on that text:

> Behalde howe deuotely sche syttes, & hyre boke lyande on a deske before hyre, & sche aparty stowpande toward hire boke & redinge pryualy wythowtyn schewyng of voyce. And I schall tell þe qwhat þow schall thynke þat sche redys. Þow schall thynke þat sche redys wordes of prophecy, howe it was sayde of Ysai þe prophete þat *a mayden schowlde bere a chylde, þe qwhylke schulde saue all man kynde*. And on þat sche ymagyned. (229–61)

The details of Mary's position and her desk, her leaning in and silently reading, lend a kind of ekphrastic tenor evoking Mary's depictions in illuminations of the Annunciation, especially like those discussed later in this chapter. Indeed, it seems the author expected Mary with a book to be a known visual image for the reader (a resonance I will address in a moment when I turn to some Book of Hours illuminations), though that same reader wouldn't know what the book was: in other words, the reader was not yet introduced to the lives of Christ tradition via Aelred or Love or other sources, where the Isaiah prophecy is mentioned (or the alternate tradition found in Goscelin of St Bertin, where Mary reads the Psalms, as in Chapter 2). Rather the *O3W* author takes charge of introducing the motif of Mary reading the prophecies and her subsequent meditation, addressing the reader in that now-familiar guiding voice: '*I* schall tell *þe* qwhat *þow* schall thynke þat sche redys' (my emphasis). For his purposes, specifying Mary's text is crucial, because it is her specific meditation on that verse that so perfectly exemplifies the meditation he wants his reader to practice: he wants her to imagine herself part of this New Testament scene just as Mary imagined herself part of the Old Testament prophecy. The forceful 'desiryng' of the Virgin's meditation instantly shortens the distance between herself and this biblical prophecy: 'And on þat sche ymagyned, desiryng þat it myght be in hyre dayes þat sche myght ones see hyre blessyde lorde þat sche hade seruede in þe tempyll in schappe of owre kynde.' She wishes that she might see the 'child' (Christ) or Lord in the shape of a human, whom she has previously served in the temple as God. Mary is not just praying; she is praying herself *into* the scriptural narrative. The beginning reader needs to learn how to make that same imaginative leap of faith. Only then could she be prepared to embark on the myriad 'many maners of thynkynges' that represent the devotional textual traditions mentally re-enacting the Gospel story and the Passion. Mary is not a merely devotional object unto herself, the end goal, but rather the means by which meditants can access the divine, just as she was the means by which the divine was made present on earth. She is the key.

This opening scene is bookended by the treatise's final section which develops this paradigm of participatory piety in finer detail by silently borrowing a motif from a visionary text, exemplifying the close relationship between that genre and the gospel meditation genre. While earlier we read only that Mary's response to reading the prophecy was that she desired to see Christ, now her inner thoughts are narrated. They are ebullient:

> Wele I wote þat fro þe tyme þat sche had redde how owre lorde god schulde take man kynde & be borne of a maydyn, sodanly sche fell into swylke a desyre of owre lorde þat sche ymagyned of þat prophecy þus in hyr saule, sayande þise wordes in hyre mynde: 'A lorde god, yf it wer þi worthy wyll þat þis thyng myght be in my tyme.' & þus sche sayde wyth-in hyr saule: 'Qwat ioy! Qwatt conforth! Qwatt blysse! Qwatt welth! Qwatt myrth! Qwatt nede myght any saule haue more þan to see & serue þat blyssede lorde beande on owre kynde, so þat bothe myght be gladdid, owre body in þe seruyce & in þe syght of his body & owre saule in þe lufe & in þe fervoure of his godhede.' And þus for gretnes of desyre, sche sayde efte sones in hir saule þise wordes of grett desyre: 'A lorde, yf itt be þi worthy wyll þat I myght be þe handmaydyn of þat maydyn þat schall bere þat chylde.' (372–400)

Mary's wish merely to see the child of the prophecy escalates first to her desire to 'serue þat blyssede lorde' and climaxes with her final wish to be 'þe handmaydyn of þat maydyn þat schall bere þat chylde'. Rather than projecting backwards to re-imagine a biblical past with one's self as an additional participant in it, as with lives of Christ or gospel meditations, she utilizes the same imaginative technique to project herself into a biblical future. In essence, she imagines the New Testament out of the Old Testament; her meditations conjure up the prophecy's fulfilment. Her devout belief in Isaiah's words foretells the fulfilment of her own prophetic desire to witness them. Such a transformation from witness to participant parallels the progression experienced by readers of lives of Christ, who begin by visualizing the biblical scenes described by the narratives before being invited by the narrators to visualize their active participation in them. The Virgin's words in this meditation thus simultaneously validate the devotional practice of imaginative, participatory piety, while also encouraging the reader to ventriloquize Mary's desiring words and emulate her desire to serve the mother of God. And just as meditations such as these might have shaped visionary experiences as in the case of Margery Kempe, so did a visionary account shape this particular gospel meditation.

O3W's 'twist' on the motif of Mary reading about Isaiah's *ancilla* – desiring to be not that maiden herself but rather 'the handmaiden of that maiden' – links *O3W* to Elizabeth's *Revelations* and its influence on late medieval English devotional culture. While it is possible the *O3W*-author picked up the motif through another intermediary or devised it himself, the *Revelations* attributed to Dominican nun Elizabeth of Hungary and Naples (d. 1322) could be a possible source of the motif. McNamer has postulated that this visionary account would have been completed in Italy around 1325,[41] giving it perhaps two decades to get to England and exert an influence on the author of *O3W*, if indeed that author was Rolle, who would have written *O3W* in the 1340s. While neither the English translations of the *Revelations* nor the Latin version extant from medieval England can be dated that early, that does not rule out the possibility that Rolle – an eager reader of visionary texts – could have obtained a copy, even in the Yorkshire moors, and used it for inspiration for *O3W*. Elizabeth's *Revelations* certainly could have been the force behind the highly developed focus of *O3W* on Mary as contemplative at the Annunciation.

The entirety of the *Revelations*, analysed in detail in the previous chapter, revolves around the Annunciation and Mary's prior reading; in particular, Mary's words to Gabriel, 'ecce ancilla domini' (Behold the handmaid of the Lord) (Luke 1:38) reverberate throughout the text. In the very opening of the visionary account, Mary invites Elizabeth the visionary to be her 'handmaydyn' or *ancilla* (I, 56), and this epithet recurs throughout the chapters; Elizabeth becomes handmaiden to the maiden that bore Christ.[42] However, this was a desire first expressed by Mary, as in *O3W*. Later, the motif's full meaning in the *Revelations* emerges with the two mentions of Mary's desires in relation to Isaiah's prophecy. First, at the young Virgin's entrance to the temple, she ascends its steps while reciting 'seven petitions to God', a theme that became popular in late Middle English versions of the life of Christ and of the Virgin.[43] Mary explains to Elizabeth the fifth petition:

> Þe fyfþe was þat he schulde make me to se þat tyme in þe qwech þe blessyd maydyn schulde be born þat aftyr tellingis of prophetic schulde bere ys Sone, and he schulde kepe myn hey3yn wyt þe wech I myte see hyre, myn eers þat I miyte heryn here spech, my tunge wyt þe qwech I myte loue here, my handys þat I myte towch here, my feeth þat I myte go to here, my knes þat I myte worschope hire and here Sone lygende in here lappe to se and to loue. (IV, 64)

---

[41] On the attribution see McNamer, *Meditations on the Life of Christ*, cxxxix–cxlvi.
[42] References are to chapter and page in McNamer, *The Two Middle English Translations*, as in Chapter 4.
[43] McNamer, *The Two Middle English Translations*, 41–2; other texts that borrow this theme include John Lydgate's long poem *The Life of Our Lady*, and the *Mary Play* of the N-Town Cycle.

The first specification that God should help Mary 'to se þat tyme in þe qwech þe blessyd maydyn schulde be born' recalls the first mention in *O3W* of Mary's wish 'þat sche myght ones see hyre blessyde lorde' (257–8, also 386–7) and 'þat þis thyng myght be in my tyme' (380–1). Both describe Mary's desire to have her own time intersect with the time of the prophecy's maiden, to have that scriptural future become her own future. In the next chapter of the *Revelations* Mary describes the actual moment when she reads the prophecy and in response thinks to preserve her 'maydynheed' or virginity for that maiden or *ancilla* in Isaiah 7:14, and 'þat I mayte in maydynheed seruyn here al þe tyme of my lyf' (V, 72). It is during her continuing prayer on this particular desire that Mary experiences an aural visitation from God, where he clarifies that in fact *she* will be the mother of God, and others will revere her as she wishes to revere another. God the Father himself responds directly to Mary's imaginative meditation on the Scripture; or rather, her imaginative meditation on Scripture stimulates direct contact with God, complete with ecstatic ravishment. Such image-based meditations might be appropriate for a beginner, as *O3W* affirms, but we also learn from both *O3W* and *Revelations* that for Mary – or those more advanced meditators who 'haue besily disposide þar lyfe many day before in prayer & in meditacyon' and are chosen by God (306–10) – it could lead to far higher levels of contemplation, even contact with the divine.

This brings us to the overriding paradigm driving this treatise, and indeed many of the medieval considerations of the Annunciation analysed in this study: that because Mary conceived Christ in her body, so can she 'conceyue þe grace of godde in hire saul' (327–9), and thus she enables all souls do the same. It was after her physical conception of Christ that Mary had the two things that facilitate meditation and ultimately ascent to God – the height of desire and the ground of meekness: 'And þise two hade sche neuyre verely ore þe tyme þat sche conceyued Cryste' (345–8). Centred in *O3W*, both structurally and theologically, is Mary's body. The female flesh that bore Christ presents not a hindrance or a distraction from spiritual progression but rather a crucial part of approaching God, just as it was crucial for God to approach humanity in the fleshly form of Christ. The corporeality of prayer recurs again and again in different ways throughout *O3W* and evokes the (in)corporation of the divine in the moment about to come, the Incarnation. We see this in Mary's uttered responses to Isaiah in *O3W* quoted above – 'owre body in þe seruyce & in þe syght of his body' (389–91) – setting up a chiasma between 'owre' common body (Mary's but also all humanity's), which in its service is able to be seen by 'his' body; humans and Christ connect through their common bodies. Eyes, ears, feet, knees: the parallel passage in Elizabeth's *Revelations* quoted above advances methodically through Mary's body parts that she wishes to direct towards Isaiah's maiden. It will ultimately, of course, be her womb that she gives in service as that maiden herself.

The polysemic power of Mary's physical and spiritual conception helps explain *O3W*'s quite unusual, detailed section on the physical and physiological changes the Virgin's body undergoes during high contemplation. The narrator instructs the reader to picture 'in þis ymagynacyon' how Mary looks away from her book and up to heaven (i.e. moving from textual meditation to contemplation), with her mouth and eyes closed, and 'no brethe passand oute of hire mouth ne noyse' (273–4). Her face becomes pale. This is because, the narrator explains, when a 'mans saule is full rauyschyde in desire of any thyng, þen all þe blode of hym is gedyrde in tyll a place of hym þer þe saule moste regnes, & þat is þe harte' (279–84). In this kind of suspended trance-like state the body seems as if it were dead, 'sauand a lityll hete & warmenesse leues in þe lymmes' (295–6). Physiological details highlight the proper bodily symptoms of contemplation as signs the readers should take note of, presumably with reference to their own contemplative practice or those around them. With this static moment of deep concentration on the body in stillness, the text's long description enforces the reader's equally slowed contemplation of the ravished body. Not only do readers learn proper reading, meditation and contemplation through Mary's example, by concentrating on Mary's flesh and blood readers are also reminded of how she shares these with Christ at the (imminent) Incarnation, as well as Christ at the Passion later in the text.

The narrator next admits that this mental imaging of Mary's 'holy body' is 'bot a bodely ymagynacyon' – that is, only the concrete images for meditation, but that he will now explain the spiritual side:

> Butt nowe I wyll tell þe, as gode & owre lady gyffes me grace to schewe vn-to þe for þi prophete, yf þow wyll do þer-eftyr, & othyr mens also þat redis þis tretice, qwhatekynd a considracyon þow schall haue gostely in þi saule off hyr preuy wyrkynge in hire saule; and howe sche disposede hire for to conceyue þe grace of godde in hire saul. And þerfore I conseylle þe fore to dispose þe in þi saule in gostely wyrkynge, yf þow desyre tyll haue þe grace of godde wonande in þe. And wytte þow wele, wyth-owtyne þis manere of disposycyon schalle neuyr man taste in hymselfe verely þe swetnes of contemplacyon & of Christes luffe. And þerfore herkyn besily, for þis itt is. (312–40)

This 'disposycyon', we learn in the next sentence, is the desire and meekness that 'sche neuyre verely ore þe tyme þat sche conceyued Cryste' (345–8). Mary sets the best model of literate devotion for this reader new to the practice: her body, having conceived Christ, can now conceive the grace of God in her soul – and if you 'dispose' your soul like Mary's, the narrator instructs, you too can 'grow' the grace of God in your soul. Her female, pregnant body, in other words, enables 'þe swetnes of contemplacyon & of Christes luffe' to be experienced by any Christian. For *O3W* and other lives of Christ, as well as Julian of

Norwich and other visionaries, that is why meditation on this particular scene – Mary at the Annunciation, or just before, in this case – suits the beginning of the soul's journey towards Christ: it shows how humanity, body and all, can meet the divine, through the transformative power of the Word.

Of Three Workings' subsequent influence

O3W demonstrates the porosity between the genres of gospel meditations and visionary texts. With its invitation to the reader to join Mary in her prayer as a solitary contemplative, the treatise taps into the precedent of lives of Christ like Aelred's *De Institutione*; as in those texts, the scene serves to prepare the reader to embark on their meditative practice, with Mary as the ideal model. At the same time, its precise details about her meditation seem to be inspired by the details presented in the Marian visions of holy woman Elizabeth and preserved in her *Revelations*, where Mary herself comes to resemble a female mystic. *O3W*, I have discovered, also exerted its own influence back on the representation of Mary in the later lives of Christ tradition in England. The vividness of *O3W*'s Annunciation scene struck one reader enough for him to interpolate it into a new vernacular compilation he composed in the late fourteenth or early fifteenth century. *Meditaciones domini nostri* (hereafter *MDN*), an example of the many surviving gospel meditations produced in late medieval England that has not received much modern attention, borrows nearly the entire *O3W* meditation describing Mary's reading and prayer.[44] In *MDN*, Mary's meditative scene joins interpolated excerpts from the visionary accounts of Elizabeth and Birgitta of Sweden that almost all relate to Mary's

---

[44] Edited by Elisabeth Blom-Smith, 'The Lyf of Oure Lord and the Virgyn Mary edited from MS Trinity College Cambridge B.15.42 and MS Bodley 578' (PhD diss., King's College, London, 1992); a full PDF can be found online at https://kclpure.kcl.ac.uk/portal/files/2926635/418745.pdf (accessed 17 August 2019). She uses Trinity as the base text, supplementing with Bodley when gaps occur. For the first notice of this borrowing, where some of the points made here are detailed, see Laura Saetveit Miles, 'An Unnoticed Borrowing from the Treatise *Of Three Workings In Man's Soul* in the Gospel Meditation *Meditaciones Domini Nostri*, *Journal of the Early Book Society* 20 (2017): 277–84. Elizabeth Salter includes this life of Christ in her work on Love's *Mirror* and other translations of the *MVC*, where she grouped it with the *Speculum Devotorum*, a similar text; see chapter IV in *Nicholas Love's 'Myrrour of the Blessed Lyf of Jesu Christ'*, Analecta Cartusiana 10 (Salzburg: Institut fur Anglistik und Amerikanistik, 1974), esp. 106, n. 188. Roger Ellis and Barry Windeatt both mention it in passing as part of their discussions of Birgitta's revelations in medieval England; see Ellis, 'Flores ad Fabricandum ... Coronam: An Investigation into the Uses of the Revelations of St Bridget of Sweden in Fifteenth-Century England', *Medium Aevum* 51 (1982): 180; and Windeatt, '1412–1534: Texts', 199.

life, greatly extending the focus on Christ's mother in this 'life of Christ', and strongly endorsing women as spiritual *auctrices* and mystical models.

MDN survives in two early fifteenth-century manuscripts: Oxford, Bodleian Library, MS Bodley 578, containing only this text and of unknown provenance; and Cambridge, Trinity College, MS B.15.42 (fols 5–42v), a larger religious miscellany with vernacular and Latin texts, suggesting a clerical origin, confirmed by the 1468 ownership inscription of a certain brother ('frater') William Caston.[45] Like many of the compiled lives of Christ from this period, this text weaves together a myriad of sources. Although *MDN*'s Latin prologue claims that what follows presents 'meditaciones de vita et passione et resurreccione et in celum ascecione Ihesu Christi secundum Bonaventuram ex tertia sua et brevissima licet fortisissima edicione' (a meditation on the life and passion and resurrection and ascension into heaven of Jesus Christ according to Bonaventure out of his third, and shortest – though best – edition), in fact less than half the text derives from the pseudo-Bonaventuran *MVC*, and a large portion actually focuses on Mary and not on her son.[46] *MDN* incorporates Bible verses translated directly from the Vulgate and accompanied by careful explication, some apocryphal gospels, various patristic sources such as Jerome, excerpts from Bernard of Clairvaux's sermons and small parts of Nicholas of Lyra's *Postilla*. In addition, the compiler drew extensive material from Birgitta of Sweden's *Liber Celestis* and her *Sermo Angelicus*, as well as Elizabeth's *Revelations*, the *Legenda Aurea*, *The Pricking of Love* and Mandeville's *Travels*.[47] The composite nature of the text emerges as an explicit characteristic: the compiler rhetorically emphasizes the authority of his sources, frequently citing them by name, with the scribes of both manuscripts also drawing visual attention to *auctores* with rubricated marginal notations in the case of the Trinity manuscript, and red underlining in Bodley. In fact, out of the twelve marginal attributions, nine are to Birgitta for various borrowings, one is to Elizabeth for the seven petitions on the steps of the temple scene[48] and one is to Richard of St Victor for the excerpt from *O3W*. In other words, for the Bodley scribe's presentation, all rubricated attributions elevate either female visionary or

---

[45] Examined in detail by Laura Saetveit Miles, 'The Living Book of Cambridge, Trinity College MS B.15.42: Compilation, Meditation, and Vision', in *Late Medieval Devotional Compilations in England*, ed. Marleen Cré, Diana Denissen and Denis Renevey (Turnhout: Brepols, 2019), 287–301. MS B.15.42 also includes Rolle's *The Commandment*, a vernacular devotional piece focusing on Christ.

[46] MS Bodley 578, fol. 47v.

[47] For more on sources see Blom-Smith, 'The Lyf of Oure Lord', vii–xiv.

[48] Elizabeth's *Revelations* are likely sourced via their inclusion in the *MVC*; more work needs to be done in re-editing the *MDN* and more accurately establishing its chain of sources.

contemplative authority.[49] Even the passage attributed to Elizabeth seems to have been borrowed through its presence in the *MVC*, but the compiler has been sure to cite her name. The correspondence between Elizabeth's vision of the fifth petition on the temple steps – Mary's desire to see the maiden of the prophecy – and the parallel motif in the *O3W* borrowing becomes even more clear when brought together in such close proximity in *MDN*.

'More than 15% of the entire [*MDN*] constitutes the Annunciation to Mary,' the editor notes, suggesting the significance of the scene within the text as a whole. In the Trinity manuscript at the marginal note that identifies Richard of St Victor, the main body text reads: 'And as a gret clerk seith is called Richard of Seynt Victores in a boke that he made off contemplation. Thus glorous virgyn about the tyme of the comynge of the Angell' (fols 8r–v). What follows does *not* include the first half of *O3W* on thought, meditation and contemplation, but skips directly to the Marian meditation. So though it is conspicuously marked as Richard of St Victor's in both the text and the margins of *MDN*, nothing by 'this worthi clerke' actually remains in this borrowing – the compiler seems to have thought the meditation was also by Richard, or simply kept his name as an *auctor* to lend credentials to the passage. The result is that it now looks like Richard of St Victor, elite contemplative author, composed this detailed description of Mary as elite contemplative model.

Most of the *O3W* scene is kept except for the passage on the nature of the 'bodely ymagynacyon' and its relation to the soul, and brief moments are omitted where the narrative voice speaks directly to the reader – 'And I schall tell thee', etc.[50] These omissions fit in with the compiler's general tendencies to focus on visual details and to avoid more meta-commentary on devotional theory or process. Nonetheless, the compiler retains a few direct commands to the reader to 'busily behold', a tone that is completely different from the rest of this compilation (he has carefully scrubbed most of that kind of language from the *MVC* passages). The borrowing discards the original goal of educating meditants about contemplative theory, and instead gives

[49] This list could also possibly include another female visionary source for a curious, unattributed passage immediately before the *O3W* interpolation: 'the angell Gabriell apperid to hure to salute hyre, and as scho schewid by the reuelacion vnto a deuote seruant of hure: in the tyme that the angell come to grete hure schoo was clothid in a kurtyll of blacke gyrd abouȝt with a small gerdull and barefote and thereto nothynge on her hede, but oonly a bende that kepte hure here vp from hure yen and fro hur visage' (13). Blom-Smith is not able to make a positive identification in her edition, and the description does not match any other visionary accounts that I have seen.

[50] The omission matches ll. 303–41 in Hayes' edition: 'therafter his ioye is moche or lasse where it be. [*omitted ll. 303–41*] Moreouer this worthi clerke forseide in the forseide boke off contemplacyon seyith þat twey thyngis oure lady had in hure sowle.' See Blom-Smith, 'The Lyf of Oure Lord', 14, ll. 19–20 (fol. 8v).

the scene a new context of Mary's entire life and her spiritual development from childhood until assumption.

This unusual – perhaps unique – interpolation of *O3W* in a gospel meditation highlights some of the powerful consequences of depicting Mary as model reader and contemplative. Readers witness Mary's engaged reading of the Bible as an example that should be imitated in their own reading of devotional texts such as *MDN* itself. Its logical placement towards the beginning of the story of Christ's life becomes strategic: the scene of Mary's reading offers an opportunity for *practising* meditation before continuing on with imaginative engagement of the rest of the narrative, culminating in Christ's passion and resurrection. While the *O3W* author implies that his beginning readers will go on to practice their meditative skills when they read all kinds of meditative texts just like such a life of Christ as this or Love's *Mirror*, here the reader is doing exactly that. The reader of the *MDN* gets the opportunity to internalize this Marian model in the midst of a longer meditative exercise itself, and in the longer context of the life span of both Mary and Christ. It is more Mary's life than Christ's that shapes this narrative, however, in tandem with the authoritative voices of female visionaries Birgitta and Elizabeth. As *MDN*'s editor Blom-Smith notes, 'all the material from [Birgitta's] *Revelations* selected by our compiler concerns the Virgin Mary' and Mary is even added to narrative events from which she is absent in the source text *MVC*.[51] Birgitta and Mary, and to a lesser extent Elizabeth, are given by the compiler and the scribes a mutually reinforcing authority as holy women with privileged access to God and Christ, both spiritually and physically. Mary's model of conceiving Christ, the *Logos*, while reading the Word should be understood in the light of the compilation's excerpting from Birgitta and Elizabeth's visionary texts: holy women channel God in powerful ways, the *MDN* emphasizes, and can facilitate the reader's own spiritual conception of Christ by means of text-based meditation.

Thus in *MDN* I would identify a dramatically increased focus on Mary and her role in successful meditation, compared to other prominent gospel meditations of this period explored in Chapter 3 of this book. Mary reads in Isaiah in Aelred's *De Institutione* (c. 1160) and its later Middle English translation in MS Bodley 423, dated 1430–80, and in Nicholas Love's *Mirror of the Blessed Life of Jesus Christ*, c. 1410. In contrast, she prays without Scripture in the imported *MVC*, the Vernon manuscript translation of *De Institutione*, dated between 1382 and 1400, and the anonymous *Mirror to Devout People* or *Speculum Devotorum* written for the nuns of Syon Abbey in the 1430s. *MDN* was probably composed sometime after 1390, when Birgitta's *Revelations* would have been accessible in England in Latin if not translated already, and before when the two manuscripts could be earliest dated, mid-fifteenth century: so

---

[51] Blom-Smith, 'The Lyf of Our Lord', xiv.

essentially 1390–1425 or so. In other words, it was written in those decades during which lives of Christ flowered as a popular and influential genre. None of them, however, so emphatically and consistently as *MDN* invite the reader to gaze upon Mary as in a mirror, to re-create themselves in her image, both physically and mentally – from the Annunciation through to the very last scenes. By incorporating such a large interpolation from *O3W*, this intriguing gospel meditation confirms the importance of *imitatio Mariae* at precisely this point in a reader's devotional experience.

The Annunciation as prayer practice: the *Ave Maria* and 'Our Lady's Psalter'

O3W's interpolation into *Meditationes domini nostri* shows how this (pre-) Annunciation episode could fit so well in a life of Christ narrative. Yet one of the most interesting aspects of *O3W* gets lost in that borrowing into *MDN*: the author's original prescription of the Marian scene as a meditation, linked to the repetition of the *Ave Maria* prayer. Side by side with the booming popularity of gospel meditations like the *MVC* in the second half of the fourteenth century and first half of the fifteenth was the increased usage of repetitive prayers of seemingly endless *Pater nosters* and *Ave Marias*. These traditions intertwined to result in 'Our Lady's Psalter' or simply a Lady Psalter, a kind of early rosary, defined as 'a combination of verbal prayer and an accompanying set of mental meditations'.[52] A crucial part of understanding how *O3W* works thus lies in the precise wording of the introduction to the Marian episode, after the theoretical first half: 'And yf þow wyll vse þe in thynkyng, I wyll tell þe a maner of thynkyng, qwylke þow hase prayed me of before tyme. And it is bothe thynkynge & prayer, & it is of þe ioyes of owre blyssed lady saynt Mary, and howe þow schall thynke qhen þow sayes þi fifty Aues' (219–28). For the last phrase, so reads the base text Trinity College MS O.8.26 as well as CUL MS Dd.5.64; MS Pepys 2125 omits the 'fifty' to read simply 'þi Aues,' while the greatly abbreviated version in MS Sloane 1009 adds an additional detail: 'when

---

[52] Anne Winston-Allen, *Stories of the Rose: The Making of the Rosary in the Middle Ages* (Philadelphia: Pennsylvania State Press, 1997), 15. See also Sarah Jane Boss, 'Telling the Beads: The Practice and Symbolism of the Rosary', in *Mary: The Complete Resource*, ed. Sarah Jane Boss (London: Continuum, 2007), 385–94; John Desmond Miller, *Beads and Prayers: The Rosary in History and Devotion* (London: Burns & Oates, 2002); and Rachel Fulton Brown, *Mary and the Art of Prayer: The Hours of the Virgin in Medieval Christian Life and Thought* (New York: Columbia University Press, 2018), 54–75; and on the Lady Psalter (in relation to Lydgate's poem *Fifteen Joys and Sorrows of Mary*), Andrew Kraebel, 'Lydgate's Missing "Ballade" and the Bibliographical Imaginary', in *The Shapes of Early English Poetry: Style, Form, History*, ed. Irina Dumitrescu and Eric Weiskott (Kalamazoo, MI: Medieval Institute Publications, 2018), 191–213.

þu seyest þine ave mary or ellys owere lady sawter'.[53] Why 'fifty' Ave Marias, or not? Why add the option of 'Our Lady's Psalter'? Analysing the different traditions behind these mentions of the fifty Aves and Our Lady's Psalter helps to explain how the Annunciation – specifically the motif of Mary's contemplation at the Annunciation – functioned as a cornerstone of prayer practice in late medieval devotion, and highlights the often overlooked connections between the life of Christ genre and the rosary.

The *Ave Maria* derives from the Annunciation itself: the first part, 'Ave maria, gratia plena: Dominus tecum, benedicta tu in mulieribus', is taken from Gabriel's greeting to Mary in Luke 1:28, and seems to have been used as a prayer as early at the seventh century. Later, her cousin Elizabeth's greeting from Luke 1:42 was added, as well as other components.[54] Extended repetition of the *Ave* became a popular practice in the twelfth and thirteenth centuries as a result of two intersecting traditions. One tradition is the 'Marian Psalter', a monastic practice from *c.* 1130s where the usual antiphons between psalms recited as part of the Divine Office were replaced with specially written verses that interpreted the psalms in reference to Mary (and Christ).[55] The other tradition is an imitation of the monastic Divine Office: while (largely) literate monks might recite the 150 psalms weekly first by reading and then by memory, the (largely) non-literate lay brothers needed something more easily memorizable in order to participate. First they recited multiples of *Pater noster* in place of the Psalter and then, as the cult of the Virgin grew after the turn of the millennium, *Ave Maria* overtook in popularity within a few centuries. Around 1200, for instance, the anchoritic guide *Ancrene Wisse* frequently directed its enclosed readers to recite *Ave Maria* as part of their personal liturgy, at one point specifying 'fifty or a hundred – more or less according to how much time one has', to be followed immediately by the versicle from Luke 1:38, 'Behold the handmaiden of the Lord.'[56]

Within the thirteenth century the practice of reciting 150 *Aves* (or multiples thereof), to match the number of psalms in the Psalter, became known as 'Our Lady's Psalter'. As is typical, what began as a monastic devotional practice migrated to private use, responding to 'the demands of laity for new, more individual and private forms of religious observance'.[57] Evidence suggests this became a widespread practice among both monastic and lay people in England

---

[53] Variants as recorded in Hayes and checked against the manuscripts.
[54] Winston-Allen, *Stories of the Rose*, 14.
[55] Winston-Allen, *Stories of the Rose*, 15.
[56] Anne Savage and Nicholas Watson, trans. and intro., *Anchoritic Spirituality: Ancrene Wisse and Associated Works* (New York: Paulist Press, 1991), 63. In his *Meditation A*, Rolle instructs his readers to pray the *Pater noster* and *Ave Maria* multiple times, but not as extended as a psalter-length.
[57] Winston-Allen, *Stories of the Rose*, 4.

in this period. Around this time we also find evidence of strings of beads used to count the prayers; when Ela, Countess of Salisbury, was buried at an Augustinian nunnery in 1261, it was with a cross and beads.[58] One of the earliest of the many medieval origin stories about 'Our Lady's Psalter' survives from late thirteenth-century England: the Middle English verse with the Anglo-Norman title, 'Coment le sauter noustre dame fu primes cuntroue' ('How Our Lady's Psalter was Made'), found in Oxford, Bodleian Library MS Digby 86 (fols 130r–132r), a compendious tri-lingual manuscript dated 1272–83.[59] Here a monk especially devoted to Mary recites fifty *Aves* and is subsequently rewarded by a visit from the Virgin herself. 'Þat is riȝt mi sauter' (l. 108), she says to him, identifying his ritualized repetition of the *Ave* in three sets of fifty as 'her psalter', hence 'Our Lady's Psalter'. According to the Virgin in this poem, the first fifty are 'In tokning of þe blisse / Þat fel me mid i-wisse / Þo þe aungele to me com, / And seyde me tidinge, / Þat of me sholde springe / He þat is god and mon' (ll. 113–18). In other words, the first fifty *Aves* represent the Annunciation, Gabriel's tiding; as she continues on in the poem, the second fifty represent the Nativity; and the third fifty the Assumption. 'How Our Lady's Psalter was Made' does not explicitly specify that these are themes for *meditating* on while reciting the prayer, but that is how the practice worked, or at least came to work within the next few decades. With increasing complexity over the following centuries, each set of fifty or decade of ten became linked with meditation on a specific episode of the life of Mary and of Christ. The decades of the first fifty *Aves* were each consistently assigned the five 'joys of Mary' (Annunciation, Visitation, Nativity, Presentation/Finding, Assumption) and so on. What we now know as the 'rosary' thus coalesced in the fourteenth century; 'to pray the rosary was, and is, to visualize complex scenes from the life of the Virgin'.[60] Thus the ritualized recitation of *Ave Maria* in sets of 150 to match the Psalms – with many variations for how to demarcate each ten or fifty – was no mindless activity, but a multi-tasking prayer. This is where

[58] A. Gottschall, 'Prayer Bead Production and use in Medieval England', *Rosetta* 4 (2008): 14; 5.
[59] IMEV1840; also survives in Edinburgh, National Library of Scotland, Advocates 19.2.1 (aka the Auchinleck manuscript), dated 1330–40. Edited in F.J. Furnivall and M.A. Cambridge, eds, *The Minor Poems of the Vernon MS: Part II (With a Few from the Digby MSS. 2 and 86)*, EETS o.s. 117 (Oxford: Oxford University Press, 1901), 777–85; quotations cited by line number from this edition. Winston-Allen lists MS Digby 86 as the first instance in her table of 'elaboration of meditations', *Stories of the Rose*, 74. Hoccleve adapted the tale into a miracle of the virgin, *The Monk and the Blessed Virgin's Sleeves*, which is copied next to *The Canterbury Tales* of Oxford, Christ Church College, MS 152, and sometimes linked by modern scholars to the rosary beads carried by Chaucer's Prioress. See Beverly Boyd, 'Hoccleve's Miracle of the Virgin', *The University of Texas Studies in English* 35 (1956): 116–22.
[60] Newman, 'What Does it Mean', 16.

the gospel meditation genre comes into play, providing the detailed images of the holy family's story to accompany the rosary. While the mouth forms the words, the mind forms the images, recalling and imaginatively inhabiting Mary and Christ's life.

This historical context begins to flesh out what kind of devotional practice the *O3W* author implies in his short introduction to Mary's contemplation scene. 'It is bothe thynkynge & prayer,' he says, because the 'prayer' is the repeated utterance of the *Ave Maria*, while the 'thinking' or meditation (as he has carefully explained) is the mental image of the scene itself. He refers to the meditation as 'of þe ioyes of owre blyssed lady saynt Mary' (225–6) not just because it concerns the Annunciation as one of the joys, but because the five (or fifteen, or seven, etc.) joys of Mary were the meditative subject traditionally assigned to the first fifty *Aves* of the rosary. When the author writes that the meditation is 'howe þow schall thynke qhen þow sayes þi fifty *Aues*' with one witness adding 'or ellys owere lady sawter' it suggests the regular practice of the rosary already by the reader, which would make sense for nearly any kind of readership – lay, monastic, male, female – considering the ubiquitous usage of the 'Our Lady's Psalter' by the mid-fourteenth century. Instead of confining one's self to picturing just the biblical scene itself as expected, however, this text offers a related but innovative subject for imagining: the moment *before* Gabriel's arrival, when Mary can model the proper meditative technique the reader is supposed to be learning. Her demonstration of engaged, participative piety where the Scriptural story blends with one's own story has the potential to transform the reader's engagement with their established rosary practice. In addition to ventriloquizing Gabriel's greeting to Mary, the meditant *becomes* Mary herself, or at least emulates her instead of the angel.

Contextualizing *O3W* within the rosary tradition also helps to illuminate the end of the text. Two of the longer witnesses conclude with the greeting of the angel – or, the words of the *Ave Maria* that the meditant has been uttering this whole time: 'Aue gracia plena. Dominus tecum. Deo gracias' (425–67). In MS Pepys 2125, the scribe directs the reader straight to the Gospel itself: 'And if þu wult haue lenger meditacion of þe cuntenaunce þat was bitwixt þe angel and hire, y rede þat þu lerne hit at seynt luke in his gospell Missus est angelus gabriel' (fol. 82v). The default explanation is of course that the biblical Annunciation scene presents the logical next topic for meditation, as in the lives of Christ such as the *MDN* where indeed the compiler does precisely that when he continues to a close translation of Luke. In light of the sensitivity to Bible reading expressed by some other gospel meditations as I documented in Chapter 3, it is interesting that unmediated Scripture itself, whether in Latin or vernacular, seems to be acceptable reading material for the intended audience of Pepys when it was created around the end of the fourteenth century – aligning with its likely male, likely monastic readership. But perhaps the final line also insinuates that some meditants might not be done with their fifty *Aves* by this point: a 'lenger meditacion' of the Annunciation scene would help to fulfil their regulated allotment of time created by the fiftyfold prayer repetition.

Suspended time, reflective images and Books of Hours

The *Ave Maria* not only functioned as a psalter of prayer on its own, it also was the very first utterance of the other major personal devotional practice of the Middle Ages, also vital to the history of the Annunciation: *Horae beatae Mariae virginis*, or the Hours of the Blessed Virgin Mary. This was a series of prayers and psalms in honour of the Virgin Mary for each of the canonical hours of the day, beginning with Matins and finishing with Compline.[61] The Hours of the Virgin has many aspects in common with the rosary and together they constitute an important matrix of prayer practice linked with O_3W and its range of readers – female and male, enclosed and lay, but not exclusively a mystical or visionary elite. Both the Hours and the rosary were in imitation of the monastic Divine Office, with the Hours tradition emerging in the twelfth century, and gaining momentum alongside the rosary throughout the end of the thirteenth century. The *Ancrene Wisse* mentions its anchoritic readers saying their Hours of the Virgin as well as their *Aves*.[62] Both had a physical object to facilitate them – the rosary had its beads, the *Horae* a Book of Hours (or 'primer' as it was known in England). This small, often personalized manuscript usually included a calendar and other prayers in addition to the *Horae* itself, and would be used by an individual on their own in a private or semi-private setting on a daily basis.[63] Nuns and monks, and anchoresses, said their hours in the solitude of the cell; laypeople retreated to a bedroom

---

[61] A translation of the texts of the Hours of the Virgin, and other Books of Hours material, can be found in the appendix in Roger S. Wieck, *The Book of Hours in Medieval Art and Life* (London: Sotheby's, 1988), 157–67. Various texts from English Books of Hours are published in Charity Scott-Stokes, *Women's Books of Hours in Medieval England: Selected Texts Translated from Latin, Anglo-Norman French and Middle English with Introduction and Interpretive Essay*, Library of Medieval Women (Cambridge: D.S. Brewer, 2006).

[62] Savage and Watson, *Anchoritic Spirituality*, 64.

[63] Detailed histories of the Hours of the Virgin and Books of Hours can be found in John Harthan, *Books of Hours and their Owners* (London: Thames and Hudson, 1977); Virginia Reinburg, 'Prayer and the Book of Hours' and Wieck, 'Hours of the Virgin', both in Wieck, *The Book of Hours*; Alexa Sand, *Vision, Devotion, and Self-Representation in Late Medieval Art* (Cambridge: Cambridge University Press, 2014), 152–62; Eamon Duffy, *Marking the Hours: English People and their Prayers* (New Haven, CT: Yale University Press, 2006); Kathryn A. Smith, *Art, Identity and Devotion in Fourteenth-Century England: Three Women and their Books of Hours* (London: The British Library, 2003).

or closet, or conversely performed their hours communally with the domestic household, usually saying them all at once in the morning rather than spaced out over the course of the day as in monastic practice.[64] Many deluxe Books of Hours commissioned for wealthy aristocratic or royal patrons survive, while the increased availability of less expensive manuscript or print copies in the decades leading up to the Reformation ensured a broad swath of society could recite their hours. 'Recite' and 'perform' being the operative words here – some lay Books of Hours users only possessed a 'phonetic literacy' of the Latin *Horae*, meaning they would sound out the words syllable by syllable as a pious act that did not necessarily entail full comprehension, though sometimes vernacular rubrics and other shorter prayers would supplement the experience. (Such recitation could, however, with some guidance, lead to learning to read Latin.[65]) *O3W* seems to aim itself at precisely such readers with high vernacular literacy but low or non-existent Latin capabilities. Others such as clerics applied a 'comprehension literacy' of complete or near fluency to the Latin liturgy and prayers.[66]

Regardless of how much readers understood of the words, however, they could look at the pictures. For the nine hours there was a standard series of illustrated scenes, starting with the Annunciation for Matins.[67] Both text and image in Books of Hours, however, were subject to huge variation over time and according to local tastes, expressing idiosyncrasies in devotional practice and offering a valuable window into the formation of devotional subjects in the later medieval period through *imitatio Mariae*. When I suggested above that perhaps the author of *O3W* was counting on its readers to be familiar with the visual image of the Annunciation, a Book of Hours might be one of those key artistic sources. Devotion was a coherent sensual experience, where 'a single image in an illustrated book could inflect the experience of reading by starting a chain of mental associations – with other texts read, with sermons

[64] Duffy reproduces Hans Holbein's drawing of Thomas More's entire family with Books of Hours in hand, *Marking the Hours*, 56–7.
[65] Michael Clanchy, 'Images of Ladies with Prayer Books: What Do They Signify?', *Studies in Church Studies* 38 (2004), 111. See also Marjorie Curry Woods, 'Shared Books: Primers, Psalters and the Adult Acquisition of Literacy Among Devout Laywomen and Women in Orders in Late Medieval England', in *New Trends in Feminine Spirituality: The Holy Women of Liege and their Impact*, ed. Juliette Dor, Lesley Johnson and Jocelyn Wogan-Browne (Turnhout: Brepols, 1999), 181–8.
[66] Paul Saenger, 'Books of Hours and the Reading Habits of the Later Middle Ages', in *The Culture of Print: Power and Uses of Print in Early Modern Europe*, ed. Roger Chartier, trans. Lydia G. Cochrane (Princeton, NJ: Princeton University Press, 1989), 142. See also Clanchy, 'Images of Ladies with Prayer Books'.
[67] The standard cycle of images is described in Wieck, *The Book of Hours*, 60–6, and Harthan, *Book of Hours*, 28–9.

heard or with other images in the book owner's religious environment'.[68] Likewise, an ekphrastic passage in a text like *O3W* or another gospel meditation or visionary account sparks connections to familiar artistic representations, which in the case of the Annunciation, would almost without fail feature a book – reflecting back yet again to the act of reading. Holly Flora, among others, theorizes these multimedia connections as an act of imagination crucial to lives of Christ: 'Using her imagination, a reader/viewer would connect images, derived from a variety of sources, in her mind's eye.'[69] Interpictoriality, or intervisuality, as it is variously called, designates the layered response of a viewer to an image 'based on his/her former acts of viewing other images'.[70] This visual matrix was far larger than manuscript illuminations: sacred images such as the Annunciation surrounded medieval Christians in many media. Kathryn A. Smith describes how:

> the illustrated Book of Hours also potentially mediated its owner's experience of other imagery and texts within his/her religious environment, whether the parish church – itself a multimedia 'installation' of freestanding and relief sculpture, stained glass, wall and panel painting, embroidered vestments, hangings and altar decorations, and precious liturgical objects as well as liturgical performance and preaching – the private chapel or the bedchamber, which might be furnished with a religious statue or a carved or painted diptych, and in which one might engage in other types of devotional reading.[71]

Thus even the mention of Mary's chamber (with its desk and window), simultaneously intimate bedroom and enclosed cell, could prompt associations with interior decorative representations of the Annunciation that may be familiar to the reader from their own home. Yet it is Books of Hours that perfectly visualize the drama of the Annunciation as expressed by the unusual suspense of *O3W*, because, even more than other media, these books formed the reader as a meditant in Mary's image.

The Virgin's potential for *imitatio* in precisely such a multiplicity of sacred spaces as private bedroom and public chapel is captured by the remarkable illumination considered next. In a well-known image from a bespoke Book of Hours made in Flanders *c.* 1470–80, Vienna, Österreichische Nationalbibliothek, Codex Vindobonensis MS 1857, known as the Hours of Mary of Burgundy (step-daughter of Margaret of York), the Virgin Mary functions as the pivot

[68] Smith, *Art, Identity and Devotion*, 126.
[69] Holly Flora, *'The Devout Belief of the Imagination': The Paris Meditationes vitae Christi and Female Franciscan Spirituality in Trecento Italy* (Turnhout: Brepols, 2009), 230.
[70] Flora, *The Devout Belief*, 230.
[71] Smith, *Art, Identity and Devotion*, 4.

of the overlapping devotional function of the Book of Hours and the rosary. The full-page illumination on fol. 14v (Figure 7), the first of the manuscript, shows patron Mary of Burgundy in the foreground sitting at a window-ledge by herself with her dog in her lap, looking down at a Book of Hours with a rosary draped within reach.[72] Beyond her through the window we the viewers look into a church. Mary of Burgundy's eyes remain fixed on her book, because she too looks on this scene but with her inner eye: the view of the church can be interpreted as a mystical vision or interior imagining by Mary of Burgundy herself, in which she appears again with her ladies-in-waiting, all kneeling in veneration of the Virgin Mary and the infant Christ.

A similar illumination on fol. 43v opens the Hours of the Cross, with a Book of Hours and rosary adorning the foregrounded frame, and a scene from the crucifixion within. Eamon Duffy notes how these illuminations 'carefully locate the book within a devotional regime which included, with no apparent sense of hierarchy, the recitation of the rosary, the use of devotional images, the recitation of the liturgical office and cultivation of extended devotional meditation on the Passion'.[73] Yes, Mary of Burgundy's devotions will, eventually, turn to the Passion. Yet Duffy, like many other critics, underestimates the hierarchic primacy of devotion to, through and in imitation of Mary at the Annunciation that began daily prayer practice. Many folios before Christ is born, the medieval Christian's most extended devotional meditation will be on the Virgin Mary. The Marian image on fol. 14v serves as a frontispiece to a prayer on the joys of the Virgin Mary, ascribed to a vision shown to Thomas Beckett by the Virgin,[74] which begins with the joy of the Annunciation. A few folios later, on fol. 19v, the Annunciation illumination itself appears, with the Virgin Mary reading in prayer, in parallel to the laywoman Mary on fol. 14v. There is a reason the Crucifixion scene frame is empty while the female patron is depicted in the frame surrounding an image of the Virgin. It was in Mary that Mary mirrored herself as a reader and devotee; it was the Virgin Mary that Mary of Burgundy herself both foreshadowed and reflected. Alexa Sand examines this image and other similar ones, noting how 'the painting represents the conditions of its own viewing, and its subject reflects the viewing subject, creating a mise-en-abyme, or interior duplication, well suited to ... the confessional ideal of making the self visible to the self'.[75] When the

---

[72] For more on this spectacular manuscript see Eric Inglis, ed., *The Hours of Mary of Burgundy* (London: Harvey Miller, 1995). Online catalogue entry including full scans: http://data.onb.ac.at/rec/AC13946376 (accessed 17 August 2019).

[73] Duffy, *Marking the Hours*, 17; also 53–4. Clanchy also discusses the 'contemplative concentration' suggested by these illuminations, 'Images of Ladies with Prayer Books', 120; and Penketh, 'Women and Books of Hours', 266.

[74] Duffy, *Marking the Hours*, 51.

[75] Sand, *Vision, Devotion, and Self-Representation*, 2.

Figure 7. Mary of Burgundy at Prayer. Hours of Mary of Burgundy, Flanders, c. 1470–80. Österreichische Nationalbibliothek, Vienna, Codex Vindobonensis 1857, fol. 14v.

Virgin is the one in the mirror, however, I would argue that a confessional *looking* within is part of a larger devotional *transforming* within – a re-conception of the soul to be disposed like Mary's, to borrow the phrasing of the *O3W* author. Such a transformation is predicated on the Annunciation and Mary's own conception of the divine physically through her body and spiritually through her interpretive reading. The viewer re-sees and re-forms themselves in the image of a woman whose holiness is shaped by her literacy. 'Any work of art can prompt a vision,'[76] but because of Mary's imaginative reading, it is art of the Annunciation that trains the reader/viewer to visualize themselves *inside* that vision. It is simultaneously the same Mary, and the same Annunciation, that begins both their overall training in contemplative practice and their daily devotions.

A Reading Annunciate was the opening main illustration in nearly all of the thousands of illustrated Hours of the Virgin produced in the Middle Ages. The first hour of Matins at daybreak was all about openings: as the prayer looked upon Mary's reading, she read aloud the opening versicle, 'Domine, labia mea aperies' (Lord, open my lips). (The actual first prayer, the *Ave Maria*, was so automatic as to be almost never written out, with a 'rare exception' shown in Figure 11.)[77] Thus the devotee opened herself to the spiritual experience by seeing herself in Mary, both reading themselves into the Scriptural story, one preparing to conceive Christ spiritually in her soul just as the other conceived Christ physically in her womb. While it might seem merely chronologically logical that Mary at the Annunciation was the first illumination a devotee encountered in their Hours of the Virgin – being the first event in Christ's life – and merely convenient she too held a book, in fact this 'coincidence' was actually predicated on centuries of Mary's status as the ideal contemplative and the ideal model for channelling the divine through text-based devotion. It is the episode's importance in *Mary*'s life that takes precedence over that of her Son at this moment. Her primary significance as textual meditator and mediator – predicated on yet distinguished from her role in the Incarnation – comes to the fore when we examine specific Books of Hours Annunciations that show her *before* Gabriel has even arrived, and others that show her in closer, more intimate proximity to the patron's portrayal than to the angel.

---

[76] Jeffrey Hamburger, *The Visual and the Visionary: Art and Female Spirituality in Late Medieval Germany* (New York: Zone, 1998), 131. Also on 'the role of art in the formation of miraculous visions', including the story of a nobleman who is praying to an 'old image' of the Virgin when she suddenly appears to him, see Sixten Ringbom, 'Devotional Images and Imaginative Devotions: Notes on the Place of Art in Late Medieval Private Piety', *Gazette des Beaux-Arts* 73 (1969): 160.

[77] On the presence of the *Ave Maria* in the Buves Hours see Wieck, *The Book of Hours*, 60–1; on the details of Matins see Brown, *Mary and the Art of Prayer*, 3–4.

From the hundreds of Books of Hours' Annunciations I will focus on a few significant variations that maximize a contemplative *imitatio Mariae* in ways similar to *O3W*. Like the *O3W* author, some of these artists went a step beyond to exploit the drama of suspended time, the moment of expectation and contemplation on that expectation, by depicting Mary still absorbed in prayer and not yet interrupted by the angel. Like several of the lives of Christ authors, some of these artists have made the space and time for the reader to enter the scene and participate in contemplation with Mary, by means of the owner portrait, with varying levels of direct interaction with the biblical figures. With all the following examples, text and image combine together to teach the meditant how to exercise their *imaginatio* as Mary does in her own prayers. Yet she no longer definitively reads Isaiah 7:14 as the gospel meditations describe, nor the psalms of earlier literature, both often depicted as larger, two-columned books in eleventh- and twelfth-century Annunciation images. Now she is sometimes depicted with a smaller, single-column Book of Hours, her own *Horae*.[78] Or at the very least, her book remains ambiguous: it is both scripture, from which is drawn the liturgy of the Hours, and that liturgy itself. Her precedent of reading Isaiah's prophecies and imagining herself into them has transformed into her reading the very prayer book she is represented in – so thoroughly has she transformed into a mirror for the reader.

Luckily, the practicalities of primer manuscript production resulted in the Annunciation miniature being, 'in many Books of Hours, of a higher quality than the others'.[79] John Harthan explains that:

> It is the most important image in the whole book from a devotional point of view, and for this reason was often undertaken by the master of the workshop, the other miniatures being distributed among his assistants. In the case of manuscripts made for stock and not personally commissioned there was a more mundane reason for concentrating on the Annunciation; it came early in the book and would be one of the first pictures to catch the eye of a prospective purchaser.[80]

While he does not elaborate how the Annunciation might be the most important 'from a devotional point of view' – an opportunity I will take over the coming pages – it is relevant to consider briefly the material circumstances of the creation and circulation of the Books of Hours selected here. This subset of Books of Hours leads us from England back to France and the Low Countries and back to England again. In the heyday of the *Horae*, England imported hundreds of these manuscripts from France, especially Paris, the

---

[78] Duffy, *Marking the Hours*, 36.
[79] Harthan, *Books of Hours*, 28.
[80] Harthan, *Books of Hours*, 28.

largest producer and exporter of Books of Hours from the late fourteenth century through the Reformation, as well as from the second largest producer, the Low Countries, especially Belgium.[81] Some of these books were custom-made and represent the height of late medieval manuscript illumination; others were lower-quality 'mass-market' assembly-line productions. Because the base text of the *Horae* was in Latin no matter the vernacular of the reader, this kind of trade in Books of Hours was feasible (even though some rubrics or other prayers might be in Middle English or French). Such market exchange also highlights the continuous exchange of artistic trends between England and the Continent. Ideas, and iconography, circulated through porous cultural borders. Just as *O3W* fruitfully combined a Latin contemplative treatise written by a Scotsman who moved to France with an original Middle English meditation, so will the following examples demonstrate the profit of combining evidence from England and abroad.

Visually representing a languorous meditation on the Virgin's meditation involves only a slight adjustment of the stereotypical Annunciation scene. In a late fifteenth-century Book of Hours from Belgium, New York City, Pierpont Morgan Library, MS M. 171, fol. 30v (Figure 8) we can see an unusual visual representation of the suspense in *O3W* I examined above: on the right Mary sits with her book (not on a desk but in her lap) completely oblivious to Gabriel's airborne approach from the left.[82] She remains rapt in prayer, which becomes the foremost meaning for the image instead of the Incarnation. He reaches out his hand and sceptre in greeting but there is not yet an *Ave Maria* scroll and his mouth is closed. The emphasis rests on Mary's meditation, undisturbed for just a moment more. Not yet looking at the angel, but neither looking down at her book, she instead looks off to the right, perhaps, I would suggest, even outside the frame – as if to the words the devotee reads aloud at that moment: the first versicle of Matins, 'Domine, labia mea aperies' (Lord, open my lips), with the large initial 'D'. The artist thus crafts a connection between Mary and the reader at the expense of a connection between her and the angel, or even between her and the conception of Christ. Not only the illuminator but also

---

[81] Wieck, *The Book of Hours*, 28–30; Duffy, *Marking the Hours*, 25–30; and in more detail, Nicholas Rogers, 'Patrons and Purchasers: Evidence for the Original Owners of Books of Hours Produced in the Low Countries for the English Market', in *'Als Ich Can': Liber Amicorum in Memory of Professor Dr Maurits Smeyers*, Corpus of Illumination Manuscripts vol. 11–12 (Leuven: Peeters, 2002), vol. 11, 1165–81. On French books of hours in general see Virginia Reinburg, *French Books of Hours: Making an Archive of Prayer c. 1400–1600* (Cambridge: Cambridge University Press, 2012).

[82] The Morgan online catalogue entry for MS M.171: https://www.themorgan.org/manuscript/77349 (accessed 17 August 2019). Another example of an Annunciation just before Gabriel arrives can be found in a Book of Hours (Rouen, France, 1525), New York City, Pierpont Morgan MS M. 61, fol. 30r.

the binder of the manuscript recognized the significance of the Annunciation for the performance of the Hours of the Virgin. Made *c.* 1480–90 in Belgium, probably Tournai, for Franciscan use, this Book of Hours retains its original binding: 'brown morocco over boards stamped with panels of the Annunciation surrounded by the inscription: *Ave gracia / plena dominus tecum / o mater*

Figure 8. Annunciation. Matins, Book of Hours. Tournai, Belgium, c. 1480–90. New York City, Pierpont Morgan Library, MS M.171, fol. 30v.

dei memento mei'.[83] Leather worn smooth by generations of hands, the details are hard to discern, but in the stamped design Mary appears to be turning her head over her right shoulder to acknowledge Gabriel. Here is where the angel speaks, or rather the devotee ventriloquizes his greeting with the start of the *Ave Maria* and finishes with their own supplication, 'o mater dei memento mei' (O Mother of God, remember me).

Another equally rare iconographic tradition takes the contemplative moment prior to Gabriel's arrival and adds the owner figure, or *destinaire*, the person for whom the manuscript was originally destined.[84] The similar Annunciation illuminations of two Parisian Books of Hours – Poitiers, Médiathèque François-Mitterand, MS 53, fol. 18 (Figure 9) and Amiens, Bibliotheque Municipale, MS 2540, fol. 1 (Figure 10)[85] – show how the expected iconography can be transformed by this suspension of time. In Poitiers MS 53, dated *c*. 1490–5, Mary holds up her left hand not in greeting to Gabriel but in guidance to the female *destinaire*, with her right hand gesturing to her open book on the low table. Or is it a Book of Hours belonging to the aristocratic laywoman, the very volume in which this image is captured? Though Mary is closer to the open book, both their bodies are angled towards it, with Mary gazing in the direction of the woman and the woman gazing slightly downwards at the text, hands together in prayer. Most importantly, they remain oblivious to the approaching angel. Gabriel's wings are just inside the window frame but his legs still seem outside and his entire figure remains high above and behind the two women as they continue undisturbed in their spiritual time together. Again, the emphasis shifts completely away from the Incarnation itself and the Luke episode; by shifting the scene back in time, as in *O3W*, the artist refocuses on Mary's expertise in prayer and her private instruction of the laywoman reader.

Amiens MS 2540, from the first quarter of the sixteenth century, presents a slight variation with a more explicit visual mirroring between Mary and the

---

[83] See online catalogue entry and cataloguer notes: http://corsair.themorgan.org/msdescr/BBM0171a.pdf (accessed 17 August 2019). Image of the cover: http://ica.themorgan.org/manuscript/page/29/77349 (accessed 17 August 2019).
[84] Sand, *Vision, Devotion, and Self-Representation*, 6.
[85] Also Paris, BnF, MS. Lat. 13306, fol. 19, and Paris, BnF, MS 2225, fol. 6v. See Isabelle Delauney, 'Livres d'heures de commande et d'étal: quelques exemples choisis dans la librairie parisienne 1480–1500', in *L'artiste et le cammanditaire aux derniers siècles du Moyen Âge: XIIIe–XVIe siècles*, ed. Fabienne Joubert (Paris: Presses de l'Université de Paris-Sorbonne, 2001), 249–70; 263–4, fig. 9 is MS 53. Delauney also discusses the coats of arms and the identities of the female owners. Online catalogue entry for MS 2540: http://initiale.irht.cnrs.fr/codex/6045 (accessed 17 August 2019). Anneliese Pollock Renck mentions Poitiers MS 53 and BnF MS 2225, which she includes as figure 5, in her discussion of female owner portraits in *Female Authorship, Patronage, and Translation in Late Medieval France* (Turnhout: Brepols, 2018).

Figure 9. Annunciation. Matins, Hours of the Virgin. Book of Hours, use of Paris and Le Mans. Paris, France, c. 1490–5. Poitiers, Médiathèque François-Mitterrand, MS. 53 (292), fol. 18r.

Figure 10. Annunciation. Matins, Hours of the Virgin. Book of Hours. Paris, France, 16th century. Amiens, Bibliothèque Municipale, MS 2540, fol. 1r.

destinaire, now each with their own Book of Hours. As in Poitiers MS 53, the Virgin guides the woman as the spiritual authority; both illuminations suggest this by the way the Virgin is physically slightly higher in the composition, in a spatial position of power. This might be the only visual cue to suggest the laywoman imitates Mary and not the other way around: the ambiguity highlights how much the biblical woman has come to reflect her devotees even as they model themselves on her. Gabriel has come a bit closer to the pair than in the other illumination. He is entirely within the window in their domestic space, still in the background though visually overlapping with the laywoman. Crucially, he is prior to them chronologically: he does not disrupt their prayer.

Annunciation representations where Gabriel has not yet arrived, such as Poitiers MS 53 and Amiens MS 2450, have been previously unstudied, like their textual counterpart *O3W*. These two manuscripts take the opportunity of the Matins miniature to establish *imitatio Mariae* as the ground of this prayer practice; so does *O3W* establish *imitatio Mariae* as the ground of meditation and higher levels of contemplation. The images play off the usual iconographic tradition in an innovative, dramatic way, just as *O3W* pushes beyond the typical gospel meditation text like *MVC*. *O3W* and these illuminations bend space and time to re-present Mary's prayer as not just imitable, but inhabitable. Participatory piety brings the devotee in to pray *with* and *as* Mary, not just *to* Mary. But does this work any differently than other owner portraits elsewhere in Books of Hours? Representing the owner figure or *destinaire* has a more profound semiotic charge in the Annunciation scene than in other scenes, I would argue, because of the scene's role in forming the devotional approach of the reader, as we see with *O3W*. Though she does not analyse the Annunciation in depth, Alexa Sand has done some important work on the power of owner portraits in religious manuscripts in general as 'reflexive images'. She writes that 'such pictures form a recursive loop between subject and object – the viewer sees herself seeing and thereby attains a heightened awareness of her own visibility and her own vision'.[86] Vision here applies to the act of seeing through the eyes as well as the spiritual act of receiving visions from divine sources. Sand notes that 'frequently, the depicted book owner participates in a mystical revelation, seeing and being seen by God, the Virgin, or another saint: a pictorial nudge that seems to suggest that with proper application to her devotion, the embodied owner might experience what her pictorial double does'.[87] Such an identification with visionary experience certainly applies to the illuminations above in Figures 9 and 10, as it does to the illumination from Mary of Burgundy's Book of Hours discussed initially. But representing the owner alongside Mary at the Annunciation also carries with it the history of

---

[86] Sand, *Vision, Devotion, and Self-Representation*, 4.
[87] Sand, *Vision, Devotion, and Self-Representation*, 17.

Mary herself as a contemplative and, often, as a visionary. Visionary women such as Birgitta and Elizabeth describe in their accounts a Virgin with special mystical abilities, a reputation that seeped into lay Marian belief. When the owner sees herself represented alongside Mary, the reader is thus *able* to register that depiction as a kind of vision because of Mary's role as visionary model in the first place. *Imitatio Mariae* shapes how the reader interprets what she reads and sees as reflective of themselves (like Mary reflecting herself in the prophecies) and, ultimately, as transformative (like Mary was transformed at her conception of Christ). Such reading and viewing functions as exegetical in its own way; the Gospel, as Word, is reinterpreted by and for each individual soul, when they enter it mentally to participate in Mary's devotion by means of their imagination.

It is worth turning to a few other examples from both the Continent and England in order to elaborate how the development of imaginative prayer practice linked with the Annunciation scene might challenge artists to represent their patrons in more creative, surprising ways than in other biblical scenes. In several instances it is not Gabriel that is about to interrupt the shared contemplation of owner and Virgin, but the owner that actively participates in the interaction between the Virgin and Gabriel. The Buves Hours from Belgium (Baltimore, Walters Art Museum, MS W.267), *c.* 1450–60, divides up the Annunciation into a diptych over two pages, fols 13v–14r (Figure 11).[88] On the right Mary kneels at a private altar with her book open, her body facing outwards, arms crossed in acceptance as handmaiden, and face turned slightly towards Gabriel – a typical set-up. But intercepting her gaze across the page gutter is the female patron, kneeling in front of Gabriel and receiving his attention as well as the Virgin's. This unknown member of the Buves family wears a dress in the same brilliant blue as Mary's cloak, and kneels at a covered desk with an open book conspicuously matching Mary's; both are detailed with red covers, equating them directly with each other and with the Buves Hours itself, whose original fifteenth-century red velvet binding survives. Close inspection reveals both painted books begin with a common legible letter: the rubricated initial 'E' – for Mary evoking Isaiah 7:14 'Ecce virgo concipiet' (Behold, a virgin shall conceive), and evoking for the patron, Mary's own 'Ecce ancilla domini' (Behold, the handmaid of the Lord) response to Gabriel (Luke 1:38). Mary and the laywoman utter 'Ecce' together, the image suggests. Gabriel, meanwhile, places a guiding hand on the owner's shoulder as he waves his word scroll in

---

[88] In *The Digital Walters* catalogue: http://www.thedigitalwalters.org/Data/Walters-Manuscripts/html/W267/ (accessed 17 August 2019). Found in Wieck's catalogue as #40, *The Book of Hours*; discussed in Sandra Penketh, 'Women and Books of Hours', in *Women and the Book: Assessing the Visual Evidence*, ed. Jane H.M. Taylor and Lesley Smith (1997); and Clanchy, 'Images of Ladies with Prayer Books', 112–13.

Figure 11. Annunciation. Matins, Hours of the Virgin. Book of Hours, known as the Buves Hours. Hainaut, Belgium, c. 1450–60. Baltimore, Walters Art Museum, MS W.267, fols 13v–14r.

the other, as if to urge her on in her ventriloquization of his greeting in her prayers. Of all the images examined in this book here is the only moment of physical touch. The entire emphasis shifts from the Christ's Incarnation to the devotional subject who sees herself benevolently encouraged by the biblical figures. The scribe's text corroborates this unison by including, unusually, the full text of the *Ave Maria* underneath the verso half of the diptych, with the opening versicle for Matins following underneath the recto half. For this Annunciation, in contrast to Poitiers MS 53 and Amiens MS 2450, the traditional timing after Gabriel's arrival enables the devotional emphasis to be on the devotee's performance of his words – but by copying them out the scribe refocuses on the act of reading behind the prayer, aligning the female reader again with Mary the reader.

A female owner figure in a slightly earlier English Books of Hours similarly distracts Mary from Gabriel while she imitates the Virgin's reading. The Beauchamp Hours (Part 2 of BL Royal 2.A.XVIII) was made in London *c.* 1430 for Margaret Beauchamp, Duchess of Somerset (and mother of Margaret Beaufort, grandmother of Henry VII), and represents its female patron in the Annunciation illumination beginning Matins (Figure 12).[89] For this instantiation, Mary and Gabriel retain their usual framed scene with Mary on the right, kneeling at her open book and arms crossed in the gesture of acceptance; to the left Gabriel (same scale and plane as Mary) kneels calmly on one knee, directly in front of her, his 'Ave Maria' word scroll unfurling from his right hand. Mary, however, ignores him. Instead she looks down, outside the edge of her own illumination, into the initial 'D' for 'Domine'. There kneels the female patron. She is at a slightly smaller scale than the other two figures, as if to show her existence in an entirely different dimension than them. As in the Buves Hours, the patron's blue dress matches precisely the Virgin's blue cloak, and their books are identical with red covers (unfortunately the manuscript's medieval binding is lost, though we might speculate it was red too). These details align the two female figures in a visual *imitatio Mariae*, while at the same time the owner issues a word scroll out of her hand in imitation of Gabriel. But it is not the *Ave Maria* – she prays off script! Instead the illuminator has introduced an entirely distinct prayer: 'Mat[er] ora filium ut post h[oc] exiliu[m] nob[is] donet gaudiu[m] sine fine' (Mother, pray thy son that after this exile he may

---

[89] Online catalogue entry: http://www.bl.uk/catalogues/illuminatedmanuscripts/record.asp?MSID=6543&CollID=16&NStart=20118 (accessed 17 August 2019). Another example of a female owner portrayed reading just outside the frame of an Annunciation can be found in a late fourteenth-century English book of hours linked to the Bohun family, now in Copenhagen, Royal Library, Thott 547, 4°; see Marina Vidas, *The Copenhagen Bohun Manuscripts: Women, Representation, and Reception in Late Fourteenth-Century England* (Copenhagen: Museum Tusculanum Press, 2019), 56–8; Plate 1, Figures 1 and 2.

Figure 12. Annunciation. Matins, Hours of the Virgin. Book of Hours, known as the Beauchamp Hours. England, c. 1430. London, BL, MS Royal 2.A.XVIII, part 2, fol. 34r.

grant us joy without end).⁹⁰ I cannot find that this supplication has any other connection to the Annunciation, but is rather linked to the Nativity. It is documented as the refrain of a macaronic carol for Christmas, replacing 'sine fine' with 'beatorum omnium,' with the first verse beginning 'Fayre mayden who is this barn / That you beriste in thyn arme?', as found in Richard Hill's commonplace book (Oxford, Balliol College, MS 354), dated to the first third of the sixteenth century.⁹¹ Such a curious departure from the normative *Ave Maria* prayer with a replacement that conjures up the concern of exile, quite foreign to the themes of the Annunciation, suggests that the prayer had some other meaning for the woman depicted, presumably Margaret Beauchamp. Was it a personal favourite? Was 'exile' a resonant theme for her or her family? Its insertion highlights the personal flavour that could inflect owners' portrayals at the Annunciation, as they saw themselves reflected in both the Virgin and Gabriel, and formed themselves as devotional subjects, finding their own voice with which to pray.

So far, women readers have dominated this targeted history of Annunciation illuminations in Books of Hours, as would be expected: the majority of owner portrayals in prayer books are women, but certainly not all.⁹² In some ways, then, this history parallels the story of the treatise *O3W*. If Rolle was the author, as I discuss above, then it seems likely his intended audience was a female religious reader. Later scribes, however, adapted the text for male and mixed gender audiences, both monastic and lay. The inclusion of men into devotional artistic tropes developed predominantly for women can also be seen in certain Annunciation illuminations with male owner figures. What changes in the image when the gender changes, when a man inhabits a position typically inhabited by a woman? Annunciations with male devotees added are unusual, but the opening illumination to Matins from another late medieval Parisian Book of Hours from the same artistic tradition as Poitiers MS 53 and Amiens MS 2540 offers a relevant comparison: Poitiers, Médiathèque François-Mitterand, MS 1096, fol. 43 (Figure 13).⁹³ As in the Beauchamp Hours,

---

⁹⁰ Note that the BL catalogue entry incorrectly expands h[oc] to h[unc].
⁹¹ Roman Dyboski, ed., *Songs, Carols and Other Miscellaneous Poems from the Balliol MS. 354, Richard Hill's Commonplace Book*, EETS o.s. 101 (London, 1907, issued in 1908), carol # 2; online catalogue entry for MS 354: http://archives.balliol.ox.ac.uk/Ancient%20MSS/ancientmsslist8.asp (accessed 17 August 2019).
⁹² On women and Books of Hours see, for example, Scott-Stokes, 'Interpretive Essay: Women and their Books of Hours,' in *Women's Books of Hours*, 148–61; Sand, *Vision, Devotion, and Self-Representation*, 211–15; Smith, *Art, Identity, and Devotion*; Penketh, 'Women and Books of Hours'; Bell, 'Medieval Women Book Owners'.
⁹³ Another example would be the Annunciation in Part 1 of BL Royal 2.A.XVIII., fol. 23v, where a husband and wife flank the architectural frame surrounding Gabriel and Mary; see the relevant discussion in M. Rust, *Imaginary Worlds in Medieval Books: Exploring the Manuscript Matrix* (New York: Palgrave, 2007), 1–5.

Figure 13. Annunciation. Matins, Hours of the Virgin, use of Poitiers. France, 15th century. Poitiers, Médiathèque François-Mitterand, MS 1096, fol. 43.

the Virgin and Gabriel stay in an upper framed space, while the owner figure is enclosed in a separate space below; here, the two spaces are partitioned within a single, larger frame. The Annunciation above is, in all respects, straightforward: on the right Mary kneels in front of a draped desk with her own book on top (binding clasps evident), while opposite the desk on the left, Gabriel kneels on one knee, with his greeting written in gold as streaming directly from his mouth (which is closed).

But this normality means that there is no interaction with the frame below. Mary looks at Gabriel and does not match the gaze of the male owner figure looking up in devotion from the frame below. There is a disconnect between the two scenes, in contrast to the connection between Mary and the female figure below her in the Beauchamp Hours. The male owner figure, though kneeling like Mary, most closely parallels Gabriel visually; the two figures align vertically, and his red robe tinged with gold matches the angel's. Behind the male owner figure stands John the Baptist with his signature beard and lamb; perhaps his inclusion suggests he was a namesake for that patron. John the Baptist raises his right hand slightly as if to guide the meditant in his prayers, reminiscent of Gabriel's gesture in the Buves Hours (Figure 11).[94] It is striking how the male owner has a much more intimate spatial connection to the male figure of John, and a more obvious visual alignment with the male-presenting Gabriel, than he has a connection to Mary, beyond her being the object of his devotional gaze. The ultimate effect is that any sense of *imitatio Mariae* suggested by the shared book feels overridden by the male triangulation of Gabriel–John the Baptist–owner and their shared objectification of the only woman. Compared to the previous examples examined in this chapter, this instance shows how one artist did not so explicitly encourage Mary as a mirror for a devotee of the opposite gender. Of course, this is only one artist. But this illumination suggests how the kind of male access to *imitatio Mariae* enabled by O3W's scribes was not necessarily universally offered across devotional traditions.

Conclusions

O3W weaves together many of the strands of this study. In an unusual way, however, it maximizes the power of the Annunciation scene's literary and contemplative *imitatio Mariae* by putting off entirely Gabriel's arrival – now cast as an interruption – so the Incarnation itself becomes peripheral while Mary's meditative reading takes centre stage. Obviously Christ's actual conception remains vital to the Annunciation episode, but Mary's metaphorical

---

[94] Thank you to Laura Katrine Skinnebach for this identification.

function of allowing each Christian to conceive Christ in their soul takes over the devotional effect of the scene. The vector for that conception is the book – book as weighty authority, as devotional object, as transformative tool, as mirror, as Word, as *Logos*. In *O3W*, the book begins as Richard of St Victor's 'boke þat he made of contemplacion' but it quickly shifts to Mary's hands, the Old Testament scriptures. Then as the reader practises seeing themselves through and as Mary, her book melds with their book. Even if they are a beginner on the contemplative ladder, with rudimentary vernacular literacy, this sacred connection through the text becomes the cornerstone of their devotional practice. The same shift in view transforms the user of a Book of Hours who sees themselves represented as special guest right next to Mary the expert reader. The fact that certain Book of Hours Annunciation illuminations from the Continent perfectly visualize the shared quiet moment between Virgin and reader as described in the English *O3W* demonstrates how it is a kind of logical conclusion, the best way to capture the importance of Mary as model of literary prayer.

The vivid re-enactments of the Annunciation found in *Of Three Workings of Man's Soul* and the rich illuminations in many Books of Hours gave readers and viewers an opportunity to use their 'deuote imaginacioun' and mentally place themselves at Mary's side. These devotional fantasies, whether conjured by the meditant or delivered by the divine, nevertheless remain in the mind – a mental, spiritual and emotional experience – and solitary, as in an anchoress's cell, where Mary was imagined to be. The Shrine at Walsingham, however, offered something quite different: the chance to physically enter, body and mind, into Mary's chamber at the Annunciation, or at least a reconstructed 'authentic replica' of it, alongside a gaggle of fellow pilgrims. Next I will examine the pilgrimage tradition that brought the Virgin's two-dimensional bookish devotions into three dimensions, where private prayers are said side by side with strangers, and where the Annunciation comes alive.

Figure 14. Copper alloy pilgrim badge from the shrine of Our Lady of Walsingham. Late 15th century. Diameter 37 mm. Museum of London, Item ID 78.84/19.

6

Inhabiting the Annunciation: The Shrine of Our Lady of Walsingham and the Pynson Ballad

The Virgin's book at the Annunciation endured as a symbol not only of the divine *Logos* made flesh in a woman's womb, but also as a symbol of how each Christian could access God through the Word. The previous chapters have surveyed the many ways in which Mary's reading modelled devotional and contemplative practices for centuries across medieval England. We can see its pervasive influence in Mary's presence as an interpretive, intellectual authority whose power is not cancelled out by her motherhood but rather enabled by it. As we saw with the Books of Hours illuminations in the previous chapter, nearly every single medieval artistic representation of the scene clearly features a book. The largest medieval physical representation of the Annunciation space is survived by perhaps one of the smallest reading Annunciate images from pre-Reformation England: a fifteenth-century copper alloy pilgrim badge from the Shrine of Our Lady of Walsingham (Figure 14), an artefact now at the Museum of London.[1] No bigger round than the top two joints of a finger, the badge depicts Gabriel kneeling on one side with a scripted phylactory extending from his hand, the lily in the centre and Mary on the opposite side behind an open book on a desk or prie-dieu. This tiny Annunciation scene, while entirely typical and resembling any Books of Hours illumination or altar painting, would remind the badge's owner of something very special: their visit to the life-size reproduction of the Annunciation

---

[1] Brian Spencer, *Pilgrim Souvenirs and Secular Badges: Medieval Finds from Excavations in London* (London: Boydell Press, in association with Museum of London, 2010), discusses these types under 'Annunciation Badges', 141–5. See also a second similar surviving badge at the Museum of London, Item ID 81.284/1, Online record: https://collections.museumoflondon.org.uk/online/object/29183.html (accessed 17 August 2019).

Figure 15. Lead alloy pilgrim badge from the shrine of Our Lady of Walsingham. Late 14th-early 15th century. Height 37 mm, width 31 mm. Museum of London, Item ID 88.53.

space, a shrine built in the small village of Walsingham in Norfolk. For their visit, the pilgrim would have entered first into the larger, later protective stone chapel, and then into the smaller, earlier wooden building around which it was built: the Holy House, claimed to perfectly represent the original Holy Land structure within which Gabriel found Mary and the Incarnation occurred. This edifice is depicted in another late fourteenth-century pilgrim badge with stylized architectural elements and a still tinier Annunciation on the upper floor (Figure 15), also preserved at the Museum of London.[2]

[2] Spencer, *Pilgrim Souvenirs*, discusses this particular surviving badge in the section 'The Holy House', along several other similar and related badges. As far as research

Tiny as they are, the architectural details of these badges actually give us some important clues about what Walsingham's Holy House may have looked like: the shrine itself was utterly destroyed at the Reformation. We have little physical evidence or archeological remains to show precisely what kind of interior space was experienced by medieval pilgrims when they stepped into the reconstructed Annunciation room. Neither do we have any pre-Reformation visual depictions. We do, however, have some intriguing contemporary textual descriptions. William of Worcester, reporting on his visit to the shrine in 1479, reports that the room itself was about 23 ft 6 in by 12 ft 10 in (7.16 m x 3.91 m): 'about the area of the ground floor of an ordinary, early medieval town house', which, considering the thousands of pilgrims that flocked there especially in the fifteenth and early sixteenth century, likely felt relatively small and intimate.[3] Erasmus, visiting *c.* 1512, describes the shrine in his *Peregrinatio Religionis Ergo*, translated into English in 1536: 'ther is a lytle chapell seelyd ouer with woode, on ether syde a lytle dore wher ye pylgrymes go thorow, ther is lytle light, but of ye taperes, with a fragrant smell'.[4] So we can picture a rectangular structure through which pilgrims walked in one end and out the other; presumably along the length of the room would have been an altar with some kind of statuary or art, in front of which pilgrims would have stopped to pray. While the precise details of the shrine might elude us because of gaps in the architectural record, I propose that we turn to the history of the Annunciation as focused on Mary's reading as the foremost devotional model in order to reconstruct what it might have been like to pray at Walsingham. We can begin with its art and statuary.

---

has shown, it was only the shrine at Walsingham that produced badges featuring the Annunciation (or was associated specifically with the Annunciation in any way in medieval England).

[3] J.C. Dickinson, *The Shrine of Our Lady of Walsingham* (Cambridge: Cambridge University Press, 1956), 77–8, gives these dimensions, derived from William of Worcester's note (for which see J.H. Harvey, *William Worcestre: Itineraries* [Oxford: Oxford University Press, 1969]); Spencer, *Pilgrim Souvenirs*, 137, makes the comparison to house size.

[4] Desiderius Erasmus, *Peregrinatio Religionis Ergo* (Basle, 1526), translated into English and printed London, *c.* 1536, *A dialoge of communication of two persons, deuysyd and let forthe in the late[n] tonge, by the noble and famose clarke Desiderius Erasmus intituled ya Pylgremage of pure devotyon* (STC 10454), 17; for lack of page numbers, all quotations are by image number of page spreads from the 1540 second edition copy in the British Library, available on EEBO: http://gateway.proquest.com/openurl?ctx_ver=Z39.88-2003&res_id=xri:eebo&rft_id=xri:eebo:citation:99846697 (accessed 17 August 2019), followed by page number from the modern English translation by Craig R. Thompson, trans., *The Colloquies of Erasmus*, in *The Collected Works of Erasmus*, vol. 40 (Toronto: University of Toronto Press, 1997), 619–74. For one extended discussion of the work in the context of the shrine's history see Gary Waller, *Walsingham and the English Imagination* (London: Ashgate, 2011), ch. 3, 'Walsingham's Chaucer: Erasmus's Peregrinatio Religionis Ergo'.

The figure of the Virgin most strongly associated with the Shrine of Our Lady of Walsingham is an enthroned Mary with an infant Christ seated on her lap (or standing beside her lap), with a book held in his arms – the well-known modern official statue. This image can be found on the earliest seals of the priory connected to the shrine, dating from the mid- or late twelfth century, and closely resembles the imagery of Our Lady of Rocamadour.[5] Unfortunately no precise description or drawing survives that preserves exactly what the statue itself may have looked like. Early witnesses are somewhat vague. Erasmus found it hard to discern the statue: he writes of the Virgin Mary that 'the lyght ... was but little, and she stode at the ryght ende of the aultre in the derke corner'.[6] Royal household accounts specify the value of various gifts given over the years 'at the statue of Blessed Mary' or 'Our Lady', without describing said statue.[7] A few surviving late medieval pilgrim badges also feature the enthroned Our Lady, but in comparison to the Annunciation motif, 'the miraculous image of [the] Lady of Walsingham is only rarely represented on pilgrim badges from the fourteenth and fifteenth century'.[8] Nor was it only Walsingham that produced badges of the enthroned Mary with young Christ: similar signs are linked with Our Lady Undercroft, Canterbury, and others survive in England from the French shrine of Our Lady of Rocamadour.[9] Not to mention, it was an official stipulation that every parish church had to have a statue of Mary. Indeed, the English history of this statue of Mary enthroned and its actual prominence in Walsingham's medieval shrine is so murky that Dickinson speculates that 'not only may it be rather later in date than the chapel, but it does not seem probable that a chapel commemorating the Annunciation would be provided with a statue of Our Lady showing her seated on a throne with the infant Christ on her arm'.[10] Despite the fact that it is the enthroned Virgin that typically dominates both modern critical discussion and modern branding of the shrine, we know little for certain about

---

[5] Dickinson, *Shrine*, 111–12. On the general history of the enthroned Virgin see Hans Belting, *Likeness and Presence: A History of the Image before the Era of Art*, trans. Edmund Jephcott (Chicago: University of Chicago Press, 1994), 299–300.

[6] Erasmus, *Peregrinatio*, 25 (*Colloquies*, 629).

[7] Dickinson, Shrine, 39–43, lists several examples, such as from the records of Edward I, Edward III and Henry VII.

[8] As stated by Michael P. Carroll, 'Pilgrimage at Walsingham on the Eve of the Reformation: Speculations on a "splendid diversity" only Dimly Perceived', in *Walsingham in Literature and Culture from the Middle Ages to Modernity*, ed. Dominic Janes and Gary Waller (Farnham: Ashgate, 2010), 37; and seen evidenced in the section on 'The Statue' in Spencer, *Pilgrim Souvenirs*, 136, where he identifies many fewer badges of the enthroned Virgin than of the Annunciation scene itself.

[9] On badges from Our Lady Undercroft, Canterbury, see Spencer, *Pilgrim Souvenirs*, 131–3, figures 136–7; on Our Lady of Rocamadour see 234–7, figure 245.

[10] Dickinson, *Shrine*, 9.

the history of the Mary with Christ statue at Walsingham before the shrine's obliteration at the Reformation. That is, while it is possible that there was a statue of the Virgin enthroned with Christ in her lap, a statue that visitors worshiped and ascribed miracles to, I would like to challenge the assumption that this was the only or even the most important devotional statuary within the shrine. Why couldn't the central statue have been the Annunciation itself, with Mary and her book?

In the enthroned Mary statue, Christ holding the book while seated in Mary's lap suggests the significance of scripture as part of the incarnational symbolism of the Word made flesh, appropriate for devotion at a house commemorating the original location of Mary's conception of the Word. But the devotional experience of pilgrims, I suggest, was likely more directly shaped by imagery of Mary in her own devotional experience, modelling Christ's polymodal conception – physical, spiritual, mental – before he is visible to the world. I suspect that more likely than the enthroned Our Lady statue, the Annunciation episode itself – and the book in *Mary's* hands, not her Son's – must have figured prominently in the iconography within the medieval shrine, as it does in the surviving pilgrim badges.[11] No other English shrine seems to have produced badges of the Annunciation; no other pilgrimage destination in England derived so much of its power from not just Mary but specifically her role in the Incarnation and the moment when divinity took materiality. Though not discussed by modern commentators, surely the Annunciation scene was a part of the visual experience of pilgrims and shaped their devotion there. Medieval sources suggest its presence. Several of the same royal account records that describe offerings made 'at the statue of Blessed Mary' also list offerings 'at the statue of the blessed Gabriel in the same chapel'.[12] In the fourteenth century Henry, earl of Lancaster, gave to the shrine some kind of Annunciation picture with precious stones ('salutationem angelicam cum lapidibus pretiosis').[13] In his commonplace-book testimony about his visit to Walsingham sometime in the last quarter of the fifteenth century, Robert Reynes of Acle, Norfolk, mentions the Annunciation scene for which the

---

[11] Regarding the medieval shrine, Spencer states that 'by the late 13th century the Holy House is known to have contained at least one representation of the Annunciation and to have had others bestowed on it during the 14th century', but does not cite sources or evidence (*Pilgrim Souvenirs*, 139). In the modern Anglican Walsingham shrine a large frieze of the Annunciation adorns the back wall, and there is an Annunciation with Mary holding a book on the front altar left-hand panel. See Simon Coleman, 'Purity as Danger? Seduction and Sexuality at Walsingham', in *The Seductions of Pilgrimage: Sacred Journeys Afar and Astray in the Western Religious Tradition*, ed. Michael A. Di Giovine and David Picard (London: Ashgate, 2015), 58.

[12] See especially for Edward I; Dickinson, *Shrine*, 39.

[13] John Capgrave, *Liber de illustribus Henricis* (London: Longman, Brown, Green, Longmans & Roberts, 1858), 164; also cited by Dickinson, *Shrine*, 39.

shrine was built: 'Gabriel gretyng Our Lady; in the myddes of the tabyll at the avter stante Our Lady, on eche syde of her stante an angell ... alle clene gold'.[14] From this brief description of an artistic representation of the Annunciation scene – beginning abruptly, 'Gabriel gretyng Our Lady' – it is unclear if it is a framed painting, or wall-painting, or rather free-standing sculptures (as his language seems to suggest in the description of Mary and the angels). Regardless, we might speculate that this representation of Gabriel greeting Mary matches those captured in the various pilgrim badges, including the typical props helping to identify the scene – lily in the middle, desk and book in front of Mary. In other words, Walsingham was special in that it was the only English shrine focused on the Annunciation, but it promoted an entirely traditional Annunciation scene: one where Mary read.

The overwhelming artistic tradition of the reading Annunciate is justification enough for speculating that the shrine depicted Mary with a book. But in terms of specific artefact evidence, it seems extremely likely that the interior shrine of the Holy House presented to pilgrims a reading Mary because of proof of the pilgrim badges, but also because of the relevant evidence of the unusually frequent depiction of Annunciations (all with a book) in the Norwich school of stained glass surviving from the region around Walsingham, dating to the fourteenth and fifteenth centuries. Only six miles from Walsingham, the parish church of All Saints, Bale, contains on the south side of the nave a large stained glass window that appears to be a modern amalgamation of at least five distinct medieval Annunciation scenes, with four instances of Mary reading.[15] The window is a twentieth-century reconstruction combining together fragments from different original medieval windows from within All Saints Church, Bale (or perhaps even a combination of churches in the Norwich area). Whatever their more recent history, they represent a regional emphasis on the Annunciation scene no doubt linked to the shrine's prominence in the area. A detail from the main-light panel shows one of the representations of Mary, with her book clearly open in front of her as the dove approaches (Figure 16). While the pieces might be slightly jumbled by recent

---

[14] Cameron Louis, ed., *The Commonplace Book of Robert Reynes: An Edition of Tanner MS 407* (New York: Garland, 1980), Entry 116 on 323, notes on 502. On dating and provenance of the manuscript see 24–7. This description is discussed by Gibson, *Theater of Devotion*, 141 and Carole Hill, 'St Anne and her Walsingham Daughter', 104.

[15] See entries under Bale: All Saints in 'Corpus Vitrearum Medii Aevi (CMVA): Medieval Stained Glass in Great Britain', Online Stained Glass Archive, http://www.cvma.ac.uk/index.html (accessed 17 August 2019); in addition to CMVA inv. No. 005130, other relevant entries include no. 015459 and 015455. For more information on the Norwich school, Sarah Crewe, *Stained Glass in England c. 118–1540* (London: HM Stationery Office, 1987). This window is mentioned in Carole Hill, 'St Anne and her Walsingham Daughter', 107.

Figure 16. Detail of Annunciation, stained glass. c. 1460–70. Main-light panel (part), South window, Nave, All Saints Bale parish church, Norfolk, UK.

restoration, there is no doubt that originally the book was no afterthought but integral to the composition, reflecting its central symbolic significance for the medieval understanding of the Incarnation.

Occluded as it has been by the shrine's destruction and a more recent lack of scholarly attention, the reading Annunciate's importance emerges in my analysis as the central driving devotional imagery behind the shrine at Walsingham. Recovering Mary's reading as part of the iconography of Walsingham recuperates the shrine's role in a long and lively cross-media devotional tradition centred around the Virgin's book at the Annunciation – and transforms how we understand the medieval pilgrim experience at the shrine. By reaching back to the long textual history of the Annunciation as a model meditative scene, we can see the ways in which the Virgin as a contemplative, interpretive reader powered an *imitatio Mariae* also at work in the Walsingham shrine. For instance, in his twelfth-century devotional treatise *De Institutione Inclusarum*, Aelred of Rievaulx, like several other gospel meditation authors, urges his readers to use their imaginations to actively participate in the Annunciation and 'cum beata Maria, ingressa cubiculum, libros quibus uirginis partus et christi prophetatur aduentus euolue' (with blessed Mary, enter the bedroom, open the books in which the virgin birth, even the arrival of Christ, is prophesied).[16] Reading in meditation was how fifteenth-century readers found the Virgin in Nicholas Love's *Mirror of the Blessed Life of Jesus Christ*, 'þe virgine Marie, þat was in hire pryue chaumbure þat tyme closed & in hir prayeres, or in hire meditaciones perauentur redyng þe prophecie of ysaie, touchyng þe Incarnacion'.[17] Thus when medieval readers left home and became pilgrims, when they entered the simulacrum of Mary's 'pryue chaumbure', suddenly that Annunciation devotional fantasy came dramatically alive. There they were in the realistic company of the mother of God and the angel they had imagined so many times; the miniature Mary and Gabriel from their Book of Hours illuminations suddenly writ large, lively under the shadows of candlelight. When they saw Mary depicted with her book inside the shrine, they might recall their own reading about her reading, when they learned from her example how to interpret the Word of God such that they became participants in the biblical story instead of just witnesses.

Mary's room was an intimate, familiar space. As in illuminations from the French Books of Hours discussed in the previous chapter, reader-pilgrims had been present in the room before, virtually, in their mind's eye, in their contemplative trance – just like Mary had been virtually present as the handmaiden of the handmaiden of Isaiah, as in the visions of Elizabeth and Birgitta, and

---

[16] From 'The Latin text of De Institutione Inclusarum', ed. Talbot, l. 889–90; my translation. See the discussion above in Chapter 3.
[17] Sargent, *The Mirror: Full Critical Edition*, 23, ll. 14–16.

in the devotional treatise *Of Three Workings in Man's Soul*. The example of Margery Kempe, who even went to far as to pre-empt Gabriel's announcement to Mary in a vision, ties together these related performative modes of participative piety, visionary activity, and physical pilgrimage when Margery 'gon to Walsyngham and offeryn in wirschep of owr Lady'.[18] With her hometown of Lynn only ten miles from Walsingham, visiting the shrine would be a logical expression of her devotion to Mary and use of the Annunciation to express her privileged access to the holy family (as discussed above in Chapter 4). Margery professed her own illiteracy, immersing herself in religious books by hearing them read aloud by confessors and friends; regardless of her actual level of literacy, she demonstrates how pilgrims with varying levels of reading ability and access to books were aware of the trends developing in devotional texts. Even those poorer, illiterate visitors would be deeply familiar with the imagery of Mary's reading and its symbolic power for inspiring an *imitatio Mariae* of the spiritual conception of Christ.

Thus inhabiting the Shrine of Our Lady of Walsingham constituted a devotional experience both alike and different from visiting shrines dedicated to other biblical or historical events. As with pilgrim sites also featured in life of Christ texts, the Holy House would trigger the deployment of the devotional practices undertaken by the reader in their previous reading at home – the text would come alive, their devotional fantasies come true. Of course the wide range of classes and education levels of pilgrims produced a wide range of experiences. Not all pilgrims could read, but even those illiterate devotees would likely have been familiar with the method of imaginative prayer promoted by the immensely popular gospel meditation tradition based on the *MVC*. Mental, interiorized pilgrimage to the distant past had prepared medieval readers to become pilgrims to the 'real thing', whether a historical site around the world or a reconstruction in their own backyard. But the image of the book in the Annunciation scene connected their personal, book-based devotions to the shrine in a way unique among pilgrim destinations.

The crucial difference between, for example, the Passion on the Mount with its imaginative modelling of compassion, and the Annunciation at Walsingham, is that what devotees learned at the Annunciation scene – and from Mary herself – was *how* to imaginatively model themselves on and in a text, *how* to read themselves into the scene. The Annunciation provided the mimetic methodology necessary to engage devotionally in both the reading and the pilgrimage experience. Inside the Holy House, pilgrims would be primed to mime the roles of Mary or Gabriel, perhaps uttering aloud the *Ave Maria* prayer, or to observe silently the visual depiction as it simultaneously played out in their imagination. A rare survival of a personal prayer specifically

---

[18] Windeatt, *The Book of Margery Kempe*, Book II, 393.

prayed at Walsingham survives, which exemplifies the vitality of the *imitatio Mariae* centred around the Annunciation – ironically enough, preserved by the man who helped fuel the iconoclasm that would later destroy the shrine. Erasmus writes about his personal devotions at Walsingham:

> And therefore whan I was within the chapell I mayd my prayers to our lady after thys fashio[n]. Oh chefe of all women Mary the mayd, most happy mother, moste pure virgyne … we pray thy that thy sone may grante this to vs, that we may folow thy holy lyffe, and that we may deserue thorow the grace of the holy ghoste, spirytualy to co[n]ceyue the lord Jesus Christ, + after that conception neuer to be separat frome hym, Amen. This done I kyssed the aultre. (25)

This prayer combines two ancient, powerful themes long shaping medieval devotion to the Annunciation moment: imitating Mary ('folow thy holy lyffe') and in turn imitating her physical conception with the devotee's spiritual conception of Christ in the soul ('spirytualy to co[n]ceyue the lord Jesus Christ'). As discussed in Chapter 1, over twelve centuries before Erasmus, Origen urged his congregation to 'hunc fide concipite, operibus edite; ut quod egit uterus Mariae in carne Christi, agat cor vestrum in lege Christi' (conceive [Christ] by faith … so that your heart may be doing in the law of Christ what the womb of Mary did in the flesh of Christ).[19] Guerric of Igny, Meister Eckhart and Bridget of Sweden, among many theologians and writers, developed this theme, maximizing its dramatic power to encapsulate the Incarnation's modelling of metaphor – the divine made man, the spiritual made physical. Erasmus, dedicated as he was in the early part of his life to the Virgin and her cult, taps into this history to demonstrate how prayer at Walsingham was not just any prayer to the Virgin, not even about her intercession or mercy: it was about her motherhood and how imitating her role in the Incarnation could transform the self.

Praying at the altar in Walsingham likewise could prompt a specific kind of identity formation. We should not underestimate the power of performing a deeply personalized recreation of the Incarnation within its own authenticated sacred space. As their Saviour is conceived, so does each devotee conceive themselves as a devotee. This operates on multiple overlapping levels. As Mary is transformed into a mother by her conception of Christ, so the pilgrim is transformed into her likeness by his spiritual conception of Christ. But this transformation was powered not only by the singular experience of kneeling at the altar like Erasmus and gazing on the reading Mary and praying like her. For many pilgrims their prayer within the shrine was also the ultimate fruition of years of private meditative exercises with book in hand – the imagined version of this very same Annunciation room in which they had mentally conceived of

---

[19] Augustine, Sermon 192.2, PL 38: 1012; trans. Lawler, *St Augustine*, 114. See discussion in Chapter 1.

themselves as devotional agents, fashioning themselves after Mary, the perfect meditant. Thus their experience at the shrine relived their previous reading experiences learning how to pray from Mary, perhaps prompting a kind of nostalgia for a devotional fantasy where they found themselves transformed spiritually as Mary had been transformed physically with the conception of Christ. Back home from their pilgrimage, devotional manuscript or Book of Hours back in hand, readers could also integrate their Walsingham experience into their regular prayers – both mentally and physically. Pilgrimage souvenirs like cards and even metal badges have been found pasted into East Anglian Books of Hours. In this way, we could imagine that Mary's book could be preserved inside the pilgrim's book, and 'the devotions of the shrine were thus transplanted into the daily piety of the book owner'.[20]

The shrine as simulacrum was also a special strength. In that it was understood as a replica of a holy place instead of the holy place itself, Stella Singer points out, 'Walsingham's status reflects the popular late medieval phenomenon of mimetic pilgrimage, whereby a hill-top chapel anywhere might become "a substitute Mount Sinai".'[21] She argues that 'the significance of place, essential to the phenomenon of pilgrimage, was changing: it was becoming, in a sense, reproducible and portable'.[22] As a sacred portal in time and space, the Walsingham shrine represents not only a mimetic pilgrimage but endorses a transformative opportunity for devotional mimesis, and in a different way than on-site pilgrimages to the actual Holy Land. Simon Coleman and John Elsner describe how 'Walsingham itself – "England's Nazareth" – has made its name as an East Anglian appropriation and transformation of a place in Palestine: the village provides not merely a flexible stage for pilgrimage performances, but also easy if vicarious access to a mythically charged, biblical landscape.'[23] So through its uniquely fluid 'vicarious access' to the far-away Holy Land, connected yet disconnected, the English shrine becomes a floating

[20] Eamon Duffy mentions an example of an indulgenced hymn and prayers from the shrine at Bromholm, pasted in the Lewkener Hours at Lambeth; see 'The Dynamics of Pilgrimage in Late Medieval England', in *Pilgrimage: The English Experience from Becket to Bunyan*, ed. Colin Morris and Peter Roberts, (Cambridge: Cambridge University Press, 2002), 173; for another example see B.W. Spencer, 'Medieval Pilgrim Badges', *Rotterdam Papers: A Contribution to Medieval Archaeology* (Rotterdam: Rotterdam Papers, 1968), 148, pl. 1.

[21] Stella A. Singer, 'Walsingham's Local Genius: Norfolk's "Newe Nazareth"', in *Walsingham in Literature and Culture from the Middle Ages to Modernity*, ed. Dominic Janes and Gary Waller, (Farnham: Ashgate, 2010), 24. See also Katherine J. Lewis, 'Pilgrimage and the Cult of St Katherine in Late Medieval England', in *Pilgrimage Explored*, ed. J. Stopford (York: York Medieval Press, 1999), 51, 37.

[22] Singer, 'Walsingham's Local Genius', 26.

[23] Simon Coleman and John Elsner, 'Performing Pilgrimage: Walsingham and the Ritual Construction of Irony', in *Ritual, Performance, Media*, ed. Felicia Hughes-Freeland (London: Routledge, 1998), 60.

signifier, available for devotional fantasy and for metaphorical interpretation of its functions.

It is in the interiority of the Holy House space itself rather than its geographical locatedness that its transformative power lies. Rather than being centred on a location *where* an action occurred – like the spot in Canterbury Cathedral where Thomas Becket was stabbed – the Walsingham shrine offers a re-creation of the room *within which* was the body *within which* was the womb *within which* Christ was incarnated. Its intimate proportions, a homely house unlike the soaring spaces of other shrines like Canterbury, evoke the most intimate enclosure of Christ within Mary, paradoxically 'heven and erthe in lytyl space' as the fifteenth-century Middle English lyric articulates it.[24] Modern pilgrims have reflected on this connection between womb and room in their own feelings inside the shrine, feelings that might well have been shared by their medieval counterparts many centuries before: 'the experience of entering the modern Holy House, going into an enclosed space filled with dim candle-light, is frequently described by visitors as like going into a womb'.[25] Moreover, the architectonically layered medieval shrine complex – a stone outer chapel *within which* was the wooden Holy House *within which* was the statue(s) of Mary *within which* was the conceived Christ, invisible but imagined – reinforces yet again the enclosure motif. Thus another difference from other pilgrim sites is that the Holy House at Walsingham not only contained Mary's body, but metaphorically *became* Mary's body, a womb within which pilgrims could be born again and could conceive Christ within themselves in mimesis of the Mother of God. Gail McMurray Gibson gestures towards this congruence when she writes that Walsingham

> had become a canonical image of the sacred house that had enclosed the Virgin – in whom God himself had been enclosed. ... its sacramental and symbolic power was none the less real for being a mimetic representation of the indwelling of God. Indeed, no better example exists of the image theology of the late Middle Ages than the Walsingham shrine, a replica or stage setting that pilgrims saw as proof of the Virgin's accessibility, the place where Mary – particularized, localized, in bodily likeness – had made her home, and had heard the angel's message.[26]

I would add that the shrine's enclosedness makes it more than a replica or stage setting, because the shrine was also a devotional fantasy made reality;

---

[24] Known as 'There is no rose', this well-known lyric is cited in full and discussed in Douglas Gray, *Themes and Images in the Medieval English Religious Lyric* (London: Routledge & Kegan Paul, 1972), 88.
[25] Coleman, 'Purity as Danger?', 66.
[26] Gibson, *The Theater of Devotion*, 142.

it was a womb for giving life to literary texts like gospel meditations or *Of Three Workings in Man's Soul*. The history of the Annunciation scene further demonstrates that the 'Virgin's accessibility' also relates to her imitable interaction with divine text: to read, interpret, pray and incarnate the Word of God. In its symbolic representation of Mary's womb, then, the shrine room enables pilgrims to be in the place of Christ as what is conceived in the Virgin's body.

Such an opportunity as Walsingham offered, to be both physically and spiritually centred in the transformative act of the Incarnation, granted special access to the conception of Word made flesh. This view of the shrine gives a deeper meaning to the general idea that 'pilgrimage is, in important sense, an incarnational experience'. Gary Waller elaborates on the concept of pilgrimage as incarnational in that:

> its very materiality reinforced the belief that bodily activities like walking, kneeling and prostrating before the image of the Virgin and holy relics were all part of an opening of the self to new possibilities as well as reinforcing existing beliefs and practices. Pilgrims were led to acknowledge the possibility of personal intimacy with the Virgin, not merely as a distant historical figure but there, in the details of the village, at the priory and its shrine, in the material as well as the spiritual accoutrements of a particular place.[27]

Corporal pilgrimage to the built building of the Annunciation enabled the body to join with the soul in what the soul had previously experienced in a purely imaginative way. Body and soul are unified in their access to the Incarnational moment, thus parallelling what happened when the Holy Spirit 'took flesh' of Mary and God became man. The letter and spirit, the text and the practice, of devotional books are likewise unified.

The shrine also presented to all its pilgrims a momentary experience of that enclosure which promoted communion with the divine for so many vowed men and women enclosed in anchorhold or cloister cells. Generally speaking, 'pilgrimage also provided a temporary release from the constrictions and norms of ordinary living, an opportunity for profane men and women to share in the graces of renunciation and discipline which religious life, in theory at least, promised'.[28] But again, specific to Walsingham in particular, the shrine's Annunciations room offers an intimate scale of construction that taps into the centuries-long association of Mary's *cubiculum* with the sanctified enclosure of the monastic cell or anchorhold, thus sharing its metaphoric significance as womb-room. While those vowed religious inhabitants might not be able to leave their cells or cloisters, they could mimetically conflate their room with Mary's, and make all the more powerful their participative prayer. We saw

---

[27] Waller, *Walsingham and the English Imagination*, 30.
[28] Duffy, 'The Dynamics of Pilgrimage', 191.

this at work in the eleventh- and twelfth-century texts examined in Chapter 2, especially the *Liber confortatorius* by Goscelin of St Bertin, written for an anchoress, and the *vita* and Psalter of Christina of Markyate. A contained, permeable yet impermeable, heterotopic space: both Mary's womb and her room, her *cubiculum*. Both can enclose the pilgrim, whether she journeys there on foot or in her mind, never leaving her own little room. Both offer a privacy and a sanctity parallel to the cell. But now those lay people or non-cloistered holy men and women who would have had the freedom to visit the shrine at Walsingham are also able to participate in a parallel mimetic conflation where the shrine's room transforms into the Annunciation room (doubling as anchorhold or cell) they had imagined in their prayers. While not living an enclosed life, they could vicariously experience religious seclusion for at least a moment by entering the Holy House.[29]

But the shrine was also profoundly different from the monastic cell or anchorhold. Unlike the paradoxically open and closed Annunciation room of devotional texts – open to the angel, open to the Holy Spirit, open to the interloping devotee, but closed to sin, other humans and any disruption – the Walsingham shrine was dramatically permeable in its accessibility by the public. Indeed, later medieval visitors to the popular shrine likely experienced what has been described as 'the bustling turmoil of an overcrowded resort'.[30] We should assume the flocks of pilgrims more often filed through the shrine in groups rather than singly. Likely they knelt or stood in prayer in front of the altar as described by medieval eye-witnesses like Reynes and Erasmus and, during high traffic periods, this pious encounter was in the midst of many others; Erasmus's account definitely gives the sense of 'animated congestion', as Spencer puts it.[31] What was at home and in their imagination an intimate, personal engagement with the Annunciation scene now became a public, shared moment. This tension between private devotion and public access parallels the sacred intimacy of the Annunciation moment itself, the moment when a short conversation between angel and girl brings the hope of salvation to all mankind. Walsingham pilgrims performing those otherwise typically private motions – kneeling, praying, imagining themselves in the scene – all suddenly found themselves united in their shared common devotional gestures that had previously brought them together only virtually through their shared

---

[29] Such a bodily experience vicariously tapping into monastic enclosure parallels the late medieval genre of texts of spiritual advice that translated 'the most iconic structures of monastic life (rule and cloister) into literary form for the guidance of lay readers'. See Nicole Rice, *Lay Piety and Religious Discipline in Middle English Literature* (Cambridge: Cambridge University Press, 2008), esp. Chapter 1, 'Translations of the Cloister: Regulating Spiritual Aspiration', 17–46, here at 17.
[30] Spencer, *Pilgrim Souvenirs*, 135.
[31] *Pilgrim Souvenirs*, 138.

experiences of reading those gospel meditations. Even if a pilgrim had previously read or heard a text like Love's *Mirror* as part of a group, their imaginative inhabitation of the Annunciation was still individual – that is, each imagined him or herself alone with Mary and Gabriel. But now pilgrims *en masse* inhabited the Holy House, physically sharing Mary's room as they metaphorically shared her womb. The particularity and universality of the Incarnation's role in human salvation thus played out in Walsingham's communal devotions based on the Annunciation scene.

Yet such a symbolic inhabitation of the womb was not so much an *imitatio Christi* as an *imitatio Mariae* – indeed Christ seems to be nearly absent from Walsingham discourse, in effect replaced by the pilgrim in his relationship to his mother. Mary's dominant role in the shrine at Walsingham recalls how a strong part of her cult focused on her qualities as a holy woman apart from Christ. Her powers to intercede with Christ were rarely emphasized in texts and images associated with the Annunciation; rather it was Mary as reader, interpreter, contemplative, visionary and mystic that was set up for *imitatio Mariae*. Erasmus, in his *Peregrinatio* poem on Walsingham, suggests her mimetic authority: to the question 'How wold she be worshipyd?' is the response, 'The most acceptable honor, that thou canste doo to her is to folowe her lyuynge.'[32] Her living, as captured in the Annunciation scene memorialized at the shrine, modelled not only a pious life, but also a *literate* contemplative one. This emphasis on literacy and contemplation (as the chapters above argue) marks one of the biggest divergences between the cult of Mary and the cult of Jesus or Christocentric devotions in this period. The Shrine of Our Lady of Walsingham reflected the strong Marian emphasis of medieval English religious culture from the twelfth century up to the Reformation, co-existing with devotion to Christ.

It is not surprising that Mary's exemplary reading, interpretation and devotion have been overlooked as a major part of the shrine's history, considering how the role of Mary herself is undervalued. For instance, when modern scholar Michael P. Carroll probes the question, 'What would have made the Holy House and its association with the Annunciation especially popular with pilgrims?', he cites Eamon Duffy's claims concerning the 'expanding lay market for traditional religious material', no doubt one very general factor, but then specifies that 'the rising demand for religious materials that Duffy describes as occurring throughout the fifteenth century was, in other words, a demand pervaded with a strongly *Christocentric* emphasis' (emphasis original).[33] Quite

---

[32] Erasmus, *Peregrinatio*, 34 (*Colloquies*, 640); cited and discussed in Waller, *The Virgin Mary*, 92.
[33] Carroll, 'Pilgrimage at Walsingham', 37-38; referencing Duffy, *The Stripping of the Altars*, 78–80.

the contrary: rather the shrine testifies to the influential *Mariocentric* motivation behind late medieval religiosity in England. Aside from the Christ child in Mary's lap of the Walsingham seal and statue, Christ plays very little part in the shrine's piety and history. Mary is no sidekick to Christ in this cultural history. Certainly pilgrims 'could connect themselves to the Gospel narratives in a manner that was both concrete and experiential', as Carroll argues, but it was not the narratives in general or even Christ's life *per se* to which they connected – it was very specifically their mimesis of Mary and Gabriel at the Annunciation into which the shrine tapped.[34] It was the Virgin and 'her lyuynge', her own imaginative, participative piety exemplified by her reading, that drove the popularity of Walsingham. Miracles associated with the shrine are likewise presented in medieval sources 'as distinctly Mariocentric. Christ is not explicitly mentioned. The Virgin's miracles are her own, even if their details are kept vague.'[35] Waller recognizes the need to emphasize that 'these miracles do not reflect the new Christocentric humanist learning: they are directly attributed to the power of the Virgin, not to God or even Christ. They are brought about by the Virgin herself.'[36] To overlook the immense power the Virgin wielded at the shrine, intertwined with influential devotional traditions gendered female because of the Virgin's central role, constitutes a misogynstic and anachronistic critical stance. How she developed into the distinctive Our Lady of Walsingham – working her distinctively Marian miracles, encouraging distinctively Marian contemplative devotion and appearing in distinctively Marian visions – is a story best exemplified by a single late medieval poem, the Pynson ballad.

The Pynson ballad: Rychold the visionary

The so-called 'Pynson ballad' linked to Walsingham confirms the shrine's unabashed Mariocentric motivations, and ties it into the main themes that drive the Annunciation tradition in medieval England: vision, interpretation, exegesis and women's devotion. Printed by London printer Richard Pynson sometime around 1496 and likely written during the preceding half-century, this poem uniquely survives in a four-page pamphlet (Cambridge, Magdalene College, Pepys Library, Book 1254).[37] After opening with a four-line stanza,

[34] Carroll, 'Pilgrimage at Walsingham', 38.
[35] Waller, *The Virgin Mary*, 92.
[36] Waller, *The Virgin Mary*, 90.
[37] STC 25001; see C.S. Knighton, ed., *Catalogue of the Pepys Library at Magdalene College, Cambridge: vol. 1, Census of printed books* (Cambridge: D.S. Brewer, 2004), 124, item 1254(6). On the dating of the poem see Dickinson, *Shrine*, Appendix 1, 124–5. The poem has been edited in Dickinson, *Shrine*, Appendix 1, 124–30; citations here are by stanza number.

twenty stanzas of seven lines each describe the shrine's origin story (stanzas 1–13), miracles (14–16), importance for England's Marian heritage (17–20) and conclude with a petition to the Virgin. The poem opens by explicitly identifying the foundation of the shrine in a particular year, 1061: 'A thousande complete syxty and one / The tyme of sent Edward kyng of this region' (1), and putting at the centre of the story 'A noble wydowe, sometyme lady of this towne, / Called Rychold' (3) whose visionary visitations from Mary led to the building of the shrine. However, according to Dickinson, 1130–1 is the earliest reference to a Richold or Richeldes attested in historical sources, so Waller notes that 'most modern historians (as opposed to pious readers of the ballad eager to accept its tale as historically accurate) date the beginnings of a private chapel that became an Augustinian priory in the mid twelfth century rather than Pynson's date of 1061'.[38] Waller points out the fifteenth-century political importance of dating the shrine's origin to before the Norman Conquest, thus affirming its native English quality, and that no other sources supplement the poem's account and dating. Some critics since Dickinson, such as Waller and Carroll, have now entirely discounted as mythical the poem's story about the visionary woman Rychold and declared that 'the simplest explanation is that there is no reference to it before the late fifteenth century because it does not emerge until then'.[39] Carroll goes so far as to call the ballad's account of the foundation an 'invented tradition' reflecting late medieval concerns rather than actual eleventh-century history.[40] Nonetheless, some recent authors digging behind Dickinson's conclusions to re-examine eleventh-century sources have unearthed some intriguing evidence that might support the story's early historical validity.[41] Suffice to say that the identification of Rychold and the foundation's dating bears further scrutiny; the case is far from closed.

---

[38] Waller, *The Virgin Mary*, 84; on the sources concerning Richeldes de Faverches, and the facts of the priory foundation and the early chronology of Walsingham in general see Dickinson, *Shrine*, 3–9. I will use the poem's spelling of the name Rychold, as opposed to Richeldes, the spelling of the twelfth-century historical figure, who may or may not be synonymous with the foundress described in the poem.

[39] Michael P. Carroll, 'Pilgrimage at Walsingham', 39. Carroll suggests the Walsingham legend is based on a similar legend about the Casa Sancta at Loreto. The similarities are legitimate, but the Walsingham legend's power and relevance to both eleventh- and fifteenth-century medieval England still hold.

[40] Carroll, 'Pilgrimage at Walsingham', 40; for a similar view see Waller, *Walsingham and the English Imagination*, 15–22.

[41] Bill Flint, *Edith the Fair: Visionary of Walsingham* (Leominster: Gracewing, 2015) puts forth a quite extended argument for the identification of Rychold as Edith, wife of King Harold; his theories deserve closer examination. Using different evidence, D.J. Hall, *English Medieval Pilgrimage* (London: Taylor & Francis, 1965) also argues that it could have been as early as the poem claims (107–8). In any case the *terminus ante quem* remains *c*. 1153, when the priory was founded.

In fact, from a literary-cultural point of view, there is no reason to connect exclusively the Pynson ballad's 'invented' story of a Marian vision with the religious trends of the fifteenth century. The poem's events and its claim of 1061 as the shrine's foundation, or even the rival dating in the twelfth century, fit in with the early medieval rise of the cult of Mary in England as outlined in the previous chapters.[42] It was in the eleventh century that the art and literature of England and Europe began to promote the cult of the Virgin in earnest and that women and their special connection to the Annunciation first found a prominent place in that tradition. Rychold, as the poem describes her – a pious woman with a special devotion to Mary and experiencing divine visions – aligns with other contemporary holy women like Eva (of Goscelin's *Liber*, 1080–3), Christina of Markyate (d. 1155) and the anchoress sister of Aelred of Rievaulx, for whom he wrote *De Institutione Inclusarum* (c. 1160). Considering Rychold as simultaneously an early medieval *and* late medieval figure allows us to connect her to those holy women as well as to fourteenth- and fifteenth-century visionaries such as Julian of Norwich, Margery Kempe and Birgitta of Sweden, all of whom engaged with a fiercely authoritative and hermeneutically expert Virgin like the one that Rychold meets in her vision. That Rychold was a laywoman like Margery Kempe shows how broad an appeal the Annunciation commanded, beyond the specialized interest demonstrated by enclosed religious women and their texts. In sum, the shrine's foundation story in the Pynson ballad certainly reflects the fifteenth century's continued, energetic interest in Mary and her propensity to appear in visions and offer expert interpretation – yet also the cultural evidence supports the possibility that Rychold's experience could be an authentic survival from four hundred years earlier.

Regardless of her historicity or fictionality, the protagonist and her presentation in the poem reward analysis. Rychold is depicted as a consummate 'deuout woman' (6); her model prayer practices facilitate a series of visions and divine intercessions by means of which she develops a close and supportive relationship with the Virgin Mary, who calls her 'doughter' (4). Like the late medieval visionary women I discussed in Chapter 4, Rychold requests and receives special attention from Mary. According to the ballad, Rychold 'desyred of Our Lady a petycyowne / Hir to honoure with some werke bountyous' (2). Her request was rewarded with a visionary pilgrimage. Mary led Rychold 'in spyryte' to Nazareth 'and shewed hir the place where Gabryel hir grette' (4), the Holy House of the Annunciation – not to the foot of the cross, or even the nativity bed, but back to where it all began: the 'rote of mankyndes gracyous redempcyon' (5), but also the moment when and where Mary discovered

---

[42] See also Miles, 'The Origins and Development', for a corresponding historical account of the cult's rise and women's role in it.

her identity as Mother of God. Now it is by means of the Annunciation that Rychold forms her own new identity: creator of the building of a miraculous shrine, made possible by her extreme devotion and belief in Mary's visionary appearances.

Whatever the status or accessibility of the original Holy House in the Holy Land, within this visionary space Mary's room remains intact and ready to be re-created by Rychold. In the vision, Mary commands Rychold to take carefully the measurement of the house so that she could build 'another lyke thys at Walsingham' (4). According to the poem Rychold witnessed this vision three times, each time 'in mynde well she marked both length and brede' of the little house (6). To construct the building the noblewoman called upon 'hir artyfycers full wyse'. They pre-fabricated the structure, and then were shown a sign of where to build it: in a meadow of dew one morning, two miraculously dry spaces appear, both in the correct dimensions for the structure. Rychold picks one of the two dry spaces as the site of her new Annunciation building, but her carpenters cannot get the pieces of the house to fit together despite their best efforts. So she turns to Mary for help.

The ballad describes Rychold's prayer on the night after the failed build: the widow 'prayed Our Lady with deuoute exclamacyon, / As she had begonne, to perfourme that habytacion' (11). The 'she' refers back to Our Lady: as Mary had started the whole project by showing the original house in the vision, Mary should help perform, or complete, the new house. In the following stanza we learn that:

> All nyghte the wydowe permayninge in this prayer
> Oure blyssed Lady with heuenly mynystrys,
> Hirsylfe beynge here chyef artyfycer,
> Areryd this sayd house with aungellys haudys. (12)

While Rychold prays her appeals are granted by Mary with her angel crew. Rychold's nocturnal 'deuoute exclamacyon' is set up as an efficacious, exemplary mode of private worship, where her female voice finds validation from the Virgin – a pious act long linked to the Annunciation event. In his eleventh-century anchoritic treatise, Goscelin of St Bertin tells the story of Mary's own singing of the psalms in the middle of the night at that very moment that 'the Archangel Gabriel entered with heavenly splendor, so that the Virgin appeared to be receiving him with this greeting'.[43] Christina of Markyate's 'reading and singing of the psalms by day and night' similarly functions as marker of her extreme piety and mirroring of the Virgin at the Annunciation, a performance effective enough to drive away demons. Rychold's 'exclamacyon' likewise recalls the performance prompt in Aelred of Rievaulx's meditational guide, where the

---

[43] Otter, trans., *The Book of Encouragement and Consolation*, 100.

reader is supposed to 'cry out and say' the *Ave Maria*, further emphasized in the fourteenth-century translation as 'cry þu as lowde as þu myȝt'.[44] Founded in the devotional history of the Annunciation scene, the lesson in this stanza from the ballad is that vocal prayer pleases the Virgin. While Rychold prays, Mary works, generating the shrine as she generated Christ in her womb. Like Mary's prayer at Gabriel's arrival, Rychold's generative prayer is also imitable. Her model devotion can be emulated by the pilgrims who come to the shrine. A few stanzas later, the poem turns to directly address the reader: 'Therfore euery pylgryme gyue your attendaunce / Our Lady here to serue with humble affeccyon' (17), thus matching both the vocal affection of Rychold and the 'humylyte' with which Mary describes herself bearing Christ (5).

Rychold's status as a laywoman functions as an important bridge between the monastic tradition and the devotional lives of regular people. Though she lives in the world, as far as the poem tells us, her Holy House could function for her like a *cubiculum*, a temporary anchorhold or monastic cell. Mary in effect gives Rychold the sacred space within which she can pray *like* an anchoress, that model contemplative figure, and thus pray like Mary – often portrayed as an enclosed contemplative at the Annunciation in anchoritic texts like Aelred of Rievaulx's *De Institutione Inclusarum*, Goscelin's *Liber confortatorius* and the *Ancrene Wisse* (as explored in Chapter 2). The laywoman Rychold would probably not have had such a reclusive space otherwise available to her. Yet the ballad poet never leads us *inside* the shrine room: its small space is left a mystery open only to those pilgrims who enter in. It is somehow untranslatable into verse. The wooden shrine becomes its own sacred universe, wholly distinct from the English countryside around it, mystically transporting both Rychold and the pilgrim back right into the scene with Mary and the angel – indeed, back into the mystical womb of the Virgin itself. Waller rightly suggests that Walsingham 'embodied a particular female source of power rooted in the female body represented by the Virgin'.[45] Yet while it might be Mary's womb that is mimetically represented by the enclosure, its origin story emphasizes not the female body but female holiness, wisdom and determination. The Annunciation once again allows for the peaceful reconciliation between women's biological reproduction and women's intellectual and devotional production, or even the primary importance of those abstract capacities. In the Holy House – as in the poem itself – Rychold fully inhabits her new identity as devout sponsor of the shrine. Her noblewoman status is now defined by her sanctity. Her progeny are the thousands of pilgrims who, passing through the likeness of Mary's room and womb, exit re-born.

---

[44] See the Vernon translation in Aelred of Rievaulx's *De Institutione Inclusarum*, ed. Ayto and Barratt, ll. 555–61.
[45] Waller, *Walsingham and the English Imagination*, 61.

The Pynson ballad: Mary the interpreter

In the entire poem, Mary makes the only mention of Christ: the Annunciation was when she would 'goddys sonne conceyue in virgynyte' (5). Actually the Mary that became Our Lady of Walsingham has very little to do with her relationship to Christ explicitly, and much more to do with her powers of prognostication, prophecy, sign-making and interpreting, all rooted in the symbolic power of her reading at the Annunciation and the transformation of the Word of God in her womb. The ballad's story of the shrine's building hinges, in fact, on the connection between sign and signified, between Old Testament and New Testament, that underlies the Incarnation itself.

Once Rychold is ready to re-create the house shown to her in her visions, the morning reveals two completely dry places on a meadow otherwise 'wete with dropes celestyall / And with syluer dewe sent from hye adowne'. The poem explains that 'this was the fyrste pronostycacyowne / Howe this our newe Nazareth here shold stande' (7). As a prognostication – a sign or token of a future event[46] – it is fitting that the lack of dew recalls, as the poem makes a point of explaining, 'the flees of Gedeon in the wete beynge drye' (8). The Old Testament story of Gideon's fleece comes from Judges 6:36–60, when Gideon sought a sign from God:

> Dixitque Gedeon ad Deum: Si salvum facis per manum meam Israel, sicut locutus es, ponam hoc vellus lanae in area: si ros in solo vellere fuerit, et in omni terra siccitas, sciam quod per manum meam, sicut locutus es, liberabis Israel. Factumque est ita. Et de nocte consurgens expresso vellere, concham rore implevit. Dixitque rursus ad Deum: Ne irascatur furor tuus contra me si adhuc semel tentavero, signum quaerens in vellere. Oro ut solum vellus siccum sit, et omnis terra rore madens. Fecitque Deus nocte illa ut postulaverat: et fuit siccitas in solo vellere, et ros in omni terra.
>
> (And Gideon said to God: If thou wilt save Israel by my hand, as thou hast said, I will put this fleece of wool on the floor: if there be dew on the fleece only, and it be dry on all the ground beside, I, shall know that by my hand, as thou hast said, thou wilt deliver Israel. And it was so. And rising before day wringing the fleece, he filled a vessel with the dew. And he said again to God: let not thy wrath be kindled against me if I try once more, seeking a sign in the fleece. I pray that the fleece only may be dry, and all the ground wet with dew. And God did that night as he had requested: and it was dry on the fleece only, and there was dew on all the ground.)

Like the sign of the dry fleece granted by God, the dry patches in the dewy field at Walsingham are 'assygned by myracle of holy mayde Marye' (8). With this

---

[46] OED, *prognostication*, n. 3.

prognostication right out of scripture, Mary exhibits her deep knowledge of the Old Testament and its use as typology: she not only chooses a sign whose meaning can only be unlocked by reference to the Gideon and the fleece story, with the dew motif she also evokes several other prophetic passages which are often linked to the Incarnation. Foremost among them is Isaiah 45:8: 'Rorate, cæli, desuper, et nubes pluant justum; aperiatur terra, et germinet salvatorem, et justitia oriatur simul: ego Dominus creavi eum' (Drop down dew, ye heavens, from above, and let the clouds rain the just: let the earth be opened, and bud forth a saviour: and let justice spring up together: I the Lord have created him). The morning dew, as a symbol of new beginnings and natural fecundity and purity, was often invoked as an allegory of the Incarnation.[47] Featured prominently at the opening Office of the Mass of the Blessed Virgin Mary in the Sarum Use, this verse from Isaiah would have been heard daily in English Lady Chapels from Advent to Christmas.[48] It was also an antiphon for the Purification of the Virgin.[49]

The portrayal of Mary's prognostication as one of the Old Testament prophecies that foretells her own pregnancy taps into her role as interpreter of scripture, the first reader to conceive the ultimate meaning of those prophecies, physically conceived within her body at that moment of mental understanding. With this web of scriptural associations hovering in the background of the Pynson ballad, Mary as expert interpreter – female creator and reader of signs – emerges as Our Lady of Walsingham. This new house of the Annunciation, representing the space where the Word was made flesh and the New Testament began, literally and figuratively rests on a foundation of Old Testament verses, operating as signs, which prognosticate that Incarnation.

But why then must Rychold *incorrectly* interpret the sign? Why does she fail? She certainly tries to choose wisely between the 'tweyne quadrates of egall space' (8), as the poem carefully explains that 'the wydowe thought it most lykly of congruence / This house on the fyrste soyle to bylde and arere' (9). Yet the builders could not get the house to go up. 'For no pece with oder wolde agre with geometrye', causing them to be 'full of agonye / that they could nat ken neyther mesure ne marke / To ioyne togyder their owne proper werke'

---

[47] Other Old Testament occurrences of the dew motif typologically linked to the Incarnation include Hosea 14:6: 'Ero quasi ros; Israël germinabit sicut lilium, et erumpet radix ejus ut Libani' (I will be as the dew, Israel shall spring as the lily, and his root shall shoot forth as that of Libanus).

[48] *The Sarum Missal in English* (London: The Church Press Company, 1868), 521. Dew also features as a motif in several Middle English Marian lyrics like 'I syng of a mayden'; Carleton Brown, *Religious Lyrics of the XV Century* (London: Clarendon Press, 1939), 119; cf. Eamon Duffy's discussion in *The Stripping of the Altars*, 256–7.

[49] *Corpus antiphonalium officii*, ed. by René-Jean Hesbert and René Prévost, 6 vols (Rome: Herder, 1963–79); no. 4441.

(10). Rychold's all-night prayer to the Virgin was in response to this disaster, and we could initially think that the prayer itself was the desired result of the failure. Mary first wanted this house – she could figure it out, the poem tells us the noblewoman thought. Sure enough,

> Oure blyssed Lady with heuenly mynystrys,
> Hirseylfe beynge chyef artyfycer,
> Areyed this sayd house with aungellys haudys [handys],
> And not only reyred it but set it there it is,
> That is, two hundred fote and more in dystaunce
> From the fyrste place bokes make remembraunce. (12)

Modern critics usually assume that the final location of the Holy House is on the *second* dry patch of meadow, but in fact the poem is vague; maybe Mary directed it to be built on another random spot entirely. However, it would be logical (optimistic?) to assume that Mary presented Rychold with a 50/50 chance of choosing correctly. Regardless, this story seems to be a kind of inherently unfair game-show contest: asked to pick between two identical doors, the poor contestant doesn't realize that she can never pick the right door – only the host knows.

There are several intersecting ways to understand such a perplexing scenario. Most obviously, Rychold's second devotion to Mary comes about because of her initial wrong choice, and this model 'deuoute exclamacyon' is important for its inspiration for the pilgrims and readers of the poem. In another way, the impossible choice Mary sets out for the widow partly evokes the late medieval tradition of Madonna as trickster, most thoroughly researched as it emerged in Italy.[50] In those Marian cult stories sometimes the Virgin made people lame or otherwise temporarily incapacitated them in order to convince others to believe her miracle. Our Lady of Walsingham does not display such malevolence here, but she definitely sets up the two plots as some kind of a test which Rychold seems bound to fail, perhaps with a motive of convincing others of the miracle of the shrine (though precisely how that motive works seems a bit unclear at first). Dickens has suggested that the point of the wrong plot is that Rychold had to show that she would 'submit to the request of Mary and try to accomplish it obediently'.[51] Certainly obedience to Mary is at play here. But in fact Rychold does submit to Mary's every request from the beginning and tries to accomplish them quite submissively. Also, Mary never stipulates

---

[50] As in Michael P. Carroll, *Madonnas that Maim: Popular Catholicism in Italy since the Fifteenth Century* (Baltimore, MD: Johns Hopkins University Press, 1992), 58, 71, 82.
[51] Andrea Janelle Dickens, *Female Mystic: Great Women Thinkers of the Middle Ages* (New York: I.B. Tauris, 1999), 15.

which of the two plots to use: they simply appear as signs without any signal as to which is the 'right' one. So the plot twist is not really in response to any lack of devotion or obedience on Rychold's part; in contrast, I think the whole story demonstrates the laywoman's consistent, humble acceptance of Mary's control over the situation. Rather I would argue something else entirely can explain the story of the two dry plots and the house that wouldn't hold.

When Mary's miracle presents itself as a manifestation of the Old Testament story of Gideon's fleece, also alluding to the Isaian prophecies foretelling the Incarnation, this is a signal to us – the pilgrims and readers – that this story is actually about Mary's authority as interpreter of both signs and scripture. Mary, reader of the Word at the Annunciation, proves to be the better 'reader' of her *own* prognostications. She both creates and interprets supernatural signs. By surrendering legibility to Mary the story acknowledges her superior power of interpretation. While in general Mary operates as intercessor between mankind and Christ, in this situation she intercedes between sign and signified, just as her body interceded between Word and Word made man. She creates this physical recapitulation of Luke's story by re-entering the intermediary space between Old and New Testament, the space of interpretation. Just as the events of the New Testament Gospel are foreshadowed by the Old Testament, so is the new location of her house miraculously revealed through shadow – that which preserves the dew around it. Just as Mary fulfilled the prophecies by giving flesh to Christ in her womb, so does she fulfil the sign of the dewless field by giving form to the house of her Annunciation. In the medieval world, form – meaning – structure – falls apart without divine intervention (as in the Incarnation) and our submission to it.

Of course Rychold cannot read the signs correctly, as divine signs are illegible to fallen humanity without the grace of God. She is bound to 'see through a glass darkly', while it is only Mary, having born the Word in her body, that can directly see the divine (i.e. the meaning behind the sign) 'face to face' (1 Cor 13:12). In many ways Rychold's failure parallels the failure of the servant in the Lord and servant parable of Julian of Norwich's *Revelations* or Long Text (discussed in chapter 4). In Julian's vision (which she laboured long to interpret), a servant rushes to do the command of the Lord and in his eagerness falls into a ditch, where the Lord must rescue him. The servant fails, like Rychold, but only while trying to obey, like Rychold. Each Christian must fail, 'fall' like the servant in Julian's parable, in order to be saved – in order to earn salvation through Christ, or in the case of Rychold and the shrine, through Mary's intercession and miracle-working. Yet in the Pynson ballad Mary intercedes with her own power; there is no interceding to Christ, because Christ is absent from this story. Mary reigns: she is, as the ballad asserts, the 'chyef artyfycer', commanding her own crew of 'heuenly mynystrys' with their 'aungellys haudys' (12).

Mary's epithet 'chyef artyfycer' is intriguing. Earlier in the poem, we also read about Rychold's 'artyfycers full wyse' whom she called to build the chapel (6, again in 13). According to both the MED and the OED, the term 'artificer' (from the Old French) had a dominant meaning of 'one who practices a craft or trade' or 'an artisan, a craftsman' in use throughout the fifteenth century, towards the end of which the Pynson ballad was composed and printed.[52] In addition an artificer can be 'a constructor, a manufacturer'.[53] These definitions of 'craftsman' and 'constructor' fit well with the mortal builders and with Mary as the immortal builder, all of whom attempt construction with differing levels of success. Yet the Virgin is the *chief* artificer. With her special skills both in craftsmanship but more importantly in making and interpreting signs (and managing angel workers), she is no average artisan. Perhaps here the poem evokes another connotation of the word 'artificer', 'a practitioner of (any of) the sciences or liberal arts; a scientist; a scholar', attested as early as 1449. Mary was well known in the Middle Ages as queen of the liberal arts and, as the original expert Old Testament scholar *sina qua non*, surely she fulfils this next level of the artificer title, far beyond the craftsmen who labour in vain to build the building.[54]

Those same hapless craftsmen return the next morning to discover the second miracle of the angel-built chapel: 'They founde eche parte conioyned sauns fayle / Better than they coude *conceyue* it in mynde / Thus eche man home agayne dyd wynde' (13, my italics). Again, human failure is set up in order to emphasize Mary's superior powers: this time, of *conception*. Predictably, the craftsmen could not satisfactorily conceive of or picture what the house would look like or how it would be constructed – that is, conceive as in 'to form (an intention, design, etc.) in the mind'.[55] Mortal men cannot fully conceive the divine in their minds, much less a divinely revealed structure shown in a vision, which like all visionary experience would be impossible to relay adequately in speech (not to mention in well-drawn section and elevation building plans dictated by an untrained noblewoman). But again here is where Mary's tripartite model of conception, centred around her physical conception of the Word as Christ, underlies the poem and its deployment of the Annunciation tradition. The entire shrine memorializes that moment 'whan Gabryell gaue to me relacyon / To be a moder through humylyte, / And

---

[52] MED, *artificer, -ier* (n.); OED, *artificer* (n.) 1.
[53] OED, *artificer* (n.) 4.a.
[54] On Mary as Queen of the liberal arts see Donavin, *Scribit Mater*. An additional definition provocatively links the tradition of Mary as trickster to her role in the poem as chief artificer: OED *artificer* (n.) 3., 'an artful, cunning, or devious person, a trickster, a dissembler' attested as early as the 1430s; however, I do not necessarily think it is in play here because its uses are too derogatory for reference to the Virgin.
[55] OED, *conceive* (v.) I.1.a.

goddys sonne *conceyve* in virgynyte' (5). Having conceived God in her body, she is better able to conceive (designs, plans, interpretations) in her mind than any other person. And while Rychold's workmen may not be the sharpest tools in the shed, the poet's author gives his pilgrim-readers the benefit of the doubt in his final devotional directions:

> Therfore euery pylgryme gyue your attendaunce
> Our Lady here to serue with humble affeccyon,
> Your sylfe ye applye to do hir plesaunce,
> Remembrynge the great ioye of hir Annunciacion,
> Therwyth *conceyuynge* this bryef compylacyon,
> Though it halte in meter and eloquence,
> It is here wryten to do hyr reuerence. (17, my italics)

Now, in remembering the Annunciation – the moment when Mary conceived Christ – readers can also conceive, or comprehend in the mind, the poem itself. In a way, they can internalize 'this bryef compylacyon' spiritually, bringing alive the story in themselves like Christ was brought alive in Mary, and can be brought alive in each Christian's soul. Employing all the connotative levels of the verb *to conceive* highlights how the interpretive action at the centre of the Annunciation – Mary's conception of Word as Christ – reverberates through the physical building of the shrine of Walsingham, the textual monument of the Pynson ballad and the reader-pilgrim's act of inhabiting the Annunciation room in their mind, through reading, and with their body, through pilgrimage.

Coda:
Mary and her Book at the Reformation

On 14 July 1538, on the order of Thomas Cromwell, royal commissioners removed the statuary of Our Lady of Walsingham as well as all the gold and silver in the chapel.[1] Within a few days, the Marian items were taken to London along with other images of the Virgin from various churches in order to be burned (the metal valuables went straight into the royal coffers).[2] By 4 August, the chapel and priory would be completely shut down, surrendered to King Henry VIII.[3] Within a year, the entire site had been sold on into private hands. Soon scant ruins remained.

The loss was keenly felt by those devoted Christians who had gone on pilgrimage to Walsingham; 'its memory was long a-dying', Dickinson writes. Around the end of the sixteenth century, when any hope of a successful counter-reformation had long ago died out, an anonymous poet 'poured out the bitterness which the deed had brought to those to whom the cult of Our Lady stood as an ennobling force in a crude society':[4]

> Weepe, weepe, O Walsingam, whose dayes are nightes,
> Blessings turned to blasphemies, holy deeds to dispites.
> Sinne is wher our Ladie sate, heaven turned is to hell,
> Sathan sits where our Lord did swaye, Walsingam oh farewell.[5]

---

[1] According to the letter of Ric Vowel of Walsingham to Cromwell, entry no. 1376, in 'Henry VIII: July 1538, 10–15,' in *Letters and Papers, Foreign and Domestic, Henry VIII, Volume 13 Part 1, January–July 1538*, ed. James Gairdner (London, 1892), 510. *British History Online*, http://www.british-history.ac.uk/letters-papers-hen8/vol13/no1/pp507-513 (accessed 17 August 2019). See also Dickinson, *Shrine*, 65.

[2] Dickinson, *Shrine*, 65.

[3] See entry no. 31, 'Henry VIII: August 1538 1–5,' in Gairdner, *Letters and Papers*, part 2, p. 11. *British History Online*, http://www.british-history.ac.uk/letters-papers-hen8/vol13/no2/pp1-14 (accessed 17 August 2019).

[4] Dickinson, *Shrine*, 67.

[5] Last lines of the ballad found in Bodleian Library MS Rawl. Poet. 291, fol. 16r-v, perhaps by Philip, Earl of Arundel, printed in *The New Oxford Book of Sixteenth Century Verse*, ed. E. Jones (Oxford: Oxford University Press, 1991), 550–1.

Indeed, farewell not only to blessings and holy deeds, but also to precious evidence of an important chapter in a nation's own religious history. The shrine at Walsingham's medieval cultural heritage, dispersed and destroyed in the waves of the English Reformation, can never be fully known or recovered. Some short weeks of iconoclastic fever devastated nearly five centuries of sacred art, artefacts and manuscripts. Martin Luther rejected extreme iconoclasm such as this, writing, 'no one who sees the iconoclasts raging thus against wood and stone should doubt that there is a spirit hidden in them that is death-dealing, not life-giving'.[6]

While religious institutions all over England and Europe suffered similar annihilation, those connected to the Virgin Mary experienced a particularly targeted desecration, due to the Virgin's problematic position for the Reformers. Widespread beliefs in Mary's power to intercede with Christ, her elevated position as Queen of Heaven, her real presence in her statues, her focus for pilgrimages and her ability to effect miracles were all seen as dangerous heterodoxies by Protestant thinkers.[7] The problem with Mary was deeply connected to everything from lay devotional practices and the authority of women, to the very nature of the Incarnation and the definition of the Eucharist – aspects whose links to the Annunciation I will examine in this coda. By no means did Mary disappear during the Reformation centuries, but her significance was dramatically redefined at all levels of the church. The Annunciation shows how this redefinition put the Virgin at the centre of 'an attack which was not limited to the cult of saints, but struck at the heart of the Catholic system of access to sacred power'.[8] With the Virgin and her book a central part of that medieval system, giving access to the divine through both text and body for so many different types of people but especially women, the way the Annunciation scene

---

[6] *Luther's Works*, vol. IX, ed. Jaroslav Pelikan (St Louis, MO: Concordia Press/Fortress Press, 1960), 80; a quote discussed by many scholars, among whom Margaret Aston, *England's Iconoclasts: Vol.1, Laws Against Images* (Oxford: Clarendon Press, 1988), 6, and Miri Rubin, *Mother of God: A History of the Virgin Mary* (New Haven, CT: Yale University Press, 2009), 373. On the complexities of the Reformation and iconoclasm see Sergiusz Michalski, *The Reformation and the Visual Arts* (London: Routledge, 1993), and Joseph Leo Koerner, *The Reformation of the Image* (Chicago: University of Chicago Press, 2004).

[7] On Mary at the English Reformation generally see Diarmaid MacCulloch, 'Mary and Sixteenth-Century Protestants', *Studies in Church History* 39 (2004): 191–217; Christine Peters, *Patterns of Piety: Women, Gender and Religion in Late Medieval and Reformation England* (Cambridge: University of Cambridge Press, 2003), esp. ch. 9 'The Virgin Mary and the Saints', 207–45; Waller, *The Virgin Mary*; Lilla Grindlay, Queen of Heaven: *The Assumption and Coronation of the Virgin in Early Modern English Writing* (Notre Dame, IN: University of Notre Dame Press, 2018); and, more briefly, Rubin, *Mother of God*, 367–70.

[8] Peters, *Patterns of Piety*, 207.

survived the Reformation offers a complex case study for what happened to the Mother of God in these tumultuous years.

For the leaders of the Reformation, Mary's role as the woman who gave birth to Christ could not be ignored; yet at the same time, she must not be allowed to usurp veneration due to God alone, and her intercessory powers must be curtailed.[9] Erasmus's colloquy on Walsingham, *Peregrinatio Religionis Ergo*, captures this tension in the Virgin's own words, from an imagined letter written by herself: 'But as for me thou canst not cast owt, except thou cast owt my sone, whiche I holde in myne armes. I wyll nat be seperat frome hym, other thou shalt cast hym owt with me or else thou shalt let vs bothe be, except that you wold haue a temple withowt a Christe.'[10] So would many agree who resisted the Reformation's demotion of the Virgin. Despite her imagined protestations, and Erasmus's own Marian devotion, his text was to have a vital role in the casting out of the Our Lady from the shrine of Walsingham, and indeed the iconoclasm wreaked across England. All part of the plan: Cromwell likely approved the English translation of the Latin work, and probably made sure to add on the severely anticlerical and antipapal preface.[11] The *Peregrinatio* both captures and sets up for derision those trends in late medieval religion most reviled by reformers, which were foundational to the cult of the Virgin: images, relics, pilgrimage and miracles. MacCulloch gets to the heart of the matter, for Erasmus particularly, but also perhaps pertaining to so many of the highly educated elite men who led the reform efforts:

> Famously, in [Erasmus'] *Colloquies*, he turned his pilgrimage to Walsingham and Canterbury into light comedy for the public. This was part of a vigorous debunking of the physicality and tactility of late medieval popular piety which reflected Erasmus's distaste for lay devotion; for all his loudly proclaimed vision of the labourer reading the Bible at the plough-tail, and his strictures on the clericalism of his age, he was profoundly repelled when he observed the everyday reality of Western Christendom's layfolk grasping at the sacred. His nausea would become naturalized in Protestantism, particularly in its Reformed variety.[12]

---

[9] Peters, *Patterns of Piety*, 218–19.
[10] Erasmus, *A dialog of communication of two persons*, 15; for lack of page numbers, all quotations are by image number of page spreads from the 1540 second edition copy in the British Library, available on EEBO: http://gateway.proquest.com/openurl?ctx_ver=Z39.88-2003&res_id=xri:eebo&rft_id=xri:eebo:citation:99846697 (accessed 17 August 2019).
[11] Thompson, *Colloquies*, 620. See also James K. McConica, *English Humanists and Reformation Politics under Henry VIII and Edward VI* (Oxford: Oxford University Press, 1965).
[12] MacCulloch, 'Mary', 194.

We might extrapolate and suggest that for many reformers a theological concern for the over-reaching intercessory powers of the Mother of God was entangled with this strong 'distaste for lay devotion', captured by the style and atmosphere of publicly accessible shrines like Walsingham. The Virgin did not stand a chance against such an overwhelming combination of Protestant objections.

Another major factor in Mary's reduced position was that so many of the stories of her life were apocryphal, and the newly reformed faith was to be solely based on God's word in the canonical scriptures – so all those non-canonical Marian traditions had to go, according to Luther and other like-minded reformers. Thus both private prayer and devotion were reshaped as well as communal celebrations of Marian feasts. Personal devotion was redirected away from the medieval traditions of imaginative, participative piety which made vivid Christ's and Mary's humanity for devotees. The genre where Mary had received so much attention, lives of Christ or gospel meditations, fell out of favour. For instance, John Daye's 1578 officially sponsored *Booke of Christian Prayers* included mostly new Reformation prayers that shied away from depicting the Crucifixion as an 'imagined reality'.[13] Yet at the same time, as Peters justly notes, 'such habits of mind were, though, hard to break': Daye's *Booke* also included translations of pre-Reformation affective prayers that selectively preserved earlier Catholic modes of devotion.[14] Their efficacy (or ability to sell copies) could not be so easily dismissed.

Likewise those enormously popular medieval feasts of Mary's Conception, Birth and Assumption, which had evolved from the apocryphal gospels over several centuries, quickly fell to the reformist movements. However, other Marian feasts based on the Bible were retained, such as the Annunciation: 'thanks to their biblical foundation they were appreciated by Lutherans and enjoyed the attention of preachers, artists and composers of church music. These feasts demonstrated Mary's virtues: at the Annunciation her humility was manifest, her openness to God's word.'[15] Protestants and Catholics at least agreed on the historicity of the Annunciation scene as the moment of Christ's incarnation.[16] The retention of the feast of the Annunciation, but with a renewed emphasis on Mary's humanity and submission, in many ways captures how her role transformed in the new Protestant church. Mary did not so much fade away as a model for Protestant women (and men), as the mimetic possibilities simply shifted – or rather, became circumscribed, with a

---

[13] Eamon Duffy, 'Devotion to the Crucifix and Related Images in England on the Eve of the Reformation', in *Bilder und Bildersturm im Spätmittelalter und in der frühen Neuzeit*, ed. R. Scribner (Wiesbaden: Harrassowitz, 1990), 32.
[14] Peters, *Patterns of Piety*, 212.
[15] Rubin, *Mother of God*, 369.
[16] Waller, *A Cultural Study*, 133.

more limited range of models offered by the reformed Virgin.[17] Humility was of course always an important factor in *imitatio Mariae*; but, as this study has shown, in the medieval church it was combined with Mary's powerful authority as mother of God, as intercessor and queen, as reader and interpreter of the Bible. After the Reformation, Sarah Boss explains, 'over time, devotion to the Virgin changed its emphasis in that it became less interested in Mary's authority and glory as Mother of God and more concerned with her spiritual role as mother of Christians, and subsequently with her *moral* example as the recipient of God's Word' (my emphasis) – moral vs mystical, devotional or intellectual.[18] Boss tracks how in the sixteenth and seventeenth century, in both England and France, authors often 'assume that the influence of a mother ought to be confined to the nursery' so that 'Mary's motherhood is thereby stripped of any authority.'[19] Instead of her divinely anointed motherhood elevating all earthly mothers, Mary's motherhood was brought down to size, to the lowest common denominator of a humble, modest woman whose passive submission was her main moral virtue. The Virgin's survival in the Protestant church 'depended on denying her power of intercession and on reducing her to a more human level, whether by insisting upon her physical plainness or by denying her bodily Assumption into heaven'.[20]

We have seen how Mary's immense influence in medieval culture was fostered by pilgrimage sites like the Shrine of Our Lady at Walsingham, and how those sites in turn fostered a devotional culture where women could participate fully and under their own authority – as modelled by Rychold and Margery, the visionaries.[21] Protestant aversion from Mary was never merely doctrinal; it was often a thinly veiled outlet for misogyny. There were several gendered dimensions to iconophobia and its focus on Marian shrines. Generally speaking, reformers considered idolatry as a kind of metaphorical adultery, with the seduction of images leading Christians into various sins figured as spiritual fornication.[22] So the offending sculptures, etc., were already feminized in their

[17] MacCulloch, 'Mary', 215. Similarly, Peters argues that 'it is oversimplistic to see an attack on Marian veneration as getting rid of the Virgin Mary to the detriment of women and their access to a female role model'; *Patterns of Piety*, 223.
[18] Boss, *Empress and Handmaid*, 52.
[19] Boss, *Empress and Handmaid*, 50.
[20] MacCulloch, 'Mary', 243–4.
[21] On women's independent and influential engagement in pilgrimage practices in general see Susan Signe Morrison, *Women Pilgrims in Late Medieval England: Private Piety as Public Performance* (London: Routledge, 2000); and on Walsingham in particular, ch. 1, 'The Milky Way: Women Pilgrims and Visual Art', 10–42.
[22] On this issue in other arenas see Huston Diehl, *Staging Reform, Reforming the Stage. Protestantism and Popular Theater in Early Modern England* (Ithaca, NY: Cornell University Press, 1997), esp. ch. 6, 'Iconophobia and Gynophobia: The Stuart Love Tragedies'; and Sarah Stanbury, 'The Vivacity of Images: St Katherine, Knighton's

dangerous threat. Specifically, as well, statues of Mary and Marian shrines associated with the female and often subversive power of the Virgin came to represent the danger of women's independence from the authority of male clerical authority. Certainly some medieval clerical authorities had always felt threatened by and sought to control this female independence linked to Mary and to pilgrimage, but the Reformation witnessed a stark shift to zero tolerance for female 'overreach' linked to Mary. While medieval holy women such as Birgitta of Sweden and Julian of Norwich had found in Mary inspiration for asserting their own spiritual authority, reformist sermons, for instance, emphasized her humility as demonstrated by scriptural references to 'her obedience to lawfully constituted authority'.[23]

When looking for their own female figures to emulate, activist Protestant women turned away from Mary and back towards the strong women of the Old Testament, particularly Judith and Esther.[24] Obviously Mary was far 'too hot' and much too Catholic, but most of all, in the Protestant tradition she modelled little of the female authority she once wielded centuries before. Her position as mother of God was securely domesticated and deflated. Peters considers one way of understanding the consequences of Mary's changing image:

> Perhaps paradoxically, the effect of deflecting attention from Mary as Queen of Heaven was to make the model of Mary more accessible, and more powerful, for godly men and women. The image of a humble, modest, and even plain Mary filled with divine grace bestowed upon her by God could be the image of the godly layperson. In such an image the role of merit was conveniently glossed over ... and the Virgin Mary at her prayer desk in portrayals of the Annunciation was also the godly protestant reading in the closet.[25]

Mary as accessible to the godly layperson might ring true in the Protestant world. Yet Peters' argument overlooks how an accessible Mary also rang true in the Catholic pre-Reformation world – and was incredibly powerful. For more than a millennia Mary had been imitable via *imitatio Mariae* by the godly layperson, even as she was simultaneously the most elevated of women,

---

Lollards, and the Breaking of Idols', in *Images, Idolatry, and Iconoclasm in Late Medieval England*, ed. Jeremy Dimmick, James Simpson and Nicolette Zeeman (Oxford: Oxford University Press, 2002). My thanks to Fionnuala O'Neill Tonning for her insights regarding iconophobia and gender.

[23] MacCulloch, 'Mary', 215

[24] Peters, *Patterns of Piety*, 228; MacCulloch, 'Mary', 216. On early modern women and scriptural reading more generally see Femke Molekamp, *Women and the Bible in Early Modern England: Religious Reading and Writing* (Oxford: Oxford University Press, 2013); Erica Longfellow, *Women and Religious Writing in Early Modern England* (Cambridge: Cambridge University Press, 2004); and Michele Osherow, *Biblical Women's Voices in Early Modern England* (Farnham: Ashgate, 2009).

[25] Peters, *Patterns of Piety*, 224.

the Queen of Heaven and the *mediatrix* to the Saviour. She was also a woman who liked to sit and read and pray, a way of being that medieval women found accessible and relevant. The Virgin contained multitudes. What is more paradoxical, however, is what Peters briefly refers to: how the motif of Mary reading at the Annunciation fitted into the Protestant agenda.

Generally post-Reformation England does not offer evidence of rejection of the motif of Mary holding a book. On the contrary, the iconography persists continuously in artistic representations of the Annunciation up to the present day. Although the creation of (any kind of) new images trailed off, there is little evidence Annunciations were systematically destroyed. As I noted above, the feast of the Annunciation survived in the post-Reformation calendar because of its basis in scripture; likewise, typical representations of the Annunciation did not come under so much scrutiny as more dangerous statues of Mary enthroned, for instance, projecting the intercessory power that reformers feared would detract from her Son. The Annunciation does, after all, document the moment of the Incarnation of Christ, who was and remained the sole source of salvation. Certainly other Protestant anxieties were triggered by specific aspects of some Annunciation art. For instance, in 1511 German artist Lucas Cranach the Elder produced a woodcut of the Annunciation, book in the Virgin's lap, but including below the image a prayer with an indulgence. It was later reprinted in 1524 without the prayer: indulgences violated Reformist beliefs, but certainly representations of the biblical scene itself did not, and neither did Mary directly accessing the Word of God.[26] In the same Lutheran artistic traditions we even see quite emphatic embracing of medieval-style representations of Mary's erudition as in, for example, a 1584 altarpiece by Lucas Cranach the Younger, with an Annunciation painting where Mary reads at a four-sided desk with three open books on view.[27]

Unquestionably heterodox for Reformers was the somewhat common iconographical detail of the infant Christ descending on a sunbeam to the Virgin's womb. This motif is mentioned by one of the English interrogatories from 1560:

> Whether all aulters, images, holy water stones, pictures, paintings, as of th'assumption of the blessyd virgin, *of the descending Christ into the virgin in the forme of a lyttel boy at th'annunciation of the aungel*, and all other superstitious and daungerous monuments; especially paintings and images in waul, boke, cope, banner, or elsewhere, of the blessed Trinitye, or of the

---

[26] Lucas Cranach the Elder, *Annunciate*, Rijksmuseum, Amsterdam. See Koerner, *The Reformation of the Image*, 63, illus. 24. On Cranach the Elder generally see Bonnie Noble, *Lucas Cranach the Elder: Art and Devotion of the German Reformation* (Lanhan, MA: University Press of America, 2009).

[27] Koerner, *The Reformation of the Image*, 214, illus. 98.

Father, (of whom there can be no image made) be defacide and removyd out of the churche, and other places, and are destroied.[28] (my italics)

The image of the Christ Incarnate as 'a lyttel boy at th'annunciation', a homunculus, floating down to his mother on beams of light was already controversial in the late medieval period because it suggested Christ's flesh did not come from Mary; after the Reformation, the iconography egregiously breached the limits of appropriate representation of the divine.[29] Likewise, representations of the Virgin's Assumption, the Trinity together and God the Father receive Protestant ire in this query – yet again, the Annunciation itself is not problematic. Neither, evidently, was Mary's book at the Annunciation worthy of mention in this list of offensive iconography. Even if her act of reading was apocryphal – nowhere mentioned in Luke or the other gospels – and thus potentially problematic, it otherwise fitted well enough into Protestant prioritization of the Word that it appears not to have received much negative attention. The medieval tradition identifying her reading as the Old Testament prophecies such as Isaiah 7:14 foretelling the conception and birth of Christ also did not violate Reformist understandings of the relation between the Old and New Testaments. Catholics, Protestants and Lutherans all continued to affirm the typological reading of Isaiah 7:14; such an interpretation was endorsed by Calvin himself: 'there can be no doubt that the Prophet referred to Christ', he wrote about the verse.[30]

Crucially, with her reading Mary demonstrated scriptural access to her Son through the Bible. Just as Christ was centred in post-Reformation belief, so was the Word of God, and the ability of each Christian to come closer to Christ by reading the scriptures unmediated – especially in the vernacular. Access to the Bible in the vernacular became a hallmark of the reformist agenda, so an image of a lay person by herself with the scriptures could be seen to support

---

[28] Recorded in John Strype, *Annals of the Reformation and Establishment of Religion and Other Various Occurrences in the Church of England During Queen Elizabeth's Happy Reign* (Oxford: Clarendon Press, 1824), vol. 1, part 2, 497. See also Margaret Aston, *Broken Idols of the English Reformation* (Cambridge: Cambridge University Press, 2016), 566, and Peters, *Patterns of Piety*, 222.

[29] A well-known example of an Annunciation with the homunculus (intact) is the fifteenth-century Flemish Merode Altarpiece at The Cloisters, the Metropolitan Museum of Art. An example from England is the late fifteenth-century alabaster carving panel representing the Incarnation with a Christ figure being sent down from the Father to Mary, kneeling in front of an open book (Gabriel not preserved); Victoria and Albert Museum, #A.58-1925, online catalogue entry http://collections.vam.ac.uk/item/O71601/the-incarnation-and-the-parliament-panel-unknown/ (accessed 17 August 2019). On the medieval history of the Christ homunculus see Jacqueline Tasioulas, '"Heaven and Earth in Little Space": The Foetal Existence of Christ in Medieval Literature and Thought', *Medium Ævum* 76(1) (2007): 24–48.

[30] Waller, *A Cultural Study*, 134.

that agenda. Chapter 2 showed how a woman reading the Bible alone could cause enough concern in the fifteenth century to be omitted from a textual description of the Annunciation. The same conservative climate was behind the mixed success Wycliff and Tyndale had in their respective vernacular Bible translation projects; while their lives were cut short because of their efforts, their books' influence spread, despite official restrictions on English scriptures. In 1536 Thomas Cromwell somewhat prematurely endorsed parish-level ownership of vernacular bibles, but broad access to the Word in English was not truly a reality until after both Henry VIII and Mary, with the first complete Edwardian bible in 1549 and even more so Elizabeth's Bishops' bible first printed in 1568.[31] The Protestant Geneva bible of 1579 explicitly encouraged individual Christians to read it 'everie day, twise at the least', and included extensive reading aids that testify to the engaged reading practices endorsed for early modern readers studying on their own.[32] The counter-reformation Doaui-Rheims bible in 1582 and 1609–10 then offered an updated English bible for Catholic readers.[33]

Mary's solitary reading could therefore persist as a fluid model available to both Protestant and Catholic readers, where perhaps for those readers less inclined to Marian devotion it was her act of reading that carried meaning apart from its agent (whose historicity could not, nonetheless, be denied). When Peters suggests 'the Virgin Mary at her prayer desk in portrayals of the Annunciation was also the godly Protestant reading in the closet', we realize what longstanding medieval allusion has been reinvented that of Mary as the vowed, enclosed holy woman, living a life of solitary prayer. With England's monasteries dissolved in 1538, the trope of enclosure was no longer contemplative in a monastic sense, but secretive in a Protestant sense of adhering to a faith intermittently illegal during the periods of counter-reformation resurgence. Yet during Protestant rule, Mary's isolation could also represent the illegal Catholic reading in *their* closet, unofficially cloistered behind domestic doors. After all, her book's contents were illegible to viewers. Each could project their own preferred scriptural language back onto the blank pages.

Mary's reading, as it had for nearly a thousand years, continued to function as a concrete demonstration of literal devout reading as well as a theological metaphor of the *Logos* coming into the world. The idea that Mary's book

---

[31] Kevin Killeen and Helen Smith, '"All other Bookes ... are but Notes upon this": The Early Modern Bible', in *The Oxford Handbook of the Bible in Early Modern England, c. 1530–1700*, ed. Kevin Killeen, Helen Smith and Rachel Willie (Oxford: Oxford University Press, 2015), 5.

[32] Molekamp, *Women and the Bible in Early Modern England*, 19; see also Femke Molekamp, 'Genevan Legacies: The Making of the English Geneva Bible', in *The Oxford Handbook of the Bible in Early Modern England*.

[33] Killeen and Smith, 'The Early Modern Bible', 5.

represented the Incarnation of the Word made flesh played into the new Protestant shift of emphasis away from Christ's body and onto Christ as Word. Michael O'Connell explains this shift: 'For Erasmus – and for humanism more generally – "Christ as text" replaces the painted, sculpted Christ. For succeeding reformers Christ's real presence as text would also eclipse his real presence in the visible, tactile Eucharist.'[34] Many Protestant churches replaced crucifixes – the body – with the Word: literally, scripture written on the walls. By representing God made man with the metaphor of the Book instead of with his actual human form, the Annunciation scene bypassed central iconoclastic concerns – even as the scene recorded that moment in which the Incarnation made it possible to have images of God at all. Indeed, the moment of the Annunciation highlights one of the key theological pressures fracturing Christianity in Europe: that the iconoclasm of the Reformation 'emerged from tensions in the relation of image and word that inhere in the central religious doctrine of Christianity, the incarnation, the belief that God, in taking on a human form, became subject to representation as an image', O'Connell writes.[35] The reformist discomfort with the misuse of holy images links tightly to their discomfort with the belief in transubstantiation, because in both the physical and spiritual coalesce. Mary, giving flesh to God, became implicated in the dangers of both representation and transubstantiation.[36]

For many Protestant sects, such a Mariolatry phobia competed with the acceptance of representing a historical, scriptural scene foundational to Christ's life and Christian salvation. Images of the Annunciation somewhat escaped the wrath of the iconoclasts in sixteenth- and seventeenth-century Reformation England. The Virgin's dedication to scripture at Gabriel's arrival might have redeemed her role in reformers' eyes. Yet conservative Protestant reformers allowing images of Mary's reading – or at least ignoring it – were likely doing so quite unaware of the powerful affective devotional tradition surrounding the motif in the Middle Ages. For the readers of fourteenth-century *Of Three Workings in Man's Soul*, for instance, Mary's body, reverently described as rapt in contemplation, became an effective example of how to gain access to the divine through the meditative training of both body and soul (see Chapter 5). Readers were simultaneously using their imaginative *imaging* of Mary's body at the Annunciation as a means of direct encounter with

---

[34] Michael O'Connell, *The Idolatrous Eye: Iconoclasm, and Theater in Early-Modern England* (Oxford: Oxford University Press, 2000), 37.

[35] O'Connell, *The Idolatrous Eye*, 10.

[36] 'The Swiss reformer Zwingli coupled Mary and the Eucharist when he likened the notion that Christ was present in the bread and wine at the altar to the prevalent belief that Mary was present in her statues. Since both were wrong, he concluded, the mass required reform and statues of the Virgin should be removed from churches,' writes Rubin, *Mother of God*, 370.

God, while Mary was imagining herself as serving the Saviour as handmaiden to the maiden that would bear him, according to the scripture inspiring her devotions. Like *Of Three Workings in Man's Soul*, other participatory piety texts such as *Meditationes vitae Christi*, Love's *Mirror of the Blessed Life of Jesus Christ* and *Speculum devotorum* are part of medieval devotional affective traditions that focus on the human body of Christ, serving his bodily needs – the body that iconoclasts were so loath to represent to believers, lest they worship the representation instead of what it represents, or worship the man instead of the God. 'Anxiety about idolatry is associated with anxiety about physicality in general – our human physicality and, indeed, the physicality of God in Christ Incarnate.'[37] Mary's body, too, must of course be occluded.

While post-Reformation Mary was still commonly depicted reading in Anglican artistic representations of the Annunciation, textual descriptions of what and how she was reading are more sparse. Like the bloody body of Christ on the cross that disappeared from English churches, Mary as intellectual, visionary contemplative by and large was forgotten by Protestant readers, and along with it faded the full potential of Mary's book as a textual model for transformative reading. But it did not disappear completely. In one unusual seventeenth-century Anglican text, the studious, prophetic Mary reappears. Anthony Stafford's 1635 prose tract *The Femall Glory; or, the Life, and Death of our Blessed Lady, the holy Virgin Mary, Gods owne Mother*[38] taps into medieval Marian imagery that had been dormant for nearly a century, and his text was not without controversy.[39] Stafford describes Mary's time as a young girl in the temple as occupied by writing, reading, meditation, just like an enclosed religious woman or 'a pretty Nun' (22). These seem to have been aspects that had been censored by other Protestants, but which Stafford reaffirms with the help of marginal notes citing established authorities:

> Let us then imagine that this holy Recluse confined her body to this sacred solitude, and a spare diet, and warily kept her soule from the surfets to which carnall delights invite all things humane. And it is consonant both to

---

[37] Clare Snow, '*Maria Mediatrix*: Mediating the Divine in the Devotional Literature of Late Medieval England', unpublished PhD dissertation, Center for Medieval Studies, University of Toronto (2012), 187.

[38] Anthony Stafford, *The Femall Glory; or, the Life, and Death of our Blessed Lady, the holy Virgin Mary, Gods owne Mother* (London: Thomas Harper, 1635).

[39] STC 231123. *The Femall Glory* is available open access at https://archive.org/details/TheLifeOfTheBlessedVirgin as well as in Early English Books online, at http://gateway.proquest.com/openurl?ctx_ver=Z39.88-2003&res_id=xri:eebo&rft_id=xri:eebo:citation:99853008 and transcribed in its Text Creation Partnership site: https://quod.lib.umich.edu/e/eebo/A12816.0001.001/1:11?rgn=div1;view=toc (all accessed 19 August 2019). Citations here are given by page number (preface material pages are unnumbered).

reason and truth, that her exercise there, was pious like the place. They who goe about to take away her writing, and reading tongue are impiously ridiculous, since it evidently appeares that she was well read in the Scriptures by her divine Hymne uttered in *Zacharies* house.* On her reading attended Meditation, on her Meditation Prayer, or her Prayer Action, as the louely fruit of the precedent. (23)

*Ancient and eminent Authors affirme her to have beene learned in the Hebrew tongue, all which you shall finde quoted in *Cedrenus*.

Like in the long medieval tradition of devotional texts examined in Chapters 2 and 3, the Virgin is a 'holy Recluse' whose body and soul are kept intact by her solitude and the reading, meditation and prayer it enables. When he mentions 'they who goe about to take away her writing, and reading tongue' Stafford seems to be countering some kind of contemporary claim that Mary did *not* read or write (perhaps more than merely the passive omission of such a fact). Echoing Shakespeare's Lavinia, Stafford's Mary is metaphorically mutilated without her literary abilities, for him an 'impiously ridiculous' silencing obviously contradicted by her Magnificat or 'divine Hymn' at the Visitation with her cousin Elizabeth. While Stafford does not elaborate on Mary's reading at the Annunciation in the text itself, she does hold a book in the accompanying etching of the 'Salutation' (an alternate name for the Annunciation) (Figure 17). As the first of only four illustrations in the volume, the representation of the book in her lap establishes the Virgin's literacy as a central attribute of her holiness. It also links it to medieval representations of the scene.

Stafford likewise uses *The Femall Glory* to reply to critics that seek to deny Mary's status as mystic or visionary: 'And why should we with difficulty beleeve that this white spotlesse soule was illuminated with Revelations by the divine object of her chaste vowes?' (21). In other words, there should be no problem in believing Mary received revelations from God, though some of his contemporaries evidently object to this idea. Later, at the Annunciation itself, he reinforces the claim that she 'clearly foresaw that she was not onely chosen to conceive the Son of God*' with a marginal note: '*Many ancient writers hold that she had the gift of prophecie' (35). This would be a Mary familiar to the medieval visionary women discussed in Chapter 4, all of whom saw Mary as having special mystical, visionary, or prophetic abilities that helped legitimate their own visionary vocation.[40] At these moments, among many others, Stafford invokes the weighty power of medieval authorities to back up these now unfamiliar details of Mary's life. In addition to the fairly obscure

---

[40] But on the Protestant female prophet Dame Eleanor Davies (*c.* 1588–1652) and her perception of and identification with Mary as a prophet see Watt, *Secretaries of God*, 148–54.

Figure 17 'The Salutation.' Anthony Stafford, *The Femall Glory; or, the Life, and Death of our Blessed Lady, the holy Virgin Mary, Gods owne Mother* (London: Thomas Harper, 1635), p. 30.

eleventh-century Byzantine author Georgios Cedrenus mentioned above, Stafford drew on multiple sources 'of those Primitive times' including Bernard of Clairvaux, Gregory the Great, Augustine, Ambrose, St John Crysostome and, as he proclaims, '[w]ould I muster up my forces I could produce many other Champions of the same worth and antiquity, that with an indefatigable zeale, doe vindicate the faith of this blessed Virgin against some of these latter ages, who accuse her as defective in that wherin she was most accomplisht' (60). He explicitly hearkens back to a pre-Reformation history of Marian writing he feels has been neglected, and is crucial for proper veneration of the Virgin. The entire volume of *The Femall Glory* is deeply inflected by medieval traditions in many ways: before the main text, it includes a Latin verse *Meditationes poeticæ & Christianæ in annunciationem beatæ Virginis* followed by a series of vernacular poems, panagyrics echoing early medieval long Latin lists of epithets for the Virgin.

Even as an Anglican, Stafford and his *vita* represent an extreme of Protestant respect – not to say adoration – of the Virgin Mary: orthodox (licensed by Archbishop William Laud), but controversial.[41] He was accused of 'crypto-Catholicism' by puritan minister Henry Burton, among others.[42] Suzanne Trill comments that *The Femall Glory* 'situates [Mary] as an exemplar for Protestants, and, to the disdain of contemporary puritans, seeks to reevaluate her position within the English church'.[43] In the preface titled 'To the Feminine READER', Stafford describes Mary as 'a glass', 'a Mirrour of Femall perfection', invoking the medieval term *speculum* as the main conceit (pages unnumbered). As with the fifteenth-century *Speculum devotorum* and other texts, women could reflect on themselves in her matching sex, but also reshape their own lives in imitation of hers: 'Here, any Ornament you have, you may better; and any you have not, you may purchase, at the

---

[41] An 1860 reprint, *The Life of the Blessed Virgin; Together With The Apology of the Author*, ed. Orby Shipley (London), includes critical replies by Henry Burton and William Prynne, and the defences of Peter Heylin and Christopher Dow, as well as Stafford's own apology. Available online at https://archive.org/details/TheLifeOfTheBlessedVirginTogether/page/n11. On the controversies surrounding the text see John Flood, 'Marian Controversies and Milton's Virgin Mary', in *Milton and Catholicism*, ed. Ronald Corthell and Thomas N. Corns (Notre Dame, IN: University of Notre Dame Press, 2017); Sidney Lee, 'Stafford, Anthony', *Dictionary of National Biography* volume 53 (1885–1900), now online at https://en.wikisource.org/wiki/Stafford,_Anthony_(DNB00); and Arnold Hunt, *Stafford, Anthony*, entry in the *Oxford Dictionary of National Biography* (Oxford, 2004), https://doi.org/10.1093/ref:odnb/26200 (all accessed 22 March 2019).

[42] Hunt, *Stafford*.

[43] Suzanne Trill, 'Religion and the Construction of Femininity', in Helen Wilcox, ed., *Women and Literature in Britain, 1500–1700* (Cambridge: Cambridge University Press, 1996), 36.

easie rate of reading, and imitating.' Just as the medieval readers of gospel meditations could read and imitate the Virgin, as a learned holy woman, so was this option resurrected for early modern readers of *The Femall Glory*. Just as Mary herself engaged in reading and meditation on scripture in the temple, so was Stafford's text 'A treatise worthy the reading, and meditation of all modest women,' as the long title insists.

Thus in its medieval form, medieval content and medieval sources, Stafford's unique production both proves the enduring vitality of pre-Reformation traditions of Mary as a learned mystic and suggests the rarity of these views and the prejudice they faced from within Anglicanism as well as from without. Mary remains reading in modern Annunciation images more than five hundred years after the split of the western Church. But the previous eight hundred years of belief in the Virgin's interpretive, revelatory power enabled by her reading has never quite been recuperated after the Reformation fissuring.

Acknowledgements

Although this monograph is about reading and creating texts in solitude, I could never have written this book alone. I owe its fruition to the help and company of so many other scholars and friends (though any of its remaining faults are my own). First and foremost, I would like to acknowledge the great generosity, wisdom and knowledge that Alastair Minnis and Jessica Brantley put into this project from its very beginnings at Yale University – and long after. My gratitude also goes to Theresa Tinkle and Catherine Sanok, at the University of Michigan, Ann Arbor, for their feedback on the book's early transformations and for their kind mentorship.

Many other medievalists and fellow scholars have read over parts of this book in draft form or given feedback to conference papers and lectures based on this research: my deep thanks to all of you. I thank especially Jennifer Brown, Ian Cornelius, Diana Denissen, Georgianna Donavin, Rebecca Huffman, Michelle Karnes, Andrew Kraebel, Liz Herbert McAvoy, Joe Morgan, Barbara Newman, Emily Price, John Rogers, Michael Sargent, Denys Turner, Nancy Bradley Warren, Nicholas Watson, Diane Watt and Barbara Zimbalist; and all those with whom I have corresponded and conferenced about this project over the years.

I presented material from this book to various audiences and am grateful for their questions and feedback: the Middle English Graduate Seminar, University of Cambridge, 2016; the Middle English Seminar, University of Oxford, 2015; the Medieval Studies Research Group, University of Oslo, 2015; and the Medieval Philology Research Group, UiB, 2015. Several localized research groups have also directly supported my work on this book; thank you for your collegiality and help improving drafts at writing workshops. During my time at the Michigan Society of Fellows, it was the Humanities Working Group and the 2012 Michigan Medieval Seminar (co-led with Kit French); at the University of Bergen it is the UiB Literature and Religion Research Group (especially Siri Vevle, Henning Laugerud, Sissel Undheim, Erik Tonning and Fionnuala O'Neill Tonning).

My Society for Medieval Feminist Scholarship Writing Group (b. Sept. 2017) – Einat Klafter, Renáta Modráková and Ricarda Wagner – has given me both feminist sustenance and rigorous, positive criticism, and this book and all my work is better for it. During a difficult period of stalling out, this book, and me, received a much-needed jumpstart from Anne Bramley, academic coach. Thank you for giving me the practical, mental and emotional tools to learn how to prioritize research again and to finish this and so much else.

I acknowledge the support of a Whiting Fellowship at Yale and a Beinecke Research Fellowship early on in this project. My time as a post-doc at the Michigan Society of Fellows, encouraged by Don Lopez, gave me the valuable breathing room to see the *Speculum* article and this monograph emerge as distinctive entities. Much of the writing and rewriting of the book happened after I took my current position as førsteamanuensis (associate professor) in English literature at the Institutt for fremmedspråk, Universitetet i Bergen, Norway, in 2013. I am grateful to the department and chair Åse Johnsen for sabbatical leave in the autumn of 2017, which enabled massive research and writing progress, and also for funding to underwrite the publication costs of this book, especially for colour plates. Thank you to Stuart Sillars for regularly asking me 'How is the book going?' Gunn Inger Sture generously helped me to navigate befuddling French image permissions, and Emily Price efficiently and expertly compiled the index. Tusen takk also to Kari Normo at the UiB Humanities Library for faithfully fulfilling endless obscure book requests.

I feel privileged to publish this book under the careful guidance of esteemed Boydell & Brewer editor Caroline Palmer, whose professionalism, efficiency and kindness shine as a gold standard to which all press editors should aspire. The careful and constructive comments from the blind peer review process made this book far stronger – thank you for staying with multiple drafts over multiple years. My gratitude to the entire Boydell & Brewer team for their help.

Thank you to my dear parents, Margaret and Duane, and my sister Kristin, for their enduring support. Sadly my mother died just a few months before publication and I so wish she could have held this book in her hands, but it comforts me that at least she saw the cover image and was as delighted by it as she was by everything I accomplished. My thanks for the love and encouragement of my husband, Randolph; and for the spunk and patience of my daughter, Astrid, throughout this book's long gestation period, overlapping with her own. Thank you to Jack, Ginger and Loki for the company and comfort when I worked at home. Finally, I would like to thank my Grandma Proctor, to whom this book is dedicated, for her inspirational model of going back to finish her undergraduate degree in her retirement years, and for her bottomless warmth and love. I know you would be proud of this book.

Bibliography

Manuscripts

Amiens, Bibliothèque Municipale, MS 2540
Baltimore, Walters Art Museum MS W.288
Baltimore, Walters Art Museum, MS W.267
Boulogne-sur-mer, Bibliothèque Municipale, MS 11
Cambridge, Corpus Christi College, MS 402
Cambridge, CUL, MS Add. 6578
Cambridge, CUL, MS Dd.5.64
Cambridge, CUL, MS Hh.i.11
Cambridge, Magdalene College, MS F.4.14
Cambridge, Magdalene College, Pepys Library MS 2125
Cambridge, Trinity College, MS B.15.42
Cambridge, Trinity College, MS O.8.26
Hildesheim, Dombibliothek, MS St Godehard 1
Lincoln, Lincoln Cathedral Chapter Library, MS 114
London, BL, MS Cotton Tiberius E.I.
London, BL, MS Sloane 1009
London, BL, MS Additional 49598
New York City, Pierpont Morgan Library, MS M. 171
New York City, Pierpont Morgan Library, MS M. 61
Oxford, Balliol College, MS 354
Oxford, Bodleian Library, MS Bodley 423
Oxford, Bodleian Library, MS Bodley 578
Oxford, Bodleian Library, MS Bodley Eng. Poet. A.1
Oxford, Bodleian Library, MS Digby 86
Oxford, Bodleian Library, MS Laud Lat. 19
Oxford, Bodleian Library, MS Rawl. Poet. 291
Oxford, Christ Church College, MS 152
Oxford, Corpus Christi College, MS 410
Paris, BnF, MS 2225
Paris, BnF, MS Ital. 115
Paris, BnF, MS Lat. 9471
Paris, BnF, MS Lat. 13306
Poitiers, Médiathèque François-Mitterand, MS 53

Poitiers, Médiathèque François-Mitterand, MS 1096
Vienna, Österreichische Nationalbibliothek, Codex Vindobonensis MS 1857

Primary Sources

'Of Three Workings in Man's Soul: A Middle English Prose Meditation on the Annunciation'. Edited by Stephen B. Hayes. In *Vox Mystica: Essays for Valerie M. Lagorio*, edited by Anne Clark Bartlett et al., 177–99. Cambridge: D.S. Brewer, 1995.
A Mirror to Devout People (Speculum Devotorum). Edited by Paul Patterson. EETS o.s. 346. Oxford: Oxford University Press, 2016.
Aelred of Rievaulx. *La vie d'Édouard le Confesseur: poème anglo-normand du XIIe siècle*. Edited by Ölsten Södergård. Uppsala: Almqvist & Wiksells, 1948.
Aelred of Rievaulx. '"The De institutis inclusarum" of Ailred of Rievaulx.' Edited by C.H. Talbot. *Analecta Sacri Ordinis Cisterciensis* vii (1959): 167–217.
Aelred of Rievaulx. 'The Latin text of *De Institutione Inclusarum*'. Edited by C.H. Talbot, in Aelredi Rievallensis, *Opera Omnia*, CCCM 1, 637–82. Turnhout: Brepols, 1971.
Aelred of Rievaulx. *Aelred of Rievaulx's* De Institutione Inclusarum: *Two English Versions*. Edited by John Ayto and Alexandra Barratt. EETS o.s. 287. Oxford: Oxford University Press, 1984.
Aelred of Rievaulx. *Aelredus Rievallensis Sermones I–XLVI: Collectio Claraevallensis Prima et Secunda*. Edited by Gaetano Raciti, CCCM IIA, 21. Turnhout: Brepols, 1989.
Aelred of Rievaulx. *The Liturgical Sermons: The First Clairvaux Collection*. Translated by Theodore Berkeley and M. Basil Pennington. Kalamazoo, MI: Cistercian, 1989.
Albertus Magnus. *Opera omnia*. Edited by Jammy. Lyon, 1651.
Alighieri, Dante. *Tutte le Opere di Dante Alighieri*. Edited by E. Moore. 3rd ed. Oxford: Oxford University Press, 1904.
Alighieri, Dante. *Literary Criticism of Dante Alighieri*. Translated by Robert Haller. Lincoln: University of Nebraska Press, 1973.
Ambrose. *De virginibus ad Marcellinam*. PL 16: 187–232.
Ancrene Wisse. Edited by Robert Hasenfratz. TEAMS Middle English Text Series. Kalamazoo, MI: Western Michigan University, Medieval Institute, 2000.
Anselm of Canterbury. *Anselmi Opera Omnia*. Edited by F.S. Schmitt. Edinburgh, 1946–61.
Anselm of Canterbury. *The Prayers and Meditations of St Anselm*. Translated by Sister Benedicta Ward. Harmondsworth: Penguin, 1973.
Anselm of Lucca. *Prieres Anciennes de l'Occident a la Mere du Sauveur, Des origines a saint Anselme*. Edited by Henri Barré. Paris: Lethielleuz, 1963.
Apocryphal Gospels, Act, and Revelations. Translated by Alexander Walker. Edinburgh: T. & T. Clark, 1870.
Augustine. *Sermon 192: In Natali Domini, IX*. PL 38: 1012–14.
Augustine. *St Augustine, Sermons for Christmas and Epiphany*. Translated by Thomas Comerford Lawler. Westminster, MD: Newman Press, 1952.
Augustine. *The Trinity*. Translated Stephan McKenna C. SS. R. Washington, DC: The Catholic University of America Press, 1963.

Augustine. *De Trinitate libri XV, CCSL* 50A. Edited by William J. Mountain and François Glorie. Turnhout: Brepols, 1968, 2001.
Augustine. *On the Trinity: Books 8–15*. Translated by Gareth B. Matthews. Cambridge: Cambridge University Press, 2002.
Basil, St. *St Basil: The Letters*. Edited and translated by R.J. Deferrari. Cambridge, MA: Harvard University Press, 1961.
Bernard of Clairvaux. *Sancti Bernardi Opera, IV*. Edited by Jean Leclerq and H. Rochais. Rome: Editiones cistercienses, 1966.
Bernard of Clairvaux. *Homilies in Praise of the Virgin Mary*. Translated by Marie-Bernard Saïd. Kalamazoo, MI: Cistercian, 1993.
Birgitta of Sweden. *Revelaciones*. Stockholm: Kungl. Vitterhets Historie och Antikvitets Akademien, 1956–2002.
Birgitta of Sweden, *Liber Celestis of St Bridget of Sweden: The Middle English Version in British Library MS Claudius B i, together with a life of the saint from the same manuscript*. Edited by Roger Ellis. EETS o.s. 291. Oxford: Oxford University Press, 1987.
Birgitta of Sweden. *The Revelations of St Birgitta of Sweden, Volume 1: Liber Cælestis, Books I–III*. Translated by Denis Searby with introductions and notes by Bridget Morris. Oxford: Oxford University Press, 2006.
Blom-Smith, Elisabeth, ed. '*The Lyf of Oure Lord and the Virgyn Mary* edited from MS Trinity College Cambridge B.15.42 and MS Bodley 578'. PhD dissertation, King's College, London, 1992.
Book to a Mother: An Edition with Commentary. Edited by Adrian James McCarthy. Salzburg: Insitut für Anglistik und Amerikanistik, Universität Salzburg, 1981.
Brown, Carleton, ed. *Religious Lyrics of the XV Century*. London: Clarendon Press, 1939.
Capgrave, John. *Liber de illustribus Henricis*. London: Longman, Brown, Green, Longmans & Roberts, 1858.
Daniel, Walter. *The Life of Aelred of Rievaulx*. Translated by F.M. Powicke, introduction by Marsha Dutton. Kalamazoo, MI: Cistercian, 1994.
de Voragine, Jacobus. *The Golden Legend: Readings on the Saints*. Translated by William Caxton, vol. 6, reprinted. London: J.M. Dent, 1900.
Dyboski, Roman, ed. *Songs, Carols and Other Miscellaneous Poems from the Balliol MS. 354, Richard Hill's Commonplace Book*. EETS o.s. 101. London, 1907, issued in 1908.
Elizabeth of Hungary. *The Two Middle English Translations of the Revelations of St Elizabeth of Hungary*. Edited by Sarah McNamer. Heidelberg: Universitatsverlag C. Winter, 1996.
Erasmus, Desiderius. *Peregrinatio Religionis Ergo*. Basle, 1526.
Erasmus, Desiderius. *A dialog of communication of two persons, deuysyd and let forthe in the late[n] tonge, by the noble and famose clarke Desiderius Erasmus intituled ya Pylgremage of pure devotyon*. STC 10454. London, 1536.
Erasmus, Desiderius. *The Colloquies of Erasmus*. In *The Collected Works of Erasmus*, vol. 40, translated by Craig R. Thompson. Toronto: University of Toronto Press, 1997.
Evangelia apocrypha. Edited by Constantinus Tischendorf. 2nd ed. Leipzig, 1876.
Feiss, Hugh, OSB, trans. *Peter of Celle: Selected Works*. Kalamazoo, MI: Cistercian, 1987.
Foxe, John. *Acts and Monuments*. 3 vols. New York: AMS, 1965.

Furnivall, F.J. and M.A. Cambridge, eds. *The Minor Poems of the Vernon MS: Part II (With a Few from the Digby MSS. 2 and 86)*. EETS o.s. 117. Oxford: Oxford University Press, 1901.

Gairdner, James, ed. *Letters and Papers, Foreign and Domestic, Henry VIII, Volume 13 Part 1, January–July 1538*. London, 1892.

Goscelin of St Bertin. 'La légende de Ste Édith en prose et vers par le moine Goscelin'. Edited by A. Wilmart. *Analecta Bollandiana* 56 (1938): 5–101, 265–307.

Goscelin of St Bertin. 'The *Liber Confortatorius* of Goscelin of Saint Bertin'. Edited by C.H. Talbot. *Analecta monastica* series 3, *Studia Anselmiana* 37 (1955): 1–117.

Goscelin of St Bertin. *The Book of Encouragement and Consolation [Liber Confortatorius]: The Letter of Goscelin to the Recluse Eva*. Translated by Monica Otter. Cambridge: D.S. Brewer, 2004.

Goscelin of St Bertin. *Writing the Wilton Women: Goscelin's* Legend of Edith *and* Liber Confortatorius. Translated by W.R. Barnes and Rebecca Hayward. Turnhout: Brepols, 2004.

Guerric of Igny. *Sermones per Annum, in Annuntiatione Dominica II*. PL 185: 120–4.

Guibert of Nogent. *Self and Society in Medieval France: The Memoirs of Abbot Guibert of Nogent*. Translated by John F. Benton. New York: Harper & Row, 1970.

Hesbert, René-Jean and René Prévost, eds. *Corpus antiphonalium officii*. 6 vols. Rome: Herder, 1963–79.

Hilton, Walter. *The Scale of Perfection*. Edited by Thomas Bestul. TEAMS Middle English Text Series. Kalamazoo, MI: Medieval Institute, 2000.

Ildefonso of Toledo. *De Virginitate Beatae*. Edited by Vicente Blanco García, Textos latinos de la edad medina española – Sección 3. Madrid: Centro de Estudios Historicos/Rivadeneya, 1937.

Ildefonso of Toledo. *The Life and Writings of Saint Ildefonsus of Toledo*. Edited and translated by Sister Athanasius Braegelmann OSB. Washington, DC: The Catholic University of America Press, 1942.

Iohannis de Caulibus Meditaciones vite Christi, olim S. Bonaventuro attributae. Edited by M. Stallings-Taney. CCCM 153. Turnhout: Brepols, 1997.

Jones, E., ed. *The New Oxford Book of Sixteenth Century Verse*. Oxford: Oxford University Press, 1991.

Julian of Norwich. *The Writings of Julian of Norwich: A Vision Showed to a Devout Woman and A Revelation of Love*. Edited by Nicholas Watson and Jacqueline Jenkins. Philadelphia: Pennsylvania State University Press, 2006.

Libri de natiuitate Mariae: Pseudo-Matthaei Euangelium. Edited by J. Gijsel. Turnhout: Brepols, 1997.

Love, Nicholas. *The Mirror of the Blessed Life of Jesus Christ: A Reading Text*. Edited by Michael Sargent. Exeter: Exeter University Press, 2004.

Love, Nicholas. *Nicholas Love's 'Mirror of the Blessed Life of Jesus Christ': A Full Critical Edition*. Edited by Michael Sargent. Liverpool: Liverpool University Press, 2005.

Luther, Martin. *Luther's Works*, vol. IX. Edited by Jaroslav Pelikan. St Louis, MO: Concordia Press/Fortress Press, 1960.

Lydgate, John. *The Minor Poems of John Lydgate*. Edited by H.N. MacCracken. EETS e.s. 107. London, 1911.

Meditations on the Life of Christ. Translated by Francis X. Taney Sr, Anne Miller OSF and C. Mary Stallings-Taney. Asheville, NC: Pegasus, 2000.

Meditations on the Life of Christ: The Short Italian Text. Edited by Sarah McNamer. Notre Dame, IN: University of Notre Dame Press, 2018.

Meredith, Peter, ed. *The Mary Play from the N. Town Manuscript*. London: Longman, 1987.

Millett, Bella with Richard Dance, eds. *Ancrene Wisse: A Corrected Edition of the Text in Cambridge, Corpus Christi College, MS 402 with variants from other manuscripts*, 2 vols. EETS o.s. 325 and 326. Oxford: Oxford University Press, 2005, 2006.

Odilo of Cluny. *Sermon 12: De Assumptione dei genitricis Mariae*. PL 142: 1023–9.

Oliger, Livarius, ed. 'Regulae tres reclusorum et ermitarum angliae saec. Xiii–xiv'. *Antonianum* 3 (1928): 151–90, 299–320.

Otfrid of Weissenburg. *Otfrids Evangelienbuch*. Edited by Oskar Erdmann. 6th edition by Ludwig Wolff. Altdeutsche Textbibliothek 49. Tübingen: Niemeyer, 1962.

Peter of Celle. *Sermo XXVI, In Annuntiatione Dominica V*. PL 202: 720–2.

Philip de Mézières. *Figurative Representation of the Presentation of the Virgin Mary in the Temple*. Edited and translated by Robert S. Haller, introduction by M. Catherine Rupp OSM. Lincoln: University of Nebraska Press, 1971.

Quand Jésus eut douze ans. Edited by Dom A. Hoste OSB. Paris: Cerf, 1958.

Reynes, Robert. *The Commonplace Book of Robert Reynes: An Edition of Tanner MS 407*. Edited by Cameron Louis. New York: Garland, 1980.

Richard of St Victor. *De Gratia Contemplationis Libri Quinque Occasione Accepta ab Arca Moysis et ob Eam Rem Hactenus Dictum Benjamin Major*. PL 196: 63–202.

Rolle, Richard. *Yorkshire Writers: Richard Rolle of Hampole and His Followers*. Edited by Carl Horstmann. 2 vols. London: Swan Sonnenschein, 1895.

Rolle, Richard. *Writings Ascribed to Richard Rolle, Hermit of Hampole, and Materials for His Biography*. Edited by H.E. Allen. New York: MLA, 1927.

Rolle, Richard. *Richard Rolle: Prose and Verse*. Edited by S.J. Ogilvie-Thomson. EETS o.s. 293. Oxford: Oxford University Press, 1988.

Rolle, Richard. *Richard Rolle: Uncollected Prose and Verse with related Northern Texts*. Edited by Ralph Hanna. EETS o.s. 329. Oxford: Oxford University Press, 2007.

Savage, Anne and Nicholas Watson, eds. *Anchoritic Spirituality: Ancrene Wisse and Associated Works*. New York: Paulist Press, 1991.

Scase, Wendy, ed. *A Facsimile Edition of the Vernon Manuscript: A Literary Hoard from Medieval England*. With software by Nick Kennedy. Oxford: Bodleian Library, 2011.

Sedulius. *Sedulius, The Paschal Song and Hymns*. Edited and translated by Carl P. Springer. Atlanta: Society of Biblical Literature Press, 2013.

Speculum Inclusorum: A Mirror for Recluses: A Late-Medieval Guide for Anchorites and its Middle English Translation. Edited by E.A. Jones. Liverpool: Liverpool University Press, 2013.

Speculum Virginum. Edited by Jutta Seyfarth. CCCM V. Turnhout: Brepols, 1990.

Stafford, Anthony. *The Femall Glory; or, the Life, and Death of our Blessed Lady, the holy Virgin Mary, Gods owne Mother*. STC 231123. London: Thomas Harper, 1635.

Stafford, Anthony. *The Life of the Blessed Virgin; Together With The Apology of the Author*. Edited by Orby Shipley. London: E. Lumley, 1860.

Strauch, Philipp, ed. *Margaretha Ebner und Heinrich von Nördlingen. Ein Beitrag zur Geschichte der deutschen Mystik.* Freiburg/Tübingen, 1882.
Talbot, C.H., ed. and trans. *The Life of Christina of Markyate: A Twelfth Century Recluse.* Toronto: University of Toronto Press, 1998. First edition, Oxford, 1959.
The Sarum Missal in English. London: The Church Press Company, 1868.
The Vernon Manuscript: A Facsimile of Bodleian Library, Oxford, MS. Eng. poet. a.1. Introduction by A.I. Doyle. Cambridge: D.S. Brewer, 1987.
William of Malmesbury. *De Gestis Regum Anglorum.* Edited by William Stubbs. London: HM Stationery Office, 1889.
Zinn, Grover A., trans. and intro. *Richard of St Victor: The Twelve Patriarchs, The Mystical Ark, Book Three of the Trinity.* New York: Paulist Press, 1979.

Secondary Sources

Abbott, Christopher. *Julian of Norwich: Autobiography and Theology.* Cambridge: D.S. Brewer, 1999.
Aers, David. 'The Humanity of Christ: Reflections on Julian of Norwich's *Revelation of Love*'. In *The Powers of the Holy: Religion, Politics, and Gender in Late Medieval English Culture*, edited by David Aers and Lynn Staley, 77–104. Philadelphia: University of Pennsylvania Press, 1996.
Ashley, Kathleen and Pamela Sheingorn, eds. *Interpreting Cultural Symbols: Saint Anne in Late Medieval Society.* Athens: University of Georgia Press, 1990.
Aston, Margaret. *England's Iconoclasts: Vol.1, Laws Against Images.* Oxford: Clarendon Press, 1988.
Aston, Margaret. *Broken Idols of the English Reformation.* Cambridge: Cambridge University Press, 2016.
Baert, Barbara. 'The Annunciation and the Senses: Late Medieval Devotion and the Pictorial Gaze.' In *The Materiality of Devotion in Late Medieval Northern Europe: Images, Objects, and Practices*, edited by Henning Laugerud, Salvador Ryan and Laura Katrine Skinnebach, 121–5. Dublin: Four Courts Press, 2016.
Baker, Denise. 'Julian of Norwich and the Varieties of Middle English Mystical Discourse'. In *A Companion to Julian of Norwich*, edited by Liz Herbert McAvoy, 53–63. Cambridge: D.S. Brewer, 2008.
Bale, Anthony. 'Richard Salthouse of Norwich and the Scribe of *The Book of Margery Kempe*'. *The Chaucer Review* 52(2) (2017): 173–87.
Barr, Jessica. *Willing to Know God: Dreamers and Visionaries in the Later Middle Ages.* Athens, OH: Ohio University Press, 2010.
Barr, Jessica. 'Visionary "Staycations": Meeting God at Home in Medieval Women's Visionary Literature'. *Medieval Feminist Forum* 52(2) (2016): 70–101.
Barratt, Alexandra. 'Margery Kempe and the King's Daughter of Hungary'. In *Margery Kempe: A Book of Essays*, edited by Sandra J. McEntire, 189–201. New York: Garland, 1992.
Barratt, Alexandra. 'The *Revelations* of Saint Elizabeth of Hungary: Problems of Attribution'. *The Library* Sixth Series, XIV(1) (March 1992): 1–11.

Barratt, Alexandra. 'The Virgin and the Visionary in *The Revelations* of Saint Elizabeth'. *Mystics Quarterly* 42 (1992): 125–36.

Barratt, Alexandra. *Women's Writing in Middle English*. London: Longman, 1992.

Barratt, Alexandra. 'Small Latin? The Post-Conquest Learning of English Religious Women'. In *Anglo-Latin and its Heritage: Essays in Honour of A.G. Rigg on his 64th Birthday*, Publications of *The Journal of Medieval Latin* 4, edited by Siân Echard and Gernot R. Wieland, 51–65. Turnhout: Brepols, 2001.

Barré, H. 'Saint Bernard, docteur marial'. In *Saint Bernard théologien, Analecta S.O.C.* IX(3–4) (1953): 92–113.

Bartlett, Anne Clark. *Male Authors, Female Readers: Representation and Subjectivity in Middle English Devotional Literature*. Ithaca, NY: Cornell University Press, 1995.

Bastero, Juan Luis. *Mary, Mother of the Redeemer: A Mariology Textbook*. Translated by Michael Adams and Philip Griffin. Dublin: Four Courts Press, 2006.

Beadle, Richard. '"Devoute ymaginacioun" and the Dramatic Sense in Love's *Mirror* and the N-Town Plays'. In *Nicholas Love at Waseda: Proceedings of the International Conference, 20–22 July 1995*, edited by Shoichi Oguro, Richard Beadle and Michael G. Sargent, 1–17. Cambridge: D.S. Brewer, 1997.

Beattie, Tina. *God's Mother, Eve's Advocate: A Marian Narrative of Women's Salvation*. London: Continuum, 2002.

Bechtold, Joan. 'St Birgitta: The Disjunction Between Women and Ecclesiastical Male Power'. In *Equally in God's Image: Women in the Middle Ages*, edited by Julia Bolton Holloway et al., 88–102. New York: Peter Lang, 1990.

Beckwith, Sarah. 'A Very Medieval Mysticism: The Medieval Mysticism of Margery Kempe'. In *Gender and Text in the Later Middle Ages*, edited by Jane Chance, 195–215. Gainesville: University Press of Florida, 1996.

Bell, David. *What Nuns Read: Books and Libraries in Medieval English Nunneries*. Kalamazoo, MI: Cistercian, 1995.

Bell, Susan Groag. 'Medieval Women Book Owners: Arbiters of Lay Piety and Ambassadors of Culture'. *Signs* 4 (1982): 742–68.

Belting, Hans. *Likeness and Presence: A History of the Image before the Era of Art*, translated by Edmund Jephcott. Chicago: University of Chicago Press, 1994.

Bepler, Johann and Jane Geddes with codicological commentary by Peter Kidd. *The St Albans Psalter*. Simbach am Inn, Germany: Müller und Schindler, 2008.

Bestul, Thomas. *Texts of the Passion: Latin Devotional Literature and Medieval Society*. Philadelphia: University of Pennsylvania Press, 1996.

Blake, N.F. 'The Vernon Manuscript: Contents and Organization'. In *Studies in the Vernon Manuscript*, edited by Derek Pearsall, 45–59. Cambridge: D.S. Brewer, 1990.

Blamires, Alcuin. 'Women and Preaching in Medieval Orthodoxy, Heresy, and Saints' Lives'. *Viator: Medieval and Renaissance Studies* 26 (1995): 135–52.

Blamires, Alcuin. *The Case for Women in Medieval Culture*. London: Clarendon Press, 1997.

Blumenfeld-Kosinksi, Renate. 'The Strange Case of Ermine de Reims (*c.* 1347–1396): A Medieval Woman between Demons and Saints'. *Speculum* 85 (2010): 321–56.

Borgehammer, Stephen. 'The Ideal of the Recluse in Aelred's "De Institutione Inclusarum"'. In *In Quest of the Kingdom: Ten Papers on Medieval Monastic Spirituality*, edited by Alf Härdelin, 177–202. Stockholm: Almqvist & Wiksell International, 1991.

Børresen, Kari Elisabeth. 'Birgitta's Godlanguage: Exemplary Intention, Inapplicable Content'. In *Birgitta, hendes værk og hendes klostre i Norden*, edited by Tore Nyberg, 21–71. Odense: Odense Universitetsforlag, 1991.

Boss, Sarah Jane. *Empress and Handmaid: On Nature and Gender in the Cult of the Virgin Mary*. London: Cassell, 2000.

Boss, Sarah Jane, ed. *Mary: The Complete Resource*. London: Continuum, 2007.

Boss, Sarah Jane. 'Telling the Beads: The Practice and Symbolism of the Rosary'. In *Mary: The Complete Resource*, edited by Sarah Jane Boss, 64–75. London: Continuum, 2007.

Bourassé, Jean Jacques. *Summa Aurea de Laudibus Beatissimæ Virginis Mariæ*, Vol. IX. Paris: P. Migne, 1862.

Boyarin, Adrienne Williams. *Miracles of the Virgin in Medieval England: Law and Jewishness in Marian Legends*. Cambridge: D.S. Brewer, 2010.

Boyd, Beverly. 'Hoccleve's Miracle of the Virgin'. *The University of Texas Studies in English* 35 (1956): 116–22.

Breeze, Andrew. *The Mary of the Celts*. Leominster: Gracewing, 2008.

Bridges, Margaret. 'Ubi est thesaurus tuus, ibi est cor tuum: Towards a History of the Displaced Heart in Medieval English'. In *The Heart*, edited by Agostino Paravicini Bagliani, *Micrologus* 11, 501-518. Turnhout, Belgium: Brepols, 2003.

Brown, Rachel Fulton. *Mary and the Art of Prayer: The Hours of the Virgin in Medieval Christian Life and Thought*. New York: Columbia University Press, 2017.

Bruce, Yvonne. '"I am the Creator": Birgitta of Sweden's Feminine Divine'. *Comitatus* 32(1) (2001): 19–41.

Bryan, Jennifer. *Looking Inward: Devotional Reading and the Private Self in Late Medieval England*. Philadelphia: University of Pennsylvania Press, 2008.

Bynum, Caroline Walker. *Jesus as Mother: Studies in the Spirituality of the High Middle Ages*. Berkeley: University of California Press, 1982.

Bynum, Caroline Walker. *Holy Feast and Holy Fast: The Religious Significance of Food to Medieval Women*. Berkeley: University of California Press, 1987.

Bynum, Caroline Walker. *Fragmentation and Redemption: Essays on Gender and the Human Body in Medieval Religion*. New York: Zone, 1992.

Bynum, Caroline Walker. *Wonderful Blood: Theology and Practice in Late Medieval Northern Germany and Beyond*. Philadelphia: University of Pennsylvania Press, 2006.

Camille, Michael. 'Seeing and Reading: Some Visual Implications of Medieval Literacy and Illiteracy'. *Art History* 8 (1985): 26–49.

Carol, Juniper, ed. *Mariology*. 3 vols. Milwaukee, WI: Bruce, 1954.

Carroll, Michael P. *Madonnas that Maim: Popular Catholicism in Italy since the Fifteenth Century*. Baltimore, MD: Johns Hopkins University Press, 1992.

Carroll, Michael P. 'Pilgrimage at Walsingham on the Eve of the Reformation: Speculations on a "splendid diversity" only Dimly Perceived'. In *Walsingham in Literature and Culture from the Middle Ages to Modernity*, edited by Dominic Janes and Gary Waller, 35–48. Farnham: Ashgate, 2010.

Carruthers, Mary. *The Craft of Thought: Meditation, Rhetoric, and the Making of Images, 400–1200*. Cambridge: Cambridge University Press, 1998.

Catto, Jeremy. '1349–1412: Culture and History'. In *The Cambridge Companion to Medieval English Mysticism*, edited by Samuel Fanous and Vincent Gillespie, 113–32. Cambridge: Cambridge University Press, 2011.

Cervone, Cristina Maria. *Poetics of the Incarnation: Middle English Writings and the Leap of Love*. Philadelphia: University of Pennsylvania Press, 2012.

Chazelle, C.M. 'Pictures, Books, and the Illiterate: Pope Gregory I's Letters to Serenus of Marseilles'. *Word and Image* VI (1990): 138–53.

Chenu, M.-D. OP. 'Theology and the New Awareness of History'. In *Nature, Man, and Society in the Twelfth Century: Essays on New Theological Perspectives in the Latin West*, edited and translated by Jerome Taylor and Lester K. Little, 162–201. Toronto: University of Toronto Press, 1997.

Clanchy, Michael. 'Images of Ladies with Prayer Books: What Do They Signify?'. *Studies in Church Studies* 38 (2004): 106–22.

Clanchy, M.T. *From Memory to Written Record: England 1066–1307*. 2nd ed. Oxford: Blackwell, 1993.

Clayton, Mary. *The Cult of the Virgin Mary in Anglo-Saxon England*. Cambridge: Cambridge University Press, 1990.

Cleve, G. 'Margery Kempe: A Scandinavian Influence in Medieval England?'. In *The Medieval Mystical Tradition in England V*, edited by M. Glasscoe, 163–78. Cambridge: D.S. Brewer, 1992.

Coleman, Simon and John Elsner, 'Performing Pilgrimage: Walsingham and the Ritual Construction of Irony'. In *Ritual, Performance, Media*, edited by Felicia Hughes-Freeland, 46–65. London: Routledge, 1998.

Coleman, Simon. 'Purity as Danger? Seduction and Sexuality at Walsingham'. In *The Seductions of Pilgrimage: Sacred Journeys Afar and Astray in the Western Religious Tradition*, edited by Michael A. Di Giovine and David Picard, 53–69. Farnham: Ashgate, 2015.

Collins, Kristen and Matthew Fisher, eds. *St Albans and the Markyate Psalter: Seeing and Reading in Twelfth-Century England*. Kalamazoo, MI: Medieval Institute, 2017.

Collins, Kristen, Peter Kidd and Nancy Turner, eds. *The St Albans Psalter: Painting and Prayer in Medieval England*. Los Angeles: J. Paul Getty Museum, 2013.

Cooper-Rompato, Christine. *The Gift of Tongues: Women's Xenoglossia in the Later Middle Ages*. Philadelphia: Pennsylvania State University Press, 2010.

Crewe, Sarah. *Stained Glass in England c. 1180–1540*. London: HM Stationery Office, 1987.

Crook, John. *English Medieval Shrines*. Woodbridge: Boydell Press, 2016.

Davis-Weyer, Caecilia. *Early Medieval Art, 300–1150: Sources and Documents*. Toronto: University of Toronto Press, 1986.

de Lubac, Henri. *Medieval Exegesis, Volume 1: The Four Senses of Scripture*. Translated by Mark Sebanc. Grand Rapids, MI: Wm. B. Eerdmans, 1998.

de Lubac, Henri. *Medieval Exegesis, Volume 2: The Four Senses of Scripture*. Translated by E.M. Macierowski. Grand Rapids, MI: Wm. B. Eerdmans, 2000.

de Lubac, Henri. *Medieval Exegesis, Volume 3: The Four Senses of Scripture*. Translated by E.M. Macierowski. Grand Rapids, MI: Wm. B. Eerdmans, 2009.

Deanesly, Margaret. *The Lollard Bible and Other Medieval Biblical Versions*. Cambridge: Cambridge University Press, 1920.

Delauney, Isabelle. 'Livres d'heures de commande et d'étal: quelques exemples choisis dans la librairie parisienne 1480–1500'. In *L'artiste et le cammanditaire aux derniers siècles du Moyen Âge: XIIIe–XVIe siècles*, edited by Fabienne Joubert, 249–70. Paris: Presses de l'Université de Paris-Sorbonne, 2001.

Deshman, Robert. 'Servants of the Mother of God in Byzantine and Medieval Art'. *Word and Image* 5(1) (1989): 33–70.

Despres, Denise. *Ghostly Sights: Visual Meditation in Late-Medieval Literature*. Norman, OK: Pilgrim, 1989.

Dickens, Andrea Janelle. *Female Mystic: Great Women Thinkers of the Middle Ages*. New York: I.B. Tauris, 1999.

Dickinson, J.C. *The Shrine of Our Lady of Walsingham*. Cambridge: Cambridge University Press, 1956.

Didi-Huberman, Georges. *Fra Angelico: Dissemblance and Figuration*. Translated by Jane Marie Todd. Chicago: University of Chicago Press, 1995.

Diehl, Huston. *Staging Reform, Reforming the Stage: Protestantism and Popular Theater in Early Modern England*. Ithaca, NY: Cornell University Press, 1997.

Dillon, Janette. 'Holy Women and their Confessors or Confessors and their Holy Women? Margery Kempe and Continental Tradition'. In *Prophets Abroad: The Reception of Continental Holy Women in Late-Medieval England*, edited by Rosalynn Voaden, 115–40. Cambridge: D.S. Brewer, 1996.

Donavin, Georgiana. *Scribit Mater: Mary and the Language Arts in the Literature of Medieval England*. Washington, DC: The Catholic University of America Press, 2012.

Donohue-White, Patricia. 'Reading Divine Maternity in Julian of Norwich'. *Spiritus* 5(1) (2005): 19–36.

Doyle, A.I. 'Stephen Dodesham of Witham and Sheen'. In *Of the Making of Books: Medieval Manuscripts, their Scribes and Readers: Essays Presented to M.B. Parkes*, edited by P.R. Robinson and Rivkah Zim, 94–115. Aldershot: Scolar Press, 1997.

Doyle, A.I. 'A Letter Written by Thomas Betson, Brother of Syon Abbey'. In *The Medieval Book and A Modern Collector: Essays in Honor of Toshiyuki Takamiya*, edited by T. Matsuda, R. Linenthal and J. Scahill, 255–67. Cambridge: D.S. Brewer, 2004.

Doyle, A.I. 'Codicology, Paleography, and Provenance'. In *The Making of the Vernon Manuscript: The Production and Contents of Oxford, Bodleian Library, MS Eng. poet. a. 1*, edited by Wendy Scase, 3–25. Turnhout: Brepols, 2013.

Duffy, Eamon. 'Devotion to the Crucifix and Related Images in England on the Eve of the Reformation'. In *Bilder und Bildersturm im Spätmittelalter und in der frühen Neuzeit*, edited by R. Scribner, 21–36. Wiesbaden: Harrassowitz, 1990.

Duffy, Eamon. *The Stripping of the Altars: Traditional Religion in England c. 1400–c. 1580*. New Haven, CT: Yale University Press, 1992.

Duffy, Eamon. 'Dynamics of Pilgrimage in Late Medieval England'. *Pilgrimage: The English Experience from Becket to Bunyan*, edited by Colin Morris and Peter Roberts, 164–77. Cambridge: Cambridge University Press, 2002.

Duffy, Eamon. *Marking the Hours: English People and their Prayers*. New Haven, CT: Yale University Press, 2006.

Duggan, L.G. 'Was Art Really the "Book of the Illiterate"?'. *Word and Image* V (1989): 227–51.

Dutton, Elisabeth. 'Christ the Codex: Compilation as Literary Device in *Book to a Mother*'. *Leeds Studies in English* n.s. 35 (2004): 81–100.

Dutton, Elisabeth. *Julian of Norwich: The Influence of Late-Medieval Devotional Compilations*. Cambridge: D.S. Brewer, 2008.

Dutton, Marsha. 'The Cistercian Source: Aelred, Bonaventure, and Ignatius'. In *Goad and Nail: Studies in Medieval Cistercian History, X*, edited by E. Rozanne Elder, 151–78. Kalamazoo, MI: Cistercian, 1983.

Dutton, Marsha. 'Christ Our Mother: Aelred's Iconography for Contemplative Union'. In *Goad and Nail: Studies in Medieval Cistercian History, X*, edited by E. Rozanne Elder, 21–45. Kalamazoo, MI: Cistercian, 1985.

Dutton, Marsha. 'Gilding the Lily: The Enhancement of Spiritual Affectivity in a Middle English Translation of Aelred of Rievaulx's De institutione inclusarum'. In *The Medieval Translator*, vol. 10, edited by Jacqueline Jenkins and Olivier Bertrand, 109–24. Turnhout: Brepols, 2007.

Dzon, Mary. *The Quest for the Christ Child in the Later Middle Ages*. Philadelphia: University of Pennsylvania Press, 2017.

Eco, Umberto. *Semiotics and the Philosophy of Language*. Bloomington: Indiana University Press, 1984.

Eco, Umberto. 'History and Historiography of Semiotics'. In *Semiotik/Semiotics: Ein Handbuch zu den zeichentheoretichen Grundlagen von Natur und Kultur/A Handbook on the Sign-Theoretic Foundations of Nature and Culture*, 730–46. Berlin: Walter de Gruyter, 1996.

Elich, Tom. 'Using Liturgical Texts in the Middle Ages'. In *Fountain of Life: In Memory of Niels K. Rasmussen, OP*, edited by Gerard Austin, 69–83. Washington, DC: Pastoral Press, 1991.

Elkins, Sharon K. *Holy Women of Twelfth-Century England*. Chapel Hill: University of North Carolina Press, 1988.

Elliott, Dyan. *The Bride of Christ Goes to Hell*. Philadelphia: University of Pennsylvania Press, 2012.

Ellis, Roger. '"Flores ad Fabricandam ... Coronam": An Investigation into the Uses of the *Revelations* of St Bridget of Sweden in Fifteenth-Century England'. *Medium Aevum* 51 (1982): 163–86.

Ellis, Roger. 'Margery Kempe's Scribe and the Miraculous Books'. In *Langland, the Mystics and the Medieval English Religious Tradition*, edited by Helen Phillips, 161–75. Cambridge: D.S. Brewer, 1990.

Ellis, Roger. 'Text and Controversy: In Defence of St Birgitta of Sweden'. In *Text and Controversy from Wyclif to Bale: Essays in Honour of Anne Hudson*, edited by Helen Barr and Ann M. Hutchinson, 303–21. Turnhout: Brepols, 2005.

Ellis, Roger and Samuel Fanous. '1349–1412: texts'. In *Cambridge Companion to Medieval English Mysticism*, edited by Samuel Fanous and Vincent Gillespie, 133–62. Cambridge: Cambridge University Press, 2011.

Evangelatou, Maria. 'The Purple Thread of the Flesh: The Theological Connotations of a Narrative Iconographic Element in Byzantine Images of the Annunciation'. In *Icon and Word: The Power of Images in Byzantium. Studies Presented to Robin Cormack*, edited by A. Eastmond and L. James, 261–79. Farnham: Ashgate, 2003.

Falls, David J. 'The Carthusian Milieu of Nicholas Love's *Mirror of the Blessed Life of Jesus Christ*'. In *The Pseudo-Bonaventuran Lives of Christ: Exploring the Middle English Tradition*, edited by Ian Johnson and Allen F. Westphal, MCS 24, 311–39. Turnhout: Brepols, 2013.

Falls, David J. *Nicholas Love's Mirror and Late Medieval Devotio-Literary Culture*. London: Routledge, 2015.

Falvay, Dávid. 'St Elizabeth of Hungary in Italian Vernacular Literature: *Vitae*, Miracles, Revelations, and the *Meditations on the Life of Christ*'. In *Promoting the Saints: Cults and the Contexts from Late Antiquity until the Early Modern Period: Essays in Honor of Gábor Klaniczay for his 60th Birthday*, edited by Ottó Gecser et al., 137–50. Budapest: CEU Press, 2010.

Fanous, Samuel. 'Becoming Theotokos: Birgitta of Sweden and Fulfilment of Salvation History'. In *Motherhood, Religion, and Society in Medieval Europe, 400–1400: Essays Presented to Henrietta Leyser*, edited by Conrad Leyser and Lesley Smith, 251–80. Farnham: Ashgate, 2011.

Ferrante, Joan M. *To the Glory of Her Sex: Women's Roles in the Composition of Medieval Texts*. Bloomington: Indiana University Press, 1997.

Fleming, John. *An Introduction to the Franciscan Literature of the Middle Ages*. Chicago: Franciscan Herald Press, 1977.

Flint, Bill. *Edith the Fair: Visionary of Walsingham*. Leominster: Gracewing, 2015.

Flood, John. 'Marian Controversies and Milton's Virgin Mary'. In *Milton and Catholicism*, edited by Ronald Corthell and Thomas N. Corns, 169–95. Notre Dame, IN: University of Notre Dame Press, 2017.

Flora, Holly. *'The Devout Belief of the Imagination': The Paris Meditationes vitae Christi and Female Franciscan Spirituality in Trecento Italy*. Turnhout: Brepols, 2009.

Flynn, William T. 'Ductus figuratus et subtilis: Rhetorical Interventions for Women in Two Twelfth-Century Liturgies'. In *Rhetoric Beyond Words: Delight and Persuasion in the Arts of the Middle Ages*, edited by Mary Carruthers, 250–80. Cambridge: Cambridge University Press, 2010.

Foucault, Michel. 'Of Other Spaces'. Translated by Jay Miskowiec. *Diacritics* 16(1) (1986): 22–7.

Frey, Winfried. 'Maria Legens – Mariam Legere: St Mary as an Ideal Reader and St Mary as a Textbook'. In *The Book and the Magic of Reading*, edited by Albrecht Classen, 277–93. New York: Garland, 1988.

Fulton, Rachel. *From Judgment to Passion: Devotion to Christ and the Virgin Mary, 800–1200*. New York: Columbia University Press, 2002.

Gebauer, Gunter and Christoph Wulf. *Mimesis: Culture–Art–Society*, translated by Don Reneau. Berkeley: University of California Press, 1995.

Geddes, Jane. *The St Albans Psalter: A Book for Christina of Markyate*. London: British Library, 2005.

Georgianna, Linda. *The Solitary Self: Individuality in the* Ancrene Wisse. Cambridge, MA: Harvard University Press, 1981.

Gerry, Kathryn. 'The Alexis Quire and the Cult of Saints at St Albans'. *Historical Research* 82 (2009): 593–612.

Ghosh, Kantik. *The Wycliffite Heresy: Authority and the Interpretation of Texts*. Cambridge: Cambridge University Press, 2002.

Ghosh, Kantik. 'Nicholas Love'. In *A Companion to Middle English Prose*, edited by A.S.G. Edwards, 53–66. Cambridge: D.S. Brewer, 2004.
Gibson, Gail McMurray. *The Theater of Devotion: East Anglian Drama and Society in the Late Middle Ages*. Chicago: University of Chicago Press, 1989.
Gilchrist, Roberta. *Gender and Material Culture: The Archeology of Medieval Women*. London: Routledge, 1994.
Gill, Miriam. 'Female Piety and Impiety: Selected Images of Women in Wall Paintings in England after 1300'. In *Gender and Holiness: Men, Women and Saints in Late Medieval Europe*, edited by Samantha J.E. Riches and Sarah Salih, 101–20. London: Routledge, 2002.
Gillespie, Vincent. 'Anonymous Devotional Writings'. In *A Companion to Middle English Prose*, edited by A.S.G. Edwards, 127–50. Cambridge: D.S. Brewer, 2004.
Gillespie, Vincent. 'The Haunted Text: Reflections in *The Mirror to Deuout People*'. In *The Text in the Community: Essays on Medieval Works, Manuscripts, Authors, and Readers*, edited by Jill Mann and Maura B. Nolan, 129–72. Notre Dame, IN: University of Notre Dame Press, 2006.
Gillespie, Vincent. '"[S]he do the police in different voices": Pastiche, Ventriloquism and Parody in Julian of Norwich'. In *A Companion to Julian of Norwich*, edited by Liz Herbert McAvoy, 192–207. Cambridge: D.S. Brewer, 2008.
Gillespie, Vincent and Kantik Ghosh, eds. *After Arundel: Religious Writing in Fifteenth-Century England*. Turnhout: Brepols, 2011.
Gillespie, Vincent and Maggie Ross. '"With mekenes aske perseverantly": On Reading Julian of Norwich'. *Mystics Quarterly* 30 (2004): 126–41.
Goodich, Michael. '*Ancilla Dei*: The Servant as Saint in the Late Middle Ages'. In *Women of the Medieval World: Essays in Honor of John H. Handy*, edited by Julius Kirshner and Suzanne F. Wemple, 119–36. Oxford: Basil Blackwell, 1985.
Gottschall, A. 'Prayer Bead Production and use in Medieval England'. *Rosetta* 4 (2008): 1–14.
Grabes, Herbert. *The Mutable Glass: Mirror-Imagery in Titles and Texts of the Middle Ages and English Renaissance*. New York: Cambridge University Press, 1982.
Graef, Hilda. *Mary: A History of Doctrine and Devotion*. New York: Sheed and Ward, 1964.
Gray, Douglas. *Themes and Images in the Medieval English Religious Lyric*. London: Routledge & Kegan Paul, 1972.
Grayson, Janet. *Structure and Imagery in* Ancrene Wisse. Hanover, NH: University of New Hampshire, 1974.
Green, D.H. *Women Readers in the Middle Ages*. Cambridge: Cambridge University Press, 2007.
Greenspan, Kate. 'Autohagiography and Medieval Women's Spiritual Autobiography'. In *Gender and Text in the Later Middle Ages*, edited by Jane Chance, 216–36. Gainesville: University Press of Florida, 1996.
Grindlay, Lilla. *Queen of Heaven: The Assumption and Coronation of the Virgin in Early Modern English Writing*. Notre Dame, IN: University of Notre Dame Press, 2018.
Gunn, Cate and Liz Herbert McAvoy, eds. *Medieval Anchorites in their Communities*. Cambridge: D.S. Brewer, 2017.

Hale, Rosemary Drage. 'Imitatio Mariae: Motherhood Motifs in Late Medieval German Spirituality'. In *Medieval German Literature: Proceedings from the 23rd International Congress on Medieval Studies, Kalamazoo, Michigan, May 5-8, 1988*, edited by Albrecht Classen, 129-45. Göppingen: Kümmerle Verlag, 1989.

Hale, Rosemary Drage. '*Imitatio Mariae:* Motherhood Motifs in Late Medieval German Spirituality'. PhD diss., Harvard University, 1992.

Hall, D.J. *English Medieval Pilgrimage*. London: Taylor & Francis, 1965.

Hamburger, Jeffrey. *Nuns as Artists: The Visual Culture of a Medieval Convent*. Berkeley: University of California Press, 1997.

Hamburger, Jeffrey. *The Visual and the Visionary: Art and Female Spirituality in Late Medieval Germany*. New York: Zone, 1998.

Haney, Kristine L. *The St Albans Psalter: An Anglo-Norman Song of Faith*. New York: Peter Lang, 2002.

Hanna, Ralph. 'English Biblical Texts before Lollardy and their Fate'. In *Lollards and Their Influence in Late Medieval England*, edited by Fiona Somerset, Jill C. Haven and Derrick G. Pitard, 141-53. Woodbridge: Boydell Press, 2003.

Hanna, Ralph. *The English Manuscripts of Richard Rolle: A Descriptive Catalogue*. Exeter: Exeter University Press, 2010.

Hanna, Ralph. 'The Oldest Manuscript of Richard Rolle's Writings'. *Scriptorium* 70 (2016): 105-15.

Harthan, John. *Books of Hours and their Owners*. London: Thames and Hudson, 1977.

Harvey, J.H. *William Worcestre: Itineraries*. Oxford: Oxford University Press, 1969.

Hill, Carole. 'St Anne and her Walsingham Daughter'. In *Walsingham in Literature and Culture from the Middle Ages to Modernity*, edited by Dominic Janes and Gary Waller, 99-111. Farnham: Ashgate, 2010.

Hodapp, W. 'Sacred Time and Space Within: Drama and Ritual in Late Medieval Affective Passion Meditations'. *Downside Review* 115/4 (1997): 235-48.

Hollis, Stephanie. 'Barking's Monastic School, Late Seventh to Twelfth Century: History, Saint Making, and Literary Culture'. In *Barking Abbey and Medieval Literary Culture: Authorship and Authority in a Female Community*, edited by Jennifer N. Brown and Donna Alfano Bussell, 33-55. York: York University Press, 2012.

Holloway, Julia Bolton. 'Bride, Margery, Julian, and Alice: Bridget of Sweden's Textual Community in Medieval England'. In *Margery Kempe: A Book of Essays*, edited by S. J. McEntire, 203-22. New York: Garland, 1992.

Holmes, Emily A. *Flesh Made Word: Medieval Mystics, Writing, and the Incarnation*. Waco, TX: Baylor University Press, 2014.

Hoppenwasser, M. 'The Human Burden of the Prophet: St Birgitta's Revelations and *The Book of Margery Kempe*'. *Medieval Perspectives* VIII (1993): 153-62.

Hoppenwasser, Nanda and Signe Wegener. '*Vox Matris*: The Influence of St Birgitta's *Revelations* on *The Book of Margery Kempe*: St Birgitta and Margery Kempe as Wives and Mothers'. In *Crossing the Bridge: Comparative Essays on Medieval European and Heian Japanese Women Writers*, edited by Barbara Stevenson and Cynthia Ho, 61-85. New York: Palgrave, 2000.

Hudson, Anne. *Lollards and Their Books*. London: Bloomsbury Academic, 1985.

Hudson, Anne. *The Premature Reformation: Wycliffite Texts and Lollard History*. Oxford: Oxford University Press, 1988.

Hughes-Edwards, Mari. 'The Role of the Anchoritic Guidance Writer'. In *Anchoritism in the Middle Ages: Texts and Transitions*, edited by Catherine Innes-Parker and Naoe Kukita Yoshikawa, 31–46. Cardiff: University of Wales Press, 2013.

Hughes-Edwards, Mari. *Reading Medieval Anchoritism: Ideology and Spiritual Practices*. Cardiff: University of Wales Press, 2012.

Hunt, Arnold. 'Stafford, Anthony'. *Oxford Dictionary of National Biography* (2004). https://doi.org/10.1093/ref:odnb/26200

Inglis, Eric ed. *The Hours of Mary of Burgundy*. London: Harvey Miller, 1995.

Innes-Parker, Catherine. 'Subversion and Conformity in Julian's *Revelation*: Authority, Vision and the Motherhood of God'. *Mystics Quarterly* 23(2) (1997): 7–35.

Irigaray, Luce. 'Christian Mysteries as Graces in the Feminine'. In *Key Writings*, edited by Luce Irigaray, 162–4. London: Continuum, 2004.

James, M.R. *The Western Manuscripts in the Library of Trinity College, Cambridge: A Descriptive Catalogue*. 4 vols. Cambridge: Cambridge University Press, 1900–4.

Jantzen, Grace. *Julian of Norwich: Mystic and Theologian*. New York: Paulist Press, 1987; new ed., 2000.

Jeay, Madeleine and Kathleen Garay. '"To Promote God's Praise and Her Neighbour's Salvation": Strategies of Authorship and Readership Among Mystic Women in the Later Middle Ages'. In *Women Writing Back/Writing Women Back: Transnational Perspectives from the Late Middle Ages to the Dawn of the Modern Era*, edited by Anke Gillier, Alicia Montoya and Suzan van Dijk, 23–50. Leiden: Brill, 2010.

Johnson, Ian. 'Prologue and Practice: Middle English Lives of Christ'. In *The Medieval Translator: The Theory and Practice of Translation in the Middle Ages*, edited by Roger Ellis et al., 69–85. Cambridge: D.S. Brewer, 1989.

Johnson, Ian. *The Middle English Life of Christ: Academic Discourse, Translation, and Vernacular Theology*. Turnhout: Brepols, 2013.

Joliffe, P.S. *A Check-list of Middle English Prose Writings of Spiritual Guidance*. Toronto: Pontifical Institute of Mediaeval Studies, 1974.

Jones, E.A., trans. and anno. *Hermits and Anchorites in England, 1200–1550*. Manchester: Manchester University Press, 2019.

Jung, Jacqueline E. 'Chrystalline Wombs and Pregnant Hearts: The Exuberant Bodies of the Katherinenthal Visitation Group'. In *History in the Comic Mode: Medieval Communities and the Matter of Person*, edited by Bruce Holsinger and Rachel Fulton, 223–37. New York: Columbia University Press, 2007.

Karnes, Michelle. 'Nicholas Love and Medieval Meditations on Christ'. *Speculum* 82 (2007): 380–408.

Karnes, Michelle. *Imagination, Meditation, and Cognition in the Middle Ages*. Chicago: University of Chicago Press, 2011.

Katz, Melissa R. 'Regarding Mary: Women's Lives Reflected in the Virgin's Image'. In *Divine Mirrors: The Virgin Mary in the Visual Arts*, edited by Melissa R. Katz, 19–132. Oxford: Oxford University Press, 2001.

Keene, Catherine. 'Read Her Like a Book: Female Patronage as *Imitatio Mariae*'. *Magistra* 24(1) (2018): 3–38.

Kelly, Henry Ansgar. *The Middle English Bible: A Reassessment*. Philadelphia: University of Pennsylvania Press, 2016.

Killeen, Kevin and Helen Smith. '"All other Bookes ... are but Notes upon this": The Early Modern Bible'. In *The Oxford Handbook of the Bible in Early Modern England, c. 1530–1700*, edited by Kevin Killeen, Helen Smith and Rachel Willie, 1–19. Oxford: Oxford University Press, 2015.

Klafter, Einat. 'The Feminine Mystic: Margery Kempe's Pilgrimage to Rome as an *imitatio Birgitta*'. In *Gender in Medieval Places, Spaces and Thresholds*, edited by Victoria Blud, Diane Heath and Einat Klafter, 123–36. London: School of Advanced Study, University of London, 2018.

Knighton, C.S. ed. *Catalogue of the Pepys Library at Magdalene College, Cambridge: vol. 1, Census of Printed Books*. Cambridge: D.S. Brewer, 2004.

Koerner, Joseph Leo. *The Reformation of the Image*. Chicago: University of Chicago Press, 2004.

Kraebel, Andrew. 'Lydgate's Missing "Ballade" and the Bibliographical Imaginary'. In *The Shapes of Early English Poetry: Style, Form, History*, edited by Irina Dumitrescu and Eric Weiskott, 191–213. Kalamazoo, MI: Medieval Institute, 2018.

Kraebel, Andrew. 'Modes of Authorship and the Making of Medieval English Literature'. In *The Cambridge Handbook of Literary Authorship*, edited by Ingo Berensmeyer, Gert Buelens, and Marysa Demoor, 98–114. Cambridge: Cambridge University Press, 2019.

Kraebel, Andrew. 'Rolle Reassembled: Booklet Production, Single-Author Anthologies, and the Making of Bodley 861'. *Speculum* 94(4) (2019): 959–1005.

Kraebel, Andrew. *Biblical Commentary and Translation in Later Medieval England: Experiments in Interpretation*. Cambridge: Cambridge University Press, 2020.

Kristeva, Julia and Catherine Clément. *The Feminine and the Sacred*. New York: Columbia University Press, 2001.

Krug, Rebecca. *Margery Kempe and the Lonely Reader*. Ithaca, NY: Cornell University Press, 2017.

Latham, R.E., D.R. Howlett and R.K. Ashdowne, eds. *The Dictionary of Medieval Latin in British Sources*. London: British Academy, 1975–2013.

Laugerud, Henning. 'Polysemi og den dynamiske tradisjon'. In *Passepartout: Skrifter for kunsthistorie* 25 (2005): 94–103.

Lawton, David. 'The Bible'. *The Oxford History of Literary Translation in English: Volume 1 to 1550*, edited by Roger Ellis, 193–233. Oxford: Oxford University Press, 2008.

Leclerq, Henri. 'Office divin'. *Dictionnaire d'archéologie chrétienne et de liturgie*, vol. 12, cols. 1962–2017. Paris, 1935.

Leclerq, Jean, OSB. 'Mary's Reading of Christ'. *Monastic Studies* 15 (1984): 105–16.

Leclercq, Jean. *Women and Saint Bernard of Clairvaux*. Translated by Marie-Bernard Saïd OSB. Kalamazoo, MI: Cistercian, 1989.

Legge, M.D. *Anglo-Norman Literature and its Background*. Oxford: Oxford University Press, 1963.

Lewis, Charlton and Charles Short. *A Latin Dictionary*. Oxford: Oxford University Press, 1879.

Lewis, Katherine J. 'Pilgrimage and the Cult of St Katherine in Late Medieval England'. In *Pilgrimage Explored*, edited by J. Stopford. Woodbridge: York Medieval Press, 1999.

Lewis, R.E., N.F. Blake and A.S.G. Edwards. *Index of Printed Middle English Prose*. New York: Garland, 1985.

Leyser, Henrietta. 'Christina of Markyate: An Introduction'. In *Christina of Markyate: A Twelfth-Century Holy Woman*, edited by Samuel Fanous and Henrietta Leyser, 1–12. Routledge: London, 2005.

Linton, David. 'Reading the Virgin Reader'. In *The Book and the Magic of Reading in the Middle Ages*, edited by Albrecht Classen, 253–76. New York: Falmer Press, 1999.

Longfellow, Erica. *Women and Religious Writing in Early Modern England*. Cambridge: Cambridge University Press, 2004.

MacCulloch, Diarmaid. 'Mary and Sixteenth-Century Protestants'. *Studies in Church History* 39 (2004): 191–217.

Manly, John M. and Edith Rickert, eds. *The Text of the Canterbury Tales: Studied on the Basis of All Known Manuscripts*. 8 vols. Chicago: University of Chicago Press, 1940.

Manoussakis, John Panteleimon. 'On the Flesh of the Word: Incarnational Hermeneutics'. In *Carnal Hermeneutics*, edited by Richard Kearney and Brian Treanor, 306–15. New York: Fordham University Press, 2015.

McAvoy, Liz Herbert. *Authority and the Female Body in the Writings of Julian of Norwich and Margery Kempe*. Cambridge: D.S. Brewer, 2004.

McAvoy, Liz Herbert. '"For we be doubel of God's making": Writing, Gender and the Body in Julian of Norwich'. In *A Companion to Julian of Norwich*, edited by McAvoy, 166–80. Cambridge: D.S. Brewer, 2008.

McAvoy, Liz Herbert. *Medieval Anchoritism: Gender, Space and the Solitary Life*. Cambridge: D.S. Brewer, 2011.

McAvoy, Liz Herbert and Diane Watt. 'Writing a History of British Women's Writing from 700 to 1500'. In *The History of British Women's Writing, 700–1500*, edited by McAvoy and Watt, 1–30. Basingstoke: Palgrave, 2012.

McConica, James K. *English Humanists and Reformation Politics under Henry VIII and Edward VI*. Oxford: Oxford University Press, 1965.

McDevitt, Mary. '"The Ink of Our Mortality": The Late-Medieval Image of the Writing Christ Child'. In *The Christ Child in Medieval Culture: Alpha Es et O!*, edited by Mary Dzon and Theresa M. Kenney, 224–53. Toronto: University of Toronto Press, 2012.

McDonnell, K. 'Feminist Mariologies: Heteronomy/Subordination and the Scandal of Christology'. *Theological Studies* 66 (2005): 527–67.

McGinn, Bernard, ed. and introd. *The Essential Writings of Christian Mysticism*. New York: The Modern Library, 2006.

McGuire, Brian Patrick. *Brother and Lover: Aelred of Rievaulx*. New York: Crossroad, 1994.

McIlroy, Claire Elizabeth. *English Prose Treatises of Richard Rolle*. Cambridge: D.S. Brewer, 2004.

McInerney, Maud Burnett. '"In the Meydens Womb": Julian of Norwich and the Poetics of Enclosure'. In *Medieval Mothering*, edited by John Carmi Parsons and Bonnie Wheeler, 157–99. London: Garland, 1996.

McIntosh, Angus, M.L. Samuels and Michael Benskin. *A Linguistic Atlas of Late Mediaeval English*. 4 vols. Aberdeen: Aberdeen University Press, 1986.

McNamer, Sarah. 'The Exploratory Image: God as Mother in Julian of Norwich's *Revelations of Divine Love*'. *Mystics Quarterly* 15(1) (1989): 21–8.
McNamer, Sarah. 'Further Evidence for the Date of the Pseudo-Bonaventuran *Meditationes vitae Christi*'. *Franciscan Studies* 50 (1990): 235–61.
McNamer, Sarah. 'The Origins of the *Meditationes vitae Christi*'. *Speculum* 84 (2009): 905–55.
McNamer, Sarah. *Affective Meditation and the Invention of Medieval Compassion*. Philadelphia: University of Pennsylvania Press, 2010.
Meale, Carol M. '"oft siþis with grete deuotion I þought what I miȝt do pleysyng to god": The Early Ownership and Readership of Love's *Mirror*, with Special Reference to its Female Audience'. In *Nicholas Love at Waseda: Proceedings of the International Conference, 20-22 July 1995*, edited by Shoichi Oguro, Richard Beadle and Michael G. Sargent, 19–46. Cambridge: D.S. Brewer, 1997.
Meiss, Millard, intro., with intro and commentaries by Marcel Thomas. *The Rohan Master: A Book of Hours: Bibliothèque Nationale, Paris MS Latin 9471*. New York: George Braziller, 1973.
Meredith, Peter ed. *The Mary Play from the N. Town Manuscript*. London: Longman, 1987.
Mews, Constant J. ed. *Listen Daughter: The Speculum Virginum and the Formation of Religious Women in the Middle Ages*. New York: Palgrave, 2001.
Michalski, Sergiusz. *The Reformation and the Visual Arts*. London: Routledge, 1993.
Miles, Laura Saetveit. 'Space and Enclosure in Julian of Norwich's *A Revelation of Love*'. In *A Companion to Julian of Norwich*, edited by Liz Herbert McAvoy, 154–65. Cambridge: D.S. Brewer, 2008.
Miles, Laura Saetveit. 'Looking in the Past for a Discourse of Motherhood: Birgitta of Sweden and Julia Kristeva'. *Medieval Feminist Forum* 47(1) (2011): 52–76.
Miles, Laura Saetveit. 'St Bridget of Sweden'. In *History of British Women's Writing, Vol. 1: 700–1500*, edited by Diane Watt and Liz Herbert McAvoy, 207–15. Basingstoke: Palgrave, 2012.
Miles, Laura Saetveit. 'The Origins and Development of Mary's Book at the Annunciation'. *Speculum* 89(3) (2014): 632–69.
Miles, Laura Saetveit. 'An Unnoticed Borrowing from the Treatise *Of Three Workings In Man's Soul* in the Gospel Meditation *Meditaciones Domini Nostri*'. *Journal of the Early Book Society* 20 (2017): 277–84.
Miles, Laura Saetveit. '"Syon Gostly": Crafting Aesthetic Imaginaries and Stylistics of Existence in Medieval Devotional Culture'. In *Emerging Aesthetic Imaginaries*, edited by Lene Johannessen and Mark Ledbetter, 79–92. London: Lexington, 2019.
Miles, Laura Saetveit. 'The Living Book of Cambridge, Trinity College MS B.15.42: Compilation, Meditation, and Vision'. In *Late Medieval Devotional Compilations in England*, edited by Marleen Cré, Diana Denissen and Denis Renevey, forthcoming. Turnhout: Brepols, 2019.
Miller, John Desmond. *Beads and Prayers: The Rosary in History and Devotion*. London: Burns & Oates, 2002.
Millett, Bella. 'Women in No Man's Land: English Recluses and the Development of Vernacular Literature in the Twelfth and Thirteenth Centuries'. In *Women and*

Literature in Britain, 1150–1500, edited by Carol M. Meale, 86–103. Cambridge: Cambridge University Press, 1993.
Minnis, Alastair. 'Affection and Imagination in *The Cloud of Unknowing* and Hilton's *Scale of Perfection*'. *Traditio* 39 (1983): 323–66.
Minnis, Alastair, A.B. Scott and David Wallace, eds. *Medieval Literary Theory and Criticism, c. 1100–c.1375: The Commentary-Tradition*, rev. ed. Oxford: Oxford University Press, 1991, rpt 2001.
Minnis, Alastair. *Translations of Authority in Medieval English Literature: Valuing the Vernacular*. Cambridge: Cambridge University Press, 2009.
Minnis, Alastair. *Medieval Theory of Authorship: Scholastic Literary Attitudes in the Later Middle Ages*, 2nd ed. Philadelphia: University of Pennsylvania Press, 1988, rpt. 2010.
Molecamp, Femke. 'Genevan Legacies: The Making of the English Geneva Bible'. In *The Oxford Handbook of the Bible in Early Modern England*, edited by Kevin Killeen, Helen Smith and Rachel Willie, 24–38. Oxford: Oxford University Press, 2015.
Molekamp, Femke. *Women and the Bible in Early Modern England: Religious Reading and Writing*. Oxford: Oxford University Press, 2013.
Mooney, Linne R. *Index of Middle English Prose Handlist XI: Manuscripts of the Library of Trinity College, Cambridge*. Cambridge: D.S. Brewer, 1995.
Moorman, John. *A History of the Franciscan Order from its Origins to the Year 1517*. Oxford: Clarendon Press, 1968.
Morris, Bridget. 'Four Birgittine Meditations in Medieval Swedish'. *Birgittiana* 2 (1996): 167–86.
Morris, Bridget. *St Birgitta of Sweden*. Woodbridge: Boydell Press, 1999.
Morrison, Susan Signe. *Women Pilgrims in Late Medieval England: Private Piety as Public Performance*. London: Routledge, 2000.
Muir, Laurence. 'IV. Translations and Paraphrases of the Bible, and Commentaries'. In *A Manual of the Writings in Middle English, 1050–1500*, vol. 2, edited by J. Burke Severs, 381–409. New Haven, CT: Connecticut Academy of Arts and Sciences, 1970.
Mulder-Bakker, Anneke B. '*Maria doctrix*: Anchoritic Women, the Mother of God, and the Transmission of Knowledge'. In *Seeing and Knowing: Women and Learning in Medieval Europe 1200–1550*, edited by Anneke B. Mulder-Bakker, 181–99. Turnhout: Brepols, 2004.
Nerlich, Brigitte. 'Polysemy: Past and Present'. In *Polysemy: Flexible Patterns of Meaning in Mind and Language*, edited by Brigitte Nerlich et al., 49–79. Berlin: Mouton de Gruyter, 2003.
Newman, Barbara. *God and the Goddesses: Vision, Poetry, and Belief in the Middle Ages*. Philadelphia: University of Pennsylvania Press, 2003.
Newman, Barbara. 'What does it mean to say "I saw"? The Clash between Theory and Practice in Medieval Visionary Culture'. *Speculum* 80 (2005): 1–43.
Newman, Barbara. 'Liminalities: Literate Women in the Long Twelfth Century'. In *European Transformations: The Long Twelfth Century*, edited by Thomas F.X. Noble and John Van Engen, 354–402. Notre Dame, IN: University of Notre Dame Press, 2012.
Nixon, Virginia. *Mary's Mother: Saint Anne in Late Medieval Europe*. Philadelphia: Pennsylvania State University Press, 2004.

Noble, Bonnie. *Lucas Cranach the Elder: Art and Devotion of the German Reformation*. Lanham, MA: University Press of America, 2009.

Norgate, Gerald le Grys. 'Stafford, Anthony'. *Dictionary of National Biography* 53 (1885–1900). https://en.wikisource.org/wiki/Stafford,_Anthony_(DNB00)

Ó Carragáin, Éamonn. *Ritual and the Rood: Liturgical Images and the Old English Poems of the* Dream of the Rood *Tradition*. London: British Library and University of Toronto Press, 2005.

O'Connell, Michael. *The Idolatrous Eye: Iconoclasm, and Theater in Early-Modern England*. Oxford: Oxford University Press, 2000.

Ogura, Shoichi, Richard Beadle and Michael G. Sargent, eds. *Nicholas Love at Waseda*. Cambridge: D.S. Brewer, 1997.

Osherow, Michele. *Biblical Women's Voices in Early Modern England*. Farnham: Ashgate, 2009.

Otter, Monica. 'Entrances and Exits: Performing the Psalms in Goscelin's *Liber Confortatorius*'. *Speculum* 83 (2008): 283–302.

Pächt, Otto, C.R. Dodwell and F. Wormald, *The St Albans Psalter (Albani Psalter)*. London: Warburg Institute, 1960.

Parkes, M.B. *Scribes, Scripts and Readers: Studies in the Communication, Presentation, and Dissemination of Medieval Texts*. London: Hambledon, 1991.

Parkes, M.B. *Their Hands Before Our Eyes: A Closer Look at Scribes. The Lyell Lectures Delivered at the University of Oxford, 1999*. New York: Routledge, 2008.

Patterson, Paul. 'Translating Access and Authority at Syon Abbey'. In *Devotional Culture in Late Medieval England and Europe: Diverse Imaginations of Christ's Life*, edited by Stephen Kelly and Ryan Perry, MCS 31, 443–59. Turnhout: Brepols, 2014.

Paul Patterson. 'Female Readers and the Sources of the *Mirror to Devout People*'. *Journal of Medieval Religious Cultures* 42(2) (2016), 181–200.

Pelikan, Jaroslav. *Mary Through the Centuries: Her Place in the History of Culture*. New Haven, CT: Yale University Press, 1996.

Perry, Ryan. '"Some Sprytuall matter of gostly edyfycacion": Readers and Readings of Nicholas Love's *Mirror of the Blessed Life of Jesus Christ*'. In *The Pseudo-Bonaventuran Lives of Christ: Exploring the Middle English Tradition*, edited by Ian Johnson and Allen F. Westphal, MCS 24, 79–126. Turnhout: Brepols, 2013.

Peters, Christine. *Patterns of Piety: Women, Gender and Religion in Late Medieval and Reformation England*. Cambridge: University of Cambridge Press, 2003.

Pezzini, Domenico. 'Two Middle English Translations of Aelred of Rievaulx's *De Institutione Inclusarum*: An Essay on the Varieties of Medieval Translational Practices'. In *Atti del VII Convegno Nazionale di Storia della Lingua Inglese*, edited by Giovanni Iamartino, 81–95. Rome: Quaderni di Libri e Riviste D'Italia, 1998.

Powell, Morgan. 'Making the Psalter of Christina of Markyate (the St Albans Psalter)'. *Viator* 36 (2005): 293–335.

Raby, Michael. 'The Phenomenology of Attention in Julian of Norwich's *A Revelation of Love*'. *Exemplaria* 26(4) (2014): 347–67.

Ravin, Yael and Claudia Leacock. 'Polysemy: An Overview'. In *Polysemy: Theoretical and Computational Approaches*, ed. Ravin and Leacock, 1–29. Oxford: Oxford University Press, 2000.

Renck, Anneliese Pollock. *Female Authorship, Patronage and Translation in Late Medieval France*. Turnhout: Brepols, 2018.

Reynolds, Brian K. *Gateway to Heaven: Marian Doctrine and Devotion, Image and Typology in the Patristic and Medieval Periods, vol. 1: Doctrine and Devotion*. New York: New City Press, 2012.

Rice, Nicole. *Lay Piety and Religious Discipline in Middle English Literature*. Cambridge: Cambridge University Press, 2008.

Ringbom, Sixten. 'Devotional Images and Imaginative Devotions: Notes on the Place of Art in Late Medieval Private Piety'. *Gazette des Beaux-Arts* 73 (1969): 159–70.

Rivera, Mayra. *Poetics of the Flesh*. Durham, NC: Duke University Press, 2015.

Robb, David M. 'The Iconography of the Annunciation in the Fourteenth and Fifteenth Centuries'. *The Art Bulletin* 18(4) (1936): 480–526.

Robbins, Mary E. 'The Truculent Toad in the Middle Ages'. In *Animals in the Middle Ages: A Book of Essays*, edited by Nona C. Flores, 25–47. New York: Garland, 1986.

Robertson, Elizabeth. *Early English Devotional Prose and the Female Audience*. Knoxville, TN: University of Tennessee Press, 1990.

Robinson, P.R. 'The Vernon Manuscript as a "Coucher Book"'. In *Studies in the Vernon Manuscript*, edited by Derek Pearsall, 15–28. Cambridge: D.S. Brewer, 1990.

Rogers, Nicholas. 'Patrons and Purchasers: Evidence for the Original Owners of Books of Hours Produced in the Low Countries for the English Market'. In *'Als Ich Can': Liber Amicorum in Memory of Professor Dr Maurits Smeyers*, Corpus of Illumination Manuscripts vol. 11–12, edited by Bert Cardon et al., 1165–81. Leuven: Peeters, 2002.

Rosenfeld, Jessica. 'Envy and Exemplarity in *The Book of Margery Kempe*'. *Exemplaria: A Journal of Theory in Medieval and Renaissance Studies* 26 (2014): 105–21.

Roy, Gopa. 'Sharpen Your Mind with the Whetstone of Books: The Female Recluse as Reader in Goscelin's *Liber Confortatorius*, Aelred of Rievaulx's *De Institutione Inclusarum* and the *Ancrene Wisse*'. In *Women, the Book and the Godly: Selected Proceedings of the St Hilda's Conference, 1993*, vol. 1, edited by Lesley Smith and Jane H.M. Taylor, 113–22. Cambridge: D.S. Brewer, 1995.

Rubin, Miri. *Mother of God: A History of the Virgin Mary*. New Haven, CT: Yale University Press, 2009.

Rust, M. *Imaginary Worlds in Medieval Books: Exploring the Manuscript Matrix*. New York: Palgrave, 2007.

Sabbath, R. S. *Sacred Tropes: Tanakh, New Testament, and Qur'an as Literature and Culture*. New York: Brill, 2009.

Saenger, Paul. 'Silent Reading: Its Impact on Late Medieval Script and Society'. *Viator* 13 (1982): 367–414.

Saenger, Paul. 'Books of Hours and the Reading Habits of the Later Middle Ages'. In *The Culture of Print: Power and Uses of Print in Early Modern Europe*, edited by Roger Chartier, translated by Lydia G. Cochrane, 141–73. Princeton, NJ: Princeton University Press, 1989.

Sahlin, Claire. '"His Heart was My Heart": Birgitta of Sweden's Devotion to the Heart of Mary'. In *Heliga Birgitta – budskapet och förebilden*, edited by Alf Härdelin and Mereth Lindgren, 213–27. Stockholm: Almqvist and Wiksell, 1993.

Sahlin, Claire. 'Gender and Prophetic Authority in Birgitta of Sweden's *Revelations*'. In *Gender and Text in the Later Middle Ages*, edited by Jane Chance, 69–95. Gainesville: University Press of Florida, 1996.
Sahlin, Claire. 'The Virgin Mary and Birgitta of Sweden's Prophetic Vocation'. In *Maria i Sverige under tusen år. Foredrag vid symposiet i Vadstena 6–10 oktober 1994: I*, edited by Sven-Erik Brodd and Alf Härdelin, 227–54. Skellefteå: Artos, 1996.
Sahlin, Claire. *Birgitta of Sweden and the Voice of Prophecy*. Cambridge: D.S. Brewer, 2001.
Salmesvuori, Päivi. *Power and Sainthood: The Case of Birgitta of Sweden*. New York: Palgrave Macmillan 2014.
Salter, Elizabeth. *Nicholas Love's 'Myrrour of the Blessed Lyf of Jesu Christ'*. Analecta Cartusiana 10. Salzburg: Insitut für Anglistik und Amerikanistik, Universität Salzburg, 1974.
Sand, Alexa. *Vision, Devotion, and Self-Representation in Late Medieval Art*. Cambridge: Cambridge University Press, 2014.
Sanok, Catherine. *Her Life Historical: Exemplarity and Female Saints' Lives in Late Medieval England*. Philadelphia: University of Pennsylvania Press, 2007.
Sargent, Michael. 'Versions of the Life of Christ: Nicholas Love's *Mirror* and Related Works'. *Poetica* 42 (1994): 39–70.
Sargent, Michael. 'Nicholas Love's *Mirror of the Blessed Life of Jesus Christ* and the Politics of Vernacular Translations in Late Medieval England'. In *The Medieval Translator: Vol. 12, Lost in Translation*, edited by Denis Renevey and Christiania Whitehead, 205–23. Turnhout: Brepols, 2009.
Schaberg, Jane. *The Illegitimacy of Jesus: A Feminist Theological Interpretation of the Infancy Narratives*. New York: Harper & Row, 2006.
Schein, S. 'Bridget of Sweden, Margery Kempe and Women's Jerusalem Pilgrimages in the Middle Ages'. *Mediterranean Historical Review* 14 (1999): 44–58.
Schibanoff, Susan. 'Botticelli's Madonna del Magnificat: Constructing the Woman Writer in Early Humanist Italy'. *PMLA* 109(2) (1994): 190–206.
Schirmer, Elizabeth. 'Reading Lessons at Syon Abbey: *The Myroure of Oure Ladye* and the Mandates of Vernacular Theology'. In *Voices in Dialogue: Reading Women in the Middle Ages*, edited by Linda Olsen and Kathryn Kerby-Fulton, 345–76. Notre Dame, IN: University of Notre Dame Press, 2005.
Schneiders, Sandra. *Beyond Patching: Faith and Feminism in the Catholic Church*. New York: Paulist Press, 1991.
Schreiner, Klaus. '"... wie Maria geleicht einem puch": Beiträge zur Buchmetaphorik des hohen und späten Mittelalters'. *Archiv für Geschichte des Buchwesens* 11 (1971): cols. 1437–64.
Schreiner, Klaus. 'Marienverehrung, Lesekultur, Schriftlichkeit: Bildungs- und frömmigkeitsgeschichtliche Studien zur Auslegung und Darstellung von "Mariä Verkündigung"'. In *Frühmittelalterliche Studien: Jahrbuch des Instituts für Frühmittelalterforschung des Universität Münster* 24, edited by Hagen Keller and Joachim Wollasch, 314–68. Berlin: De Gruyter, 1990.
Schreiner, Klaus. *Maria: Jungfrau, Mutter, Herrscherin*. Munich: Carl Hanser, 1994.

Scott-Stokes, Charity. *Women's Books of Hours in Medieval England: Selected Texts Translated from Latin, Anglo-Norman French and Middle English with Introduction and Interpretive Essay*. Cambridge: D.S. Brewer, 2006.
Selman, Rebecca. 'Spirituality and Sex Change: *Horologium Sapientiae* and *Speculum devotorum*'. In *Writing Religious Women: Female Spiritual and Textual Practices in Late Medieval England*, edited by Denis Renevey and Christiania Whitehead, 63–80. Cardiff: University of Wales Press, 2000.
Sheingorn, Pamela. '"The Wise Mother": The Image of St Anne Teaching the Virgin Mary'. *Gesta* 32(1) (1993): 69–83.
Shoaf, R.A. 'Medieval Studies After Derrida After Heidegger'. In *Sign, Sentence, Discourse: Language in Medieval Thought and Literature*, edited by Julian N. Wasserman and Lois Roney, 9–30. Syracuse: Syracuse University Press, 1989.
Short, William. *Saints in the World of Nature: The Animal Story as Spiritual Parable in Medieval Hagiography (900–1200)*. Rome: Pontificia Universitas Gregoriana, 1983.
Singer, Stella A. 'Walsingham's Local Genius: Norfolk's "Newe Nazareth"'. In *Walsingham in Literature and Culture*, 23–34.
Smalley, Beryl. *The Study of the Bible in the Middle Ages*. Notre Dame, IN: University of Notre Dame Press, 1964.
Smith, Kathryn A. *Art, Identity and Devotion in Fourteenth-Century England: Three Women and their Books of Hours*. London: British Library, 2003.
Smith, Lesley. 'Scriba, Femina: Medieval Depictions of Women Writing'. In *Women and the Book: Assessing the Visual Evidence*, edited by Jane H.M. Taylor and Lesley Smith, 20–44. Toronto: University of Toronto Press, 1996.
Snow, Clare. '*Maria Mediatrix:* Mediating the Divine in the Devotional Literature of Late Medieval England'. PhD diss. Center for Medieval Studies, University of Toronto, 2012.
Sobecki, Sebastian. '"The writyng of this tretys": Margery Kempe's Son and the Authorship of Her *Book*'. *Studies in the Age of Chaucer* 37 (2015): 257–83.
Somerset, Fiona. *Feeling Like Saints: Lollard Writings After Wyclif*. New York: Cornell University Press, 2014.
Spencer, B.W. 'Medieval Pilgrim Badges'. In *Rotterdam Papers: A Contribution to Medieval Archaeology*, ed. J.G.N. Renaud, 137–53. Rotterdam: Rotterdam Papers, 1968.
Spencer, Brian. *Pilgrim Souvenirs and Secular Badges: Medieval Finds from Excavations in London*. London: Boydell Press in association with Museum of London, 2010.
Squire, Aelred. *Aelred of Rievaulx: A Study*. London: SPCK, 1969.
Staley, Lynn. *Margery Kempe's Dissenting Fictions*. Philadelphia: Pennsylvania State University Press, 1994.
Stanbury, Sarah. 'The Vivacity of Images: St Katherine, Knighton's Lollards, and the Breaking of Idols'. In *Images, Idolatry, and Iconoclasm in Late Medieval England*, edited by by Jeremy Dimmick, James Simpson and Nicolette Zeeman, 131–50. Oxford: Oxford University Press, 2002.
Strype, John. *Annals of the Reformation and Establishment of Religion and Other Various Occurrences in the Church of England During Queen Elizabeth's Happy Reign*. Oxford: Clarendon Press, 1824.
Tasioulas, Jacqueline. '"Heaven and Earth in Little Space": The Foetal Existence of Christ in Medieval Literature and Thought'. *Medium Ævum* 76(1) (2007): 24–48.

Temple, Liam Peter. 'Returning the English "Mystics" to their Medieval Milieu: Julian of Norwich, Margery Kempe and Bridget of Sweden'. *Women's Writing* 23(2) (2016): 141–58.
Theweleit, K. *Male Fantasies*. Translated by S. Conway, C. Turner and E. Carter, 2 vols. Minneapolis: University of Minnesota Press, 1987–8.
Thomson, J.A.F. 'Orthodox Religion and the Origins of Lollardy'. *History* 74 (1989): 39–55.
Tóth, Peter and Dávid Falvay. 'New Light on the on the Date and Authorship of the *Meditationes Vitae Christi*'. In *Devotional Culture in Late Medieval England: Diverse Imaginations of Christ's Life*, edited by Stephen Kelly and Ryan Perry, MCS 11, 17–104. Turnhout: Brepols, 2014.
Trill, Suzanne. 'Religion and the Construction of Femininity'. In *Women and Literature in Britain, 1500–1700*, edited by Helen Wilcox, 30–55. Cambridge: Cambridge University Press, 1996.
van Liere, Frans. *An Introduction to the Medieval Bible*. Cambridge, MA: Cambridge University Press, 2014.
van Nolcken, Christina. 'Lay Literacy, the Democratization of God's Law, and the Lollards'. In *The Bible as Book: The Manuscript Tradition*, edited by John L. Sharpe III and Kimberly van Kampe, 177–95. London: British Library, 1998.
Venarde, B.L. *Women's Monasticism and Medieval Society: Nunneries in France and England, 890–1215*. Ithaca, NY: Cornell University Press, 1997.
Vidas, Marina. *The Copenhagen Bohun Manuscripts: Women, Representation, and Reception in Late Fourteenth-Century England*. Copenhagen: Museum Tusculanum Press, 2019.
Voaden, Rosalyn. *God's Words, Women's Voices: The Discernment of Spirits in the Writing of Late-Medieval Women Visionaries*. York: York Medieval Press, 1999.
Waller, Gary. *Walsingham and the English Imagination*. Farnham: Ashgate, 2011.
Waller, Gary. *The Virgin Mary in Late Medieval and Early Modern English Literature and Popular Culture*. Cambridge: Cambridge University Press, 2011.
Waller, Gary. *A Cultural Study of Mary and the Annunciation: From Luke to the Enlightenment*. London: Pickering & Chatto, 2015.
Warner, Marina. *Alone of All Her Sex: The Myth and Cult of the Virgin Mary*. London: Knopf, 1976.
Warren, Ann. *Anchorites and Their Patrons*. Berkeley: University of California Press, 1985.
Warren, Nancy Bradley. *Spiritual Economies: Female Monasticism in Later Medieval England*. Philadelphia: University of Pennsylvania Press, 2001.
Watson, Nicholas. *Richard Rolle and the Invention of Authority*. Cambridge: Cambridge University Press, 1991.
Watson, Nicholas. 'The Composition of Julian of Norwich's *Revelation of Love*'. *Speculum* 68 (1993): 637–83.
Watson, Nicholas. 'Censorship and Cultural Change in Late-Medieval England: Vernacular Theology, the Oxford Translation Debate, and Arundel's Constitutions of 1409'. *Speculum* 70 (1995): 822–64.
Watson, Nicholas. '"Yf wommen be double naturelly": Remaking "Woman" in Julian of Norwich's *Revelation of Love*'. *Exemplaria* 8(1) (1996): 1–34.

Watson, Nicholas. 'Conceptions of the Word: The Mother Tongue and the Incarnation of God'. *New Medieval Literatures* 1 (1997): 85–124.
Watson, Nicholas. 'The Middle English Mystics'. In *The Cambridge History of Medieval English Literature*, edited by David Wallace, 539–65. Cambridge: Cambridge University Press, 1999.
Watson, Nicholas. 'Fashioning the Puritan Gentry-Woman: Devotion and Dissent in *Book to a Mother*'. In *Medieval Women: Texts and Contexts in Medieval Britain: Essays for Felicity Riddy*, edited by Jocelyn Wogan-Browne et al., 169–84. Turnhout: Brepols, 2000.
Watson, Nicholas. 'The Making of *The Book of Margery Kempe*'. In *Voices in Dialogue: Reading Women in the Middle Ages*, edited by Linda Olson and Kathryn Kerby-Fulton, 395–434. Notre Dame, IN: University of Notre Dame Press, 2005.
Watt, Diane. *Secretaries of God: Women Prophets in Late Medieval and Early Modern England*. Cambridge: D.S. Brewer, 1997.
Weissman, Hope Phyllis. 'Margery Kempe in Jerusalem: *Hysterica Compassio* in the Late Middle Ages'. In *Acts of Interpretation: The Text in Its Contexts, 700–1600*, edited by Mary J. Carruthers and Elizabeth D. Kirk, 201–17. Norman, OK: Pilgrim, 1982.
Wieck, Roger S. *The Book of Hours in Medieval Art and Life*. London: Sotheby's, 1988.
Williams, Tara. 'Manipulating Mary: Maternal, Sexual, and Textual Authority in The Book of Margery Kempe'. *Modern Philology* 107(4) (2010): 528–55.
Windeatt, Barry. 'Julian's Second Thoughts: The Long Text Tradition'. In *A Companion to Julian of Norwich*, edited by Liz Herbert McAvoy, 101–15. Cambridge: D.S. Brewer, 2008.
Windeatt, Barry. '1412–1534: Texts'. In *The Cambridge Companion to Medieval English Mysticism*, edited by Samuel Fanous and Vincent Gillespie, 195–224. Cambridge: Cambridge University Press, 2011.
Winston-Allen, Anne. *Stories of the Rose: The Making of the Rosary in the Middle Ages*. Philadelphia: Pennsylvania State Press, 1997.
Woods, Marjorie Curry. 'Shared Books: Primers, Psalters and the Adult Acquisition of Literacy among Devout Laywomen and Women in Orders in Late Medieval England'. In *New Trends in Feminine Spirituality: The Holy Women of Liege and their Impact*, edited by Juliette Dor, Lesley Johnson and Jocelyn Wogan-Browne, 181–8. Turnhout: Brepols, 1999.
Woolf, Rosemary. *The English Religious Lyric in the Middle Ages*. Oxford: Oxford University Press, 1968.
Woollcombe, K.J. 'The Biblical Origins and Patristic Development of Typology'. *Studies in Biblical Theology 22: Essays on Typology*, ed. G.W.H. Lampe and K.J. Woollcombe, 39–75. London: SCM Press, 1957.
Zieman, Katherine. *Singing the New Song: Literacy and Liturgy in Late Medieval England*. Philadelphia: University of Pennsylvania Press, 2008.
Zimbalist, Barbara. 'Christ, Creature, and Reader: Verbal Devotion in *The Book of Margery Kempe*'. *Journal of Medieval Religious Cultures* 41(1) (2015): 1–23.

Index

Page numbers in bold type refer to illustrations and their captions.

Abbey of St Bertin   64
The Abbey of the Holy Ghost   95
Aelred of Rievaulx   62
   De Institutione Inclusarum   10–11, 74, 80, 84–101, 108, 111, 113, 152, 189, 198, 232, 242, 243–4
   Vita Edwardi Regis   91, 106
   See also Oxford, Bodleian Library, MS Bodley 423 (Bodley manuscript), Oxford, Bodleian Library, MS Bodley Eng. Poet. A.1 (Vernon manuscript)
Æthelwold of Winchester   64–6
Albertus Magnus
   Biblia Mariana   22, 24
Alfwen (anchoress)   67, 68–70
Alighieri, Dante
   Commedia   16
Ambrose   6–7, 63, 70, 89, 264
   commentary on Luke   6, 79, 88, 105
   De Virginibus ad Marcellinam   6, 41, 46–7, 50, 59
Amiens, Bibliothèque Municipale, MS 2540   212–5, **214**, 218, 220
anchoresses   7, 10, 43–7, 44 n.5, 50–64, 68–77, 85–92, 96–7, 100–1, 121, 149–50, 181–2, 200, 203, 237–8
Ancrene Wisse   10, 50–5, 62–3, 70, 85, 92, 152, 200, 203, 244
Anne, St (mother of Mary)   8, 8 n.16, 166, 171
Anselm of Canterbury   48–9, 189
Anselm of Lucca   47–8, 189

Antoninus of Florence   22–3
apocrypha   47 n.13, 57 n.35, 58, 67, 124, 196, 254
   Gospel of Pseudo-Matthew   6, 57
Aquinas, Thomas   4, 22
Arundel, Thomas
   Constitutions of 1409   97–8, 100, 101, 103, 107–8
Augustine of Dacia   22
Augustine of Hippo   8, 27–8, 30, 66 n.56, 234, 264
   Confessions   91
   City of God   91
   De Trinitate   4, 25
Augustinian order   29, 201, 241

Baltimore, Walters Art Museum, MS W.249   **3**
Baltimore, Walters Art Museum, MS W.267 (Buves Hours)   208 n.77, 216–8, **217**, 222
Baltimore, Walters Art Museum, MS W.288   18–21, **19**, **20**
Barking Abbey   90, 91, 91 n.20
Basil, St   38
Beauchamp, Margaret, Duchess of Somerset   95 n.32, 218–20
Bede, the Venerable   6–7, 23 n.21, 79, 105
Benedictine order   23, 29
   See also Barking Abbey, Markyate Priory, Wilton Abbey
Bernard of Clairvaux   183 n.24, 264

Homiliae Quatour de Laudibus Virginis Matris 23–4, 49–51, 53–5, 70, 72, 104, 106–7, 129–30, 142, 175–7, 196
Betson, Thomas 111
Bibles 23, 90–1, 95, 97–8, 100
 post-Reformation 258–9
 See also Wycliffite Bible
Birgitta of Sweden, St 11, 28, 29, 30, 109, 116, 135, 149–50
 as *ancilla*/handmaiden 174
 as mother 116, 122, 134, 145, 147, 148
 Franciscan defense of 147
 Liber Celestis Revelationes 37, 98, 116–9, 135–49, 166, 168, 168 n.118, 169, 173–4, 184, 196
 mystical pregnancy of 25, 28, 137–8, 145–9, 173, 234
 Sermo Angelicus 135, 196
 Quattour oraciones 137–8
Birgittine order 29, 98 n.46, 109, 111, 135, 136, 148, 184–5
 See also Syon Abbey
Boethius 66n56
 Consolation of Philosophy 91
Bonaventure 4, 31, 80, 83, 102, 113 n.84, 169
 Lignum vitae 81, 112 n.82
Book to a Mother 31–5, 33 n.53
books
 circulation of 80–1, 90, 95–6, 119, 119 n.9, 121, 135, 139, 150, 168–9 n.118, 174, 189, 192, 209–10
 codices 87, 90
 on lecterns 7, 63, 73, 105
 scrolls 86–7
 women as owners of 12, 92, 205–6, 212–20
 See also Bibles, Books of Hours, psalters
Books of Hours 1–2, 203–4, 209–210, 235
 illuminations 3, 12, 17–21, **18, 19, 20**, 179, 204–9, **207**, 210–23, **211, 213, 214, 217, 219, 221**

 See also Amiens, Bibliothèque Municipale, MS 2540; Baltimore, Walters Art Museum, MS W.249; Baltimore, Walters Art Museum, MS W.267 (Buves Hours); Baltimore, Walters Art Museum MS W.288; London, BL, MS Royal 2.A.XVIII (Beauchamp Hours); New York City, Pierpont Morgan Library, MS M. 61; New York City, Pierpont Morgan Library, MS M. 171; Paris, BnF, MS Lat. 9471 (Rohan Hours); Paris, BnF, MS. Lat. 13306; Poitiers, Médiathèque François-Mitterrand, MS 53; Poitiers, Médiathèque François-Mitterrand, MS 1096; Vienna, Österreichische Nationalbibliothek, Codex Vindobonensis MS 1857 (Hours of Mary of Burgundy)
Boulogne-sur-mer, Bibliothèque Municipale, MS 11 (Boulogne Gospels) 64, 66–7
Bridget of Sweden *see* Birgitta of Sweden

Caelius Sedulius 38
Cambridge, Corpus Christi College, MS 402 50–1, 54 n.30
Cambridge, CUL, MS Dd.5.64 183, 184, 184 n.27, 199
Cambridge, CUL, MS Hh.i.11 124 n.20, 130
Cambridge, Magdalene College, Pepys Library MS 2125 182–3, 184–5, 199, 202
Cambridge, Trinity College, MS B.15.42 196, 196 n.45
Cambridge, Trinity College, MS O.8.26 183–4, 199
Carthusian order 98, 102, 106, 109, 183–4, 183 n.24
 See also Mount Grace Priory, Sheen Priory, Witham Charterhouse
Catherine of Siena, St 109, 117 n.3, 121 n.12
Cedrenus, Georgios 262, 264

Chaucer, Geoffrey
  The Canterbury Tales   103, 185, 201 n.59
Christ   51–3, 59–60, 77, 257–8
  as book/ text   2, 11, 17–21, 24, 31–3, 82, 137, 260
  as mystical spouse   46, 124, 131–2, 136, 165
  as model see *imitatio Christi*
  Passion of   5, 8, 25, 46, 80, 82–3, 155, 165, 172, 182–3, 187, 191, 194, 198, 206, 233
Christina of Markyate   67–75, 242, 243
  Vita   10, 43, 55, 62–3, 67–73, 75, 76–7, 238
  See also Hildesheim, Dombibliothek, MS St. Godehard 1 (St Albans Psalter)
Christina of Stommeln   72
Cistercian order   28, 55, 85, 178
contemplation *see* meditation
Cranach, Lucas, the Younger   257
Cromwell, Thomas   251, 253, 259

Daye, John
  Booke of Christian Prayers   254
Dodesham, Stephen   98–9, 106
Dominican order   22, 116, 120–1, 120–1 n.12, 132, 134, 148 n.65, 192
Dublin Rule   44 n.6

Eckhart, Meister   30, 117 n.3, 234
Edith of Wilton   64–6, 74
Edward the Confessor, St   91, 241
Elizabeth of Hungary and Naples (Dominican prioress)   11, 37, 39
  as *ancilla*/handmaiden   123–7, 138, 170
  Revelations   104, 106–7, 116–20, 120–1 n.12, 121–134, 138–40, 150, 168–71, 168 n.118, 173, 174, 178, 181, 192–3, 195, 196–7, 198, 216, 232
  Revelations, disputed authorship of   120–2, 133–4
Elizabeth of Thuringia (St Elizabeth of Hungary)   120, 120–1 n.12, 122, 134

Elizabeth of Töss   111, 120–1 n.12, 133
  Vita of 120
Elizabeth, St (Mary's cousin)   xii, 8, 18, 141, 200, 262
Erasmus, Desiderius   260
  Peregrinatio Religionis Ergo   227, 228, 234, 238, 239, 253
Eva (nun of Wilton and St. Laurent)   43, 47, 55–6, 58–61, 62, 64, 66, 66 n.56, 70, 76, 91, 242
Eve (biblical figure)   48, 53

Fervor Amoris (Contemplations of the Dread and Love of God)   98
Francis of Assisi, St   101–2
Franciscan order   29, 101–2, 104, 120, 121, 121 n.12, 147, 187, 211
Fulbert of Chartres   7, 79, 105

Gabriel   168 n.117
  in illuminations   1–2, 64, 212, 215, 216–22
  in New Testament   xii, 1, 15, 21, 141
  in other devotional texts   32, 47–8, 56–7, 60, 86–7, 99, 104, 105, 129, 131, 140–1, 142–3, 167–8, 171, 172, 176, 202
  in sermons   28–9, 49–50
  in statuary   229–30, 232
Golden Legend see *Legenda Aurea*
Goscelin of St. Bertin
  Liber Confortatorius   10, 29, 43, 47, 48, 52, 55–67, 70, 74, 75, 76, 77, 133, 190, 238, 242, 244
  Vita Edithae   64–6
gospel meditations   5, 11, 80–5, 101, 113–4, 155, 191, 195–9, 202, 209, 215, 232, 233, 237, 239, 254, 265
  See also *Meditationes domini nostri, Meditationes Vitae Christi, Mirror of the Blessed Life of Jesus Christ, Speculum Devotorum*
Gregory the Great, St   73–4, 128, 264
Guerric of Igny   28–9, 234
Guibert of Nogent   38–9

Handlyng Synne 96
Henry, Earl of Lancaster 229
Hildesheim, Dombibliothek, MS St. Godehard 1 (St Albans Psalter) 10, 43, 55, 67–8, 68 n.59, **69**, 73–5
Hilton, Walter
The Scale of Perfection 96–7, 100–1

Ildefonsus, Archbishop of Toledo
Liber De virginitate perpetua Beatae Mariae 124–5
iconoclasm 251–2, 260–1
illiteracy *see* literacy
imitatio Christi 17, 26, 27, 38–9, 118, 165, 172–3, 178, 239–40
imitatio Mariae 10, 26, 27–8, 38–9, 59–60, 82, 87, 89, 113–4, 177–8, 180, 190–1, 194, 198, 199, 202, 232–4, 239–40, 254–7
  for men 12, 29–30, 44–5, 179, 183, 222–3
  for women 5–6, 11, 12, 29–31, 39–40, 42, 44–5, 51, 55, 68–70, 84, 99–101, 116–8, 123, 126–7, 129, 131, 133–4, 136–41, 145–9, 151–2, 156–7, 163–7, 171–4, 206–9, 216–8, 244, 254–6, 264–5

Jacques de Vitry 61 n.45
Jerome, St 8, 23 n.21, 47, 196
John the Baptist, St 8, 141, 222
John the Evangelist, St 126, 132
Julian of Norwich 11, 15, 28, 30, 37, 44, 116, 149–50, 173–4, 194–5, 242, 256
  and Mary's pregnancy 151–6
  differences between texts 156–60
  motif of hazelnut 159–60, 162, 163
  A Revelation of Love 116–9, 149–64, 179, 189–90, 248
  A Vision Showed to a Devout Woman 149, 156–7, 158–60

Kempe, Margery 11, 116, 139, 150, 164
  as *ancilla*/ handmaiden 166–7, 169–71
  as mother 122, 134, 165, 166–7

The Book of Margery Kempe 30–1, 34, 37, 44, 116–9, 122, 164–72, 174, 191, 233, 242, 255

A Ladder of Four Rungs 95–6
Lady Psalter *see* Our Lady's Psalter
Legenda Aurea 120, 132–3, 196
Lincoln, Lincoln Cathedral Chapter Library, MS 114 147, 147 n.60
literacy 94–6, 200, 204, 233
  female 5–6, 7–8, 64, 84–5, 89–92, 96–7, 101, 112–3, 208
liturgy 57–9, 62 n.48, 75, 77, 90, 165, 200, 204, 205, 206, 209
  liturgical cycle 25–6, 75, 80, 130, 146
  Sarum Use 80, 100, 246
lives of Christ *see* gospel meditations
Lollards *see* Wycliffites
Lombard, Peter 31
London, BL, MS Additional 49598 (Benedictional of Æthelwold) 64–6, **65**, 73
London, BL, MS Cotton Tiberius E.I. 67 n.58
London, BL, MS Royal 2.A.XVIII (Beauchamp Hours) 218–20, **219**, 220 n.93
London, BL, MS Sloane 1009 183, 185, 199–200
Love, Nicholas 102
  Mirror of the Blessed Life of Jesus Christ 11, 80, 102–6, 107–9, 110–3, 122, 176, 189, 198, 232, 261
Luther, Martin 252, 254
Lydgate, John 9, 192 n.43, 199 n.52

Mandeville, John
  Travels 196
Marie d'Oignies 61 n.45, 169
Markyate Priory 67
Mary, Blessed Virgin
  as anchoress 41–3, 51–2, 55, 59, 62–3, 72–5, 114, 121, 244
  as *ancilla*/handmaiden 127, 130, 142, 150–2, 161, 166–7, 169–71, 174, 191–2, 216, 232–3

as artificer   243, 247–9
as authority figure   36, 38–9, 110, 131–3, 137, 143–5, 148, 212–5
as book   23
as exegete   21–4, 36–7, 40, 89, 113, 115, 146, 148, 177
as historical figure   1, 24–5, 41–2
as *maistress* of Scripture   5, 132, 170, 248
as meditator   178, 188, 190–1, 193–4, 261–2
as model *see imitatio Mariae*
as Mother of God   5, 27, 63, 132, 134, 136, 144–6, 162–3, 173
as prophet   4, 116, 137, 139–40, 145, 148, 190–1, 192–3, 245–6, 248, 262
as scholar   9, 114, 144, 249
as singer   29, 43, 56–7, 59–60, 62–3, 74–7
as subject   37–8
as trickster   247
as virgin   1, 41, 49, 127, 137
as visionary   11, 37, 114, 116, 122, 128–9, 239, 262
body of   30, 32, 36, 45–7, 49, 51–2, 118, 134, 160, 162, 173–4, 193–5, 236–7, 260
chamber of   41–3, 46–50, 58, 70, 71–2, 86–8, 99, 104–5, 107, 129–30, 179, 188–9, 205, 232, 237–8
feasts of   8, 18, 35, 145–6, 201, 206, 220, 246, 254, 257
humility of   137, 140–2, 152, 255
Reformation and post-Reformation conceptions of   13, 35–7, 252–65
wit of   143–4
Mary and Martha (biblical figures)   53
Mary of Burgundy   205–6
Matilda, Countess of Tuscany   47–8, 189
Mechtild of Hackeborn   109, 117 n.3
meditation   5, 11–12, 23, 42–3, 45–8, 73, 75, 81–5, 96, 100, 110, 113–4, 115, 116, 120–3, 126, 128, 133–4, 147, 166, 172, 176–9, 182–3, 185–195, 197–9, 201–2, 206, 208–10, 212, 222–3, 232–40, 260–1

Meditationes domini nostri   12, 102, 178, 195–9, 202
Meditationes vitae Christi   11, 80, 82, 83, 84, 101–5, 121, 121 n.12, 133, 139, 165, 176–7, 178, 189, 196–8, 199, 215, 233, 260
  testo breve version   102
Merode Altarpiece   258 n.29
Miriam (biblical figure)   60
misogyny   30, 31–2, 34, 37, 240, 255–6
monasticism   7, 29, 43, 58–9, 111, 130, 132–4, 179, 183, 185, 200–1, 203–4, 237–8, 259
Mount Grace Priory   102
music
  singing   42–3, 71
  timbrel/drum   60–1, 61 n.45
  See also Mary, Blessed Virgin
mysticism *see* visions and visionaries

N-Town Manuscripts   176–7, 58 n.36, 192 n.43
New York City, Pierpont Morgan Library, MS M. 61   210 n.82
New York City, Pierpont Morgan Library, MS M. 171   210–2, **211**
Nicholas of Lyra   22, 196

Odilo of Cluny   7, 61, 79, 105
Of Three Workings in Man's Soul   11–12, 177–9, 187–95, 202, 209, 215, 222–3, 260
  authorship of   178, 179–81
  dating of   181
  influence of   195–9
  intended audience of   181–7, 192, 204
Order of St. Savior *see* Birgittine order
Origen   27–28, 30, 234
Otfrid von Weissenburg   7, 47 n.13
  Evangelienbuch   63
Our Lady's Psalter   199–203
Oxford, Balliol College, MS 354   220
Oxford, Bodleian Library, MS Bodley 423 (Bodley manuscript)   98–101, 106, 107, 108, 113, 189, 198

Oxford, Bodleian Library, MS Bodley 578   196
Oxford, Bodleian Library, MS Bodley Eng. Poet. A.1 (Vernon manuscript)   33, 92–7, 111, 113, 198, 243–4
Oxford, Bodleian Library, MS Digby 86   201
Oxford, Bodleian Library, MS Laud Lat. 19   90–1
Oxford, Bodleian Library, MS Rawl. Poet. 291   251
Oxford, Christ Church College, MS 152   201 n.59
Oxford, Corpus Christi College, MS 410   105

Paris, BnF, MS 2225   212 n.85
Paris, BnF, MS Ital. 115   105
Paris, BnF, MS Lat. 9471 (Rohan Hours)   17–8, **18**
Paris, BnF, MS. Lat. 13306   212 n.85
Paul, St   27, 34
Peter of Celle   23, 23 n.23
Philippe de Mézières
    Presentation Play   56–7 n.36
pilgrim badges   1, **224**, 225–7, **226**, 228, 229–30, 235, 226–7 n.2, 235 n.20
pilgrimage   12, 127, 135, 223, 226–30, 232–3, 234–40, 244, 250, 252, 253, 255–6
Poitiers, Médiathèque François-Mitterand, MS 53   212, 212n85, **213**, 215, 218, 220
Poitiers, Médiathèque François-Mitterand, MS 1096   220–2, **221**
Pore Caitiff   95
Prick of Conscience   103
The Pricking of Love   196
psalters   10, 43, 55, 58, 62–4, 71–6, 79, 90, 238
    See also Hildesheim, Dombibliothek, MS St. Godehard 1 (St Albans Psalter), Our Lady's Psalter
Pynson ballad   9, 12–13, 240–50

Reformation   251–65
Reynes, Robert   229–30
Richard of St. Victor   22, 178, 180, 183, 185, 197, 223
    The Mystical Ark (*Benjamin major*)   11–2, 178, 186–7
Richeldes de Faverches *see* Rychold
Rolle, Richard   12, 92, 178, 179–92, 220
    The Commandment   181, 182, 184
    Ego Dormio   181, 182, 184
    English Psalter and Commentary   95, 181
    The Form of Living   181, 182, 184
    Passion meditations   182
    See also Of Three Workings in Man's Soul
rosaries   179, 201–2, 203, 206
Rychold (Richeldes de Faverches)   241-50

Salus anime see Oxford, Bodleian Library, MS Bodley Eng. Poet. A.1 (Vernon manuscript)
sermons   6, 7, 23–4, 27–30, 49–50, 53–4, 55, 57, 62, 72, 79–80, 87–8, 106, 142, 175–6, 196, 204–5, 256
Sheen Priory   98, 109
Sowlehele see Oxford, Bodleian Library, MS Bodley Eng. Poet. A.1 (Vernon manuscript)
Speculum Devotorum (*Mirror of Devout People*)   11, 80, 102, 109–13, 198, 261, 264
Speculum Inclusorum (*A Mirror for Recluses*)   44 n.6
Speculum Virginum (*Mirror of Virgins*)   29–30
Stafford, Anthony
    The Femall Glory   261–5, **263**
stained glass   1, 33, 205, 230–2, **231**
Syon Abbey   109, 111, 112, 184–5, 198

Vienna, Österreichische Nationalbibliothek, Codex Vindobonensis MS 1857 (Hours of Mary of Burgundy)   205–8, **207** visions and visionaries   8, 11–2, 25, 28, 30–1, 33, 37–9, 70, 106–7, 115–8, 122–74, 178, 191–2, 195, 198, 206–8, 215–6, 232–3, 240–5, 249, 255, 262

Walsingham, Shrine of Our Lady   9, 12–3, 225–6, 230–50, 251–3
  appearance of Holy House   227
  statuary   228–30
  See also Pynson ballad, Rychold William of Malmsbury

De Gestis Regum Anglorum   64 n.54
William of Worcester   227
Wilton Abbey   55–6, 64–6, 66 n.55
Witham Charterhouse   98
Wulfhryth of Wilton   66
Wyclif, John   96, 97, 259
Wycliffites   34, 96, 97, 103, 108
  Wycliffite Bible   95, 103, 108, 259

Zachariah, St   141–2